The Japanese Are Coming

The Japanese Are Coming

A Multinational Interaction of Firms and Politics

Yoshi Tsurumi
*Graduate School of Management
University of California, Los Angeles*

Ballinger Publishing Company • Cambridge, Massachusetts
A Subsidiary of Harper & Row, Publishers, Inc.

 This book is printed on recycled paper.

Copyright © 1976 by Ballinger Publishing Company. All rights reserved. No part of this publication may be reproduced, stored in a retrieval system, or transmitted in any form or by any means, electronic mechanical photocopy, recording or otherwise, without the prior written consent of the publisher.

International Standard Book Number: 0-88410-651-9

Library of Congress Catalog Card Number: 76-23262

Printed in the United States of America

Library of Congress Cataloging in Publication Data

Tsurumi, Yoshihiro.
   The Japanese are coming.

   Includes bibliographical references.
   1. Corporations, Japanese. 2. International business enterprises. 3. Investments, Japanese. I. Title.
HD2907.T73   338.8'8   76-23262
ISBN 0-88410-651-9

To Maia Tsurumi

Contents

List of Figures	xiii
List of Tables	xv
Preface	xix
Chapter One **The Japanese Are Coming**	1

The Rise of Japanese Investments	1
Scope of the Study	3
A Cooperative Model of Government-Business Relationships	5
"Indicative Economic Planning" after World War II	9
Implementation of the Indicative Economic Plans — Financial Lever	13
The Economic Recovery of the 1950s	16
Implementation of the Indicative Economic Plans— Technological Innovations	18
Private Entrepreneurship	24
Industrial Structure of Japan	27
Changing Patterns of Japanese Exports and Direct Investments	30
The Japanese Strategy of Riding an International Product Cycle	31
International Marketing Activities as Triggers of Japanese Investments Abroad	33

Chapter Two
The Search for Natural Resources   37

A Phenomenal Growth	37
Industrial Growth at Home and Search for Raw Materials Abroad	38
From Glut to Shortage	40
Non-Mineral Resources	42
Defensive Investments	42
Additional Motivation for Resource-Oriented Ventures Abroad	44
On-Site Processing	45
Sea Produce	46
A Group Approach to Overseas Investment: The Japanese Consortium	46
Oil Exploration	47
The Quest for Stability among Japanese Oligopolies	49
MITI's Direct Leadership	51
Private Moves of Resource Diplomacy	52
Trading Firms and Natural Resources	52
Trading Firms' Superiority	53
Japanese Firms' Challenge to International Oligopolies	55
The New Need for Vertical Integration	57
Cooperation and Competition between Japanese and Foreign Firms	60
Japan Destabilizes International Copper Arrangements	62
Responses of International Majors	64
The Japanese Government and Resource Diplomacy	67

Chapter Three
Manufacturing Firms Abroad   71

An Overview	71
Defence of Export Markets	75
Small Firms Spearhead Japanese Investments Abroad	78
Export Orientation of Small Firms	82
Overseas Manufacturing Operations of Large Firms	84
The International Extension of Oligopolistic Competition in Japan	88
The Case of the Synthetic Fiber Industry	89
The Case of Electric and Electronic Appliances	93
Offshore Production Bases of Japanese Manufacturing Firms	95
Conclusion	99

Chapter Four
Invading the United States   101

Market Penetration (I)—The Case of Industrial Products   105
Market Penetration (II)—The Case of Consumer Products   112
Export-Led Investments   115
R&D Contacts—Direct Access to Stimuli of
   American Markets   116
Material Procurement—Closer Link-up with
   Commodity Markets   119
Exchange of Hostages and Acquisition of American and
   European Firms—The "Futurology" of
   Japanese Investments?   121

Chapter Five
Large Trading Companies: Industrial
Cyclops or Maligned Phoenix?   125

General Trading Company of Japan (Sogoshosha)   128
The Ten Largest Trading Firms   128
Large General Trading Companies—
   Inevitable Development?   132
Trading Firms and Their Direct Investments Abroad   138
Manufacturing Firms vs. Trading Firms   141
The Responses of Japanese Trading Companies   145
Mitsui vs. Mitsubishi   148
Japanese Trading Companies and Developing Countries:
   A Case of the Textile Industry in Indonesia   150
The Dual Characteristics of the Indonesian
   Textile Industry   150
Japanese Trading Companies are the Promoters
   of Indonesian Textile Firms   154
The Future of Japanese Trading Firms   155

Chapter Six
Are Japanese Banks Coming?   157

Asia-Dollar Market   159
Japanese Banks Go Abroad   161
Foreign Ownership Patterns of Banks   162
Structural Instability of Early Consortia Banks   163
The Slow Internationalization of Japanese
   Financial Institutions   163

Prominent Emergence of Leading Japanese Firms 164
Counter-Thrust of the Ministry of Finance 165
Commercial Bank vs. Security House 167

Chapter Seven
The International Transfer of
Japanese Technologies 169

The Nature of Technologies 170
Japanese Technologies 171
Other Characteristics of the Manufacturing
 Technologies of Japan 176
International Transfer of Japanese Technologies 177
Choice of Requisite Technologies for Japanese
 Subsidiaries in Asian Countries 179
The Case of Japanese Subsidiaries in Indonesia:
 Orientation Toward Local Markets 182
The Case of a Japanese Offshore Plant in Korea:
 Total Orientation to Export Market 185
Host Governments' Preoccupation
 with New Machine 188
Japanese Efforts to Transfer Process-Related
 Technologies Abroad 189

Chapter Eight
The Quest for Majority Ownership 201

Ownership of Japanese Subsidiaries 201
Joint Ventures Abroad of Japanese Manufacturing Firms 204
Emerging Stresses between Local Partners and
 Japanese Investors 206
The Quest for Majority Ownership 209
Conflicts Involved in the Joint Venture 212

Chapter Nine
Japanese Corporate Culture
and Overseas Divisions 217

Japanese Corporate Atmosphere 220
Post-World War II Phenomenon 221
Long Work Time-Horizon of Employees 223
Volleyball Team Model 224
Japanese and American Corporate Culture 225
Decision-Making Processes of Japanese Firms: "Ringi
 Seido" Revisited 227

Presidential Leadership	229
The Raison d'Etre of "Kaigai Jigyobu" (Overseas Division) for the Japanese Multinational Firm	231
Functions of KJ Division	236
Group Decision-Making	238
KJ Division in Transition?	240

Chapter Ten
The "Ugly Japanese" and Their Dilemma Abroad — 243

The Viewpoints of the Developing Countries	247
Public Visibility of Japanese Investments	251
Japanese Export Drive and Host Countries' Reaction	258
Japanese Expatriate Managers	260
Cultural Insensitivity of Japanese Firms	263
The International Impact of Government and Business Relations in Japan	266
Japanese Investments in Korea	269

Chapter Eleven
Japan in a Conflicting World — 275

The Oil Crisis and All That	275
Separation of Economics from Politics	276
Post-Vietnam War Era in Asia and Japan	281
The Government and Politics of Japan	287
International Repercussions of Anti-Big Business Sentiment in Japan	297
Japanese Labor Unions and Japanese Multinational Firms	299
Conclusion	303
Notes	309
Index	325
About the Author	335

List of Figures

1-1	An Illustration of the Three-Way Links among Manufacturer, Bank and Trading Company of Japan	29
4-1	Multiple Layers of American Markets	106
5-1	Product Composition of the Indonesian Textile Industry, 1973	152
7-1	The U-Shaped Pattern of Clients and Their Purchases of Japanese Technologies	177
9-1	Japanese and American Corporate Culture	226
9-2	Evolutionary Process of KJ Division	236
9-3	KJ Division and Its Relation to Product Division	238

List of Tables

1-1	Number of Foreign Manufacturing Subsidiaries Established by Large Enterprises Based in the U.S., U.K., Continental Europe and Japan, Pre-1914 to 1970	2
1-2	Japan-U.S. Comparisons of Direct Investment Profile, March 1972	4
1-3	R&D Related Statistics of Japan for Selected Years	19
1-4	Relative Frequency of Choice of Intelligence Methods Used by 975 Japanese Companies, Classified by Size of Firm	22
1-5	Japanese Direct Investments Abroad by Area and by Industry As of March 31, 1974	34
1-6	The Number of Overseas Subsidiaries of Non-Trading Firms in Japan by Area and by Activity As of the End of 1972	35
2-1	Resource-Oriented Investments of Japan, 1951-1974	38
2-2	Percentage Ratio of Imports to Japan's Total Consumption of Key Natural Resources, 1950-1970	39
3-1	Relative Geographical Concentration of Manufacturing Subsidiaries of Large U.S., U.K., European and Japanese Firms As of January 1, 1971	72
3-2	Classification of Principal Product Line of the Largest 79 Japanese Manufacturing Subsidiaries Abroad in 1972	73

3-3	Some Product Characteristics of Overseas, Manufacturing Subsidiaries of Large Japanese Multinational Firms Classified by the Number of Subsidiaries of Parent Firms As of January 1, 1971	74
3-4	Factors Affecting the Decision of Overseas Investments of Japanese Manufacturing Firms Classified by Size of Respondent Firm	76
3-5	Balance of Trade of Japanese Manufacturing Subsidiaries Abroad by Industry, 1971	77
3-6	Overseas Manufacturing Operations Classified by the Size of Principal Parent Firm, 1951-1971	79
3-7	The Export-to-Sales Ratios of Japanese Investing Parent Firms Shown by the Size of Parent Firms and by Industry	80
3-8	Number of Manufacturing Subsidiaries by Industry and by Size of the Principal Parent Firm in Japan As of December 31, 1973	81
3-9	Competitive Investments Abroad by Teijin and Toray for Nine Countries	90
3-10	Locations, Years Entered and Activities of Overseas Manufacturing Subsidiaries of the Four Leading Electric and Electronic Appliance and Equipment Manufacturers: Hitachi, Matsushita, Sanyo and Toshiba As of the End of 1973	94
4-1	Japanese Subsidiaries in the U.S., Canada and Europe As of the End of 1973	103
4-2	Japanese Manufacturing Subsidiaries in the U.S. As of the End of 1973	104
4-3	Japanese Manufacturing Subsidiaries in the U.S. Classified by Their Initial Investment Objective, by Their Time of Entry and by Their Product	105
5-1	The Ten Largest General Trading Companies of Japan As of 1974	128
5-2	Percentage Breakdowns of Annual Turnover of Ten Largest General Trading Companies by Product and by Activity As of 1974	129
5-4	Overseas Subsidiaries of Japanese Trading Firms Established during 1950-1961 Classified by Their Function and by Their Operating Area	138
5-5	Overseas Subsidiaries of Japanese Trading Firms Established during 1950-1971 Classified by Their Year of Entry, by Their Functions and by the Characteristics of Their Parent Firms	140

5-6	Manufacturing Subsidiaries of Japanese Trading Firms Established during 1950-1971 Classified by Their Year of Entry, by Their Operating Area and by Characteristics of Their Parent Firms	142
5-7	Overseas Manufacturing Subsidiaries Established by Japanese Trading Companies, 1950-1971	148
7-1	Japan's Receipts and Payments of Technological Fees, 1950-1969	171
7-2	Japan's Sales and Purchases of Technologies, 1950-1969	172
7-3	Classification of Japanese Technologies Sold Abroad, 1950-1969, by Purchasers' Location and by Nature of Technology	173
7-4	Six Reasons Determing Products and Production Processes in Opening Subsidiaries in Developing Countries	180
7-5	A Typical Decision-Making Process of Japanese Firms in Selecting Manufacturing Technologies for Their Subsidiaries Abroad	181
7-6	Changes in Employment, Output and Worker Productivity between Plant in Japan and Plant in Korea	186
7-7	Percentage of Management Positions of Japanese Subsidiaries Abroad Filled by Japanese Expatriates	190
7-8	Average Number of Japanese Expatriates per Manufacturing Subsidiary As of the First Quarter of 1973	191
7-9	Number of Japanese Expatriates per Manufacturing Subsidiary by Product Group As of the First Quarter of 1973	192
7-10	Method of Entry of Japanese Manufacturing Subsidiaries Abroad	195
8-1	Japanese Parent Firms' Ownership Profile of Overseas Subsidiaries by Invested Area As of The End of 1972	202
8-2	Ownership Profile of Japanese Manufacturing Subsidiaries Abroad by Size of Parent Firm As of the End of 1972	203
8-3	Ownership of Overseas Manufacturing Subsidiaries by Nationality of Largest Parent Firms As of January 1, 1971	203
8-4	Contributions Expected from Local Partners Important in the Selection of Foreign Partners	205
8-5	Equity Ownership of Off-shore and Non-offshore Subsidiaries	208

8-6	Significant Factors in Seeking 51 Percent Ownership of a Foreign Subsidiary	210
8-7	Sources of Conflict with Foreign Partners	212
9-1	Relative Size of Overseas Manufacturing Subsidiaries as Compared with Parent Firms' Operations in Japan As of March 31, 1973	233
9-2	The Internal Organization of 47 Large Japanese Multinational Firms, Possessing Relevant Information on Their Overseas Subsidiaries As of Fall 1972	234
10-1	Accumulated United States and Japanese Direct Investments in Asia	252
10-2	Approved Investments in Indonesia for Asian Countries, 1967-1972	255
10-3	Import of Manufactures from Japan as a Percent of Total Imports of Manufactures of Nine Selected Countries, 1972	259
10-4	Inflows of External Funds into Korea, 1948-1969	270
10-5	Balance of Payments of Korea Related to Inflows of External Funds, Foreign Direct Investments and Foreign Technologies, 1962-1970	272

Preface

Recently, few subjects have attracted so much journalistic coverage, polemical vilification, self-adoration, public fear, investigative hearing, and study as the phenomenal growth of multinational firms. Debates over them are far from settled. With a worldwide proliferation of Japanese corporations, multinational firms—success stories to admirers of modern corporations and hateful manifestations of neo-colonialism to critics of corporate bureaucracy—now pose important issues for all of us to consider.

Even without the exposé of unsavory acts by such American multinational firms as Lockheed and ITT, the rise of Japanese multinational firms has raised nagging questions, especially among Japan's Asian neighbors. Will Japan resort, again, to military force, clandestine or otherwise, when forced to protect its economic interests outside Japan? Will clashes of economic and political interests among the world powers, including Japan, hurt the developing nations? Or are Japanese multinational firms merely paper tigers to be helplessly engulfed by the spreading nationalism of the Third World?

What motivates Japanese firms to go multinational beyond straight-forward engagements in exports and imports? What is the relationship between the rise of Japanese multinational firms and Japan's internal political and economic situation in the post–World War II era? Above all, how are Japanese multinational firms going to disrupt or accommodate the world wide oligopolistic equilibria of economic powers that the U.S.- and Europe-based multinational firms have attained in a number of manufacturing industries as well as in the exploitation of natural resources? Could Japanese multinational firms provide the Third World with a better opportunity to play off one foreign investor against another?

The behavior of U.S.-based multinational firms has already been delineated by Raymond Vernon's *Sovereignty at Bay* (New York Basic Books, 1971). Over one hundred articles and scores of doctoral dissertations and books thus far produced by the Multinational Enterprise Project of the Harvard Business School have further illuminated many dimensions of multinational firms.* This work of mine is also an integral part of the Multinational Enterprise Project. It aims to place the diverse behaviors of Japanese multinational firms in the perspective of the post–World War II development of Japan.

Compared with U.S.- and Europe-based multinational firms, Japanese firms have thus far displayed many idiosyncracies. For instance, unlike multinational investments of American and European firms, Japanese direct investments abroad were spearheaded, not by large firms, but by small- to medium-sized firms. Manufacturing firms have often included trading firms as the indivisible partners of their ventures abroad. And Japanese direct investments are also serving as a vehicle for the international transfer of manufacturing technology and managerial skill, both of which have evolved as distinctly "Japanese." These behavioral idiosyncracies of Japanese investments abroad have merely reflected the success of rapid industrialization in Japan since the 1870s.

However, many factors that have allowed for Japanese successes within and without Japan are rapidly changing. Inside Japan the national consensus that has so far presented a unified front against would-be foreign investors in Japan is breaking up. Furthermore, Japanese corporate employees, who have been the moving force behind the accelerated industrial growth of the last 25 years or so, are showing a strong sign of changing their attitude. Outside Japan, Japanese export drives are now facing efforts by both developing and developed nations to limit importation of goods produced by Japan. Even without such adverse reactions by other countries against Japanese-made goods, the rising wage level and the "labor shortage" at home have already rendered a wide range of standard Japanese products uncompetitive in the world markets. And this "labor shortage" was caused by another success of Japan in the post–World War II epoch.

After World War II, Japan demonstrated that population growth could be contained by legal abortion on demand, by effective dissemination of birth control information and by increasing public

---

*Raymond Vernon, "A Decade of Studying Multinational Enterprises," Tenth Annual Progress Report of Multinational Enterprise Project, January 1976, Harvard Business School.

preference for a smaller-sized nuclear family. As a result, the population of Japan appears to be being stabilized at the level of around 125 to 135 million for the balance of the Twentieth Century. In the next century, Japan's population is likely to fall. And, the general aging of the Japanese population has already begun. The day will soon arrive when over one-half of the Japanese population will be in their "golden" age. The ever dwindling size of the economically "productive" population will be called on to support the majority of the population.

In industrial fields, Japanese "offshore" production bases—one form of multinational investments—are increasing in number as well as in scope. These operations are tapping more abundant young labor resources in the neighboring countries in Asia. Thus, these operations could also be viewed as Japanese ad hoc responses to the problem of the aging of its entire population. In the near future, Japan's need for relying on younger and cheaper labor forces outside Japan will be intensified.

Regarding the procurement of natural resources for Japan, the time-honored methods have not only grown inadequate for Japan's current needs but have also forced resources-supplying nations to demand a greater degree of on-site processing than they did previously. Even if Japan can continue to procure as much raw materials as she needs, she is running out of domestic sites for processing plants. The archipelago is already congested with people and industry and is suffering from the worst case of industrial pollution in the history of mankind. Japanese resistance to industrial plants is making it difficult for manufacturers to expand their operations within Japan.

All told, as a result of Japan's past successes, she is now confronted with the task of drastically revising not only her industrial strategies, but also her institutional arrangements, from education to business-government relations. One direction of change is the development of multinational manufacturing activities for Japanese industries. Already many ad hoc experiments in overseas manufacturing activities have been started by Japanese firms. This book will examine the records of these past experiments. And on the basis of such examination, future courses of actions for Japanese firms will be predicted. Possible conflicts of interest between Japan and other countries will be also evaluated especially in the context of the aftermath of the oil crisis of 1973.

During the past four years, I have been aided by literally hundreds of government officials, business executives, plant workers, farmers, journalists and academics in Japan, Canada, the United States and all the other countries I have visited. While all of them remain anonymous, this book would not have been possible without candid exchanges I have enjoyed with all of them. But especially I would like to thank Mr. Yuji Naito, President of Eisai Co. in Japan, for his warm support of my field work. Without his support it would have been extremely difficult.

Throughout field research and subsequent drafting of the book, I have been most fortunate and honored to have the penetrating but encouraging and, above all, warm support of Professor Raymond Vernon. Few researchers have been so fortunate as to be able to work with their mentor, teacher and fatherly counselor of unbounded friendship as I was with Professor Vernon. Over the years, he has taught me, with his own deeds and words, that serious research cannot possibly be separated from equally serious work in teaching. In academic life, it is not unusual to encounter an institution where the insulting and lopsided supposition—"a good researcher cannot be a good teacher, but a bad researcher must be therefore, a good teacher"—still lingers. I found Professor Vernon refreshing and stimulating all around.

While I was drafting this manuscript at Harvard Business School, the MBA students, the doctoral candidates and the participants in executive programs whom I had a good fortune to meet in my classes provided stimuli and hints for the content, organization and narration of this book. In particular, I owe much to the MBA students I had in my classes in Environmental Analysis for Management from 1973 to 1975 and in my classes in Management of International Business during the fall of 1975. They tolerated and even welcomed my bouncing emerging ideas with them in class and my thinking aloud in class.

Mrs. Marie Castro has been in charge of typing my manuscripts, managing my office in my frequent absence, counselling my students and of all other vital tasks that she has so ably and patiently executed. At various stages of this book writing, I also had a very rare fortune to have the editorial assistances of Ms. Vicki Elms, Ms. Sandy Cole, and Ms. Marianne Jacobbi. Ms. Joyce Lapp also rendered valuable assistance in putting the manuscript into a final shape. Calling them able would just be the understatement of the year.

Professor Mira Wilkins of the Florida International University, Dr. Theodore Moran of the Brookings Institution, and Professor John Dower of the University of Wisconsin reviewed an earlier version of the manuscript and offered encouraging and useful comments. Ms. Susannah Heschel read Chapters 1, 10 and 11 of the earlier draft and pronounced them to be interesting and informative. Coming as it did from an accomplished student of Judaism and other religions, Ms. Heschel's pronouncement was most welcome. Dr. Hiroki Tsurumi, Professor of econometrics at Rutgers University was my technical advisor whenever I needed quantitative information. Dr. E. Patricia Tsurumi of University of Victoria, Canada, is a professor, historian, and above all a concerned citizen. She has helped me develop a sense of history of the many streams of events that I dealt with in my book. Naturally, all the weakness of this manuscript is my own.

Some of the analyses in Chapters 7 and 10 were earlier included in my article in David Apter and Louis Goodman, ed. *The Multinational Corporation and Social Change* (New York Praeger, 1976). I would like to thank Praeger Publishing Co. for the permission to expand my earlier viewpoints for this book of mine.

The research on which this book is based was financed by the Ford Foundation. This Foundation has supported the Multinational Enterprise Project of the Harvard Business School that was launched almost a decade ago under the direction of Professor Raymond Vernon. My colleagues and I are very much honored to have obtained the recognition of the Project from the Ford Foundation.

December 1975
Boston   Yoshi Tsurumi

The Japanese Are Coming

Chapter One

The Japanese Are Coming

From East to Southeast Asia, irate students, politicians and journalists characterize Japanese business as an "economic animal." In Latin America, from Mexico to Argentina, many nations have suddenly grown ambivalent about the increase of Japanese investments in commercial ventures, agricultural projects and assorted mining and manufacturing operations. In the United States and Europe, from about 1973 onward, politicians and business leaders appeared to be gripped with the uneasy sensation that a suspected rise of Japanese ownership in commercial and manufacturing ventures in their countries might already have subverted their economic and ideological fabrics.

THE RISE OF JAPANESE INVESTMENTS

Have Japanese direct investments really become a threat to similar investments abroad by U.S.-, U.K.- and Continental Europe-based multinational firms? As shown in Table 1-1, toward the end of the 1960s, manufacturing operations abroad of large Japanese firms rose sharply, pointing to a further exponential increase in the 1970s. More important, Japanese investments have already moved into the areas and industries that had long been considered exclusive domains of American and European multinational firms.

For all types of overseas ventures—from commercial sales subsidiaries to mining operations—it is estimated that during the years from 1951 to 1970, approximately 4,000 overseas subsidiaries were established by large and small Japanese firms. At the end of 1973, I estimated that the total number of Japanese subsidiaries abroad

Table 1-1. Number of Foreign Manufacturing Subsidiaries Established by Large Enterprises Based in the U.S., U.K., Continental Europe and Japan, Pre-1914 to 1970

Period	Nationality and Number of Large Multinational Parent Firms*			
	U.S. (187 Firms)	U.K. (49 Firms)	Continental Europe (94 Firms)	Japan (66 Firms)
Pre-1914	122	60	167	0
1914-1919	71	27	51	0
1920-1929	299	118	249	1
1930-1938	315	99	112	3
1939-1945	172	34	44	40
1946-1952	386	202	129	2
1953-1955	283	55	117	5
1956-1958	439	94	131	14
1959-1961	901	333	232	93
1962-1964	959	319	229	160
1965-1967	889	459	532	235
1968-1970	N.A.	729	1,030	532

Source: The Multinational Enterprise Project of the Harvard Business School
*Compiled the manufacturing subsidiaries of parent firms that were large enough to make *Fortune's Largest 400 U.S. firms in 1967* or *Fortune's Largest 200 non-U.S. firms in 1970.* In the case of Japan, the manufacturing subsidiaries of the largest 10 trading firms were also included.

passed the six thousand mark, and that the total assets held by Japanese direct investments abroad surpassed nine billion dollars. Although the oil crisis of 1973 temporarily put a damper on Japanese direct investments (capital exports from Japan), I have estimated that by the end of 1975 Japanese assets abroad surpassed the twelve billion dollar mark. While this figure still appeared small compared to the American figure of about 120 billion dollars, there was no denying that Japan had emerged as an active participant in manufacturing operations and natural resource developments abroad.

After about a quarter century Japan has suddenly become again a suspected country. The admiration for and envy of Japan's rapid economic growth of the 1950s and the 1960s have long given way to a nagging fear on the part of several host countries—a fear that sinister designs might well lie behind the rising trend of Japanese direct investments.[1] In 1957, *The Economist* noted that the rapid recovery of the Japanese economy after World War II was due to a high level of investment by the Japanese business community, and that an uncommonly well trained labor force was the driving power behind this rising productivity. It also noted that Japanese salesmen were adept at selling their various manufactured goods throughout the world. In 1962, *The Economist* again sent a seasoned observer to Japan, who in his article, "Consider Japan," exhorted the English to learn from the Japanese experience. In an article entitled "The Risen Sun," in 1967, the journal pronounced Japan to be an unquestioned industrial power. In 1973, however, the past admiring tone of the journal shifted and labelled its survey article on Japan "No One Quite like Them."

Historically, there have been similar instances where the political acceptance of Japan by the Western nations has suddenly turned to suspicion, once Japan proved her ability to outdo Western powers. This happened right after Japan's victory in the Sino-Japanese War of 1894-95, and again after her victory in the Russo-Japanese War of 1904-05. The ignominy, "the Yellow Peril (Die gelbe Gefahr)," was coined and popularized by Kaiser Wilhelm of Germany, when he suddenly found Japan to be his competitor, after the humiliation of his Russian cousin, Czar Nicholas.[2] The slur struck responsive chords in the Western World whenever interests of the United States and European nations collided with similar interests of Japan. How had this history repeated itself? Why have Japanese firms gone multinational?

SCOPE OF THE STUDY

As of the end of 1973, about two-thirds of the Japanese manufacturing operations abroad were located in Asia. Of late, however, Japanese direct investments are rising in Latin America, most notably Brazil, as well as in North America and Europe. What motivated Japanese manufacturing and trading firms to commence manufacturing operations abroad? How did Japan's corporate culture and industrial structure influence the timing and format of Japanese overseas expansion? Why were host countries alarmed at Japan's entry into overseas investment? Was there something inherent in the corporate culture or product structure of Japanese subsidiaries abroad that caused political and economic conflicts with indigenous businesses? These questions will be answered in the following chapters.

For this study, a Japanese multinational firm has been defined as a manufacturing (or mining) and trading firm that possessed at least one manufacturing or mining operation abroad as of January 1, 1971. As was not the case with other research projects of U.S.-, U.K.- or Continental Europe-based multinational enterprises, I have not limited this study to those firms large enough to make *Fortune's* 200 largest non-U.S. firms in 1970 or *Fortune's* 400 largest U.S. firms in

1967.[3] My preliminary investigations of Japanese direct investments abroad revealed a vast presence of small to medium-sized manufacturing firms.[4] In addition, trading firms, which had become unique just by having been able to survive well into the post-industrial era, were very much active in both manufacturing operations and natural resource developments abroad.

In Table 1-2, the comparative profiles of U.S.- and Japan-based multinational firms are summarized. As of spring, 1972 Japanese investments abroad still provided a distinct contrast to those of the United States. What produced this distinct profile and how is this profile going to change? How have the past successes of Japanese industrialization and resultant export behavior affected the timing and nature of Japanese direct investments abroad?

What then, are the idiosyncracies of Japanese direct investments abroad? The idiosyncracies of Japanese direct investments abroad are no doubt a product of the political, economic and cultural traits of

Table 1-2. Japan—U.S. Comparisons of Direct Investment Profile, March 1972

	Japan-based	U.S.-based
Size of parent firms	(1) 40 percent of investments by small- to medium-sized firms. (2) Large R&D intensive firms go abroad often with their small subcontractors.	(1) Large R&D intensive firms dominate overseas investments. (2) Small- to medium-sized firms may have subcontracting relations with foreign manufacturers.
Where invested	Three-quarters of investments in developing nations. Overwhelmingly in Asia.	Two-thirds in developed nations.
Organization of subsidiaries	Joint venture dominant. Many minority interests.	Fully-owned or majority controlled.
Partner, if any, of subsidiaries	(1) Many with Japanese trading firms and local partners. (2) With other Japanese firms in the same "industrial group" in Japan.	On its own or local partner.
Parent's control over subsidiary	Loose.	Close.
Parent-subsidiary relations	Disjointed. Local market oriented.	Globally integrated.

Source: Yoshi Tsurumi, "Japanese Multinational Firm," *Journal of World Trade Law* (February 1973).

Japan that have long shaped the *modus operandi* of Japanese firms both inside and outside the country, and especially their interactions with the Japanese government.

Contrary to a popular myth, the Japanese government has long restricted the overseas investments of Japanese firms. Only as recently as July 1, 1971, due to the rising demand by large and small private firms for greater freedom for their expansions abroad, did the government lift the ceilings that it had placed on the asset size of Japanese investments abroad. Private firms' initiatives have often broken out of the institutional restrictions placed on them by the Japanese bureaucracy. The Japanese model of cooperation between government and business interests had not been totally free of antagonism. During the last hundred years, government and business circles together, have continued to redefine the realms and boundaries of public and private operations. And the rapid rise of Japanese investments abroad are now forcing both business and government circles to redefine once more their mutual relationships.

A COOPERATIVE MODEL OF GOVERNMENT-BUSINESS RELATIONSHIPS

The philosophies and practices which have long shaped government-business relationships in Japan are a product of Japan's early efforts toward industrialization. In 1868 Japan emerged from the feudalistic Tokugawa period with a strong national consensus to avoid direct financial help from the Western powers. The First Opium War (1839–42) and its resultant unequal treaties of Nangking forced Ch'ing China, Japan's longtime mentor, to grant the victorious Britain humiliating economic and political concessions.* More than anything else, this historical incident warned the leaders of the emerging Japanese state about the ulterior motives of the Western powers.

Japan faced, then, a dilemma. Japan needed western technologies and institutional models. And yet the Japanese wanted to avoid political concessions to the Western powers. This conscious effort to separate technological and institutional fruits of the West from the imperialistic ambitions of the Western powers was captured at that

*In order to arrest mounting trade deficits with Ch'ing China, the United Kingdom exported opium from India to China. When China finally banned the opium trade and burned British warehouses in order to stop social, physical and moral decay caused by opium, the United Kingdom sent, in 1839, warships and marines to "protect" her trade interest. The resultant treaties of Nangking marked the beginning of the carving-out of economic and political interests in China by the Western powers and later by Japan.

time in the popular slogan, *"Wakon Yosai"* — Japanese Wisdom and Western Technology.

Under this slogan, foreign borrowing and foreign direct investment were persistently resisted. For example, in 1875 an American trader applied to the Japanese government for a permit to open a woolen plant. With the establishment of the regular standing army and navy forces, Japan's imports of woolen cloth for military uniforms were rapidly rising. Rather than having a foreigner pre-empt woolen markets in Japan, the government leaders decided to start their own woolen plant. Toshimichi Ōkubo, then Minister of Internal Affairs declared:

> ... With the application from the American investor in front of us, it is imperative for us to start our own mill immediately. With the procurement by the military forces and the police force alone, our annual consumption of woolen cloth is reaching 557,000 yen. If we add private demand for woolen cloth in the future, the potential market size is enormous. Unless we produce our own woolen cloth, the annual drain on our foreign exchange will become unbearable. But the private entrepreneurs lack at this moment both capital and technology required for the management of a woolen mill. Therefore, we should start the mill and later, at an appropriate time, sell it to the private entrepreneurs...*

The requisite technical experience for the woolen mill was supplied by Shōzō Inoue, a young staff member in the Ministry of Internal Affairs. From 1870 to 1871, he had been sent to Berlin to study military science. But he soon realized that manufacturing strength, not military science, lay behind the Prussian military might. Of his own accord, in the winter of 1872 Inoue joined the Carl Urbricht Woolen Mill to study woolmaking. In 1876 he went back to Germany. His mission was simple: study the equipment and factory layout of woolen mills and bring them back, together with German wool engineers.

As soon as Inoue's new woolen mill proved its success in 1879, he trained wool engineers and skilled workers who were then loaned to private entrepreneurs together with the government-owned equipment. A number of private woolen mills soon sprang up in Japan. In order to help the fledgling mills procure wool directly from Australia, a group of wool importers established the Kanematsu Trading Company. While Kanematsu's office is Sydney procured wool at the best possible prices its offices in Japan purchased woolen cloth from mills and distributed them inside Japan.

*Nihon Seni Sangyoshi (History of the Japanese Textile Industry), The Textile Association, Tokyo, 1958, pp. 270–271.

Similar anecdotes marked the beginning of various "modern" industries in Japan. The government would take the initiative in seeking out the fruits of Western technologies and institutions and in diffusing them widely to indigenous entrepreneurs. It had to be the Japanese themselves who would make the critical decisions on what technologies to transplant to Japan. Manufacturing technologies were brought in by Japanese who were sent abroad by the government and private firms on the mission to "search and bring back," as well as by foreign engineers and teachers who were hired on terminal contracts.

As these early attempts bore fruit, two distinct features emerged as the commitment of both government and business circles toward the industrialization process. They were: (1) both government and business circles when possible, kept foreign investments and foreign goods out of Japan; and (2) both government and business circles invested time, effort and money in gathering information on foreign markets, industrial technologies and sciences, as well as in disseminating such information to indigenous entrepreneurs and merchants through the extensive use of government-sponsored pilot plants and trade exhibitions.

This fiercely nationalistic attitude left Japan no choice but to rely on her own human resources for rapid industrialization. The conviction—almost wishful thinking at first—that improved work habits and technological knowledge and experience embodied in hard working individuals could augment the dearth of natural resources and capital (machinery), comprised the early industrial and educational policies of Japan.

Thus, it was no accident that Japan instituted publicly funded compulsory elementary school education for both male and female children in 1873, nineteen years earlier than Britain. A selected number of secondary and advanced institutes of learning and training were created at the government's expenses. Their students were selected only on the basis of highly competitive entrance examinations.[5] Young and ambitious talents were thus channeled into appropriate positions in the government administration and private firms. The technocratic society solely based on the "meritocracy" of the individuals involved was born.

In order to pay the foreign exchange costs of Japan's industrialization—a process that encompassed broad educational, commercial, social, legal and political reforms—Japanese entrepreneurs were urged to export their products. And the exportability of Japanese manufactures was accepted by both government and business as the ultimate test in determining the quality of Japanese goods. As a nationalistic service to their country, Japanese businesses, small and large and new and old, grew increasingly oriented toward export markets. Indeed, the obsession to export their products before long led government and business circles to equate "trade surplus" with a source of "national wealth." This version of Japanese "mercantilism," with an emphasis on export supremacy, became ingrained as the guiding business ideology of Japan.

In the early days of Japan's export drive, during the 1870s and 1880s, the Japanese consulate officers stationed in major foreign markets in the United States and Europe acted as the market information collectors for Japanese firms. In Japan, government and business leaders together established export clearing houses so that foreign purchasing merchants could not play one Japanese supplier off against another. Furthermore, the government and the exporters together formalized the quality test for such important export items as silk yarns. And export orders were allocated on a competitive basis according to the product quality of each firm. Thus, Japanese manufacturers' quest for export supremacy kept fanning their zeal for technological improvements required for better quality products at worldwide competitive production costs. Later, as private trading firms were established, they took over from the government overseas marketing efforts for emerging manufacturing industries.

Upon the basis of shared goals of catching up with the West, businesses expected the government to set over-all goals for the country, to allocate such scarce resources as technology and capital according to the priorities of respective industries and to keep out foreign businesses.[6] And the cooperation between government and business was all the more necessary to fight off foreign imports under the political handicap that modern Japan had unknowingly inherited. Around the mid-Nineteenth Century, the Japanese government had signed away its sovereign right to set import tariffs and to institute import quotas in the trade treaties that it concluded with such Western powers as the United States, the United Kingdom, France, Russia and the Netherlands.

Because foreign goods could not be kept out of the country through prohibitive tariffs and quotas, Japanese manufacturers, in attempting to substitute their goods for imports, had to become internationally competitive in terms of price, product quality and delivery commitment. Target products for "import substitution" had to be selected carefully. Requisite technologies had to be imported and adapted to Japanese manufacturing conditions. Both the domestic and international marketing of finished goods needed to be accomplished in direct competition with foreign goods. Government subsidies had to be channeled into a limited number of industries, upon which Japan's future critically depended. Product and process innovations as well as newly imported manufacturing technologies needed to be diffused rapidly among diverse manufacturing firms. All these efforts required implicit but close cooperation between government, business and educational circles. The humiliating reminder that Japan was tricked by the Western powers into signing unequal trade treaties, united Japanese from various walks of life to persevere in overtaking the Western powers in industrial competition.

In Japan's single-minded pursuit of industrialization, the notion of "public domain"—the government's domain—was blurred with the notion of "private domain"—what private industries did.[7] The specific roles played by either the government or by private industries were divided more by the expediency of time than by any overriding ideological demarcation of what was public and what was private. When there were no private firms financially or technologically capable of commencing target manufacturing operations, the government set them up and guaranteed a market for their products. Few businessmen doubted the government's promise to turn the operations over to private industries once they proved successful. When private entrepreneurs took their own risks, and proved that their own products were commercially and technologically viable in direct competition with foreign goods, they ran to the government for further assistance in research and development efforts as well as for help in driving foreign goods and investments out of the country.

The government accommodated such requests almost as a reward for private entrepreneurs' achievements. The Japanese automobile industry and an assortment of chemical industries were thus established during the 1920s and 1930s. Likewise, early in the 1950s the modern sewing machine industry was successfully launched, and it even blocked the reentry of Singer Sewing Machine Company into Japan. By the 1960s both leading sewing machine and automobile firms were spearheading Japanese direct investments abroad.

This convergence of government (public) and private interests was to be repeated many times over during the postwar reconstruction era of the 1950s, thus, producing a government-business relationship often characterized impressionistically by foreign observers as "Japan, Inc."—the simplistic notion that the government and various industries are respectively likened to the head office and related operating divisions.

"INDICATIVE ECONOMIC PLANNING" AFTER WORLD WAR II

The Second World War ended on August 15, 1945. Defeated, Japan was left with war-torn industries operating at, on the average, only

27 percent of the production capacities of the prewar peak era of 1935–37. While production capacities were destroyed and inventory supplies of various goods were totally depleted, over 200 billion yen worth of paper money and bank deposits (about four times as much as the gross national product equivalent at the time) were unleashed on the dissipated economy.[8] The presiding Minister of Finance, Kaya, defroze bank deposits and paid out back wages and accounts owed to military personnel and to industries, in order to diffuse the rebellious moods which reigned throughout the disorganized military forces and dejected civilian populace. As expected, galloping inflation ensued. By the end of October 1945, two months after the war had ended, black market prices for basic necessities were running twenty to thirty times higher than "officially controlled prices."

Furthermore, on September 24, 1945 the allied occupying forces promulgated that Japanese industries be even further weakened in order to deprive Japan of any strength to wage war again. At that time, Japan already had a population of about 72 million people and was bracing herself for the immediate repatriation of over 3 million Japanese citizens and over 3.5 million disarmed Japanese soldiers from former colonies and battlefields abroad. Japan's main problem was to feed, clothe, shelter and employ the estimated 80 million people who lived on the congested archipelago, only about 18 percent of which could be called arable.

Since 1930 the growing labor force had been absorbed mainly by the growth of the new machinery and chemical industries. Such new industries as steel and iron, nonferrous metals, fabricated metals, machinery and chemicals provided both additional employment and increased living standards. Textile and indigenous crafts industries, upon which the early industrialization efforts of the 1870s–1920s had depended, had not shown much growth since 1930.

These historical patterns pointed to one and only one direction for the industrial reconstruction of the country: Japan must continue to develop such infant but growth-potential industries as chemicals and machinery, and to shed other mature but obsolete industries. This reaffirmation of the Japanese "instinct," based upon the past successes in industrialization since the 1870s, emerged as the working consensus of the special study group which met during the months between August 1945 and March 1946 under the aegis of the Ministry of Foreign Affairs.[9] This study group consisted of economists, engineers, journalists and business executives from various sectors of business, government, educational and mass media circles—the opinion leaders of society. How did they implement their consensus of solving both galloping inflation and massive unemployment through rapid expansions of industrial production?

The Japanese faced the problem. The General Headquarters (GHQ) of the Allied Occupying Forces were recommending that Japan should specialize in such light goods as textiles and craft industries and reject the course of developing peaceful but heavy and chemical industries. Japan needed to diffuse politically the dictum of the conventional wisdom counselled by the GHQ.

Japanese government and business circles seized upon the recommendations that were made during the summer of 1947 to the GHQ by a group of American scientific advisors.[10] This group's official report emphasized that the development of science and technology in Japan was essential for the reconstruction of the economy, as well as for the export promotion of Japanese manufactures. The report went on to conclude that both the unit price and quality of those products succeeding in the international free competition trade markets were constantly changing. The report recommended that:

> ... some time in the future when Japan is readmitted into competitive world trade, Japan will have to rely on her scientists and engineers in order to invent new products, to identify new products early, and at the same time to reduce the production costs of existing products. Japan will also need to develop a mechanism by which competitive new and old products will be timely sent into the world market...[11]

Furthermore, the report maintained that in the long run, the Japanese standard of living could only be improved through increases in manufacturing productivity. An export drive sustained mainly by low wage rates and a low level of domestic consumption would again lead to the social dumping of Japanese goods in the world market and thus would cause chaos.

With these pronouncements for a technology-led growth of the economy and international trade, coming from none other than the GHQ advisors, Japanese government and business circles drew up a list of industries which they proposed that Japan attempt to develop further. The list clearly showed that the target industries were chosen by two main criteria: (1) a large, immediate and growing demand in Japan for the products manufactured; and (2) future export potential of the products. Japan was to foster the target industries on the basis of her perceived strengths. These strengths included: (1) a highly educated and motivated Japanese labor force; (2) potential hydroelectrical energy which could be generated by harnessing heavy rainfall and abundant running streams; and (3) available coal reserves.

It was one thing to draw up a list of candidate industries—the "national champions" of the future—but it was another to execute these plans under the dire circumstances of the time: a shortage of every conceivable industrial material, rampaging inflation, a broken public faith in governmental leadership, and political and economic restrictions imposed by the GHQ. Raw materials, capital and technologies had to be rationed carefully. Someone had to set a priority on the basis of what was good for the Japanese economy as a whole (articulation of public interest).

The combined industrial combines called *Zaibatsu*, used to allocate scarce financial and technological resources among the respective member corporations. But it was being dismantled by the GHQ as part of a prevailing postwar atmosphere of social and political reform. The government became the only body on which individual firms could rely for the allocation of resources and for the charting of Japan's future course of development. With the dissolution of the Ministry of Internal Affairs, which had run the national policy programs, and with the dissolutions of both the Navy and Army Ministries, which had controlled the key manufacturing industries producing arms and warships, the crucial task of industrial reconstruction fell on the Ministry of Trade and Commerce, the forerunner of the Ministry of International Trade and Industry (MITI)—formed late in 1950 by merging the Agency of Foreign Trade and the Ministry of Trade and Commerce.

As the effective means of guiding Japanese industries, MITI resurrected the mechanism of government-business cooperation that existed during the period of wartime control of the Japanese economy. The basic asset left for the defeated Japan was, indeed, the proven mechanism of controlling and guiding Japanese manufacturing industries. Various industrial associations were to aid MITI in guiding and disciplining, if necessary, individual manufacturers.

MITI's prestige soared in the eyes of Japanese business circles as it visibly succeeded in its first attempt at easing production bottlenecks in the economy by linking coal and steel production.[12] This link policy poured capital and necessary materials simultaneously into coal and steel production. By channeling increased steel output into coal production and increased coal output into steel production through the strict bilateral barter arrangement, MITI broke the vicious cycle of the time: less coal output was leading to further reduction of steel output which in turn curtailed coal output. Coal and steel industries that regained self-sustaining power in turn revived the machinery and chemical industries dependent on steel and coal production.

Out of this experience did emerge the basic tenet of MITI's industrial policies. Namely, MITI would aid mainly a few large and growth-minded firms in the key industries. In turn, large manufacturing firms whose economic strength was further nourished by

MITI's assistance were to pull up small- to medium-sized manufacturers clustering around a few leading manufacturing firms. As was ingrained in the early industrialization efforts of the 1870s, the principal role of the government was to intervene in the fledgling but growth-potential industries and to help a few leading firms grow even larger.

This "survival of the fittest" that the government advocated permeated industries and triggered fierce competitive scrambling by individual firms for the leading positions in the industry. The government was expected to promote this industrial Darwinism rather than to protect weak and dying industries. And the general public, that shared the national goal of "catching up with the West," actively supported the government's role as the promoter of the survival of the fittest.

IMPLEMENTATION OF THE INDICATIVE ECONOMIC PLANS—FINANCIAL LEVER

Once target industries and products were identified, the Ministry of Finance and the Bank of Japan would see to it that scarce funds be rationed to private banks, screening the loan applications of their industrial client firms. Because the funds deposited by their customers were too meager to meet loan demands, and because their own equity and asset bases had been depleted by the galloping inflation, private banks had to borrow funds from the Bank of Japan. Thus, private banks were informally organized as the effective "pass-through conduits" for government funds to target industries and firms.

Manufacturing firms whose equity capital was also depleted by galloping inflation had to rely on their banks for both long-term and short-term loans. Their extraordinarily high debt to equity ratios of three to one made them totally dependent on their banks which were in turn at the mercy of the Bank of Japan. This unique relationship between manufacturing firms and banks—the structure that evolved as a historical accident—provided the Japanese government and the Bank of Japan with effective levers to use both monetary policies (central bank's money supply) and fiscal policies (government's investments and industrial promotions). The Bank of Japan curtailed or expanded its lendings to member banks depending on the need for smoothing out the short-term cyclical fluctuations of the Japanese economy. And MITI pursued its long-term growth goal for selected industries and large firms by letting weaker firms and industries die a natural death at every downturn of the business cycle. This was the structure of the Japanese economy that *The Economist* pointed out in 1962 as the uniquely Japanese mechanism of implementing industrial policies through "indicative economic planning."

The priorities of capital rationing were set by the Ministry of Finance and were made congruent with the industrial goals promoted by MITI. These priorities of "loan needs" were published and updated as recognized needs changed, so that private manufacturing firms could adapt their growth plans to the suggested priorities. Industries were classified into four categories depending upon the government's priorities: A-1, A-2, B and C. Categories A-1 and A-2 received top priorities in their needs for both investment and working capital. Category C was barred from any access to bank loans, while Category B was screened for loan application on a case-by-case basis. A-1 industries were petroleum, coal, steel and fertilizer. A-2 industries consisted of electric and non-electric machinery, shopbuilding, sheet glass, plywoods and transportation equipment. By discouraging consumer goods industries, Japan hoped to expand her industrial base. This rather crude but effective device of capital rationing lasted well into July 1963.

As demands for both working capital and physical investment loans outstripped the Bank of Japan's resources, the government began to pour funds, through the Reconstruction Financing Agency (RFA), into various industries. As a matter of fact, during the postwar reconstruction era of the 1950s, over three-quarters of all capital investment needs of private manufacturing firms were financed by RFA loans.[13] In other words, the Japanese government underwrote almost totally the financial needs of the immediate postwar industries.

Up until 1952, this financial lever of the government was also effectively used to subvert repeated attempts by the GHQ to cure Japan of galloping inflation by implementing drastic deflationary measures (surplus budgets). Rather than inviting the open wrath of the GHQ by rejecting the surplus budgets, Japanese officialdom quietly let the Bank of Japan and the RFA increase their combined loans and offset the deflationary pressures of the surplus budgets. The success of the coal-steel linkage policy mentioned earlier, owed in fact, much of its success to the quiet subversion of GHQ-recommended deflationary policies which the Bank of Japan, the RFA and private financial communities tacitly waged.

Early in 1948, emboldened by the success of its coal-steel linkage policy, the Japanese government published its first five-year economic plan.*

In drawing up this five-year plan—a broad declaration of economic goals intended mainly to outline future scenarios for Japan—did there emerge the institutional mechanism by which business executives of leading firms and their assistants became formally involved in debating diverse social and economic issues and goals with government officials.

The Economic Planning Agency (established in 1946) feeds various economic forecasts to literally hundreds of subcommittees of advisory councils to MITI, Ministry of Finance and other appropriate ministries. Business leaders who can be counted on to cooperate with government industrial policy-makers are appointed to the subcommittees. In turn, business firms want to be involved in these subcommittees in order to obtain useful information on the Japanese economy and political readings on the thinking of key government policy-makers. Deliberations in each subcommittee help businesses comprehend the specifics of public interest (employment, growth, export, income distribution, price trend and technological growth) that MITI and other agencies articulate.

Indeed, this process of informational exchange between leading business sectors and government policy-makers would reinforce the singular utility of drawing up "five year" plans and, then updating them in two to three years. This process, having government officials appreciate private interests of industries and having private industries confirm the public policy interests they were expected to fulfill, functioned well.

The first five-year plan was distinguished by the absence of an immediate containment of inflationary pressures, and was predicated on the expectation that the United States would continue to provide Japan with necessary industrial raw materials and foods on credit or preferably on forgivable loans. The United States government was dissatisfied with this situation. In December 1948 GHQ finally ordered that the Japanese government immediately enforce a single exchange rate (360 yen to one U.S. dollar) and that a series of severe

---

*This five year plan and subsequent plans are not to be interpreted as the government's official plan of action. Each ministry is left free to define and redefine its own specific goals and actions. See Ryutaro Komiya, "Planning in Japan", in M. Bornstein, ed., *Economic Planning: East and West*, Cambridge, Mass.: Ballinger, 1975.

deflationary measures be instituted.[14] The tacit subversion tactics of the Bank of Japan and the RFA were not to be tolerated. This abrupt disappearance of government financial support plunged Japan into a prolonged depression throughout 1949 and into the first half of 1950. The early successes of the "indicative economic planning," that had put the war-torn economy back on a recovery track, appeared to be dissipating. Then, in July 1950, the Korean War broke out and revived the Japanese economy and MITI's leadership in guiding private industries.

THE ECONOMIC RECOVERY OF THE 1950s

During the 1950s, the independent Japan needed a new "great leap forward" to accelerate the industrial growth, and the potency of synchronized coordination between the Bank of Japan and Ministry of Finance on one hand, and MITI and other ministries on the other, most vividly manifested itself in the success of the "planned shipbuilding." The aim of this industrial policy was to let the shipbuilding industry spearhead the development of export-oriented heavy and chemical industries.[15] The success of this policy not only reaffirmed the converging conducts of public and private interests but established new Japanese technological innovations as the driving forces of industrial growth. And this success led to the first large-scale overseas investment by a Japanese manufacturing firm, when in 1959 Ishikawajima-Harima Industry (IHI), the leading shipbuilder and industrial equipment manufacturer, began to build a shipyard (Ishibras) in Brazil.

By 1959 IHI had become a world leader in the technology of shipbuilding. Armed with technological competence, IHI went into Brazil to provide itself with a strategic location for servicing IHI-built ships cruising around the world as well as to pre-empt the Brazilian market. IHI's entry into Brazil was eased when the Brazilian government, persuaded by IHI, adopted a policy of "planned shipbuilding" similar to that of Japan.[16] This export of not only "technology" but "intitutional experience" of the government-business relationships marked the harbinger of Japanese investment in developing countries.

More important, the means by which the government had subsidized shipbuilders and shipping firms also precipitated the groupings of various manufacturing firms around leading private banks and trading firms; thus aiding the resurrection of prewar *Zaibatsu* combines around respective "flagship" banks and trading companies. Detailed accounts of the "planned shipbuilding" policy of Japan would reveal that the government's direct involvement pattern of the 1870s was once again played out to foster a "national champion" industry through encouragement of both cooperation and competition in the industry. By channeling 100 percent government financing of ship purchases to shipping firms through a selected ten or so private banks, the government induced shipyards to gear up their production for the "planned (guaranteed) orders." But the shipyards were left to themselves to compete for orders from other shipping firms on the basis of price, quality of work and the delivery schedule. Thus, respective shipyards continued to reinvest their profits in renewing shipbuilding facilities as well as in improving their production processes. Their technological innovations set patterns of Japanese thrusts oriented to saving both labor and raw materials. In particular, welding facilities, which permitted large-scale and continuous electrowelding, were modernized to permit the building of large ships. In order to reduce production costs of ships, shipyards endeavored to reduce the amount of steel used per ship (material saving method) as well as the number of required production processes (labor saving method). For example, the amount of steel required for a standard 7000 DWT freighter with 4000 HP was reduced from 3600 metric tons in 1949 to 3000 in 1955. During the same period, the number of production processes required for this standard ship was reduced by 35 percent.

With increased investments in larger and larger dry-docks and berths, larger freighters and oil tankers were produced (product innovations). Both product- and production-related innovations were, then, freely diffused among the leading shipyards through the common schooling efforts and joint study groups of engineers working for different firms. In 1950 the government established the Ship Technology Institute in order to carry out R&D activities for shipbuilding and ship operations.

Meanwhile, steel and machinery industries, which benefited most from the expansion of the shipbuilding industry, made efforts to reduce the prices of their products as well as to improve their product quality. MITI saw to it that the key manufacturing industries linked to the shipbuilding industry would be favored by the importing of requisite technologies through licensing agreements.

By the mid-1950s, Japanese shipyards appeared technologically able to compete with the then leading shipbuilder of the world, the United Kingdom. But successful exporting required Japan to overcome the last remaining barrier to entry into the world market: overseas marketing effort. Again the government and trading companies came to help. The Export-Import Bank of Japan extended low cost and long-term loans to finance the exportation of ships. Japanese trading firms actively scanned the world and persuaded Greek shipowners to divert their orders from the United Kingdom and Norway to Japan, which was, by then, not only able to build mammoth tankers but capable of delivering them twelve to eighteen months sooner than the U.K. or Norway. In addition, trading firms and shipyards exchanged respective credit ratings on foreign customers so that customers with dubious records would be blacklisted by all the shipyards in Japan.

After the mid-1950s, ships became the leading export product of Japan. The "quality image" of tankers and freighters made in Japan helped to change the world market conception that Japanese products were shoddily made. Just as the foreign exchange costs of fostering the Japanese shipbuilding industry were financed by the export earnings from such old export leaders as textiles, toys and ceramics, the tankers and freighters exported from Japan were in turn counted on to pay for the development of subsequent target industries such as automobiles and computers. The foreign exchange regulations of the Japanese government were specifically designed to permit such allocations of export earnings. Newly selected industries (firms) were given a high priority in receiving foreign exchange needed for importation of raw materials, machinery, and technology.

IMPLEMENTATION OF THE INDICATIVE ECONOMIC PLANS— TECHNOLOGICAL INNOVATIONS

The Japanese government also rationed the importation of manufacturing technologies among Japanese firms. Japanese manufacturing firms were exhorted to steer their own R&D activities into directions deemed useful for the country. Such general R&D guidance as well as government screening of technical licensing agreements with foreign firms was carried out on the basis of a government-recommended list of new technologies for Japan. The spirit of "search and bring back" that Japan inculcated in the industries in the 1870s was applied to complex screenings of candidate technologies for Japan.

By checking her industrial structure and export composite against those of the United States and other industrialized nations, Japan was able to identify the industries (products) that she might yet have to master in order to gain international competitive strength. Those products leading to the growth of the United States economy and to the world trade of manufactured goods, were to be chosen as prime candidates for Japan's expansion efforts. By carefully checking what kind of manufacturing technologies were required for leading products, and by comparing their own stock of manufacturing technologies, government and business, individually and collectively, drew up a list of product-related technologies recommended for acquisition by Japanese private firms either from abroad or through development on their own in the near future.

The list, published annually by MITI and the EPA, was used effectively after 1950, at a time when all licensing agreements between Japanese licensees and foreign licensors were being screened by the Japanese government. All the firms were free to apply for any licensing agreement. But they needed to justify their requests according to such public policy goals as the balance-of-payments, employment and technological growth. Again, the government acted as the custodian of public interest and forced private firms to attain public goals as well.

Meanwhile, for both absorptive and innovative R&D efforts in Japan, the "human stock" of R&D personnel in Japan would have to be augmented. And Japanese educational institutions were again called upon to increase the number of graduating students in the targeted fields of science and engineering.

Table 1-3 summarizes the growth trends in selected years for such

Table 1-3. R&D Related Statistics of Japan for Selected Years (In billions of yen)

Year	R&D Expenditures		Licensing fees & royalties		R&D Personnel (researchers only)
	Total	% ratio to GNP	Total	% ratio to GNP	
1948	5.9	0.3%	0.2	—	14,500
1953	46.6	0.5	4.1	—	26,633
1955	56.2	0.7	6.5	0.07%	34,208
1957	99.9	0.9	15.3	0.13	40,953
1959	148.9	1.2	22.3	0.17	52,077
1960	184.5	1.2	34.1	0.22	82,149
1961	245.3	1.3	40.7	0.21	86,763
1962	281.2	1.3	41.0	0.19	90,967
1963	321.1	1.3	48.9	0.19	105,781
1964	381.8	1.3	56.1	0.19	114,839
1965	425.5	1.3	60.1	0.18	117,596
1966	488.7	1.3	69.1	0.18	128,928
1967	606.3	1.4	86.0	0.19	138,689
1968	767.8	1.5	113.0	0.22	157,612
1969	933.2	1.6	132.5	0.22	157,057
1970	1195.3	1.7	155.9	0.22	172,002

Sources: *Keizai Tokei Nenpo*, Bank of Japan, 1970; *Kagaku Gijutsu Hakusho*, 1961-1973; *Kagaku Gijutsu Kenkyu Chosa Hokoku.*

R&D-related statistics as annual R&D expenditures, annual payment of licensing fees and royalties, number of annual licensing agreements concluded and the number of R&D personnel (excluding technicians and supportive personnel employed). By 1970, R&D expenditures reached 1.7 percent of the GNP, while Japan's payment of licensing fees and royalties remained at 0.2 percent of her GNP.

Prior to the marked increases in R&D activities from 1965 onward, the period 1957–60 should be noted as the time when Japanese industries succeeded in raising the percentage ratio of R&D expenditures to GNP to beyond the 1.0 percent mark. A marked jump in the number of R&D researchers from 1959 to 1960 reflects Japanese firms' efforts to intensify renovative R&D efforts in an attempt to counteract import liberalizations scheduled by the government for after 1960.

Incidentally, total payments of licensing fees and royalties by Japanese licensees to foreign licensors during the period 1950–70 were approximately 2.26 billion dollars. Currently (for the years after 1971) it is estimated that Japan's annual payments of licensing fees and royalties are running $500 to $600 million annually (after the revaluations of the yen in 1971 and 1973). It was estimated that for both 1961 and 1968, Japan's R&D efforts relative to her GNP still lagged behind the United States, the United Kingdom, France and Germany. However, in terms of R&D personnel, Japan lagged behind only the United States. It proved very economical for Japan to latch onto the technological attainments of other countries, most notably the United States!

Not all the licensing agreements in a given year represent manufacturing technologies new to the Japanese economy as a whole. Seeing competitors adventuring into new product areas or new production processes through licensing agreements, other Japanese firms quickly sought and concluded similar agreements, more often than not with the same technology sources as that of their competitors.[17] Or, when some firms saw their competitors developing new products or processes themselves, they quickly sought to conclude licensing agreements with foreign technology sources out of the fear that their technological inferiority would cost them a market share in Japan.

A fierce competitive feeling among Japanese firms may be gleaned from the fact that on the average three to five competing firms obtained identical technologies from abroad, often from the same licensor. It was noted that for such competitive industries as chemicals and electrical and electronic equipment a greater number of firms than the average obtained identical technologies from abroad.

Given their reliance upon foreign technologies, how did Japanese manufacturing firms keep track of technological developments abroad and decide which technologies to import? Although slightly outdated, the 1963 MITI Report on Current State of Technologies contains the responses of 975 manufacturing firms on their methods of technological intelligence-gathering activities (Table 1-4).

Approximately 98 percent of the respondents used publicly available data that they themselves collected. About 54 percent of the firms either regularly sent research staff members abroad or had some type of research staff stationed abroad. It is evident that the larger the firm, the better it can afford not only more expensive ways of collecting information, but also more extensive uses of all possible information sources at home and abroad. More striking, however, is the fact that 95 percent of all small- to medium-sized firms (paid-in capital of 50 to 100 million yen) systematically used publicly available data published abroad, and that about one-third of that percentage even used an expensive method of stationing or intermittently sending intelligence engineers abroad; thus demonstrating the time-honored conduct of Japanese firms, of being committed to investing time and funds in searching for technological and market information abroad.

With Japanese firms, both small and large, actively engaged in competitive R&D activities at home as well as in seeking technologies abroad, the Japanese government's industrial policy was assured a reasonable success. The government's role was limited to assuring the presence of elements of competition and protection for each industry. It strove to achieve this goal by arranging to have two or more selected firms obtain similar technologies in key industries. The postwar developments of the Japanese synthetic fiber industry and automotive industry clearly attest to the success of such government policies.

For example, when Toray Co. Ltd. purchased nylon technology from DuPont in 1951 and achieved remarkable growth by grafting DuPont technology onto Toray's Amiran techniques, its competitors in Japan rushed to seek similar nylon technologies. But the government feared that there might be excessive competition in the domestic market, and allowed only Teijin Co. Ltd. to enter the nylon market. The government wanted to nurture the growth of both Toray and Teijin in the field of nylon products assuring the two firms sufficiently large markets to permit them economies of scale in both production and marketing activities.

The passenger-car sector of the automotive industry of Japan also grew after 1950 mainly on the basis of licensed technologies. The Japanese government succeeded in the 1930s in driving both General

Table 1-4. Relative Frequency of Choice of Intelligence Methods Used by 975 Japanese Companies, Classified by Size of Firm

Size of Firm (Paid-in Capital)	Publicly Available Data	Regular Staff Stationed Abroad	Private Information Services	Overseas Information Services	Japanese Trading Firm	Scientific Information Center
50–100 mil. yen (155)*	95.5%	28.4%	21.9%	7.7%	7.1%	5.8%
100–1 bil. (511)*	97.3	47.2	32.7	15.3	13.1	12.1
1–5 bil. (231)*	99.2	71.0	48.1	31.2	25.1	24.7
Over 5 bil. (78)*	100.0	88.5	66.7	41.0	39.8	37.2
For all the Respondents (975)*	97.9	53.2	36.7	19.9	17.1	16.1

*The figures in parentheses are the number of respondents in each category of size of firm.

Source: *Gijutsudoko Chosa Hokokusho* [Report on Current State of Technologies], Ministry of International Trade and Industry, Tokyo, May 1963.

Motors and Ford out of Japan. Subsequently, the government encouraged competition among four automobile manufacturers during the war, and the automobile industry concentrated on the production of trucks and buses.

As a result, the technology of passenger vehicles was left underdeveloped. The manufacturers lacked not only engineering competence in product parts development, but also in-plant experience in the assembly of passenger cars. Toyota Motors Co. Ltd. chose to transfer on its own its experience in buses and trucks to passenger cars as soon as the Japanese government permitted passenger car production in 1949. In order to catch up with Toyota, Nissan obtained in 1951, a KD assembly contract for the Austin model from the BMC (U.K.). Isuzu obtained a similar agreement for the Hilman-Minx model from Rootes Motors (U.K.), while Hino followed suit by becoming a licensee of the 4-c.v. Renault model (France).[18] These contracts were for five to seven years and forbade the Japanese licensees to export the assembled products, although it did enable them to increase the Japanese-made content of passenger cars on a predetermined schedule. By the time the contracts expired, the Japanese licensees, notably Nissan, had accumulated adequate experience in manufacturing compact passenger cars to enable them to develop and market their own models at home and later abroad.

More recently, from the late 1950s to the early 1960s, MITI undertook specific initiatives in creating the beginnings of the computer industry in Japan. One should note, again, two characteristics of MITI's industrial policies toward the Japanese computer industry. First, MITI successfully pressured IBM into making IBM's basic patents on computer technologies available to Japanese firms. The royalty of 5 percent of sales was negotiated between MITI and IBM so that MITI could prevent IBM from bidding up royalty fees by baiting one eager Japanese firm against the other. Second, once this "general rule" of Japanese firms' accessibility to IBM's basic patents was established, MITI relied on this mutual competitive spirit between hopeful entrant firms to guide the computer industry.[19]

Since the computer hardware technologies were still at a formative stage in the early 1960s, MITI permitted hopeful Japanese entrants to conclude licensing agreements with various American and European firms. At the same time, the science and technology research institution which was attached to MITI, made all its computer technologies and know-how available free of charge to competing Japanese entrants. A number of leading universities were again called into the national services to aid the growth of "Japanese computer technology."

Moreover, MITI and the infant computer firms of Japan became aware early in the 1960s of additional barriers to entry in the computer industry. The paramount barrier to entry, more than requisite hardware or costly R&D activities, were the marketing skills required in order to bring the computer to potential business customers. The trade financing which enabled computer producers to lease expensive hardware were only a fraction of the so-called marketing problems faced. This early awareness of Japanese firms and government stands out today. For instance, the French government has persistently failed throughout the years to recognize such invisible but critical barriers to entry.

In order to expose fledgling firms of the computer industry to marketing stimuli, MITI financially aided them (seven original entrant firms were later reduced to five) in jointly forming the computer lease finance company by sharing equally the equity capital of the firm. Computer producers were, however, left alone to compete with one another for both government and private computer customers. Successful marketers then drew on the financial resources of the lease finance company at the expense of less successful marketers whose equity investments in the lease company were then drained off for the "survival of the fittest."

Computer firms which emerged as successful from this process of "learning-by-doing," were later put under the strong leadership of MITI and classified into three groupings: namely, (1) Fujitsu-Hitachi, (2) NEC-Toshiba, and (3) Oki-Univac. Fujitsu, whose technological capability was then backed by Hitachi's financial and political strength, was to grow confident enough in 1972 to acquire a computer research laboratory spun-off by former IBM R&D personnel in the United States.

In short, at least throughout the 1950s and the 1960s, MITI's industrial policies were characterized by a judicious manipulation of competitive spirit between Japanese firms. Foreign firms' access to the Japanese market was severely limited by MITI's restrictions on foreign direct investments in Japan as well as on the importation of goods and technologies to Japan. Once this protective shield was erected around Japan, Japanese private firms were encouraged to compete with one another in order to demonstrate their vigor in the "survival of the fittest." When weaker competitors were shaken out of the competitive process, MITI rewarded the surviving firms with further financial and technological incentives.

PRIVATE ENTREPRENEURSHIP

Why has MITI been able to motivate Japanese firms to excel in manufacturing technologies? Obviously, the commitment by

Japanese firms to the national goal of export supremacy—the guiding philosophy of Japanese businessmen—must have driven private firms to absorb foreign technologies well and to improve on them. This individual trait of Japanese entrepreneurs at first drove foreign imports out of Japan, and later led to exporting to the countries from which the original technologies came.

A case in point is the sewing machine industry, where Japanese export successes again led to spearheading direct investments abroad. In July 1960, Janome Co. Ltd., a leading sewing machine manufacturer of Japan, purchased the New Home Co., a subsidiary of Free Sewing Machine Co. of the United States for one million dollars in cash—the first major purchase by a Japanese firm of an American firm in a product field in which the United States had long commanded unchallenged leadership in the world.[20] In March 1964, Janome opened its manufacturing subsidiary in West Germany on a 50-50 joint venture with Pfaff GMBH, one of the oldest and largest sewing machine manufacturers in Europe.

Janome's direct investments in the United States and West Germany were backed by over fifty years of Japanese struggles with Singer. To cut a long story short, Janome completely pirated Singer's standard model sewing machine back in the early 1930s. Janome's discovery evolved over a fifty-year period, when gunsmiths and blacksmiths of Japan with their simple metal-working machines, were developing lucrative repair services. These artisans were copying Singer's parts because Singer had ignored supplying them with repair parts. Janome, then, simply assembled these "carbon copied" parts into standardized sewing machines.

Once mastering how to copy a Singer product, Janome had to compete with Singer's quality image, backed up with liberal installment payment schemes. Janome had to create its own customers. Janome aimed its sales pitches at the housewives and daughters of the lower middle class, who were being ignored by Singer but were envious of the upper and middle class families who possessed sewing machines (Singer's installment payment required a rather well-to-do co-signer). There were many potential sewing machine customers who were kept out of Singer's sales plan, but who were also too poor to pay the down payment of 60 yen for a 125-yen Janome model (as opposed to Singer's 250 yen). Janome was financially too weak to extend further sales credit. No bank in Japan was willing to loan working capital to finance Janome's term payment schemes. Janome's solution turned out to be a brilliantly innovative marketing scheme.

Janome sold a "purchase reservation credit" by which a prospective customer paid, say, 5 yen per month. When the amount paid in reached 60 yen, the saver-customer had a Janome model delivered to her home. This purchase reservation credit (a prepaid installment schemer) met both the psychological and financial needs of Japanese housewives, daughters and working girls of the lower middle class.

The Japanese tradition had long required every girl to become competent in cooking and sewing. Wives were expected to make most of their own and their children's clothing as well as curtains and other such household items. The traditional notion of Japanese frugality and modesty hailed as an exemplary virtue for even well-to-do housewives, who sewed their own and their children's clothes. Even when a housemaid was hired, it was the housewife's obligation to teach her cooking and sewing. As a result, a sewing machine was increasingly considered an indispensable item in a bride's dowry. At the same time, another traditional custom frowned on anyone incurring large debts that could not be repaid in a short time. It was unacceptable for a bride to bring a large debt such as an installment contract with her into her new household. And it was among the lower middle class populace in cities, that these traditional values were most strongly preserved.

With an increased sales volume, Janome commenced the mass production of sewing machines by adapting the process used for rifles and machine guns. With this production efficiency, added to Janome's innovative marketing plan, and with the souring of Japan-U.S. relationships over Japan's invasion of China and Manchuria, Janome finally drove Singer out of Japan in 1938.

In anticipation of Singer's re-entry into Japan after World War II, Janome and three other leading sewing machine firms organized about 200 independent parts manufacturers and about 230 independent parts subcontractors to benefit from standardized parts specifications. By having each parts manufacturer and subcontractor specialize in one-, two- or three-part items, each was able to reap the benefits of a manufacturing economy of scale. In around 1948 when Singer was trying to re-enter Japan, a typical Japanese part manufacturer was producing over 500,000 units of the same part per month, while Singer's largest production run of a single part item at that time was estimated to be at best around 40,000 units per month.

Once able to hold Singer at bay, Janome and other sewing machine firms in Japan went on to innovate their products and further improve their production efficiency. The rest of the story is common history. Japanese-made sewing machines captured by the late 1950s over 30 percent of the sewing machine market in the United States. Japanese trading firms exported Japanese sewing machines to the rest of the world. Once having proved the exportability of their products, Janome and other sewing machine firms and parts manufacturers were given access to low-interest, long-term loans for capital investment by the Japanese government. And MITI supervised the sewing machine industry in order to maintain a high product quality as well as to avoid excessive price cuts in export markets. The convergence of both the public and private interests of government and business circles of Japan was again displayed.

INDUSTRIAL STRUCTURE OF JAPAN

As the preceding success of Janome reveals, small- to medium-sized manufacturing firms and subcontractors were assigned, under the leadership of large manufacturing firms, a limited number of production operations so that planned divisions of tasks could be accomplished, often along a vertically interrelated line of products and services.

Even since the outcry of "catch up and overtake the West" was heard—a cry which from around the 1870s to 1911 turned the humiliation of unequal treaties into the driving force for Japanese industrialization—the division of labor among firms and individuals has been consciously cultivated as the only means by which Japan would be able to catch up with the West. It was assumed that Japan could adapt and use the same trades begun by the West in much less time. This division of labor deeply permeated the various walks of industrial and mercantile life. Unwritten but recognizable "boundaries" or "territories" for business activities have been drawn between firms. Both competition and cooperation penetrate Japanese industries according to invisible rules governing the time-honored division of task and labor among manufacturing firms.

When labor mobility between firms was extremely limited under the Japanese practices of "lifetime" employment, and when large growing firms employed and kept a selected number of "fresh" recruits just out of school, those workers who could not initially find jobs with large firms or who had to find post-retirement jobs after being released from large firms, joined small- to medium-sized manufacturing and subcontracting firms. This dichotomy in the labor market helped produce material differences in wages and working conditions between large and prosperous firms which paid high wages, and small- to medium-sized firms which paid more poorly.[21]

As described in the case of the sewing machine industry, the structure of division of manufacturing tasks in large and small firms often permitted cost savings arising from a long production run of a selected products and operations, and from lower labor costs for small- and medium-sized firms. This dual structure of the Japanese economy—a vast number of low paying and less profitable firms coexisting beside high paying, growing, large firms—sustained, during the 1950s and up until the mid-1960s, the fast tempo of Japanese industrialization and maintained the export competitiveness of Japanese manufactures. After the mid-1960s, the disappearance of the "dual wage structure" from the Japanese industrial scene produced the migration of Japanese manufactures abroad. In Chapter 3, we will see how these characteristics shaped the early direct investments abroad by Japanese industries.

We have already seen that the two other essential but "nonmanufacturing" functions of Japanese manufacturing firms, marketing and finance, had been relegated to trading firms on one hand and banks on the other. Rather than diverting their resources in order to build up the institutional skills of domestic and international marketing and financing, manufacturing firms concentrated on building up their experience for various products. The upshot of their subsequent success, is that manufacturing firms in Japan have popularly come to be called "mēkā" (Japanese version of *maker*), and that the marketing and financing activities have come to be performed externally by a few selected trading firms and banks.

Economically, by farming out the task of physical distribution of products at home and especially abroad to trading companies, a Japanese manufacturing firm often became able to survive as a viable economic unit of a single firm even when its small production volume and its narrow range of products would have prohibited it from maintaining a minimal required scale of market coverage. Since the overwhelming majority of manufacturers in Japan were small at the outset in the field of standard industrial products, they found it adequate to rely on trading companies to obtain the necessary reactions of their potential customers. In the field of consumer goods, there were few large-scale producers dependent on trading companies for the physical distribution of their products.

The banks, more often than not, chose to channel trade financings to various manufacturing firms through trading firms. While being used as a cushion of loan risk between banks and manufacturing firms, large trading companies borrowed heavily on their own credit from banks and loaned funds out to small- to medium-sized manufacturers. In addition to such direct financial influences over manufacturing, large trading firms increased their influence over small- to medium-sized manufacturers by becoming the legal guarantors of their bank borrowings. This practice had become so widespread through the latter half of the 1960s, that the growth of annual sales turnovers, as well as the diversification of traded goods and services of the largest ten general trading companies, had become strongly and positively related to the growth of the reported amounts of loans held by manufacturers but countersigned by the ten largest trading companies. Figure 1-1 illustrates the three-way link of divided tasks among manufacturer, bank and trading company. And this three-way link is another "idiosyncracy" of Japan in addition to the convergence of government and business interests. The roles of trading firms in Japanese direct investment will be evaluated later.

Figure 1-1. An Illustration of the Three-Way Links among Manufacturer, Bank and Trading Company of Japan

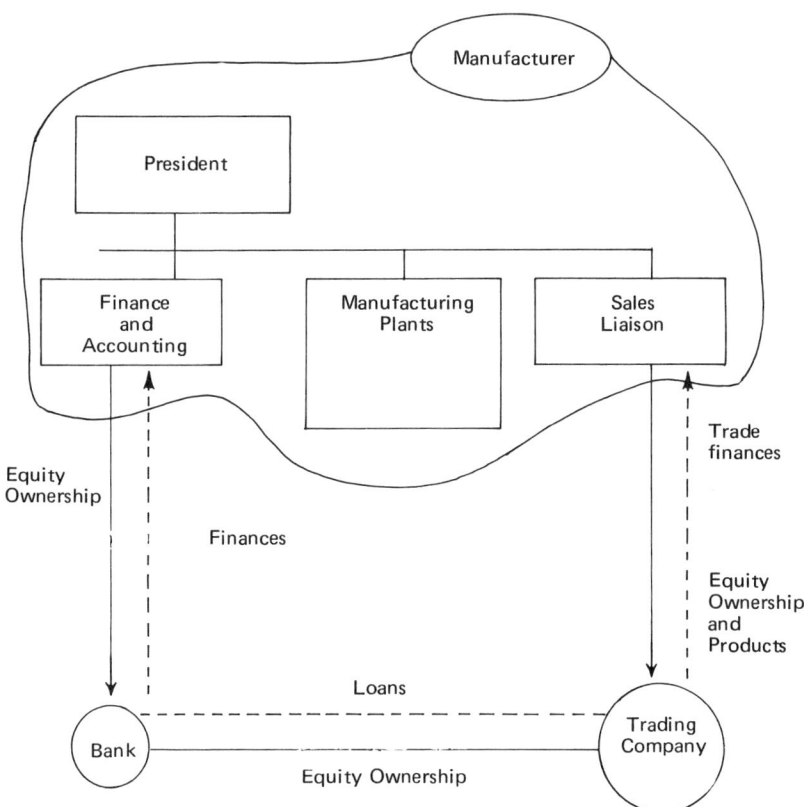

CHANGING PATTERNS OF JAPANESE EXPORTS AND DIRECT INVESTMENTS

The composite of Japanese exports changed over a period of time as the products newly transplanted to Japan later became export-competitive. Since the 1870s Japan has exploited import substitution tactics to aid her industrialization. But how has Japan's success with import substitution led to her export success in the world market? A successful import substitution does not automatically guarantee a successful exportability of newly substituted products. A "comparative advantage theorem" of international trade—Japan's export competitiveness arising from her specialization in products using the least expensive and most abundant factors of production relative to those of her trade customers—hardly offers an explanation for this success.

I found in a separate publication, that between 1950 and 1965, the change and growth of the relative competitive strength of Japanese manufacturers for a given year in the world market, was explained by the R&D efforts of Japanese industries.[22] I also found that the competitive strength of Japanese manufactures for a given year in the world market was explained by the attained level of technological competence of Japanese manufacturing industries vis-a-vis those of competing advanced nations. Neither the statistics for capital-intensity nor labor-intensity of relevant industries provided a significant explanation for the annual level or changing patterns of Japanese exports.

In addition to the above observations, there was other convincing evidence showing that over 60 percent of the economic growth of Japan during the period 1950-1965 was caused by the technological progress of Japanese industries, rather than by mere increases in the aggregate level of capital or labor in the economy.[23] In the case of Japan, whose potentially vast domestic markets were protected by the government from direct foreign competition, even mere increases in the aggregate level of capital and labor employed reflected conscious efforts on the part of manufacturers to exploit both static (increase in scale) and dynamic (cumulative manufacturing experience) economies of scale.[24] Capital investments that permitted a larger and longer production run for a given product helped reduce both the labor and raw material cost per unit of newly manufactured Japanese goods; thus making Japanese goods competitive even as regards price in the world export markets.[25] We have already noted that the export consciousness of both Japanese firms and government circles was a driving force for constant improvement in product quality. Once Japanese manufacturers were able to produce "exportable" products by concentrating their efforts on just the manufacturing task, large and small trading firms devoted themselves to cultivating domestic and overseas markets for Japanese-made goods. Trading firms invested time and money in developing extensive distribution networks and sales organizations at home and abroad, because a greater volume of sales permitted them to amortize market investment costs.

THE JAPANESE STRATEGY OF RIDING AN INTERNATIONAL PRODUCT CYCLE

Toward the end of the 1960s, Japanese manufacturers had built up technological capabilities and manufacturing experience to the point of developing new products that Japanese markets were not yet ready to accept in quantity. Rather than waiting for Japanese markets to demand these new products, Japanese manufacturer-innovators exported such new products to the United States, which was ready to purchase them in ever-increasing quantities. A few years later, when Japanese markets began to demand these products, manufacturer-innovators were not only able to continue their exports to the United States, but also to supply Japanese markets with products streamlined during earlier export-oriented production.

Thus, as innovative exporters expanded the horizons of their markets, they became able to export goods without substantial domestic market demands for these goods. And this aberration is not limited to large firms. There are many small-to-medium firms that are thriving on exports of consumer appliances that are in great demand in the United States but not yet in Japan.

For instance, from 1958 to 1969, zig-zag sewing machine models had all but replaced straight-stitching models for Japanese export. The domestic demand for this model lagged the export demand by five to six years. In other words, Japanese sewing machine manufacturers as a group went into large-scale production of zig-zag models before the domestic market was ready for this innovation. How was this possible?

The sewing machine manufacturers, who were linked closely to the major markets of the world, notably the United States, were motivated to master the manufacturing skill of zig-zag models earlier than they would have if they were predominantly preoccupied with the Japanese domestic market. When the Japanese market later caught up with the zig-zag models, manufacturers had not only already debugged zig-zag production but had also built up ample supply capacities in anticipation of an increase in Japanese demand. This behavior of a firm that is riding an "international product cycle"—a willingness to make a major shift in the product line of a domestic plant long before the domestic market becomes ready for an innovative product—is not limited to the recent experience of the Japanese sewing machine industry.

The case of the color television set manufacturers of Japan also demonstrates how a firm can use an export market to build up manufacturing skill of a new product (the old product being black and white sets). By 1964, Japan was already exporting an increasing number of black and white TV sets to the United States. This was partly because a large domestic market enabled manufacturers to produce the sets competitively, and partly because Japan's major product line of models—19 inches or smaller—happened to fit well with the portable set market or the second TV set market in the United States. American manufacturers were then forced to emphasize a new product, the color TV set, in order to fight off the Japanese competition in the black and white set. The United States' demand for color TV sets began to increase rapidly. Keenly observing the U.S. market shift, Japanese manufacturers intuitively judged that sooner or later the Japanese market demand would also shift to color. Consequently, they hurried into a developmental effort on color TV sets and soon after began exporting color sets to the United States. When the Japanese market caught up with color sets in around 1968, the manufacturer had ample capacity to meet both export and domestic demand.

However, the strategy of exploiting time lags in market demands along an international product cycle—from the United States, then to Japan, and finally even to developing nations—is but an extension of the earlier strategy of "import substitution."*

As Japanese manufacturers' technological skills are improved further, they can exploit markets along an international product cycle from the U.S. market to developing nations. For example, Sony's "video-portapack" (a compact combination of video-taping equipment and transistorized tape recorder) was first introduced in the United States. Also, the automobile firms of Japan are currently incorporating new design features and partial improvements first in the cars to be exported to North America. In both cases the prerequisites to success are the fact that manufacturers have long established their own brand names and distribution channels in the United

---

*For a theoretical and empirical treatment of this process, see Yoshi Tsurumi, "Japanese Multinational Firm," *Journal of World Trade Law* (February 1973).

States and that the final consumers of their products are essentially those who purchased their older vintage products.

INTERNATIONAL MARKETING ACTIVITIES AS TRIGGERS OF JAPANESE INVESTMENTS ABROAD

Of all the differences in the determinants of patterns of international trade between the comparative advantage theorem and the Product Life Cycle theory, the latter's recognition of exporters' marketing strategies abroad cannot be stressed too strongly. After all, a firm's intelligence in monitoring technological and market developments abroad comprises the conditions for success in the strategy of riding an international product cycle from country to country.

In other words, a firm's ability to gather vital economic and technological information abroad must also be regarded as the factor that determines the competitive advantage in international trade and investment. A firm's knowledge of various overseas territories can also be accumulated, improved and updated by its conscious investment in information-gathering activities. Japanese trading firms have performed the useful functions of monitoring foreign markets and technologies for many manufacturing firms, both large and small. For since the 1850s, Japan has been consciously investing time, manpower, and money in worldwide information-getting activities.

With these developments, Japan's export markets, both developed and less-developed nations, grew alarmed by the rapid increase in their imports from Japan. In particular, from the mid-1960s, many Asian neighbors instituted, one after another, import substitution moves in order to promote industrializations of their respective countries.

At the same time, in Japan, manufacturing firms were confronted with rapid increases in wages and the resultant disappearance of wage differentials between large firms and small subcontracting firms. Procurement needs for ever-increasing amounts of industrial raw materials for manufacturing plants in Japan were outstripping the supply of various commodities to the world export market.

At this juncture, Japanese direct investments abroad appeared to be a reactive response to changes in both Japan's export markets and the world's commodity markets. By the end of the first quarter, 1974, these reactive investments abroad by Japanese firms produced the geographical as well as industrial profile as shown in Tables 1-5 and 1-6. A comparison of Table 1-6 with similar tables of previous years reveals that from 1971 to 1974, both resource-oriented investments and market-oriented investments of Japan more than doubled

Table 1-5. Japanese Direct Investments Abroad by Area and by Industry As of March 31, 1974 (In Millions of U.S. Dollars)

	North America	Latin America	Asia	Middle East	Europe	Africa	Oceania	Total
I. Resource-oriented Investments	*509*	*247*	*779*	*1,158*	*48*	*184*	*451*	*3,376*
Agriculture	20	24	80	1	0	0	26	151
Fishery	16	15	23	0	1	13	10	78
Timber and Pulps	219	19	71	0	0	0	54	363
Mining	254	189	605	1,157	47	171	361	2,784
II. Market-oriented Investments	*1,919*	*1,560*	*1,641*	*61*	*1,132*	*47*	*185*	*6,545*
Manufacturing	367	1,038	1,140	51	155	43	98	2,892
Foods	27	40	47	1	24	7	23	169
Textile	37	183	483	15	6	30	3	757
Chemicals	28	343	76	24	36	1	13	521
Metals	152	159	99	0	28	4	43	485
Machinery	35	93	49	1	37	0	2	217
Electric and Electronics	60	69	183	3	7	1	5	328
Transportation Equipment	6	125	77	1	4	0	8	221
Others	22	26	126	6	13	0	1	194
Construction	12	41	71	0	1	0	0	125
Commerce[a]	824	120	74	1	143	1	34	1,197
Banking and Insurance	251	211	128	9	237	1	20	857
Others[b]	465	150	228	0	596	2	33	1,474
Total I and II	2,428	1,807	2,420	1,219	1,180	231	636	9,921

[a] Sales subsidiaries.
[b] Hotels, real estate developments and recreational facilities.
Source: *Wagakuni Kigyo no Kaigai Jigyo Katsudo* (Overseas Activities of Japanese Firms), The Ministry of International Trade and Investment, Tokyo, November 1974, p. 78.

Table 1-6. The Number of Overseas Subsidiaries of Non-Trading Firms in Japan by Area and by Activity as of the End of 1972

Activity	Location of Subsidiaries						Total Number
	North America	Europe	Asia	Latin America	Mid. East/ Africa	Oceania, S. Africa/ Dominions	
Resource-Seeking	35 (15.0%)	6 (2.5%)	87 (36.8%)	33 (14.0%)	24 (10.1%)	51 (21.6%)	236 (100%)
Manufacturing	50 (3.9%)	40 (3.0%)	974 (76.2%)	130 (10.2%)	56 (4.4%)	29 (2.3%)	1,279 (100%)
Sales	413 (47.7%)	185 (21.4%)	180 (20.8%)	41 (4.7%)	9 (1.0%)	38 (4.4%)	866 (100%)
Others[a]	103 (36.65%)	24 (8.4%)	107 (38.0%)	25 (8.7%)	12 (4.2%)	11 (4.2%)	282 (100%)

[a]Travel Agencies, hotels, entertainment; some agricultural and fishing projects fall in this category.
Source: The data were gathered in Japan mainly through the author's field work in 1972.

and that during the same period, industrial and geographical composites of Japanese direct investments also changed. How have the idiosyncracies of Japanese industrial structures influenced the changing profile of Japanese direct investments abroad? How are Japanese direct investments likely to change in the future? The next three chapters will answer these questions.

 Chapter Two

The Search for Natural Resources

A PHENOMENAL GROWTH

As shown in Table 2-1, since the end of the 1960s, Japanese investments seeking captive supply sources of natural resources abroad—timber, pulp, mineral ore and oil—have increased markedly. As of the end of 1974, Japan was annually opening over one hundred resource-oriented development projects abroad and was pouring over half a billion dollars into such projects. Even the "oil shock" of 1973 failed to reverse completely the increasing trend of Japanese investments in natural resources abroad.

Japanese investments in agricultural products and fishing activities abroad are also on the rise. By the early 1970s, the resource-oriented investments in terms of cumulative equity investment out-flows from Japan, overtook such market-oriented investments as manufacturing and mercantile activities abroad. I estimate that by 1980 over two-thirds of the total direct investments of Japan abroad will be of the resource-oriented type.

The demarcation between resource-oriented and market-oriented investments naturally will become blurred in the future. Lumber mills would add logging operations, and processed lumber products would be sold to local markets. Thus, what might have started as a resource-oriented venture could also acquire the dimension of a market-oriented operation. Likewise, when an overseas copper ore mining operation adds a new copper smelting operation, manufacturing activity becomes an integral part of the resource-oriented venture.

Table 2-1. Resource-Oriented Overseas Investments of Japan, 1951-1974

Year	Number of Projects			Equity Invested ($000s)		
	Timber and Pulp	Mining and Oil	Total	Timber and Pulp	Mining and Oil	Total
1951-1957	3	25	28	15,556	17,176	32,732
1958-1959	1	9	10	33,291	24,658	57,949
1960-1961	10	15	25	1,697	148,716	150,413
1962-1963	2	15	17	9,337	59,900	69,237
1964-1965	3	16	19	14,284	54,580	68,864
1966	5	17	22	36,419	72,147	108,566
1967	4	14	18	2,360	58,625	60,985
1968	5	15	20	17,280	158,681	175,961
1969	6	31	37	3,315	297,301	300,616
1970	14	38	53	73,815	234,955	317,770
1971	14	33	47	49,270	228,592	277,862
1972	29	26	55	34,474	917,386	951,860
1973	79	61	140	66,396	511,218	575,614
1974	52	67	119	61,000	466,000	527,000
Total	227	382	610	418,494	3,256,945	3,675,429

Source: *Nihon Kigyo no Kokusaiteki Tenkai*, the Ministry of International Trade and Industry, Tokyo, 1974.

INDUSTRIAL GROWTH AT HOME AND SEARCH FOR RAW MATERIALS ABROAD

When Japan embarked upon an industrialization in the 1870s, her immediate needs for natural resources were adequately met through domestic sources. During the 1890s and the 1900s, when Japan added such heavy and chemical industries as steel and iron works, dyes and explosives, and non-ferrous metals, domestic supply sources still adequately met the limited needs of the time. Only Japan's importation of materials for light industrial use, such as cotton and wool, was increasing. And these commodities were easily procured abroad by Japanese trading firms.

Taiwan, acquired in 1895 from China, provided her with such agricultural commodities as sugar, tea, camphor and jute. By the 1930s, however, the growing scale and widening variety of Japanese heavy and chemical industries had outpaced the supply capabilities of most domestic resource industries. In retrospect, Japan's imperialistic expansion into neighboring countries was partly motivated by her quest for captive supply sources of raw materials. During the 1930s, Japan's *de facto* annexation of Manchuria and the subsequent inclusion of North China under her military influence, continued to provide Japan with her increasing needs for industrial raw materials including coal, oil and iron ore.[1]

After the end of World War II, the Japanese government and business circles expanded the heavy and chemical industries throughout the 1950s and 1960s. Japan's pursuit of heavy and chemical industries made her inevitably dependent on natural resources. Japan's entry into petrochemicals and her commitment to synthetic fibres increased Japan's importation of crude oil. Furthermore, the declining costs of imported crude oil toward the end of the 1950s, relative to those of coal and hydroenergy sources in Japan, precipitated Japan's choice of imported oil as her major source of energy.[2]

By the mid-1950s, Japan emerged as a processor of raw materials almost all of which had to be procured abroad. The import tariffs and excise taxes were structured in such a way as to permit the importation of raw materials and to discourage the importation of even such semi-processed materials as aluminum ingots, blister coppers, steel ingots and petroleum products.

In addition, foreign producers were either forbidden outright or discouraged from opening their own manufacturing operations in the raw material processing industries. Technological licensing agreements and raw material supply contracts were often the only two feasible forms of involvement foreign firms were allowed in Japan.

In Table 2-2, the increasing dependence of Japan on imported raw materials is shown for selected key commodities from 1950 to 1970. From 1950 to 1970, Japan's annual consumption of copper ores and blister coppers expanded over eight times. The consumption of lead increased by seven times; zinc by eleven times; iron ores by sixteen times; coal by six times; and oil by sixty-eight times.[3] From the end

Table 2-2. Percentage Ratio of Imports to Japan's Total Consumption of Key Natural Resources, 1950-1970

	Copper ores and blister coppers	*Lead*	*Zinc*	*Iron ores*	*Coals*	*Oil*
1950	18%	53%	0%	47%	n.a.	90.0%
1955	11	33	2	55	30%	97.3
1960	51	55	26	68	36	98.6
1965	58	52	38	81	55	99.5
1970	76	55	55	88	79	99.7

Source: Computed from *Shigen Mondai no Tenbo*, 1971, the Ministry of International Trade and Industry, Tokyo, 1973, p. 359.

of the 1950s, the annual increases in Japan's industrial consumption of raw materials were met almost totally by increased imports. During the 1960s, Japanese imports of raw materials continued to expand and were absorbing a greater and greater portion of the natural resources available in the world export markets.

Toward the end of the 1960s, what was inevitable became obvious. Japan faced increasing problems of procuring adequate supplies of necessary materials. Vast quantities of raw materials were needed to satisfy the ever-increasing processing capacities of Japanese firms. These firms, like other manufacturing firms of Japan, had built up their large-scale operations inside Japan mainly with borrowed funds. The highly leveraged financial structure of the Japanese raw materials industry required that processors maintain a high rate of capacity utilization just to stay above the high break-even point of production rate. These firms began to fret over the prospect of holding their expensive plants idle, because of the lack of necessary raw material supplies from abroad.

The emergence of Japan as a processor of imported raw materials was predicated upon the assumption that Japan would be able to procure abroad ever increasing amounts of necessary raw materials both in quantity and for prices deemed advantageous. Under the prevailing glut conditions of the 1950s and early 1960s, Japanese importing firms had only to guarantee their oversees suppliers bulk purchases on long-term purchase contracts (often for a ten-year period), in order to obtain adequate supplies of raw materials. Japanese importers saw to it that the annual purchase prices of such contracts were to be negotiated with a reference to the price quotations of the London Metal Exchange, where applicable. In this way, Japanese importers engaged the best of two worlds: namely, a guaranteed supply and lower prices.

FROM GLUT TO SHORTAGE

After the mid-1960s, however, what was dreaded became reality. Starting with copper ores and blister coppers and coals—which were beginning to register frequent shortages on the world markets— overseas suppliers often cancelled altogether their promised shipments to Japan or unilaterally reduced by 10 to 15 per cent shipments initially promised. Japanese firms' long-term purchase contracts with international majors, who controlled the world supplies of raw materials, were frequently cancelled or reduced with no recourse available to the purchasers. And this period of "unreliable" long-term purchase contracts with independent foreign suppliers coincided with the time when Japanese processing firms were increasing their processing capacities in Japan. And to both business and government circles, the availability of raw materials became their overriding concern.

In pursuit of secure sources of supplies, Japanese firms sought to supplement the straightforward importation of necessary resources with loan-related procurement contracts. Their rationale was as follows: overseas suppliers repaying borrowed funds to Japanese creditors would be motivated to fulfill the supply contracts they had made. Besides, overseas explorations and the development of raw materials abroad were still deemed too risky and time-consuming by Japanese firms. Thus, Japanese firms extended loans at lower interest rates than those available internationally, and the Japanese creditor-purchasers in turn hoped they would be rewarded with favorable volume-discount prices for bulk purchases.

Since these loans were made only to secure preferential access to natural resources, the Japanese creditors often accepted the repayment in kind. Nor was a Japanese loan limited to funds. Management skill and requisite mining technologies were also extended by the Japanese purchasers who guaranteed the Japanese market for the foreign developers of natural resources.

By 1970, some successes in loan-related procurement contracts were seen for copper, nickel, iron ores and coals. In around 1970, from 15 to 10 percent of Japan's imports of these commodities were supplied by overseas mines to which Japanese trading firms and raw material processors had extended long-term loans. In the case of copper ores, by 1975, the loan-related importation contract was estimated to account for more than 30 percent of Japan's total imports of copper ores. By 1980, I predict that for loan- and investment-related procurements, about 60 percent of imported copper ores will come from Japan's captive supply sources abroad. The Japanese government and industries were hoping that by 1980, about 40 percent of imported bauxite, about 50 percent of imported nickel, and about 20 percent of imported zinc and lead would come from captive supply sources abroad. As seen from 1976, however, Japan's success in securing expected imports from captive supply sources appears rather uncertain for metal ores other than copper.

As shown in Table 2-1, Japanese trading and manufacturing firms have also been increasing their own equity participations in overseas subsidiaries engaged in the exploration and development of natural resources. These direct investments are seen by investors as providing a greater degree of assured access to raw materials. Investor-purchasers have been known to obtain greater price discounts compared with firms dealing in either long-term purchase contracts or loan-related procurements. Moreover, investor-purchasers are also entitled to dividends on the invested equity in the mining subsidiaries. According to my own computations, based on my field work in Japan during 1971–73, the effective prices of the investment-related import of copper ores coming from the eleven existing projects were at least one-half of the comparable prices charged for straightforward import purchases from the spot market. I also noted that the effective prices of the loan-related imports of copper ore from the fourteen existing projects were receiving about a 40 to 50 percent discount compared to the prices charged for straightforward imports.[4]

On closer scrutiny, this apparent profitability of the investment-related procurements turned out to be a visionary illusion. For every "lucky strike," there were ten unlucky strikes that consumed investors' funds. For instance, during the years 1953–1970, of 102 copper mining explorations undertaken abroad by Japanese firms, only 14 projects turned out to be successful. Thus, as far as the investors were concerned, the price discounts and dividends that they received from successful mining operations were the risk premiums for unsuccessful ventures.

NON-MINERAL RESOURCES

Toward the end of the 1960s, the general shortage spread to timber, corn and other animal feeds, and pulp. Japanese began to scramble for direct investments abroad in logging operations, pulp making as well as in large-scale agricultural projects. In 1975, Japan's annual importation of up to 30 percent of her total food and animal feed needs meant that as many agricultural fields abroad as those used inside Japan had to be earmarked for producing foods and feeds for Japan. Japan's importation of foods and feeds, including beef and sea food, was still growing rapidly in 1975. Many trading firms were contracting out agricultural production including cattle grazing to foreign ranchers and farmers. Both loan and investment-related procurement of foods and feeds were also on the rise.

DEFENSIVE INVESTMENTS

Even with the presently planned increases in investment-related procurements of industrial materials, Japan will continue to rely on straightforward imports for the bulk of her importation needs for various raw materials. For instance, as in the case of copper and iron ores, Japanese lumbering and trading firms will continue to purchase tropical timbers from logging firms in Indonesia and elsewhere, operated by investors from the U.S., Korea, the Phillipines and Malaysia. Moreover, the maize and corn that Japanese firms plan to grow in Indonesia and elsewhere will at best supply less than one-tenth of the future needs of Japan. What then, motivates Japanese firms to expand their direct investment abroad in natural resources? Comments made in the spring of 1973 by two separate active investors in Indonesia, and repeated later to me by other investors engaged in either similar ventures or in oil drilling and mining ventures elsewhere may provide a clue:

From a Japanese logging operator:
We still continue to buy 80-90 percent of the tropical timbers we ship to Japan from independent logging firms. However, the fact that we are also in the logging operation itself gives us a good chance to develop friendly feelings with independent firms, through industrywide meetings and joint negotiations with the government. Besides, we now can estimate the logging cost of timber with a fair degree of accuracy. This gives us an additional edge in negotiating with independent firms.

From a Japanese corn, maize and tobacco grower:
The U.S. still practically has a monopoly on these commodities in the world market. Rather than being totally at the mercy of the U.S. suppliers, we intend to have our own source of supply that will eventually produce enough to enable us to hold off our purchase feelers to the U.S. until their offering terms become more acceptable to us.

The key messages contained in the preceding quotations are three-fold. Namely, the investor-operator of a logging camp, farm or mine can obtain business and industry information that a firm cannot otherwise obtain. Second, this involvement in the operation sensitizes the investor-operator to subtle changes and developments in the industry worldwide. Third, even a 10 to 20 percent rate of "self-sufficiency" for vital materials is perceived to be far more useful for strengthening a purchaser's bargaining position than total reliance on outside suppliers. In particular, if the outside suppliers are such international oligopolists as those now in the fields of nickel, bauxite and even oil, the marginal bargaining strength that a purchaser's own supply source accords him must not be dismissed too lightly.

ADDITIONAL MOTIVATION FOR RESOURCE-ORIENTED VENTURES ABROAD

Over 110 million Japanese are living in a space of approximately 140,000 square miles as opposed to 200 million people in over 3.6 million square miles in the United States. This makes Japan susceptible to industrial pollution. When the net national income per square mile is computed for five industrialized but geographically rather small nations, Japan, the United Kingdom, West Germany, France and Italy, Japan ranks behind West Germany and the United Kingdom. But when the Japanese national income per square mile is adjusted to account for the fact that only 20 percent of Japan's 140,000 square miles are arable or habitable, the net national income per habitable square mile of Japan jumps to the highest in the world; thus making Japan most vulnerable to industrial pollution.

A visible deterioration in the environmental quality of life in Japan has prompted the public to question the growth of the GNP at all costs. Never before in the history of Japanese industrialization did Japanese firms face visible public indignation. The public was raising its voice against firms accused of destroying the ecology or of victimizing fisherman, farmers and consumers. Consequently, early in the 1970s, manufacturing plants in general, and plants of such raw materials processing operations as pulp, petrochemicals, non-ferrous smelting and steel making in particular, faced resistance from local communities whenever they attempted to expand their operating capacities. Provincial governments, which had previously invited plants of heavy and chemical industries to locate in their areas, began to cancel their standing invitations.

Meanwhile, existing firms processing raw materials in Japan were finding it less costly to install required anti-pollution devices in new plants than in old plants. Thus, a number of firms simultaneously sought to solve two problems: namely, expansion of supply capability and mitigation of pollution.

In October 1973 a group of Japanese oil refineries and non-ferrous smelting processors was planning to set up a combination of oil refinery, aluminum smelting and sodium producing plants in the Skeikdom of Abu Dhabi in the Persian Gulf. The oil refinery was to use a simple topping process to separate "white ingredients," including naphtha, from "black" heavy oil. The plant was scheduled to ship only the "white" products for further processing to plants in Japan. In this way, the existing refinery in Japan was to double its final production capacity without physically expanding its existing plant site. Also the aluminum reducing and sodium producing ventures, both of which were finding it difficult to continue their polluting operations in Japan, would be able to take advantage of lower electricity costs in Abu Dhabi, where electricity was to be generated by heat energy discharged by the oil refinery.

Likewise, a group of Japanese firms consisting of trading firms and petrochemical firms was concluding, in the fall of 1974, joint ventures with the Iranian government, in the development of Iranian petrochemical industries. In 1974 another group of Japanese petrochemical firms were undertaking development projects in the tar and sand areas in Alberta, in the northern part of Canada. These firms were intending to process oil extracted from the tar sand into petrochemical intermediates and then export them to Japan.

ON-SITE PROCESSING

During the 1970s and 1980s, iron, copper and nickel processors will expand processing raw materials abroad. Poor quality ferrous and non-ferrous ores are now increasingly used, and as the metal content of ore drops below a certain percentage, say 1 percent, it becomes economically unfeasible or unwise to transport bulky ores to Japan for processing. In order to solve this problem, on-site processing of raw materials will have to be undertaken so that only condensed ore contents or semi-processed materials need be shipped to Japan and to processors in the rest of the world.

At the present time, a number of nickel mat-making projects in Indonesia—attempting to utilize laterite ore—are the leading examples of such ventures. On-site processing of bauxite into alumina might be contemplated by Japanese investors as well. In terms of freight cost per ton, shipping costs of alumina were estimated even in 1974 to be less than one-half the shipping costs of bauxite.

Besides, from Australia and Canada to Zaire and Indonesia, both developed and developing nations that possess raw materials are binding foreign investor-developers to prearranged schedules for increased on-site processing of raw materials.

A case in point is the copper ore mining concession that a group of Japanese firms headed by Nippon Mining Co. has been developing in Zaire since November 1971. The Japanese group has agreed to commence smelting operations as soon as Japanese importations of copper ores from the mine reaches the equivalent of 50,000 copper tons per year (about 2 million tons of copper ore per year with a copper content of 2.6 percent). Chances are that the Japanese investors will expand their on-site plants to produce blister copper in

Zaire as their smelting operations in Japan are threatened with closure or reduction because of public opposition to polluting operations.

The moves toward on-site processing of raw materials are not limited to large scale operations of ferrous and non-ferrous metals. In lumber yard operations and related plywood manufacturing fields, similar moves will become increasingly apparent during the 1970s and 1980s. In pursuit of tropical timbers, processors of boards and wooden plates will be moving to Sawarak in Malaysia, and especially to East Kalimantan in Indonesia.

In search of prefabricated housing materials, a number of housing constructors would set up processing plants in British Columbia and the northwest corner of the United States where logging operations provide vital lumber materials. These moves would be precipitated as the governments of the United States and Canada come to demand greater degrees of domestic value-added in their lumber-related operations.

SEA PRODUCE

Industrial and human wastes that have been discharged into the sea all over Japan destroyed coastal fishing and shell fish produce. While small- to medium-sized fishing fleets as well as individual fishermen were abandoning their trade, large-scale companies engaged in sea produce have set up fishing bases and cold storage abroad. Shrimp caught near Mexico, Africa and Indonesia as well as tuna and seabream shipped in from remote corners of the world are practically the only "fresh seafood" the Japanese can buy. Large fishing companies and large trading firms have come to dominate supplies of sea produce to Japanese markert. Ironical as it is, as in the case of industrial raw material, the past rapid industrial successes of Japan that destroyed her coastal sea have rendered Japan vulnerable politically and economically to adverse reactions of foreign countries.

A GROUP APPROACH TO OVERSEAS INVESTMENT: THE JAPANESE CONSORTIUM

For both loan-related and investment-related projects abroad that Japanese firms have undertaken, except for a small-sized project of $10 million to $20 million, between three and seven Japanese firms often participated in the same project. This cooperative investment behavior of Japanese firms could partially be necessitated by the small size of the Japanese investors. Compared with a leading international firm in oil and non-ferrous areas, even the largest Japanese firm was in 1975 at best one-tenth the size, as measured by sales assets or any other economic indicator.

The smaller size of a Japanese processing firm means that it alone cannot use enough natural resources to permit an economical scale of operation in overseas mines. Smaller size also implies severe financial constraints for the firm when resource-oriented investments abroad must be undertaken alone. Even if a firm could afford to invest in one, or at best two projects abroad, its financial and technological resources could not be stretched to cover similar ventures in other parts of the world. Since Japan's resource-oriented investments were concentrated in developing nations, investors' concern over growing "resource nationalism" and political uncertainty in host countries led them to avoid, wherever possible, being locked into one or two sources of supply. A "group approach" permitted the sharing of all the risks and opportunities.

As a result, even when the largest mining and processing firm decided to invest alone abroad, its smaller competitors at home maneuvered MITI into pressuring that leader-firm into forming a partnership with smaller followers. The smaller firms wanted to equalize their competitive strength with one another and with the leading firm by sharing the same supply source of raw materials. The leading firm, wishing to obtain government long-term loans and diplomatic assistances for its overseas project, has so far accommodated MITI's requests to allow smaller followers to participate in overseas ventures. At least in the early 1970s MITI protected the vested interests of smaller firms in Japan. MITI was hoping to expedite merger moves among small and large firms with those moves being made by a few designated leaders of respective industries. It remains to be seen whether the interlocking of economic interests of large firms with those of small- to medium-sized competitors would help realize MITI's goal or would help preserve the current stability between large and small firms. Take the case of oil explorations, for instance.

OIL EXPLORATION

Under the direction of a government agency, the Petroleum Development Public Corporation (SKK), Japanese oil prospectors have been grouping together into oil development corporations to be organized for each exploration project abroad.* The consumers of fuel oil, financial institutions and trading firms have also joined the development projects as equity holders. As of September 1971, the breakdown of combined equity capital holdings, totaling 100 billion yen, for 23 oil-related overseas subsidiaries, produced, on the average, the following mosaic partnership among assortments of private and public corporations:[5]

Holder of Equity	Total Capital of 100 Billion Yen combined (for all 23 subsidiaries)
Petroleum Development Public Corp.	21.0%
Oil explorations and oil refiners	23.1
Trading firms	13.0
Utility, steel and iron firms	14.9
Financial institutions	7.1
Other Manufacturers	20.9
	100.0%

There is no denying that this joint ownership helped preserve the stable relationships that had evolved between oil suppliers and users. But this group approach is not without flaws. For one thing, new oil exploration and development subsidiaries are incorporated in Japan on the basis of one new subsidiary to one overseas project. Also, it is only after a feasible overseas project is offered from abroad that groups of various investor firms will be hastily incorporated into the new subsidiary. Because of this time consuming process of organizing participants in today's extremely competitive bidding situation for oil concessions in the world market, Japanese groups have lagged behind other firms in obtaining promising oil concessions.

But this group approach was also necessitated by one investment bottleneck of Japanese oil firms. Because Japan has long ignored her own oil exploration and development projects, she now suffers from an acute shortage of scientists, engineers and technicians possessing internationally competitive skills for oil development and research. As of 1973, the approximate number of oil engineers in Japan was a mere 400. At the currently projected growth rate of overseas oil developments, it was estimated that Japan would need at least 1000 such technical personnel by 1985. Nevertheless, Japanese universities

---

*With respect to oil exploration, this kind of arrangement is not unique to Japan. Eight oil companies of West Germany have jointly formed the DEMINEX, which received direct financial assistance from the government of West Germany and engages in overseas exploration and production of crude oil and even in the acquisition of existing oil wells abroad. The French government operates the ERAP to facilitate crude oil developments abroad.

were producing at most 30 technical personnel in oil-related engineering fields annually. Second, the scarce technical personnel are scattered too thinly among too many oil exploration projects that various groups of trading companies and banks of Japan are undertaking.

As a way out of this predicament, the number of permanent oil exploration and development corporations was to be limited so that especially relevant information and technical personnel could be pooled to bear upon promising projects. Late in June 1974, the Petroleum Development Public Corporation (SKK) publicly sent up a trial balloon statement, saying that it would discontinue lending its own technical experts to various private projects. This statement was interpreted as a signal that the Japanese government, most notably MITI, had decided to assume leadership in oil explorations abroad more directly. The time-honored convergence of public and private "domains" has again manifested itself in Japan's concerted efforts to develop captive sources of oil.

However, unprecedented moves are also observed on the part of a few private Japanese oil firms. Many of them are even avoiding the government's initiatives and joining overseas exploration projects with foreign developers. From the viewpoint of these developers, the financial risks could be spread by obtaining Japanese investors. At the same time, the Japanese partner would provide an immediate and direct contact with the Japanese market when oil was discovered. Already in 1974, three Japanese oil firms, which had been scrambling for such tie-ups in competition with Japanese trading firms, had commenced joint exploration projects for crude oil and natural gas with foreign oil companies. In spring 1975 Mitsubishi-Shell, Idemitsu-AMCO and Teikoku-Exxon were exploring continental shelves around Japan for oil and natural gas. Similar ventures may well be extended to overseas exploration projects. These developments point to the present trend that more and more private Japanese firms, growing accustomed to going around MITI's intended grip, are interlocking their interests with foreign firms.

THE QUEST FOR STABILITY AMONG JAPANESE OLIGOPOLIES

Unlike the oil industry which is fragmented among over thirty firms, the oligopolistic firms of the copper and aluminum industries are counting on group approaches to maintain their industrial stability. Within each group project, one strong leader firm is taking the initiative, on a rotational basis, in given overseas ventures. Although MITI did pressure large investing firms to accommodate partnerships with smaller domestic competitors—even when the initial desire of the larger firm was to invest alone—the larger firm nevertheless does maintain an unquestioned leadership position in deciding key issues as prices, production volume, development schedule and staffing of the overseas project.

A case in point is the copper ore mining project in Zaire which Nippon Mining Co. Ltd. is overseeing. Holding 60 percent of the equity interest of the mine (85 percent is owned by the Japanese group and 15 percent by the government of Zaire), Nippon Mining Co. is the sole representative of the Japanese group to the government of Zaire. While the other three copper companies (Furukawa, Mitsui and Sumitomo) station one or two of their mining engineers in the subsidiary, Nippon Mining Co. has sent in 150 of its engineers and technicians. The other Japanese partners have only the privilege of accepting their portion of the subsidiary's exports (based on their equity share of the firm) at the price negotiated annually between the government of Zaire and Nippon Mining Co. Likewise, in Northern Sawarak, the other large-scale copper mining venture is run by its project leader, Mitsubishi Kinzoku Co. The Japanese group owns 51 percent of the equity interest of the mining subsidiary, but the Mitsubishi Kinzoku Co. is solely entrusted with the management of the subsidiary.

In the case of bauxite development, in which the Japanese group has either majority or 100 percent ownership, one sees an arrangement similar to the two copper mining subsidiaries. Requisite technology for mining bauxite and producing alumina can easily be obtained from the five leading Japanese producers of primary aluminum, and these five firms have for some time stabilized their respective market shares. In December 1971, with MITI's blessing, Japanese aluminum companies jointly established the Light Metal Resource Development Co., Ltd. in order to pool funds and technologies for overseas bauxite and alumina operations. The leadership of this overseas project was to be rotated among the five producers of primary aluminum. The rotational turn at the leadership position in their overseas joint projects has enabled the oligopolistic firms to develop the structure of the "shared monopoly"—a few leading firms working covertly and overtly to protect the joint interest of the group. For one thing, the rotational leadership permits the member firms to exchange a hostage, as it were, with one another. Second, the joint ownership lets the member firms obtain the same operational information on all the projects. Any possibility of surprise moves on the part of any one of the firms is virtually eliminated. The end result is the stability of the mutual relationships among the member firms.

MITI'S DIRECT LEADERSHIP

In July 1975 MITI concluded an agreement with the Indonesian government, whereby about one billion dollars would be spent to harness the Asahan River in Northern Sumatra for hydroelectricity. Alumina plants and primary reduction facilities of aluminum would also be built. Japan was to own 90 percent of the "Asahan Development Corporation" and was to be entitled to two-thirds of the aluminum and alumina products. MITI rounded up five Japanese primary aluminum firms as well as six leading trading firms so that each of the five aluminum firms and the trading firm(s) subgroup would be entitled to and equally responsible for 20 percent of the required investment. At the same time, eight leading city banks, which are also closely related to the aluminum and trading firms, were brought in to guarantee or underwrite long-term loans for the Asahan project.

According to one knowledgeable source, "Just prior to President Suharto's visit to Japan, MITI needed to put together the Asahan project." The same spokesman continued:

> ... late in 1973, Sumitomo Chemicals, which was the second largest aluminum producer in Japan, suddenly salvaged the Asahan project after two American firms, ALCOA and Kaiser, had long withdrawn from it because of the colossal investments required for the basic infrastructure. Sumitomo Chemicals brought in four other Japanese aluminum producers. Then, MITI persuaded aluminum firms to bring in six leading trading firms...[6]

One could speculate that the sheer size of the Asahan investment would require that guaranteed access to a substantive portion of the Japanese aluminum market must remain, in order to make the project commercially feasible. Both Sumitomo's willingness to bring in four outside competitors and MITI's "invitation" to six leading trading firms, were indeed a calculated scheme to set aside about one-quarter of the Japanese market for the Asahan project.

This alliance between MITI and Sumitomo Chemicals turned out to be a marriage of convenience. After the oil crisis of 1973, MITI reasserted its direct roles in securing the "economic security" for Japan. Under the slogan of "resource diplomacy," the Japanese government searched for opportunities to conclude direct government-to-government long-term deals for procuring natural resources for Japan. On the other hand, Sumitomo Chemicals was earlier jolted by

Mitsui's group acquisition of 50 percent ownership in AMAX's aluminum division. We will shortly evaluate this AMAX-Mitsui tie-up. For the time being, it will suffice to know that Sumitomo's need for aluminum and alumina projects abroad was expediently seized upon by MITI out of its own political need for establishing a record in resource diplomacy. Internal politics of Japan were thus mingled with international politics of natural resources.

PRIVATE MOVES OF RESOURCE DIPLOMACY

Apart from MITI's initiated projects, groups of private Japanese manufacturers and trading firms often jointly hold minority participation in the equity of a mining subsidiary abroad that is controlled by foreign aluminum producers. In 1969, Showa Denko and Sumitomo Chemicals, which at that time were the second and third largest aluminum firms in Japan, acquired a 48 percent ownership of COMALCO (Hong Kong), a sales subsidiary of an Australian bauxite project, COMALCO, of the United States. While the largest aluminum producer in Japan, Nippon Light Metals, was 50 percent owned by ALCAN and was thus assured of access to ALCAN's bauxite and alumina, Showa Denko and Sumitomo Chemicals counted on their minority equity ownerships in COMALCO (Hong Kong) to provide a direct access to Australian bauxite.[7] In 1971, Showa Denko and Sumitomo Chemicals again together obtained a 50 percent equity interest in New Zealand Aluminum Smelters, which COMALCO had newly opened in New Zealand. Aluminum ingots produced by New Zealand Aluminum Smelters were to be purchased by the three investors in proportion to their respective equity ownerships.

Just as in the case of Japanese oil firms, the second and the fourth largest aluminum producers, Sumitomo Chemicals and Showa Denko, have paired themselves up to obtain the two firms' own direct access to aluminum ingots and alumina abroad. Long gone are the days when five aluminum producers remained resigned to maintaining the stable relationships among themselves. Later in this chapter, we will return to this new breaking-up of the Japanese oligopolies' stability.

TRADING FIRMS AND NATURAL RESOURCES

As of 1974, iron ore mining subsidiaries abroad, in which Japanese trading firms maintain an equity interest, have not attracted the participation or attention of steel companies in Japan. At most, the common group arrangement for iron ore ventures abroad was one where a group of steel companies would guarantee the investor trading firms a long-term purchase of ores from the trading firms' mines abroad.

The Japanese steel industry is dominated by five producers who attempt to equalize each respective firm's access to raw materials abroad. The large trading firms like Mitsui, Mitsubishi, C. Itoh and Marubeni have long cultivated their own business ties with client steel firms by procuring iron ores, scrap iron and coal for them. And these trading firms are financially capable of purchasing a minority interest in foreign investors' iron mines abroad. It appears that all that they need, however, are the guaranteed purchases by Japanese steel firms.

This "state of equilibrium" between large Japanese trading companies and large Japanese steel producers may be broken in the future, however, if and when steel producers venture abroad in order to process iron ores, say, into blister irons. It is the steel companies, not the trading firms, that possess requisite and proprietary technologies required for such processing operations. In addition, ore processing operations abroad will have to be linked far more closely with steel fabricating operations in Japan. When this need arises, each steel company will demand a greater role than its client trading firm and its overseas manufacturing operation.

TRADING FIRMS' SUPERIORITY

Trading firms have demonstrated their ability to maintain their leadership vis-a-vis Japanese manufacturers when the products involved do not require sophisticated technology, but rather shrewd traders' skill and organizing ability. Nowhere is this demonstrated more than in overseas procurement of corn and other feed grains for Japanese manufacturers.

The Japan-Thailand Agreement on Maize of 1961 was the very first commodity agreement by which Japanese trading firms linked the Japanese market for food stuffs contractually with the supplying nation. Under the initiative of Mitsui and Mitsubishi, the two largest trading firms, Japanese importers helped the host government organize the Thai Board of Trade of corn (maize) as the sole negotiator of prices, quantity, and other logistical details of Thai's annual export of corn to Japan. The Thai Board of Trade assumed the responsibility for assembling corn for export.

Prior to this "collective bargaining" arrangement, Japanese trading firms scrambled for whatever corn they could assemble in Thailand. But every time the domestic price of corn in Thailand exceeded export prices, Thai farmers and corn traders reneged on delivery promises. The resultant scrambling for available corn by Japanese trading firms and Thai exporters produced volatile price fluctuations in Thai corn prices that became susceptible to manipulative speculations by a few Thai traders. At this juncture, the Japanese trading firms felt a need for the "long-term purchase agreement" as well as the machinery of "collective bargaining." The long-term purchase agreement in this sense is nothing but a mutual understanding of maintaining a special buyer-seller relationship that accords mutually first-rejection-and-offer right. Under this spirit of "long-term business relationship," Japanese trading firms and their client feed grain manufacturers as represented on rotation by a leading trading firm, currently C. Itoh Co., annually concludes a firm purchase deal for all other Japanese trading and feed grain firms.

However, differently put, the Japan-Thailand Agreement on Maize Trade could also be viewed as the device which enabled the Thai merchants, not necessarily subsistence corn farmers, and the Japanese importers to reap the benefits of two earlier accomplishments of American economic and military aid to Thailand. From the late 1950s to early 1960s, United States military and economic aid prompted Thailand to build the "Friendship Highway" stretching northeast from Bangkok to deeper hinterlands bordering Laos and Cambodia. This highway was intended to help the Thai government extend its administrative influence to the neglected northeast region, but it also brought vast farming areas along the highway into direct contact with the mercantile activities and export facilities in Bangkok. Around the same time, the Rockefeller Research Institute in Thailand developed a corn seed particularly suited for the terrain and soil condition of the newly opened northeast region. Farmers migrating from the Menam River delta area in the southwest to the northeast region along the "Friendship Highway" were taught to plant the new Rockefeller strain of corn, Guatemala. However, the crop had to be exported since there was little domestic market for corn in Thai.

About this time, Japanese trading firms were seeking additional sources of corn imports. Intuitively, Japanese trading firms were trying to lessen their dependence on the United States for the anticipated needs for feed grains in Japan. Thus, the long-term strategies of the Japanese trading firms led by Mitsui and Mitsubishi and Thailand's need for rectifying increasing trade deficits with Japan converged in a timely fashion in 1961 to produce the Japan-Thailand Agreement on Maize. And this commodity agreement that a group of

Japanese private firms designed and concluded with the sovereign government of Thailand became the harbinger of the so-called *"Kaihatsu Yunyu"* (Overseas Development for Import)—a newly coined phrase describing Japanese firms' efforts to help develop foodstuffs and natural resources abroad for guaranteed exports to Japan.

Furthermore, the Japan-Thailand Agreement on Maize produced an unexpected turn of events in the business and government relations in Japan. The Fair Trade Commission (FTC) which is the antitrust body of Japan, objected to the Agreement requiring a group of Japanese trading firms to act in open unison. FTC charged that the Agreement smacked of "open collusion" by the large trading firms.

In retrospect, this was the case in which FTC of Japan tried to establish a precedent for the extraterritoriality of its antitrust ruling. Trading firms painstakingly persuaded both the FTC and other Japanese officialdom into a precedent setting consensus: when the national interest of Japan was clearly served better by orderly coalition of Japanese firms vis-a-vis foreign governments and traders, the extraterritorial application of the antitrust ruling would not be invoked. Thus, the Japan-Thailand Agreement on Maize vividly demonstrated that increased activities abroad of Japanese private firms would reshape even the relationships between government and business.

Trading companies acted to attain what was good for the coalition firms as a whole. Once annual negotiations between Thailand and Japan were thus institutionalized into the "collective bargaining," the leading trading firms effectively precluded any single feed grain manufacturer from going directly to Thai corn farmers. The timehonored division of task between trading and manufacturing firms was carefully maintained.

JAPANESE FIRMS' CHALLENGE TO INTERNATIONAL OLIGOPOLIES

The trans-pacific tie-up which was concluded in August 1973, between Mitsui & Co. of Japan and AMAX's aluminum subsidiary in the United States, Alumax, was the harbinger of what we may expect to see happen in the coming decade. Three months earlier, in May 1973, AMAX offered a 50 percent equity interest of Alumax for cash to Mitsui & Co., a leading trading firm which had been acting as the organizer of overseas investments in the Mitsui industrial group.[8]

AMAX's move was motivated by its need for cash for simultaneous expansion of production in molybdenum, copper, lead, zinc, oil, coal and aluminum. Because of a tight money market in the

United States and because of the depressed stock prices of the New York Stock Exchange Market, AMAX could not hope to raise the cash necessary for simultaneous expansions of all the mineral business either from bond markets or from equity capital markets. Thus, AMAX chose to sell a portion of its own assets; namely a 50 percent equity interest in Alumax.

Being an independent and medium-sized operator in the world aluminum industry, AMAX already had a joint aluminum venture in the U.S. with Pechiney of France. Accordingly, AMAX feared that newer joint ventures with Pechiney or with other leading aluminum firms in the U.S. might invite the intervention of the Federal Trade Commission. The new prospective partner, therefore, must be found not only outside the U.S. but also among less prominent firms in the aluminum field. Hopefully, the new Japanese partner would help AMAX obtain a strong toehold in one of the largest markets not only of aluminum, but of other non-ferrous products as well.

On the other hand, the Mitsui group had lagged behind other Japanese companies in Japan, notably such rival groups as Sumitomo and Mitsubishi, in primary aluminum reduction operations. In order to catch up with the leaders of the aluminum industry in Japan, Mitsui needed not only greater primary reduction capacity but also reduction technologies. Within the context of MITI-inspired "harmony" of the five aluminum firms inside Japan, the Mitsui group had long been resigned to a distant fifth place. Besides, the expansion of primary reduction capacities needed a guaranteed supply of bauxite, alumina and aluminum ingots. AMAX had a development lease on bauxite deposits in Australia as well as long-term purchase contracts for alumina with ALCOA of Australia. And AMAX was about to double its own aluminum reduction capacities in the U.S. With the purchase of a 50 percent equity interest in AMAX's aluminum subsidiary, Mitsui obtained all the ingredients necessary to make it an overnight contending "offshore" force to reckon with in the aluminum industry in Japan. It was no accident, therefore, that Mitsui was willing to pay $135 million, a 25 percent premium over and above the book value of Alumax for speed of entry into the worldwide aluminum industry. The price was a fraction of what it would have cost if Mitsui had had to overcome alone the financial and technological barriers to entry in the aluminum industry of the world.

Mitsui's acquisition of Alumax immediately motivated Sumitomo Chemicals to lobby before MITI in order to realize the Asahan project in Indonesia. Showa Denko ran to the government of Venezuela in 1974 and agreed to become a minority participant in the Venezuelan government's project for producing aluminum ingots.

Showa Denko was hopeful that the Venezuelan project would provide an additional access to aluminum ingots, made with inexpensive electricity through an oil-burning thermal power plant. Thus, through cooperative joint participations and through competitive scramblings for access to bauxite and aluminum ingots abroad, Japanese aluminum producers were vertically integrating their operations into such upstream operations as bauxite and alumina projects abroad as well as obtaining captive access to aluminum ingots abroad.

Indeed, we have already seen that not only aluminum firms but also oil and copper firms of Japan were for the first time in their history vertically integrating into raw materials development abroad. In the case of internationally-known foreign firms involved in copper, aluminum, nickel, oil and even steel, worldwide integrated operations from raw materials development to production, and to the marketing of the final product have long become the general rule rather than the exception. Historically, some foreign firms that started out as producers of raw materials integrated downstream into successive stages of manufacturing and marketing operations.[9] Other foreign firms, that started out as processors and marketers of oil and non-ferrous products had integrated upstream into the development of raw materials. Why, then, have Japanese processors of raw materials been able to remain vertically non-integrated for so long, specializing in only the processing of raw materials?

THE NEW NEED FOR VERTICAL INTEGRATION

Manufacturing firms are motivated to integrate vertically, upstream or downstream, when a competitive market mechanism is not present or is not functioning in the respective product market. For instance, raw material producers find it necessary to develop markets for the products of successive processing stages, or even for final delivery of products to end-users, when these downstream markets are not developed enough to permit the expansion of raw materials production. By the same token, processors of raw materials find it necessary or advantageous to develop captive sources of raw materials supplies in order to guarantee undisrupted processing operations, or to have an easier and cheaper access to raw materials than competitors. At each stage of the product market, such barriers to entry as technology, the large investment required for a minimally economical scale of operation and access to end-users tend to limit the number of successful entrants.

As we saw in Chapter 1, direct foreign competition was kept out of the Japanese market. Inside the Japanese market, requisite technology and necessary capital were "apportioned" by the government among a limited number of firms, especially for such primary raw materials processing operations as steel-making, copper smelting and reduction of primary aluminum, and oil refining. At the successive stages of downstream operations of these industries, less formidable barriers to entry in terms of technology, and finance and market contact, permitted a greater number of entrants than the primary processing stage allowed. There was no lack of entrants in respective downstream operations. Conscious division of tasks was soon arranged among large and small firms.

In particular, the fabrication stage of processed raw materials requires far more labor-intensive operations than the primary processing stage. Therefore, given the dichotomy of the Japanese labor market, small- to medium-sized subcontractors, who paid lower wages for harsher working conditions than large processors of raw materials, found themselves assigned to the task of fabricating metal products. This explains why large processors of raw materials invariably chose to set up their own "captive" subsidiaries rather than incorporate their downstream operations into the same corporate entity. Even when they were related to large processors of raw materials, small- to medium-sized subcontractors and subsidiaries were socially and politically permitted to pay lower wages than large parent firms.

Given the general condition of glut prevailing during the 1950s and 1960s in various commodity markets of the world, Japanese trading firms were able to procure necessary raw materials in quantity and at prices acceptable to Japanese processors. Competition among trading firms assured that Japanese processors would be able to obtain equal terms for their raw material supplies. Accordingly, there was no need for processors like steel and aluminum firms to get involved in risky and costly ventures of raw materials abroad.

Moreover, under this glut situation, foreign major and independent firms, which had developed their own raw materials, were eager to supply Japanese processors not only with raw materials but with requisite processing technologies or even with finances. Japan, who was demanding greater and greater amounts of raw materials, was an attractive customer for foreign major and independent firms which were eager to sell surplus raw materials. Closer business relationships between foreign firms and Japanese processors meant guaranteed sales of additional raw materials.

The Japanese government and MITI consciously shaped the structures of resource-based industries as well. More often than not, MITI attempted to keep the structures of resource-based industries fragmented by discouraging the vertical integration of large processing firms into downstream operations. Up until the oil crisis of 1973, MITI often counted on the fragmented structure of resource-based industries to provide price competition among numerous nonintegrated firms. The oil industry of Japan was a prime example of MITI's "structuralist" approach.[10] In order to permit large oil users like steel, power utility and petrochemical firms—key manufacturing industries in the eyes of MITI—to wield "monopsonistic" powers, scores of oil refining firms were permitted to enter the field. In order to keep each stage of oil industry separate, Arabia Oil—Japan's first and only oil producer abroad—was not permitted by MITI to integrate its operations into refining and marketing activities in Japan, to the great disappointment of the governments of Saudi Arabia and Kuwait, which each owned 10 percent of Arabia Oil incorporated in Tokyo.

In the case of aluminum, as of 1975 there were five firms in Japan engaged in the primary reduction of aluminum, fourteen firms (ten separate firms and four primary reducers) engaged in the secondary reduction of aluminum, and over sixty separate fabricators of aluminum products. Further on downstream, there were over two hundred smaller scale fabricators and recasters of aluminum products. A cursory review of the history of the aluminum industry in Japan would reveal that the Japanese government permitted new entrants in primary and secondary reduction stages, only as the expanding market enabled them to operate profitably.

The fabrication of aluminum was historically begun by local coppersmiths at copper foundries, who then expanded into aluminum products. On the other hand, the primary and secondary reduction of aluminum was started in the 1930s and was later expanded during the 1950s and 1960s by existing chemical firms. The difference in technological and financial competence required for each stage of operation separated these two industries from each other, as well as the difference in historical backgrounds. These differences facilitated the drawing of "business boundaries"—division of tasks—between the two groups of firms. MITI was quick to exploit such differences between firms in its "divide-and-rule" manipulation of the industry as a whole. Similar situations existed in the steel, iron and copper industries.

Moreover, up until the end of the 1960s Japanese processors of raw materials had competed with one another on the basis of their respective successes at technological innovations designed to reduce production costs and raw material inputs per unit of production. But they reached the practical limits on technological innovation. Thus, it became suddenly vital for the Japanese processors to obtain direct accesses to cheaper sources of raw materials than their competitors. This change in Japanese processors' perception occurred when foreign major firms showed a sign of entering the Japanese market. Without access to captive and cheaper sources of raw materials, could Japanese processors compete in Japan with foreign major and large independent competitors which had long integrated their operations vertically and which had long obtained resource development concessions from many foreign countries?

COOPERATION AND COMPETITION BETWEEN JAPANESE AND FOREIGN FIRMS

As of the end of 1972, I ascertained that of 236 Japanese overseas investments seeking industrial materials and foodstuffs, two-thirds of them were located in developing nations. North America and Oceania (mainly Australia) received one-third of the Japanese investments. The geographical spread of these Japanese investments reflected the fact that over two-thirds of the various natural resources available for the world export market, were coming from developing nations. As far as those investments were concerned, about 40 percent of all the projects were located in North America and Oceania; thus, indicating that Japanese investors preferred politically stable areas, if a choice was available.

Japanese investors were venturing into areas already secured by the leading foreign firms dominating each raw material market. Being the latecomers who were preoccupied with the guaranteed availability of raw materials, Japanese investors were eager to offer better concession terms of price, loan, ownership and technical assistance than foreign majors. Japanese firms seeking their own sources of raw materials abroad were destined to act as the "maverick rate busters" via-à-vis international majors.

A first Japanese rate-busting tactic was demonstrated as early as January 1953 by a maverick oil company, Idemitsu Kosan, when the president of the firm, Sazo Idemitsu, dispatched the firm's tanker to Abadan, Kiran, and broke through the Iranian oil boycott being held by international oil majors. The Anglo-Iranian Oil Company, whose Abadan oil refineries were expropriated in 1951 by the Iranian government, threatened to capture the Idemitsu tanker on its way back to Japan. But the threat was not carried out. Sazo Idemitsu thus punctured the two-year boycott against Iranian oil held by international majors, and opened the way to the world recognition of

Iran's sovereignty over her own oil resources. Idemitsu later recalled, "I wanted to loosen the tight grip of the international majors on the crude oil supply to Japan. When I discovered that the American government was quietly maneuvering to have American oil majors cut into the British firm's (Anglo-Iranian Oil) hold over Iranian oil, I decided to buy direct crude oil from Iran. I had to dispatch my own tanker because no shipping firms in Japan wanted to risk probable seizures by the British Navy."[11]

A second attempt by Japanese business circles to cut into the sphere of influence held by international majors also took place in oil concessions. After about one year of negotiations, in March 1958, a group of Japanese crude oil users, headed by "Manchuria Taro" Yamashita, established the Arabia Oil Company in an 80-10-10 joint venture split among the Japanese investors, the Kuwait government and the Saudi Arabian government. Arabia Oil Company obtained an oil exploration and development concession from the two foreign partners. Not only did this concession establish the precedent of an "equity participation" by host country governments, but it also confirmed the 49-51 split between foreign concessionees and host governments. Both of these terms of oil concessions were at that time frowned upon by international major oil companies.

In the field of copper, Nippon Mining Co. (NMC) of Japan was setting a new precedent in the fall of 1974 in copper ore mining concessions. As the leader of copper smelting in Japan, NMC had been actively capturing ore mining concessions in Zaire, Ethiopia, Peru and Chile in direct competition with U.S.-based major firms. In the fall of 1974, NMC was sounding out the Peruvian government as to whether the latter would take over, free of charge, NMC's wholly-owned copper mine in Peru. The profitable subsidiary, Cia Minera Condestable, was established by NMC in 1963. By 1969, the annual production of the mine's crude copper ore, with a 1.9 percent copper content, had been expanded to 180,000 tons equivalent of copper. And it was estimated in 1974 that the mine still had over 750,000 tons equivalent of copper ore available. NMC made this offer voluntarily, without any pressure from the Peruvian government. And it promised to continue buying copper from the mine. Being secure in the Japanese market, NMC could easily separate the legal ownership of the mine from the physical availability of necessary copper ore.

NMC was at the same time asking the Peruvian government's permission to develop newer prospects of crude copper deposits. Furthermore, at about the same time, NMC was negotiating a joint venture in Chile with a Chilean company, Enrique Escola Barros, for the development of a copper mine in the northern part of the country. The mine was estimated to possess about 100 million tons of crude copper ore with a copper content of 1.2 percent, far superior to the Peruvian venture, Cia Minera Condestable.

Accordingly, NMC's offer to give Cia Minera Condestable to the Peruvian government, was a strategic move to cultivate a favorable rapport with the governments of Latin America, where NMC wished to obtain copper ores. The desire to outmaneuver other international competitors led NMC to set a precedent in the relationships between foreign investors in natural resources and host governments. NMC would not have minded at all if its voluntary relinquishing of Cia Minera Condestable to the Peruvian government could place it in a more favorable light vis-à-vis European-based and U.S.-based international investors, as seen from the vantage point of developing countries in Latin America, Africa and Southeast Asia.

JAPAN DESTABLIZES INTERNATIONAL COPPER ARRANGEMENTS

In spring 1975, world news networks reported that a group of Bougainvillians battled with the security guards of Rio Tinto Zinc's huge open-pit copper mine in Bougainville in the South Pacific. Not only stones but such quaint objects as spears and arrows were reportedly thrown at the guards. The reported incidents were but the latest in an escalating animosity between Bougainvillians and a foreign owner (Australian subsidiary of the British firm) of copper mines.[12]

Judged against the soaring price of copper and against concomitantly soaring profits of the foreign copper mine, the original terms of the mining concession, which provided income tax exemptions, capital write-offs, and other developmental incentives, came to be viewed by the Bougainvillians as too "one-sidedly" in favor of the foreign firm. Long gone was the host country's original perception of tremendous uncertainty and operational risks felt prior to the initial development of the mine.

Once the mine proved itself to be commercially successful, political pressures for renegotiating the mining concession developed. As Rio Tinto Zinc's original concern over the financial and operational risks of the venture dissipated in the midst of ever increasing cash revenues, the host residents' perceptions concerning the various political and social "costs" of tolerating Rio Tinto Zinc's operations rose. No doubt the mining operation did cause a tremendous societal change by bringing a "money economy" to the primitive "barter trade" economy of the Bougainville Archipelago. The mining operation also produced visible destruction of the natural environment of the island. Silt from the mine was raising river beds. Discharge from the mining plants was destroying coastal fishing grounds.

At first, Rio Tinto Zinc counted on the needs of Papua New Guinea for further foreign direct investments to moderate the host government's demand for the renegotiation of the contract. Indeed, Kennecott, a large U.S.–based multinational copper company, was reported to have been negotiating with the Papua New Guinean government for a possible copper mining operation on the Papua side of the country. And Kennecott was closely watching what might happen to Bougainville Copper Ltd.

By spring 1975, however, the political climate of the Papua New Guinean government changed in reaction to Rio Tinto Zinc's persistent delaying tactics so much that the host government stiffened its demand for majority ownership of its joint venture with the foreign investor.

At this juncture, Kennecott was reported to have abandoned its desire to invest in Papua. Kennecott feared that once signed, the new concession terms demanded by Papua New Guinea would encourage other governments to renegotiate Kennecott's existing concessions. Strangely enough, international rumors were spouting out the story that the government of Papua New Guinea grew bold because of Japan's eagerness to fill any vacuum left by the departure of Rio Tinto Zinc and Kennecott.

True, both the Japanese government and copper companies had extended a large amount in loans to Rio Tinto Zinc's mine in Bougainville. The copper ore concentrates of Bougainville Copper Ltd. were being exported almost entirely to Japan. The colossal development venture of the Bougainville mine was initially made feasible only when the Japanese copper processors guaranteed not only loans, but long-term purchase contracts. Therefore, even if Bougainville Copper Ltd. were nationalized, Japan, which had no equity interest in the venture, could continue to purchase copper from Bougainville.

Elsewhere, in North America, Japanese firms seeking direct access to natural resources are offering financial and technical assistance to small- and medium-sized mines and resource development projects. There have also been a number of Japanese acquisitions of both minority and majority interests in such firms in the United States and Canada. These small- to medium-sized firms appear to prefer business tie-ups with Japanese firms, thus having direct access to the Japanese market and at the same time avoiding being absorbed into the orbits of large American firms. Thus, Japanese firms are invading the hard-core sphere of influence American majors have held, and are eroding the majors' powers to discipline the behaviors of smaller independent firms.

RESPONSES OF INTERNATIONAL MAJORS

The responses of international major firms to Japanese "rate buster" investors are essentially twofold. First, they are entering the Japanese market in the processing and fabrication of raw materials so that they might be in a position to invoke the strategy of "exchange of threats." Second, they are at the same time inviting Japanese firms into international consortia so that the interlocked economic and political interests between Japanese and foreign firms might moderate Japanese "rate busting" conduct.

For instance, the 50-50 joint venture in Nagoya, Japan, between Dowa Kogyo and International Nickel Co. (INCO) of Canada that was concluded late in 1973, is a harbinger of the strategy of "Exchange of threats." INCO has agreed to supply the joint venture with nickel ingots which will be processed into special metal alloys for the Japanese market. From Dowa's point of view, it has obtained a guaranteed source of supply of nickel. From INCO's point of view, the joint venture provided it with an additional opportunity to expand its market contacts in Japan, over and above the 30 percent equity interest its former tie-up with Shimura Kako had provided. Second, Dowa-INCO (Japan) gives INCO an additional presence in the Japanese nickel processing industry where it can maintain business pressures upon Japanese processors. With INCO in their own backyard, Japanese competitors may become restrained from disturbing INCO's position in markets abroad for both finished products and raw materials.

As seen earlier in this chapter, international oil majors have concluded new tie-ups with Japanese oil firms in exploring and developing natural gas and oil in the continental shelves of Japan. In the case of oil, MITI, which was badly shaken by the oil crisis of 1973, abandoned its past policy of seeking independence from international major crude oil suppliers in the summer of 1974. Instead, MITI now actively seeks ways to closely interlock Japanese oil interests with those of U.S.- and Europe-based large oil firms.

In the case of aluminum, the international interlocking of economic and political interests is now taking shape for newly contemplated bauxite and alumina ventures among Japanese, European and American firms. Not only does this arrangement work in fostering the exchange of economic hostages between Japanese and foreign firms, but it also provides help for new ventures. Because of the colossal costs of infrastructure investments today, the large-scale development of bauxite and alumina operations in remote areas of developing nations requires a large initial guaranteed market for the projects. The inclusion of Japanese firms in these projects, is therefore becoming an almost necessary factor for foreign firms and governments planning the development of their bauxite deposits.

In the case of the Bougainville Copper Mine cited earlier, the British firm, Rio Tinto Zinc, rejected Japanese equity participation, although it borrowed heavily from both Japanese government and business, and counted on Japanese purchases of ore. As a result, perhaps, the existence of "independent" Japanese purchasers encouraged the Bougainvillian government to take a stronger stand against Rio Tinto Zinc.

As of fall 1975, the actual formation of international consortia between Japanese latecomers and international majors in the developing countries is still rare. However, I do sense such moves taking shape in the world aluminum industry. Mitsui's trans-Pacific acquisition of a 50 percent interest in Alumax that was mentioned earlier is leading Alumax (now 50 percent owned by Mitsui) and Japanese trading and aluminum firms—all of which are medium-sized compared to such international majors as ALCAN, ALCOA and Pechiney and previously had no captive sources of bauxite—to coalesce for the development of their own bauxite and related alumina sources in the Kimberley region of Western Australia. Independent Australian interests and an aluminum subsidiary of Shell Oil, Billiton Aluminum Australia, have been invited to participate in the Kimberley project together with three Japanese firms, Sumitomo Chemicals Co., Sumitomo Shoji Kaisha (a trading firm) and the Marubeni Corporation (a trading firm having close business ties with Showa Denko).

Interestingly enough, Alumax and Japanese aluminum firms currently have long-term purchase contracts for alumina with ALCOA of Australia. In the mid-1960s, ALCOA of Australia first rejected AMAX's (then the sole owner of Alumax) request for alumina supplies. Only when the government of Western Australia and business partners of ALCOA of Australia pressured ALCOA to expand its production of both bauxite and alumina in Australia, did ALCOA reluctantly agree to supply Alumax with alumina. It is in the context of ALCOA's attitude toward Alumax and marginal customers in Japan, that the Kimberley project is kept "alive" by Alumax. If ALCOA or other majors cut Alumax off from alumina supplies, Alumax would be forced to open the Kimberley project up to other potential customers. With the backing of Japanese customers, the

Kimberley project would become a large-scale operation, a low-cost "supplier" of bauxite and alumina, and could threaten the current positions of ALCOA and other majors. Thus, the mere existence of the Kimberley concession could be counted on by the participants as an insurance against ALCOA's sudden change of mind about supplying Alumax and others with alumina.

Meanwhile, ALCAN is inviting the Japanese government and aluminum firms jointly to establish an alumina plant with ALCAN and a primary aluminum reduction plant jointly with the Brazilian government in the Amazon area of Brazil. ALCAN would like to exclude Japanese participation from the bauxite and hydroelectric projects that Rio Doce, a Brazilian government development corporation, and ALCAN are jointly developing. But the Japanese participants have been offered minority interests in a three-way joint venture alumina plant between ALCAN, Rio Doce and Japanese firms. This primary aluminum reduction plant is expected by the Brazilian government to produce annually about 600,000 metric tons of aluminum ingots. And the Japanese minority participants would be obligated to purchase all these ingots.

It should be noted that such international maneuvers by Japanese aluminum firms, such as Mitsui's acquisition of 50 percent ownership of Alumax, caused Nippon Steel, a firm long hoping to enter into the primary reduction stage, to interlock itself with Mitsui's aluminum venture. Early in the 1960s, Nippon Steel planned to form an aluminum firm integrated from primary reduction to fabrication operations jointly with Kaiser (U.S.). Kaiser was interested in following ALCAN into Japan. But this move was torpedoed by the vigorous oppositions of the existing aluminum firms in Japan. And Nippon Steel was permitted by MITI to open only a fabrication plant jointly with Kaiser and Showa Denko, the third largest aluminum firm in Japan. Showa Denko was expected to restrain Nippon-Kaiser ambitions from within. Since this time, Nippon Steel was feared by Japanese aluminum firms to have been invading the primary reduction stage. During 1974, Mitsui sold its 5 percent equity interest in Alumax to Nippon Steel. This move by Mitsui was seen as a motivation for containing Nippon Steel's interest in entering the primary reduction business at home or abroad. By guaranteeing Nippon Steel a direct access to Alumax's aluminum ingots, Mitsui was rumored to be dissuading Nippon Steel from thinking of primary reduction operations.

As Japan opened its doors to foreign direct investments in the 1970s, MITI was not longer counted on to contain Nippon Steel's entries into the primary reduction stage, either jointly with Kaiser or with other foreign aluminum firms. In addition, Mitsui's tie-up with AMAX might have motivated foreign major aluminum firms to enter the Japanese market with the help of a firm like Nippon Steel. At the same time, Nippon Steel might have preferred implicitly to make an understanding of "no raiding" with the Mitsui group, which had not previously entered blast furnace operations inside or outside Japan.

All told, the cooperation and competition between Japanese processors of natural resources and international majors are taking on more and more complexity. And these complexities are multiplying as the host governments participate actively in the development of their natural resources by foreign consortia.

THE JAPANESE GOVERNMENT AND RESOURCE DIPLOMACY

As the cases of the Asahan and Amazon aluminum projects indicate, large overseas investments of Japanese firms seeking natural resources are bringing both the Japanese and host governments into direct "resource diplomacy." In the case of oil exploration abroad, the oil crisis of 1973 painfully reminded the Japanese government and business that the politics of oil could not be separated from economics. During the Arab oil embargo Arabia Oil Co.—the sole producer abroad of Japan—actually suffered from the greater "mandatory production and export cut" than the international majors who had wells in the same Persian Gulf region. Neither the Japanese majority ownership nor the joint venture status with the governments of Saudi Arabia and Kuwait permitted Arabia Oil to supply Japan with crude oil. Only when the Japanese government began to support the Arab countries' positions on the Arab-Israeli conflict, was Japan taken off the list of "unfriendly nations." The crude oil flow to Japan was then restored to the pre-crisis level.[13]

Until the oil crisis of 1973, the role of the Japanese government in resource-oriented investments abroad by Japanese firms was limited to underwriting the financial risks of developmental costs, as well as to promoting the "group" approach by Japanese would-be investors. In the case of oil alone, from 1967 the Petroleum Development Public Corporation (SKK) was empowered to undertake its own oil and natural gas explorations abroad as well as to provide financial and technical assistances to private Japanese developers.

The involvement of the Japanese government in the oil industry was still dwarfed by the governments of France and Italy. Compared with the ERAP of France, the cumulative spending of the Petroleum Development Public Corporation (SKK) of Japan reached a level only one-fourth that of ERAP. The number of square kilometers comprising exploration concessions for France and Japan outside their national boundaries pointed out this difference. In around 1970, eighteen million square kilometers were held outside national boundaries by firms based in the U.S., the U.K., France, Italy, West Germany, and Japan, about three-quarters of which were held by U.S.- and U.K.-based firms. France-based firms held about 18 percent of this total, while Japan-based firms obtained barely 2 percent of these oil concession areas.[14]

Anxious to score a visible success, in 1974 the SKK concluded a deal with the Shah of Iran for the exploration and development of natural gas in Iran. It was reported that the SKK agreed to terms shunned earlier even by other late comers such as Germany's DEMINEX. In spring 1976, the SKK project was reported to have hit the largest gas deposit ever discovered. While the economics of the SKK project in Iran remained uncertain, there was no denying that the Japanese government's direct hand in the international intricacy of oil and gas developments had already made Japan diplomatically vulnerable to the political fate of the Shah of Iran.

For the procurement abroad of non-ferrous metal ores, the Public Corporation to Promote Non-ferrous Metal Ores Explorations (Kinzoku Kōbutsu Tankō Sokushin Jigyōdan) was established in 1968 by the Japanese government. This Corporation provides long-term loans for ten years at an interest cost of 6.5 percent per year. These loans provide up to 50 percent of the total costs for exploration projects located in the industrially developed nations. Only the exploration of copper, lead, zinc, manganese, nickel, uranium and bauxite qualify under the terms of these loans. For projects located in developing nations, the Overseas Economic Cooperation Fund provides long-term loans (three to five years) for up to 70 percent of the total exploration costs at an interest cost of 5 to 6.5 percent per year.

Increased investments abroad by Japanese firms seeking industrial raw materials and foodstuffs have inevitably linked foreign governments closely with the Japanese government. In the past, when Japan was merely procuring necessary natural resources from the "world export markets," both fluctuating prices and the volumes of Japanese purchases could ostensibly be attributed to the vagaries of the world markets. Now that overseas suppliers are directly linked to Japanese investors, Japanese businesses are liable for charges of unfairly and selfishly either exploiting foreign suppliers or abruptly reducing the amount of purchases. And every time such issues arise, the Japanese government will be brought into the scene. Aggrieved foreign suppliers would run to their own governments. And irate host governments would take up these issues with the Japanese government.

Such incidents happened a number of times during 1972 when Japanese purchasers of copper ores reduced their importations because of a slack in the Japanese copper market. From 1974 to 1975, as the Japanese economy continued to suffer from the post oil crisis stagflation, Japanese importers of iron ores, non-ferrous ores, and beef steers either reduced or cancelled their earlier commitments with Australian exporters. In particular, Australian cattle ranchers, who had increased their supply of beef cattle—especially groomed and fed to meet the Japanese taste—found themselves left with thousands of pounds of surplus frozen steer, whose taste and texture were disliked by Australian consumers. This "beef incident" became a sore issue in Australian domestic politics. In no time, the incident grew to become the larger issue of the "costs of foreign investments in Australia."

In August 1975, the Amazon aluminum project mentioned earlier was almost blown up into a major political incident between Brazil and Japan. Since both MITI and Japanese aluminum and trading firms had committed themselves to a project of over one billion dollars in the Asahan in Indonesia, they lost interest in the Amazon project. But the Brazilian government was counting on Japan to make a firm commitment prior to the Brazilian president's state visit to Japan, scheduled for early 1976. The Vice Prime Minister of Japan, Fukuda, who was invited to Brazil in August 1975, was expected to bring an affirmative response of the Japanese government to the Amazon project. Late in July 1975, when the aluminum firms of Japan informally told their negotiating counterparts in Rio Doce about their intention to postpone the Amazon project, the Brazilian government reacted swiftly. Informally but firmly, Fukuda's state visit to Brazil and the Brazilian president's visit to Japan were to be postponed indefinitely unless Fukuda brought an affirmative answer to the Amazon project. And Japan was not to count on the Brazilian government for further assistance in Japanese firms' investments in Brazil. An eleventh-hour meeting among the top echelon of the Japanese bureaucracy and the ruling party produced the official statement that the Japanese government was positively interested in the Amazon project. And Fukuda visited Brazil in mid-August 1975.

The list of similar incidents is no doubt growing by day and by month. We will return to look at the politics of the host countries' reactions to Japanese investments later in Chapter 10.

Chapter Three

Manufacturing Firms Abroad

AN OVERVIEW

Compared in Table 3-1 with U.S.- and Europe-based multinational firms, large Japanese manufacturing firms revealed relatively heavy concentration in developing countries throughout Asia and Latin America. As of January 1, 1971, of 479 manufacturing subsidiaries of large Japanese firms, about two-thirds were located in Asia. The growth of Japanese investments throughout Asia appeared to provide *prima facie* evidence of "geographical proximity" as the determinant of direct investments abroad, leading to the speculation that Japanese manufacturing firms simply spilled out of Japan into neighboring nations. If this is the case, how can one explain the fact that at the same time, about one-fifth of the Japanese manufacturing subsidiaries abroad were found in Latin America, an area thousands of miles away from Japan?

Earlier, in Tables 1-5 and 1-6, the market-oriented investments abroad of Japanese firms such as manufacturing, sales, and service activities were broken down by geographical area. For all Japanese investments the profiles clearly showed that both in terms of cumulative assets and number of subsidiaries, over 80 percent of the manufacturing activities were located in Asia and Latin America, and the sales subsidiaries and services were concentrated in the industrialized countries of North America and Europe. The relative concentration of sales subsidiaries in North America and Europe reflected Japanese firms' export drives in the various regions. And the concentration of

Table 3-1. Relative Geographical Concentration of Manufacturing Subsidiaries of Large U.S., U.K., European and Japanese Firms[1] (As of January 1, 1971)

Parent Firm's Nationality	Location of Manufacturing Subsidiary					Total Number of Subsidiaries
	North America	Europe	Latin America	Asia and Oceania	Africa and Middle East	
U.S.A. (as of Jan. 1, 1968)	13.0%	39.0%	27.0%	15.0%	6.5%	4246
Japan	4.8	3.3	18.0	65.0	8.6	479
U.K.	13.0	29.0	6.1	27.0	25.0	2265
Germany	9.9	53.0	18.0	9.8	9.8	788
France	7.1	51.0	17.0	6.1	19.0	425
Italy	6.2	45.0	33.0	5.4	10.0	129
Belgium and Luxemburg	21.0	62.0	4.8	1.5	11.0	272
The Netherlands	23.0	54.0	8.5	8.7	5.4	425
Sweden	4.2	68.0	14.0	9.0	4.2	167
Switzerland	10.0	64.0	14.0	7.9	4.1	393

Source: Vaupel and Curhan, *The World's Multinational Enterprises* Harvard University Press, 1973, p. 122.
1. The sample of this table is limited to those manufacturing subsidiaries which were established by parent firms sufficiently large to make *Fortune's* 200 Largest Non-U.S. Firms in 1970, and *Fortune's* 400 Largest U.S. firms in 1967.

manufacturing subsidiaries in Asia and Latin America may also be related to the export-supremacy conduct that has long characterized Japanese firms.

In order to confirm these suggestions, the largest 79 Japanese manufacturing subsidiaries—as measured by their annual sales for the year 1972—were ranked by size and by host country. Forty-seven of the subsidiaries, or about 60 percent, were located in Asia, while eighteen, or about 23 percent were located in Latin America. Thailand, with a total of eighteen, hosted the greatest number of subsidiaries, followed by Taiwan with thirteen, and Brazil with nine. These findings corroborated the suggestions that Japanese manufacturing activities abroad expanded most not only in Asia and Latin America in general, but in developing countries with large domestic markets such as Thailand, Taiwan and Brazil.

A product profile of the largest 79 subsidiaries provided a further clue to the emigration patterns of Japanese manufacturing firms. As shown in Table 3-2, such standard manufactures as textiles, electric and electronic appliances, galvanized iron sheets and wire drawings dominated the product lines of Japanese subsidiaries. Aside from the

Table 3-2. Classification of Principal Product Line of the Largest 79 Japanese Manufacturing Subsidiaries Abroad in 1972

Product	No. of Subsidiaries
Electric & electronic appliances	25
Apparels, textile yarns, weaving & dyeing	19
Galvanized iron sheets, wire drawings & pipes	13
Knock-down assembly of trucks & passenger cars	9
Pulp, lumber & plywood	4
Non-ferrous & iron ores pelletizing	3
Cement & sheet glass	2
Sewing machine assembly	1
Polyvinyl chloride	1
Aluminum fabrication	1
Vegetable oil	1

Source: *Kaigai Shinshutsu Kigyo Soran*, Toyokeizai, Tokyo, 1973.

simple knockdown assembly line production of trucks and passenger cars, the remaining products were spread over a limited range of manufactured goods which also fell into the category of standard and least skill-intensive products.

Table 3-3 supports the findings of Table 3-2 as well. Table 3-3 groups Japanese parent firms—those which were sufficiently large to make *Fortune's* list of the 200 largest non-U.S. firms in 1970—according to the number of manufacturing subsidiaries owned abroad. The 35 Japanese parent firms owning more than ten overseas manufacturing facilities as of January 1, 1971, were dominated by synthetic fiber firms like Toray, Teijin and Kanebo, with their own subsidiaries of weaving and dyeing operations in Japan. Steel firms like Nippon, Kobe and Kawasaki, which had their own subsidiaries in Japan producing galvanized iron sheets, were also found in the category of parent firms with manufacturing subsidiaries abroad. Electric and electronics firms like Hitachi, Matsushita, Toshiba and Sanyo—which were producing such consumer goods as dry batteries, transistor radios, and electric fans—were on the forefront of Japanese multinational firms as well.

On the other hand, in the field of electric and electronic appliances, Sharp and Sony—both of which were exporting such technology-intensive products as desktop calculators, portable calculators, color TV sets and hi-fi sets—did not have any overseas manufacturing subsidiaries in January 1971. Neither did Fujitsu, which was exporting FACOM computer main frames and peripherals,

Table 3-3. Some Product Characteristics of Overseas Manufacturing Subsidiaries of Large Japanese Multinational Firms Classified by the Number of Subsidiaries of Parent Firms (As of January 1, 1971)

Number of Overseas Manufacturing Subsidiaries of Each Listed Parent Firm

0	1-8	10-15	16-31
Shipbuilding Hitachi Mitsui	*Automotive* Toyokogyo Honda Nissan Bridgestone Tire Kawasaki	*Galvanized Iron Sheets and Storage Tanks* Kobe Steel Nippon Steel Kawasaki Steel Mitsubishi Heavy Ind.	*Textiles* Toray Teijin Kanebo
Electronic and Electric Appliances Sharp Sony	*Galvanized Iron Sheets and Steel Tanks* NKK Sumitomo Metals	*Textiles* Toyobo Unitika Mitsubishi Rayon	*Electronic and Electric Appliances* Hitachi Matsushita Toshiba
Computer Fujitsu	*Shipbuilding* IHI	*Electronic and Electric Appliances* Sanyo	*Automotive* Toyota
Other Kirin Beer Ube Chemicals	*Electronic and Electric Appliances* NEC	*Other* Takeda Drugs Sekisui Chemicals	
	Other Asahi Chemicals Snow Brand Dairy		

Source: Data Bank of the Multinational Enterprise Project, Harvard Business School.

even though the average Japanese manufacturing firm already possessed two to three overseas manufacturing subsidiaries.

All 35 "largest of large manufacturing firms" in Japan were actively engaged in export activities. On the average, 22 percent of the total sales of these firms in 1971 consisted of export sales. A number of firms recorded that over 40 percent of their sales came from exports. By any indication, with the exception of Kirin Beer, the remaining thirty-four firms could be safely characterized as "export minded." And yet, depending on the major product lines, the propensity for firms to open overseas manufacturing subsidiaries, as measured by the number of subsidiaries, varied from zero for Sharp, Sony and Fujitsu to over sixteen for Toray, Teijin, Kanebo,

Hitachi, Matsushita, Toshiba and Toyota (complete knock-down assembly operations). The greater the respective firm's reliance on standard and mature products in Japan for business, the greater was the propensity of the firm to commence manufacturing activities in Asia and Latin America. Indeed, typical manufactured products involved were footwear, apparel, cotton and synthetic cloth weaving, printing and dyeing goods, simple tools, galvanized iron sheets, iron bars and wire drawings, iron pipes, boilers and metal containers, plastic mouldings, drug packaging, paper boxes, soap, transistor radio assemblies, dry batteries, electric fans, fertilizer, and limited and complete knock-down assemblies of automobiles, agricultural machinery and such electric appliances as compact refrigerators, black and white TV sets, and electric fans.

DEFENSE OF EXPORT MARKETS

During the 1960s, and especially toward the end of that decade, the developing countries in Asia and Latin America began to restrict the import of light manufactured goods, with the expressed hope that foreign firms and indigenous manufacturers would substitute local productions for imports. Japanese manufacturing and trading firms, large and small, in most instances dominated the imports of light manufactured goods to developing countries. Japanese manufacturing and trading firms faced the threat of losing their export markets. In order to defend the markets, they began to migrate to Asia and Latin America.

For instance, a survey of 385 Japanese manufacturing subsidiaries abroad, conducted by the MITI during the first quarter of 1971, revealed that regardless of the type of investing industry, such export-market-oriented considerations as (1) continuing exports from Japan, (2) defending local markets, and (3) developing local markets, explained 96 percent of the cases of Japanese overseas manufacturing activities, with the greatest of these considerations being the defense of previously established export markets.[1]

During the fall of 1972 I surveyed the factors motivating Japanese firms to locate manufacturing subsidiaries abroad. The respondents were asked to rate (in descending order on a seven-point scale from 6, very important, to 0, no importance whatsoever) the relative importance of six possible reasons leading to the decision to open a manufacturing subsidiary abroad. The results are summarized in Table 3-4, according to the size of the responding parent firms.

The picture which emerged from Table 3-4 was that Japanese manufacturing firms had substituted local production aimed at local

Table 3-4. Factors Affecting the Decision of Overseas Investments of Japanese Manufacturing Firms Classified by Size of Respondent Firms

Reasons for Overseas Investment	Size of Respondent Firms*	
	Large[1]	Small-to-medium[2]
(a) Host country's import restriction	4.64	4.71
(b) Host country's market size	4.81	4.94
(c) Japanese competitors' move to open a manufacturing plant in the same host country	2.82	2.97
(d) Lower wage level of host country compared with Japan	3.80	4.40
(e) Host country's economic concessions to foreign investment	4.79	4.29
(f) Plants in Japan operating at capacity	1.63	2.41
Number of Respondent Firms	93	42

1. The paid-in capital is over 1 billion yen (3.6 million in U.S. dollars), which is the required minimum amount in order to be listed on the First Market of the Tokyo Stock Exchange.
2. The paid-in capital is less than 50 million yen (180 thousand U.S. dollars). Most of these firms are too small to be listed on the Tokyo Stock Exchange.
*The median scoring of respective firms is based on a seven-point scale from 6, very important, to 0, of no importance whatsoever.

markets for former export operations; and that two factors, lower wage levels and economic concessions offered by the host country, also influenced their investment decision. In view of the fact that the respondents' estimates of local market size (Reason (b)) were based on their records of their past exports to these local markets, the investors' desires to defend their export markets can be said to have strongly influenced their decisions to commence overseas manufacturing activities.

For both large and small firms, one can see the relative importance of Reasons (a), (b), (d) and (e) as opposed to Reasons (c) and (f). One should note, however, that small firms gave a higher degree of importance than large firms to Reasons (d) and (f), thus indicating that smaller Japanese manufacturing firms specializing in labor-intensive light manufactures were pressured out of Japan by the rise in wages more strongly than their larger counterparts. In the next section, we will return to this propensity of small Japanese firms to spearhead in Japanese investments abroad.

That Japanese manufacturing operations abroad were for the most part motivated by Japanese firms defending their export markets in developing countries in Asia and Latin America may also be gleaned from Table 3-5. In 1971, of 1423 overseas manufacturing subsidiaries that were held by 610 parent firms, 524 of the subsidiaries reported their export and import activities attributable to their overseas operations. Except for pulp and paper operations, which were oriented more toward the development of raw materials and semiprocessed materials for Japan, the remaining manufacturing operations abroad of Japanese firms imported more than they exported.[2] Electric and electronics equipment industries registered a slight surplus of exports over imports, indicating that by 1971, some of the manufacturing subsidiaries abroad were explicitly given "offshore" production tasks for markets in Japan and the United States.

Table 3-5. Balance of Trade of Japanese Manufacturing Subsidiaries Abroad by Industry, 1971 (In Millions of Yen)

Industry	No. of Subsidiaries	Balance-of-Trade of Subsidiaries		
		(A) Aggregate Exports	(B) Aggregate Imports	(C) Exports/ Imports
Textile	101	32,124	41,290	0.778
Pulp & Paper	11	1,882	969	1.940
Chemicals	46	1,177	4,782	0.246
Ferrous & non-ferrous products	46	5,542	33,035	0.167
Electric & electronics equipment	111	35,072	34,145	1.027
General machinery	32	3,375	3,787	0.891
Transportation equipment	28	8,568	40,109	0.214
Precision equipment	21	2,291	4,348	0.527
Miscellaneous	128	24,597	27,932	0.881
For all the industries	524[1]	114,628	190,397	0.602

Source: The MITI Survey, 1973, p. 93.

Since the bulk of imports, if not all, of overseas subsidiaries came from Japan, as of 1971 these overseas manufacturing activities were safely viewed as preserving export markets for investing Japanese firms. Even in the "miscellaneous" industries, which dealt mainly in footwear, plastic mouldings and rubber products, imports exceeded exports. These industries typically imported plastic pellets and other necessary chemicals from Japan and processed them into various daily-use products for local markets. Plastic sandal shoes were, for example, the most common product of this industry category. Product designs and moulds were imported from Japan together with semi-processed materials and necessary equipment. Labor and fuel were two major input items that were procured locally. Some products were exported to the United States. But in the main, operations remained oriented to local markets.

The orientation of Japanese manufacturing subsidiaries to their respective local markets is also captured by the survey that I conducted during the fall of 1972 for the Multinational Enterprise Project of the Harvard Business School. While we surveyed only the largest 39 manufacturing firms that made *Fortune's* list of the 200 largest non-U.S. firms in 1970, and the ten largest general trading firms as well, their manufacturing subsidiaries were found, in the fall of 1972, to be predominantly oriented to local markets.

Of 526 manufacturing subsidiaries that were surveyed, about 80 percent, 415 operations, were principally oriented to local markets. Even when local manufacturing subsidiaries were oriented to export markets, their export markets rarely reached beyond the neighboring countries.

SMALL FIRMS SPEARHEAD JAPANESE INVESTMENTS ABROAD

Of 1140 overseas manufacturing subsidiaries of Japanese firms established during the period 1951-1971, 479 of the operations, or about 42 percent, were undertaken by small-sized parent firms. Combined with the overseas manufacturing subsidiaries of medium-sized parent firms, as shown in Table 3-6, small- to medium-sized parent firms accounted for about one-half of all the investments in manufacturing operations abroad in the early 1970s. This Japanese phenomenon stood in marked contrast to the U.S.- and Europe-based multinational firms, where large firms dominated the overseas investments.[3]

Furthermore, it should be noted that the propensity for a firm to establish a manufacturing subsidiary abroad was greatest among small-sized and large-sized firms. Medium-sized firms are rather distinguished by their relative absence from manufacturing activities abroad. What has produced such a pattern?

I have maintained that the size of a manufacturing firm in Japan is closely linked to specific products (and requisite technologies), as well as to the export performance of the respective products. The division of tasks among various-sized manufacturing firms has become a basic characteristic of the Japanese industrial scene. For example, in Table 3-7 one can observe the difference in export activity as measured by the export-to-sales ratio from one industry to another, as well as the difference in export activity of each industry depending on the size of the firm. For the same industry, typical

Table 3-6. Overseas Manufacturing Operations Classified by the Size of Principal Parent Firm, 1951-1971

		Other Japanese Investing Partner		
Size of Principal Parent Firm	Total Number of Manufacturing Subsidiaries Abroad 1951-1971	None (Invested Alone)	Other Japanese Manufacturing Firms	Other Japanese Trading Firms
Small	479	310	54	115
Medium	63	43	3	17
Large	598	284	70	244
Total	1,140	637	127	376
(%)	(100%)	(55.9%)	(11.1%)	(33.0%)

Source: Compiled from the author's field investigations in Japan.

Table 3-7. The Export-to-Sales Ratios of Japanese Investing Parent Firms Shown by the Size of Parent Firms and by Industry (1972)

Industry	Export-to-Sales Ratios by Size of Investing Parent Firms			Overall Average Export-to-Sales Ratios for All the Responding Firms[3]
	Small[1]	Medium[1]	Large[1]	
Textile	48.1%	6.1%	19.5%	17.4%
Chemicals	6.6	9.2	9.4	8.8
Steel & iron non-ferrous products	4.0	29.1	19.7	14.4
Electric and electronic machinery	68.3	44.0	22.3	15.8
General machinery	6.1	15.5	14.6	12.2
Transportation equipment	0	8.6	22.4	23.0
Precision tools & equipment	35.0	26.4	28.9	28.1
Miscellaneous manufactures & processed foods	26.0	8.5	9.4	11.7
No. of Respondent Firms Surveyed[2]	94	70	179	343

1. The size of parent firms corresponds to the size definitions of Table 3-4: small firms (paid-in capital less than ¥ 50 million); medium firms (paid-in capital between ¥ 50 million and ¥ 1 billion); large firms (paid-in capital over ¥ 1 billion).
2. 343 firms out of 606 firms that responded to the *MITI Survey, 1973* have produced the export-to-sales ratios.
3. Average figure weighed by export and sales figures.
Source: Data restructured and re-computed from the *MITI Survey, 1973*, p. 23.

products of small-sized firms are different from those of large- and medium-sized firms. Small chemical firms produce and export glues and non-organic chemicals, whereas large chemical firms produce and export plastic resins and fertilizer.

For such industries as chemicals, steel and iron, non-ferrous products and transportation equipment, the relatively low ratio of export-to-sales of small parent firms was due to the well-known nature of these industries in Japan. These industries required a large-scale operation beyond the financial and technological resources of small- and even medium-sized firms. On the other hand, the industry group labelled "miscellaneous manufactures and processed foods," dominated by footwear, plastic mouldings, instant noodles and leather products was one in which small firms of Japan specialized. Large firms in this category were mainly those of food canning and food additives.

In Table 3-8, the number of Japanese manufacturing subsidiaries that were found to be operating as of the end of 1973 are summarized by industry, as well as by the size of respective parent firms. The three industries, namely textile, electric and electronics machinery, and miscellaneous manufactures, that showed a high export-to-sales ratio for small-sized parent firms also showed a large number of manufacturing subsidiaries established abroad by these small-sized firms. This again supported our earlier deduction that small-sized firms ventured into overseas manufacturing operations in order to defend their export markets for standard manufactures.

Table 3-8. Number of Manufacturing Subsidiaries by Industry and by Size of the Principal Parent Firm in Japan As of December 31, 1973

Industry	No. of Overseas Manufacturing Subsidiaries	
	Principally established by small-sized firms	Principally established by large- and medium-sized firms
Textile	84	146
Chemicals	62	151
Steel and iron, non-ferrous products	52	77
Electric and electronic machinery	86	252
General machinery	68	93
Transportation equipment	19	84
Precision tools and equipment	32	48
Miscellaneous manufactures and processed foods	218	114
TOTAL	621	965

Source: Multinational Enterprise Data Bank, Harvard Business School

Up until the mid-1960s, annual wage increases in Japanese firms, small or large, did not outstrip annual increases in aggregate labor productivity. Even small-sized manufacturing firms were benefiting from expansions of the Japanese market and their export sales which permitted them to expand their production scales.[4]

Up until the mid-1960s, a majority of Grade 9 Junior High School graduates (the last level of compulsory education) were still seeking immediate jobs. And small-sized firms were able to recruit many of these fresh graduates. Because of the continued supply of a young labor force, employers were able to contain their total wage payments under the Japanese seniority-based wage system.[5]

All these situations changed after the mid-1960s. From that time onward, a number of separate but important social and economic changes began to converge. For example, an ever-increasing portion of the Grade 9 graduating class began to choose further schooling rather than immediate jobs. When this happened, after the postwar "baby boom" generation had already grown up, the supply of the fifteen- to eighteen-year-olds available to the labor force suddenly dwindled. At the same time, the Japanese economy began to show a number of bottlenecks impeding further growth. For one thing, the rate of technological innovation that sustained the rapid growth of the economy during the 1950s and the early 1960s began to level off in such key industries as steel and other raw material processing industries, in petrochemicals and in synthetic fibres manufacturing.

In order to contain production costs, large and small firms in Japan competed for the ever-dwindling supply of young male and female workers. Consequently, the wage differentials for the younger labor forces between small and large firms quickly disappeared. In fact, small- and medium-sized firms were paying greater starting salaries for young workers than large firms. The high level of business activities induced by the Vietnam war immediately pushed up the prices of plant sites in Japan. By the mid-1960s, potential plant sites in Japan were growing scarce. The prices of all real estate were soaring as land speculators and manufacturing firms competed for limited land available throughout Japan. The inability to obtain suitable plant sites was one of the causes of the industrial bottlenecks that Japanese manufacturing industries were experiencing.

Unlike large firms, small firms found it increasingly difficult to afford the soaring prices of plant sites in Japan, which were necessary for the expansion of production capacity (Reason (f) of Table 3-4). And this all coincided with the adoption of import substitution moves by the developing countries in Asia and Latin America. As a result, small-sized firms which were active in the export trade were forced to consider overseas manufacturing operations earlier than larger manufacturing firms.

THE EXPORT ORIENTATION OF SMALL FIRMS

In Table 3-6 it can be seen that about 65 percent of the manufacturing subsidiaries abroad of small-sized firms were undertaken alone, while the corresponding percentage for large-sized firms was about 46 percent. Furthermore, only one-quarter of the subsidiaries of small-sized firms were jointly established with Japanese trading firms, while the figure for large-sized firms was over 40 percent.

In Japan small firms have historically had to seek export growth as the only feasible avenue for overall growth of sales. Their domestic markets were crowded by many competitors, and the opportunities for product diversification at home were often usurped by medium- and large-sized firms. Larger firms often possessed the financial and technological resources enabling them to pre-empt the product diversification ideas or even product innovations which might have originated with some enterprising small firms. Once small firms had proven the market success of new products, large firms often moved in, squeezing out the small early entrants; small manufacturing firms were thus left to concentrate on export markets.

Even when small firms were ignorant of export opportunities, or lacked managerial and financial resources to overcome such ignorance, there were literally thousands of Japanese trading companies which scanned overseas market prospects and helped connect small firms with potential markets. The end result was the same: a substantial number of small manufacturing firms have been sensitized to overseas markets and have commenced overseas manufacturing activities when their export markets were threatened by the host governments' strategies of import substitution.

Consider the case of S. Noodle P.T. Indonesia, a Southeast Asian story typical for many equally enterprising small firms of Japan:

S. Noodle P.T. Indonesia

Early in the 1960s, the firm introduced "instant" noodles to the Tokyo market, which was increasingly favoring ready-to-eat snacks and light meals. The product proved to be a distinct success.

To cut a long story short, by the mid-1960s a number of leading medium- to large-sized food processing firms had entered the growing market for instant noodles in Japan. By pouring in massive advertising money for cultivating brand loyalty among consumers, and by resorting to massive sales promotions aimed at luring away retail outlets from small competitors, the new entrants soon captured a lion's share of the market.

As a result, the sales of the Japanese parent of S. Noodle P.T. were so drastically reduced that one of its two continuous production processes had to be laid idle. The firm could not afford to leave the new one idle too long because it had just borrowed money to install that very production process. The only way out of this plight was to move the idle production process "as is" to a new market abroad. After scanning East and Southeast Asian markets, where the firm used to export through Japanese trading firms, the parent firm of S. Noodle P.T. chose Indonesia, only because the Indonesian market had not yet been cultivated. At first Thailand was considered but was abandoned out of the well-founded fear that other small Japanese competitors would follow suit. A cursory check of Indonesian dietary habits gave the firm a strong gut feeling that it would succeed in Indonesia. Besides, the Indonesian government was intimating that it would limit the number of foreign competitors' entries into the same market, as an investment inducement to early comers.

The history of S. Noodle P.T. Indonesia depicts a small enterprising firm of Japan leapfrogging potential competitors into a developing country, in anticipation of the inevitable import-substitution moves by host governments. Examples like the one above are abundant in the early history of Japanese direct investments abroad.

The case of S. Noodle P.T. Indonesia also points out both entrepreneurial and economic factors that motivated a number of small-sized Japanese manufacturing firms to commence overseas productions. First, a firm that was both export-minded and growth-minded ventured abroad either to defend its export market, or to extend the economic life of the product on hand by taking it to developing countries. Second, both process-related and product-related technologies are simple enough to permit an international transfer from Japanese manufacturing settings to developing countries. Third, the threat by host countries to cut off latecomers in the same product category often induced small-sized manufacturers to scramble for an early entry.

When a number of enterprising and export-oriented small firms faced the rising wage costs in Japan after the mid-1960s, the developing countries' import restrictions triggered many small firms to expand their business horizons beyond simple export activities. The spread of "mini" multinational firms based in Japan was indeed an outgrowth of the rapid changes taking place in Japanese economic conditions and of the developing countries' aspirations for industrial growth via import substitution.

OVERSEAS MANUFACTURING OPERATIONS OF LARGE FIRMS

In Table 3-7 it could be seen that large- and medium-sized parent firms were also active abroad in textiles and electric electronics machinery industries. Were they then competing with small-sized Japanese firms abroad?

The products that emigrated out of Japan during the 1960s were often light manufactures which were becoming mature and standard in Japan. According to the Japanese division of manufacturing tasks, small- to medium-sized processors and fabricators, not large-sized manufacturing firms, were put in charge of such standard and mature products. And yet, as shown earlier in Table 3-3, such leading steel firms of Japan as Nippon Steel, Kawasaki Steel, NKK, Sumitomo Metals and Kobe Steel, were actively involved in the overseas production of galvanized iron sheets. In Japan, these five steel firms had been producing only such intermediate materials as steel and iron coil sheets, which were sold by trading firms to fabricators of galvanized iron sheets. Large textile firms were found actively involved abroad in weaving and dyeing operations, which often had been sub-contracted out to other small- to medium-sized firms at home. Leading manufacturers of electronics and electric appliances were involved in the production of dry batteries and electric parts abroad which they had also allocated to their subsidiaries or outside subcontractors in Japan. There was an interesting discrepancy between the products made by overseas subsidiaries of the large firms and those made in Japan in the plants of the parent firms. How then, did large Japanese firms react in defending the export markets of standard and mature products, when they themselves were not involved in either the production or the export of such products to the developing countries?

In Chapters 1 and 2, it was repeatedly pointed out that the division of tasks among manufacturing firms can be broken down by the size of the respective firm. The use of a division of tasks was precipitated during the 1950s and the 1960s by large manufacturers that had continuously been absorbing newer and newer products and process technologies. It became more and more necessary for them to shed old standard or obsolete products and technologies and at the same time cultivate new markets for new products. Such dual needs of large firms produced many hierarchical groupings of firms operating in the same industry. At the apex of each hierarchy was the largest firm of the group. It goes without saying that the conscious capital rationing schemes of the Bank of Japan, as discussed in Chapter 1, helped create the hierarchical groupings of large-, medium- and small-sized firms around the product and technological links in each manufacturing industry.

As a result, each large firm listed in Table 3-3 had accumulated on the average over 100 related subsidiaries. Matsushita, for example, had 536 related subsidiaries. Hitachi possessed 150 subsidiaries, followed by Kobe Steel with 72 subsidiaries. In the textile industry, each synthetic fibre firm had accumulated from 60 to 89 domestic subsidiaries which in turn processed yarns into various textile materials. A careful cross-tabulation of the number of overseas manufacturing subsidiaries held by respective large firms and the number of domestic subsidiaries owned by each large firm produced a pattern: the greater the number of domestic subsidiaries a given large firm owned, the more likely it was to have invested in manufacturing operations abroad.

This trend among the large manufacturing firms of Japan is statistically supported below. The Chi-square test, showing the difference in the average number of domestic subsidiaries between two groups of large firms, indicated that the group whose firms possessed more than ten overseas manufacturing subsidiaries also possessed a significantly larger number of domestic subsidiaries. Since the products and industry composites of the two groups were roughly the same, it followed that overseas direct investment by the large manufacturing firms of Japan owning domestic subsidiaries was positively influenced by the firms' hierarchical structure of essentially vertically integrated operations. Why is this so?

		Average Number of Domestic Subsidiaries
Group I:	Firms with less than 8 overseas manufacturing subsidiaries	89
Group II:	Firms with more than 10 overseas manufacturing subsidiaries	121

N.B.: The Chi-square test of the difference between the average number of domestic subsidiaries of Group I and Group II reveals that the difference is statistically significant at the probability level of 0.02; leading one to infer that Group II, more active in overseas direct investments, also owned a greater number of domestic subsidiaries in Japan.

The Japanese corporate culture places a high value on hierarchical relationships among employees and related corporate members of a given firm's group, much like the relationship seen in clannish family groupings, with the filial obligations of the "children" (subsidiaries and employees) directed towards the "family master" (the leading manufacturing firm and the management). The position of a large manufacturing firm of Japan as the leader of its own industrial "domain" dictated that the parent be alert to potential threats to the business fortune of its subsidiary members. Likewise, in view of the fact that the leader firm was often the supplier of intermediate products to its subsidiaries' products (they were all vertically interrelated), a decline in the subsidiary's business tended immediately to hurt the leader's business.

Since both small- and large-sized member firms engaged in

manufacturing activities have been strongly export-minded, large firms have often taken the initiative in establishing processing operations abroad which were formerly run by small domestic subsidiaries for the purpose of export. This is why even the largest manufacturer of steel and iron products in Japan, Nippon Steel, has been spearheading in the overseas production of such standard products as galvanized iron sheets, formerly manufactured for export domestically by its small- to medium-sized subsidiaries. In this way, Nippon Steel has assured itself continuous sales of iron sheets or iron coils.

In theory, the small subsidiary of Nippon Steel possessed the technologies required for the production of galvanized iron sheets, and could well have opened its own overseas subsidiary in order to protect its export market. In reality, however, such subsidiaries often lack the financial and managerial resources required for unfamiliar overseas ventures and look to the leader-manufacturer, in this case, Nippon Steel, to assume the managerial responsibilities of the new ventures abroad. Also, in the context of the filial obligations of the subsidiary firm to its leader-manufacturer, it is the natural function of the large firm to assume leadership in ventures new to the entire group.

Until July 1, 1971, when the Japanese government began automatically to provide permits to Japanese firms for overseas investment, investing firms had to negotiate with the various agencies of the Japanese government for the necessary allotment of foreign exchange funds. This task could often be undertaken only by the leader-manufacturer; it being the only one with the requisite contacts and experience with the government. The government itself preferred to make the leader-manufacturer, rather than the subsidiary, managerially and financially responsible for the overseas ventures of the entire manufacturing group. And the government agencies often prefer to deal with the familiar personalities of large manufacturers.

A similar story unfolds in the spreading pattern of overseas investments of the leading synthetic fiber manufacturers such as Toray, Teijin and Kanebo. As the governments of developing nations increasingly expanded their strategies of import substitution to include intermediate products, say, from apparel-making to cloth printing and dyeing operations, leading textile firms of Japan took the initiative in organizing overseas manufacturing operations for their own manufacturing groups. A group usually included at least one leading trading company which was active in the distribution of manufactures of its related firms at home and abroad.

In contrast, such leading manufacturers of synthetic fibre raw materials as DuPont of the U.S. and ICI of the United Kingdom have on the whole remained independent suppliers of raw materials to equally independent yarn manufacturers. Yarn manufacturers in turn sell their products to independent weavers. In contrast to Japan, the textile industry in the U.S. and the U.K. consists of many independent yarn manufacturers, weavers and dyers. And having lost their international competitive position to the Japanese, the textile firms of the U.S. and the U.K. have become totally reoriented to their own domestic markets.

Consequently, they have been isolated from the stimuli for overseas investment arising from the import substitution strategies of the developing nations. When the markets for synthetic yarns or even raw materials for these yarns were opened up by the successful entry of Japanese weavers and dyers to developing nations, these markets became "pre-empted" or "owned" by the leading Japanese textile manufacturers that had cultivated them. The *de facto* vertically integrated large firms of Japan, which had their international competition, and especially threats of import substitution from a foreign government, are prone to go "multinational" sooner than the firm without such exposure to competition.

The previous examples explain how large manufacturing firms of Japan became sensitized to defending the export markets of their domestic subsidiaries. Medium-sized firms, on the other hand, were often one stage removed from the products whose exports were threatened by the import substitution moves of developing countries. While medium-sized firms remained inactive or behind the scene in Japanese manufacturing operations abroad in the 1960s and the early 1970s, small- and large-sized firms became involved, whether alone or with trading firms, in the proliferation of Japanese manufacturing activities abroad.

THE INTERNATIONAL EXTENSION OF OLIGOPOLISTIC COMPETITION IN JAPAN

Leading electronics and electric appliance firms as well as large synthetic fiber firms of Japan, first became involved in overseas ventures as their respective industrial groups became exposed to the import substitution moves of the developing countries in Asia and Latin America. Their expansions abroad, however, increasingly took on a rivalry between a few large oligopolistic firms in the same industry in Japan. The moment one leading firm moved to open a manufacturing operation in a foreign market where other leading Japanese firms were exporting, the rival firm(s) not only followed suit, but often tried to beat the leader firm to the next country market.

THE CASE OF THE SYNTHETIC FIBER INDUSTRY

In the 1950s, MITI helped develop the synthetic fiber industry, mainly for the production of nylon and polyester.[6] Since no synthetic fiber firms or chemical firms of Japan possessed the product technologies necessary to manufacture nylon and polyester, Japanese firms that hoped to enter this industry had to obtain requisite technologies through licensing agreements with DuPont, ICI or other foreign firms. By merely denying these licenses to other hopeful firms, MITI was able to develop an essentially duopolistic structure in the nylon and polyester industry between Toray and Teijin.

Only later, in the 1960s, when the Japanese markets for synthetic fibers—including newly discovered products like acrylic fibers—grew further in size, were other competitors like Kanebo, Toyobo, Mitsubishi Rayon and Asahi Chemicals permitted to enter the synthetic fiber industry.

In terms of adaptability as apparel, however, it is polyester, not nylon, that is the leader in both men's and women's clothing, shirts and underwear. Toray and Teijin competed with each other in the polyester markets of Japan. Teijin, which had lagged far behind Toray in entering nylon products markets, banked its business fortune on polyester. Their competition extended to their overseas ventures as well. Competition between Toray and Teijin has been waged throughout East and Southeast Asia (see Table 3-9) and in the mid-1970s there is every sign that similar competition will be carried over into Brazil and other Latin American nations, or even into Africa.

By the end of 1973, Teijin had been actively involved in 18 overseas manufacturing subsidiaries in 9 countries handling polyester-related products, while Toray had opened 35 overseas manufacturing operations in 15 countries involved in polyester and nylon products. In Table 3-9, the nine countries in which both Teijin and Toray have established manufacturing operations are listed in descending order according to the date of entry for each firm, along with the type of fibre operation established. The close parallels between the two firms are obvious.

A glance at Table 3-9 immediately reveals the following four trends: (1) the order of countries entered according to date-of-entry

90 *The Japanese Are Coming*

Table 3-9. Competitive Investments Abroad by Teijin and Toray for Nine Countries

Country Entered (Descending Order)	Leader, Time, & Operation Entered (1)	Follower, Time, & Operation Entered (1)	No. of Manufacturing Subsidiaries in Operation as of Dec. 31, 1973	
			Teijin	Toray
1. Australia	Teijin & Toray simultaneously purchased 0.3% each of the equity of Dunlop Australia in 1963 for exports of synthetic yarns.		1	1
2. Srilanka	*Teijin*, 1964 weaving & dyeing of synthetic fibers	*Toray*, 1965 spinning, weaving & dyeing of nylon fibers	1	1
3. Thailand	*Toray*, 1964 weaving & dyeing of polyester fibers	*Teijin*, 1965 weaving & dyeing of polyester fibers	5	7
4. Taiwan	*Teijin*, 1967 spinning & weaving of polyester fibers	*Toray*, 1968 weaving & dyeing of polyester fibers	2	5
5. Singapore	Both firms entered at the same time. *Teijin*, 1968 = spinning, weaving & dyeing of polyester fibers	*Toray*, 1968 nylon socks. Entered Malaysia 1971 for weaving & dyeing of polyester fibers	1	2
6. Korea	*Teijin*, 1969 polyester filament yarn making 21 ton /day	*Toray*, 1971 polyester filament yarn making 21 ton/day	2	2
7. Hong Kong	*Toray*, 1969 polyester, added knit dyeing, 1971	*Teijin*, 1971 polyester, knit dyeing	2	2
8. Indonesia	Both firms entered at the same time. *Teijin*, 1971 = spinning, weaving & dyeing of polyester fibers	*Toray*, 1971 spinning of polyester yarns, added weaving & dyeing, 1972	1	5

Table 3-9 continued

Country Entered (Descending Order)	Leader, Time, & Operation Entered (1)	Follower, Time, & Operation Entered (1)	No. of Manufacturing Subsidiaries in Operation as of Dec. 31, 1973	
			Teijin	Toray
9. Brazil	Teijin, 1972 spinning of polyester yarns	Toray, 1973 spinning of polyester yarns	1	1

N.B. (1) The date of entry marks the actual commencement of manufacturing operations.
(2) In addition to the above listed 9 countries, Toray has entered Malaysia (1971), Venezuela (1967), Ethiopia (1966), El Salvador (1967), Kenya (1965), and the U.K. (1972).
Source: The Data Bank of the Multinational Enterprise Project, Harvard Business School, and the author's field work.

for both Toray and Teijin was identical; (2) the time-lag between the entry of one firm and the following of another was negligible; (3) the firm which was second to enter one country became the first entrant in the next; and (4) the specific manufacturing operation established by the second entrant to a country was the same type of operation established by the first entrant to that same country. These regularities were too overwhelming to be coincidental. What then, were the strategic considerations of the two contending oligopolistic firms which produced the above patterns of competitive investment in eight Asian countries and in Brazil?

Of various plausible explanations, in-depth interviews with representatives of these two firms have led me to hypothesize that "risk minimizing" considerations—a form of defensive investment—were the principal motivating forces behind the competitive spread of Japanese direct investments throughout Asia and recently in Brazil. The stimulus from abroad which triggers the first entrant's move may well be the local government's move to inhibit importation of certain manufactures, say, textile cloth materials or transistor radios, from Japan. Once one alert Japanese firm makes a move to set up a manufacturing subsidiary in its traditional export market area, its competitors in Japan become suddenly aware of similar investment opportunities. But why do they enter the same country?

For this question, it would be revealing to examine the very first Japanese acquisition of equity interest in a manufacturing operation of synthetic fiber abroad, namely, the simultaneous purchase in 1963 of 0.3 percent each of Dunlop Australia Ltd. by Teijin and Toray. Although this purchase was nothing more than an attempt to acquire a captive export market, both Teijin and Toray made sure that neither firm gained any advantage or potential maneuvering position over the other.

A similar desire to balance their competitive situations operated in their moves to Thailand, their traditional and substantive export market. In Thailand, the two firms at first shared the ownership of subsidiaries engaged in weaving and dyeing operations of polyester-based cloth materials, although they divided equally the number of subsidiaries in which each would be a majority stockholder. Later, in 1972, when both firms expanded their operations in Thailand as possible bases for exporting operations, Toray and Teijin relinquished the "hostage" shares of stock they held in the jointly-owned subsidiaries and became independent of each other. And they were ready to compete with each other.

Thus changes in the relationship between the two firms, from "accommodation" to "competition," have been evident not only from one country to another, but also within such large market areas as Korea, Thailand, Taiwan and Indonesia. In 1974, Brazil appeared to be the scene for a new phase of their competition. Teijin, which had been outpaced by Toray in Indonesia, may well attempt to pre-empt the Brazilian synthetic fiber market in the future. Thus, the strength of Toray in Indonesia may be balanced globally by Teijin's moves in Brazil.

So long as these two oligopolisitc firms competed in domestic markets, or in export markets supplied from domestic sources alone, they remained on an equal footing with each other. They knew each other very well and were able to play a market-share maximization game in a familiar environment. But since technological progress in both product- and process-related technologies of nylon and polyester has been arrested, and since both Teijin and Toray have come to acquire similar degrees of technological competence, competitive advantage could not come only from marketing strength, or, more specifically from control over markets at home or abroad.

In view of the fact that both Teijin and Toray have each cultivated their own hierarchical grouping of many firms related to synthetic fiber processing, both firms appear to be bent on maintaining their market positions for their respective groups as a whole. Above all, neither Teijin nor Toray wishes to take risks that might jeopardize, through surprise retaliation from the competitor, a member of their "empire."

Accordingly, when one firm opens a manufacturing base outside

Japan, the other is strongly motivated to "follow the leader" as a precaution against being "out-supplied" by the competitor who has acquired potentially more or better supply sources. The best strategy for the follower, therefore, is to open an identical supply base right next to the leader's plant immediately after the former's move.[7] Until all the possible supply bases for strategic markets are equally divided, firms will be under strong pressure to keep opening plants abroad with the idea that being first is a temporary advantage over the competition; or at least a precaution against similar moves by the competitor. And of course the leader will be followed.

This kind of oligopolistic spread of Japanese investments in Asia and Latin America is also precipitated by the Japanese character trait that triggers fierce competition among various groups. Group loyalty, which is strong among Japanese employees and management of the same corporate group, produces competition among different corporate groups for the supreme position of leader. Another Japanese trait, success-orientation, often manifests itself in the form of devotion to the cause of the group, in direct competition with an outside group identified as the prime competitor.

In the case of synthetic fibre industry, only other Japanese manufacturers are now capable of competing with the large Japanese firms. Teijin and Toray view themselves as contenders for the world leadership position. The other Japanese firms in the field, Toyobo, Kanebo, Unitika, Asahi Chemicals and Mitsubishi Rayon, attempt to only keep toeholds in the large markets of Taiwan, Thailand, Indonesia and Brazil by imitating, where possible, the examples of Toray and Teijin. In order to find a viable market niche, however, these follower firms are focusing their overseas operations upon synthetic fiber materials which are related to the traditional product lines of cotton or rayon blended with polyester, or upon straightforward cotton and rayon products.

THE CASE OF ELECTRIC AND ELECTRONIC APPLIANCES

Defensive investment behaviors can also be identified among the four leading Japanese manufacturers of electric and electronic appliances and equipment—Matsushita, Hitachi, Sanyo and Toshiba. The combined number of manufacturing subsidiaries abroad of these four leading firms was 68 by the end of 1973 and involved 26 countries. Twenty-two of the 26 host countries were in so-called developing nations. With the exceptions of Tanzania, Nigeria, Iran and Spain, the remaining developing nations were located in Asia and Latin

America. Table 3-10 summarizes the entry patterns of the four Japanese manufacturers for the thirteen nations that have hosted overseas manufacturing operations of at least two of the four firms.*

Matsushita has led the other three firms in being the first entrant seven times. A singular development in this industry, was that toward the end of the 1960s and into the 1970s, Singapore, Malaysia, Taiwan and Korea were attracting offshore production bases of

Table 3-10. Locations, Years Entered and Activities of Overseas Manufacturing Subsidiaries of the Four Leading Electric and Electronic Appliance and Equipment Manufacturers: Hitachi, Matsushita, Sanyo and Toshiba (As of the End of 1973)

Country	Hitachi 1965	Hitachi 1970	Matsushita 1965	Matsushita 1970	Sanyo 1965	Sanyo 1970	Toshiba 1965	Toshiba 1970	First Entrant
Hong Kong	×(1)				○(2)				Sanyo
Taiwan	×○	○×○	○	○	○		×	×	Matsushita Toshiba
Korea				○		○		○	Toshiba
Malaysia		○	○	○	×			○	Matsushita
Singapore		×○			○	×		○	Sanyo
Philippines	×		×		×		×		Matsushita
Thai	×	×				×		×	Matsushita
S. Vietnam				×	×				Matsushita Sanyo
Indonesia				×	×				Matsushita
India	×	×			○				Hitachi
Mexico		×	×				×	×	Matsushita
Brazil	×	×		×	×	×		×	Hitachi
Canada					×	×			Sanyo

N.B. (1) The cross (×) denotes manufacturing operations operated exclusively to the market of the host country.
(2) The circle (○) denotes the "offshore" manufacturing operations from which products were being exported as of the end of 1973.
Source: The Data Bank of the Multinational Enterprise Project, Harvard Business School; and the author's up-dating field work.

*Unlike Sony, these four firms have historically competed with one another mainly on the basis of lower production costs of products innovated by foreign firms and Sony. In their approach to the U.S. market, they are also distinguished from Sony by their past emphasis on the bulk sales of private brand products to U.S. firms.

Japanese firms. These places acted as exporting platforms from which finished goods were exported to outside markets, often to the U.S., Europe and Japan. And all four firms, Hitachi, Matsushita, Sanyo and Toshiba, have come to possess "offshore" manufacturing bases in these four Asian nations so that the labor costs and manufacturing efficiencies of the offshore production bases will be influenced by socioeconomic environments common to all four firms. Here again, as in the synthetic fiber industry, one can detect oligopolistic moves calculated to equalize the competitive situations among all four firms.

OFFSHORE PRODUCTION BASES OF JAPANESE MANUFACTURING FIRMS

Toward the end of the 1960s, there appeared a new investment behavior, different in its initial impact, from the defensive moves of the earlier period which were designed to counteract the import substitution policies of the developing nations. In particular, the firms that were making electric and electronic household appliances began to move such labor-intensive processes as assembly of standard products like radios and black and white TV sets to newly-built plants in Korea, Taiwan, Malaysia and Singapore. Under the seniority-based wage system of Japan, the general "aging" of the entire work force of a firm, as well as the rising wages, motivated Japanese firms to move the labor-intensive processes of their products to neighboring countries.

In addition, a number of Japanese overseas manufacturing subsidiaries, which had all been initially set up in order to supply the local markets of the developing countries, increasingly encountered political pressures from the host governments to make substantive contributions to the hosts' exports. In the face of this pressure, many investing parent firms of Japan began to regroup their manufacturing subsidiaries, scattered particularly throughout Asia, so that a number of them could be expanded and streamlined to permit offshore production operations.

During the 1960s, the developing nations in Asia and Latin America adopted the strategies of import-substitution as a short-cut toward industrialization. There was even the romantic assumption on their part that the manufacturing operations created by the import-substitution policies would automatically grow, and in due time be able to assume exporting activities for them. One developing country after another appeared to turn to this hope. Toward the end of the 1960s, however, this assumption increasingly changed to disappointment. Not only their domestic manufacturers, but also foreign investors had failed to grow within a short enough period of time to acquire the international competitive strength necessary for exportation to the world market. And the developing nations often felt insistent political pressures to create jobs for their growing population of urban unemployed.[8]

As a partial solution to this problem, the developing nations began to extend special economic incentives to foreign manufacturing firms which would agree to open offshore production bases and export from them. In addition to such standard concessions as income tax exemptions, duty-free importation of necessary input materials and equipment, and free plant sites, the host governments eased their restrictions on the ownership of subsidiaries of the four leading electronic appliance firms of Japan. They were able to form fully-owned subsidiaries in the very same developing nations that often required foreign investors to conclude joint ventures with local partners.

As noted earlier, there are many Japanese manufacturing firms involved in the textile and electric and electronics industries which find it necessary to open offshore production bases for standard and labor-intensive products in nearby developing nations. In particular, sporting goods, toys, Christmas tree decorations, footwear, ceramics and the like, which spearheaded Japan's exports to the U.S. from the end of the 1940s to the early 1950s, are now increasingly exported to the U.S. and even to Japan from the offshore production bases of Japanese subsidiaries located elsewhere in Asia.

As of the mid-1970s, there have appeared three types of offshore production ventures by Japanese manufacturers. Although these types were not necessarily mutually exclusive, the origins of their investment and their future growth potentials appear to differ. Furthermore, when making predictions about the political reactions of the host nations to Japanese manufacturing subsidiaries, these differences—between the types of offshore manufacturing bases—will become important.

Type I—Total Emigration

Both product- and process-related technologies have emigrated out of Japan to the neighboring nations in Asia principally because they have no longer been economical to make in Japan, whose wage level is passing the average of the EEC nations. Most manufacturers of "miscellaneous" products like footwear, sporting goods, ceramics and toys fall into this category. These products were often moved to developing nations in Asia in order to counteract the host country's moves toward import substitution. As local entrepreneurs successfully imitated the requisite technologies of these standard products, and began pressuring the host governments to ban Japanese subsidiary operations, a number of the subsidiaries reoriented their production to service export markets. In light of these developments, the next generation of standard manufactures, such as galvanized iron sheets, nails, wire drawings, and dry batteries, is likely to face a similar fate.

One variation of the offshore production base pattern of Type I is a plant supplying such standard products as transistor radios, apparel, TV sets and electric parts to such major markets as the U.S. and the EEC countries. Japanese manufacturing subsidiaries which are located in Puerto Rico, Spain, Malta, Portugal and Ireland are dominated by Japanese offshore production bases engaged in the production of the same standard products mentioned above for the U.S. and the EEC. In addition to an abundance of labor and lower wage costs than available in Japan, the U.S. or the EEC, these host countries often offer special duty-free or reduced duty-rate access to the U.S. and the EEC. The commonwealth of Puerto Rico vis-a-vis the U.S., as well as the EEC associate membership of Spain and Portugal, attracts Japanese manufacturers eyeing the markets in the U.S. and the EEC. In 1972 Ireland joined the EEC and appeared in 1975 to be attracting Japanese manufacturers interested in the EEC market.[9]

Type II—Regional Integration

As the assembly operations of automotive products and electric and electronic products expanded simultaneously in more than two developing nations, political pressures from host governments demanding backward (vertical) integration moves by the assemblers or by parts suppliers mounted. However, the market size of any single country was yet too small to permit an economically viable production-run of necessary intermediate goods. And yet each host government was pressuring Japanese subsidiaries to export their products. One logical solution to this dilemma was to establish a regional production base from which the downstream manufacturing operations scattered in the neighboring region would be supplied with necessary intermediate input materials. Singapore and Malaysia have often been selected for these regional supply bases.

In the synthetic fiber industry of Japan, Toray was in the mid–1970s leading its competitors by setting up a large-scale nylon and polyester plant in Malaysia, from which its downstream operations in the region would be supplied with raw materials. In order to insure stable demand for a large amount of input materials of synthetic fibres, Toray may well find it necessary to enter apparel-making operations in neighboring nations—and these operations would have to be aimed exclusively at export to Japan, the U.S. and Europe in order to satisfy the host governments. Thus, there would appear in the future to be an inevitable link-up to Type I and Type II offshore production activities. Similar linkup operations also appear plausible for the electric and electronic appliance industries.

Type III—Partial Emigration of Production Processes

The most typical example of partial emigration of production process is the bonding and assembling operations of electronic parts such as semiconductors and integrated circuits which are moved from a plant in Japan to a plant in, say, Korea or Taiwan. Of all the production processes for semiconductors, the capital-intensive and technology-intensive processes, such as pellet-making, are completed in Japan. After that, the bonding and assembling operations are performed at offshore production bases. The finished products are again shipped back to plants in Japan.

In these plants in Japan, the final testing of product quality is performed on the imported products before they are assembled into appropriate electronic equipment in Japan. The whole production of certain parts and of intermediate products like vacuum tubes and standard condensers has been moved to offshore production bases by many leading electronics firms and parts manufacturers. And yet, what distinguishes the offshore operations of Type III from those of Type I and even Type II is the fact that the products made by the offshore plants of Type III are often used by domestic manufacturers of intermediate products, which are passed on to other plants in Japan for final assembly.

As in the case of semiconductors and integrated circuits, the overseas manufacturing plants (offshore bases) are nothing but branch plants to which partial production processes have been subcontracted. In view of the fact that these branch plants need close and frequent communication with their parent plants in Japan, Hong Kong, Taiwan and especially Korea have been preferred, because of their geographical proximity, for the locations of the branch plants.

The emigration of Type III is not limited to electronic products. Any labor-intensive intermediate manufactures like die-cast products and plastic mouldings which Japanese plants continue to use will be moved increasingly out of Japan into neighboring countries in Asia.

No doubt, the boundaries of the preceding categories of offshore production bases are likely to become increasingly blurred in such a way that any surviving operations of Type I will become regrouped either into Type II or III. Type I operations may well be blended with Type III so that a greater degree of interdependence among the Japanese manufacturing subsidiaries located at least throughout Asia will be increasingly realized through extensive crosshaulings of products among them.

CONCLUSION

In retrospect, Japanese manufacturing activities abroad have developed in two distinct stages, presented below. During the balance of the 1970s, we will probably see a rapid disappearance in Asia of Japanese investment patterns typical of Stage I. Those firms which have not experienced Stage I themselves, will attempt to leapfrog to Stage II by emulating earlier pioneers. Otherwise, those firms which belatedly decide to attempt investment in Asia for the reasons given in Stage I will either be taken over politically by host-country firms or outmaneuvered by emerging "multinational" activities of firms based in Hong Kong, Taiwan and Singapore.

Stage I (up to around 1970)—Ad hoc Responses to Import Substitution by Developing Nations

In order to evade the import restrictions of the developing nations, many manufacturing firms of Japan have scattered a number of limited-scale—rather than a single large-scale—manufacturing operations in Asia and in Latin America. Immediate, expedient defenses of their export markets have been the prime considerations of Japanese direct investments abroad. In order to share investment risks Japanese firms often chose to split the ownership of their overseas manufacturing subsidiaries with other Japanese firms. Trading companies often oversaw and organized such direct investments.

Stage II (from around 1971 Onward—Toward Conscious Multinational Strategies

Toward the end of the 1960s, and especially early in the 1970s, an increasing number of Japanese investors abroad began to integrate separate subsidiaries producing related products within the same country. These moves were aimed at improved efficiency in subsidiary operations, and were often triggered by Japanese parent firms which had recognized the strategic value of efficient "offshore" production bases. In addition, outright "offshore" production bases were opened mostly in neighboring Asian countries by Japanese firms in textiles, electric and electronic products, and miscellaneous products such as footwear.

Since 1971, when the Japanese yen was revalued vis-a-vis the U.S. dollar, Japanese direct investments in the U.S. and in Europe have become an expanding reality. Meanwhile, many Japanese firms have grown conscious of their direct competition with leading American and European firms, not only in the U.S. and Europe, but also in Asia.

Chapter Four

Invading the United States

Invading the United States

On a fine spring day in 1974, town dignitaries and local celebrities were gathering at a barren field outside the upstate New York town of Auburn. The ground-breaking for a mini-steel plant was about to begin. The mayor and his supporters had brought the Japanese firm to Auburn. The plant would hopefully stem, at least partially, the tide of industrial depression that had long plagued the area. Along with the mayor and his supporters, Japanese delegates from the two parent firms, Ataka Trading Firm and Kyoei Steel, were equally exuberant over the fact that the first Japanese "steel mill" was about to come ashore, as it were, to the United States.[1] Indeed, the life-long dream of the Japanese entrepreneur, Takashima, who had started the Japanese parent mini-steel mill right after World War II, was about to be realized. Since the days when he had seen Imperial Japan crumble under the military and industrial might of the United States, Takashima had vowed to himself that he would someday "conquer," peacefully that is, the American industrial market.

Just when the long awaited ground-breaking was about to begin, a few dissident town residents, led by a well-known local "protester," suddenly appeared. They were waving signs, "JAPANESE - PAY YOUR SHARE OF TAXES." Taken aback with this painful reminder that not all the townspeople welcomed their steel mill, the Japanese delegates grew apprehensive about the prospect of becoming involved in the vicious political infighting that often raged in small towns like Auburn.[2]

On March 20, 1975, the *San Francisco Chronicle* carried an article with the headline, "New Japanese Export a Hit in U.S." By "new Japanese export" the newspaper was referring to a "Japanese management-employee practice" and to its underlying philosophy. The article gave a summary of the research findings of two Stanford Business School professors.[3] The two researchers had concluded that Sony's plant in San Diego had a recorded employee absenteeism rate that was 25 to 50 percent less than other electronic firms in the same area. An American manager in the Sony plant was quoted: "You get the feeling here (at Sony) that they care about people. In my experiences with American companies, they cared only about output and profits." Similar observations were made at other Japanese plants as well. Mitsubishi in Texas, Kikkoman in Wisconsin and Matsushita in Illinois.

As many observers of American management and industrial practices became aware, the increasing number of Japanese firms in the United States brought the increasing transferrability of Japanese management practices into the American environment. With Japanese firms coming ashore into various corners of the United States, the Japanese corporate culture would also be brought ashore. American managers and business educators would be confronted with reevaluation of what they had long taken for granted as the axioms of "efficient management practices," particularly in the area of management-employee relations. For better or worse, Japanese invasions of the American industrial scene have already sown many seeds for controversy in both political and business circles of the United States.[4]

Fear over the imagined prospect of "foreign domination" of the economy—a euphemism hinting at Japanese or Arab takeover—was being raised in the United States. Various regulatory measures were proposed, ranging from "disclosure requirements" for foreign subsidiaries to outright prohibition of foreign takeover of American firms.

Foreign direct investments in the United States were around 15 billion dollars at the end of 1972; only one-seventh the size of U.S. direct investments in foreign countries.[5] Three years later in 1974, even after the worldwide energy crisis had made the United States a relatively more attractive place to invest, the total value of foreign direct investments in the United States was still hovering at the 20 billion dollar level. From 1972 to 1975, however, two interesting observations were made concerning the trend of foreign investments in the United States: namely, (1) foreign manufacturing activities in the United States increased most markedly during this time period, to account for around 55 to 60 percent of the total foreign direct investments in the United States by 1975; (2) the original EEC-based countries combined overtook Canadian investments in the United States in 1972, and almost caught up with those of the United Kingdom by 1975. As late as 1975, the total Japanese investments (realized) in the United States were, at most, 1 billion dollars; and the total assets of manufacturing investments (realized) hardly exceeded 200 million dollars.[6] And yet, one newspaper after another throughout 1975 reported events like a grain elevator in the Midwest being purchased by Japanese investors. The public visibility of Hawaii and a couple of vacant condominium apartments in Miami being purchased by Japanese investors. The public visability of Japanese investments, confirmed or speculative, was undeniably rising in the United States. Were the Japanese really invading North America and Europe?

After August 15, 1971, when the Japanese yen was revalued vis-à-vis the U.S. dollar, a number of Japanese manufacturing firms were indeed attempting to open manufacturing subsidiaries in the U.S., Canada and Europe. Table 4-1 shows various types of Japanese subsidiaries confirmed to be operating at the end of 1973 in the U.S. Canada and Europe, classified by the primary activity of each.

The Japanese subsidiaries in Spain and Portugal were principally offshore production bases aimed at selling to the EEC markets. In

Table 4-1. Japanese Subsidiaries in the U.S., Canada and Europe (As of the End of 1973)

Country or Area	Primary Activity of Subsidiary				Total No. of Subsidiaries
	Manufacturing	Services[1]	Resource Seeking	Sales	
U.S.	67	73	22	522	684
Canada	6	1	29	42	78
EEC	28	19	2	276	325
Spain	4	0	2	4	10
Portugal	7	0	0	2	9
Other Europe[2]	5	2	0	49	56

1. These subsidiaries are engaged in restaurants, retailing (department stores), hotels, warehousing, and housing developments (real estate).

2. Malta, Greece, Austria, Switzerland, Liechtenstein, Finland, Sweden and Ireland.

Source: The Data Bank of the Multinational Enterprise Project, Harvard Business School: The data were updated by the author through his fieldwork in Japan during the summers of 1973 and 1974.

Canada, resource-seeking ventures outweighed manufacturing activities. Japanese manufacturing subsidiaries in the U.S. and the EEC countries revealed an interesting pattern of Japanese direct investments in the advanced nations in general. Table 4-2 breaks down the Japanese direct investments in the U.S. according to size of the investing parent firm, and the time period of effective start of operations. The entry format of the Japanese parent was classified according to one of two types: joint ownership with a Japanese trading company; or single ownership, as far as the Japanese investor was concerned. The time periods for effective commencement of operations were purposely recorded in order to highlight the marked increase in Japanese direct investments in the U.S. after the 1971 revaluation.

In Period II of Table 4-2, large Japanese manufacturing firms replaced small ones as the dominant forces on the U.S. scene. As was not the case in Asia and Latin America, Japanese trading companies were not actively involved in manufacturing subsidiaries in the U.S. Compared with large manufacturing firms of Japan, small ones were more actively investing in the U.S. without assistance from the Japanese trading companies. How can one explain this phenomenon?

Table 4-2. Japanese Manufacturing Subsidiaries in the U.S. (As of the End of 1973)

The Ownership of Japanese Investing Parents	Effective Commencement of Manufacturing Operation			
	Period I[1] 1958-1970		Period II 1971-1973	
	By Large Firms	By Small Firms	By Large Firms	By Small Firms
Single Ownership of Manufacturing Firm	1	11	29	15
Joint Ownership with a Japanese Trading Company[2]	2(1)	1	8(4)	1
Total Number of Subsidiaries	15		53	

1. The first manufacturing subsidiary was set up in 1958. The rest came after 1965. Six subsidiaries were opened in 1970; reflecting a marked increase in Japanese direct investment in the U.S. in the 1970's.

2. The figure in the parenthesis indicates the number of manufacturing subsidiaries ostensibly owned only by Japanese trading companies.

Source: The Data Bank of the Multinational Enterprise Project, Harvard Business School: The data were updated by the author through his fieldwork in Japan during the summers of 1973 and 1974.

Are there clues lying behind the data of Table 4-2 which might point to the future direction of Japanese direct investments in the U.S. or even Europe?

The sample of 68 Japanese manufacturing subsidiaries which were operating in the U.S. as of the end of 1973 consisted of three types of investments, according to the initial business objectives of the respective subsidiaries. Table 4-3 groups these 68 manufacturing subsidiaries according to what primarily motivated their investment in the U.S., and then splits the firms into consumer or industrial (intermediate) production categories.

MARKET PENETRATION (I)—THE CASE OF INDUSTRIAL PRODUCTS

Japanese direct investments in the U.S. were led by industrial product groups and small manufacturing firms. In Period II, the production of industrial products by Japanese subsidiaries increased markedly in number, and large manufacturing firms came to be the leaders in this category of investment. The successful sales of industrial products requires a great degree of constant, detailed services

Table 4-3. Japanese Manufacturing Subsidiaries in the U.S. Classified by Their Initial Investment Objective, by Their Time of Entry and by Their Product

Initial Business Objectives of Investment	Period I up to 1970		Period II 1971-1973	
	Consumer Product	Industrial Product	Consumer Product	Industrial Product
I. Market penetration	1	11[a]	11	26
II. R & D contact	0	2	1[b]	9
III. Material procurement	0	1	3[c]	3
Total No. of Subsidiaries	15		53	

[a]A network of zipper-assembly plants of Yoshida K.K. is counted as one subsidiary.

[b]Electronic calculator: this product may well be classified as an industrial product.

[c]Three food products: soy sauce, dairy products, and instant noodles.

Source: The Data Bank of the Multinational Enterprise Project, Harvard Business School: The data were updated by the author through his fieldwork in Japan during the summers of 1973 and 1974.

for customers. Purchasing decisions on industrial products are influenced not only by the price and quality, but also, and more important, by prompt guaranteed supplies of the product. Personal, trusting relationships between salesmen and purchasers are vital for successful sales; these relationships are an "insurance," so to speak, of interlocked interest between purchaser and supplier. In addition, it is essential that sellers of industrial products provide prompt engineering services to meet the product specifications of the purchasers.

Only when products are standard, catalogued items with standard specifications, are they eligible for export sales from production bases in Japan. Even this export of standard catalogue items often requires extensive product inventories and in-plant consignment sales in the U.S. in order to guarantee a steady supply of the product. Figure 4-1 schematically segments the U.S. market into two parts: a surface layer for standard products, and bottom layers for special products. In order to penetrate the bottom layers, a foreign firm is often forced to establish a manufacturing base physically closer to the market. The constant technical communication required between customers and suppliers often rules out an exporting approach to these markets.

Barriers to entry are not so formidable for industrial products as they are for consumer products. Customers of standard industrial products are less likely to be influenced by advertisements. So long as Japanese firms can guarantee regular supplies of quality products for acceptable prices in competition with American small- to medium-sized firms, they have been given the chance to penetrate the American markets. This is one of the reasons why industrial products, not consumer products, have spearheaded the Japanese investments in the United States and Europe.

Figure 4-1. Multiple Layers of American Markets

Appropriate Approach	Market	Market Characteristics
Export from Japan with warehouses in ⇒ the U.S.	Standard Catalogue Item	Demand: most price-sensitive. Competition: keen for small local firms and foreign firms. Customer: weak loyalty to any given supplier.
Locating Plant in the U.S., with the ⇒ Capability of Engineering Services	Special Products, Vital Intermediate Products	Demand: sensitive to product quality, suppliers' engineering services and guaranteed product supply. Competition: less keen from foreign firms. Customer: strong loyalty to steady suppliers.

The early predominance of small firms of Japan in direct investments can be attributed mainly to two factors. First, relative to manufacturing technologies held by small manufacturing firms of the U.S., a number of the small Japanese firms possessed competitive, if not superior, technologies which were related to production processes. When such small Japanese firms joined American competitors in regional markets in the U.S., they often commanded an advantage over their American competitors. Japanese subsidiaries had access to the Japanese markets, from which the Japanese parent firms obtained financial and technological resources. This is why, in Periods I and II, those industrial products and services which did not economically lend themselves to large-scale operations emigrated to the U.S. Photo process-plates which were used in printing processes, and rotary bearing components which were assembled into precision instruments are but two examples.

In this regard, such operations as plastic tool- and die-making, and the knock-down assembly operation of the Takara chair used in barber shops and beauty salons fell into the same category as the zipper assembly operation of Yoshida, K.K., and as the final cutting and reshaping of stainless steel sheets by the Sumitomo Trading Company. The diverse needs of various customers outside Japan could not be held in abeyance. Accordingly, the final production process of zippers, barber chairs and stainless steel sheets were moved to the United States where final assemblies of products could be made to meet customers' orders.

The emigration of Mitsubishi Heavy Industry to Texas in the late 1960s is another illustration of the way in which Japanese exporters to the United States were drawn into "direct investments." Mitsubishi arranged earlier to have its own light aircraft, the MU-2, exported to the American market for private planes. Since Japan had practically no need for private planes, Mitsubishi had to come to the United States in order to market test its first successful light aircraft model. Mitsubishi was known for its famed "zero fighter" during World War II. But after the war, the aircraft industry did not immediately recover from the destruction which resulted. By first repairing and servicing, and later assembling American-made jet fighters for the Japanese self-defense force, Mitsubishi was regaining its footing in the design and manufacturing of aircraft with short- to medium-range cruising capability.[7] The MU-2 was the product of such cumulative efforts by Mitsubishi Heavy Industry.

In its efforts to tap the American market, Mitsubishi concluded an arrangement with a Texas aircraft firm whereby the Texas importer would build fuselages for the MU-2, in order that the other vital components could be housed and shipped from Japan. Two years later, the Texas firm went bankrupt. Rather than sacrifice its previous contact with the American light aircraft market, or risk a defeated retreat from the United States, Mitsubishi Heavy Industry took over the bankrupt firm "lock, stock and barrel." Texans were at first fearful of the "Japanese invasion." But one year later, when reporters from *Business Week* visited the town, they heard nothing but praise for Mitsubishi's respect of its employees' welfare.[8]

Second, the number of employees per Japanese manufacturing subsidiary established during Period I ranged from 13 to 250 persons, but most frequently, this figure ranged somewhere between 40 and 50 employees; this supports the view that Japanese early comers to the United States were dominated by small-scale corporations, often small- to medium-sized firms. There were many entrepreneurs from small Japanese firms who preferred to export or invest abroad in order to achieve growth in sales and profits, rather than stay bound at home, where they were feeling a competitive squeeze by other small and large firms. When they encountered the import restrictions of the U.S., enterprising firms chose to penetrate the deeper layers of American markets by establishing small branch plants in the U.S.

The success story of NMB, a young and aggressive producer of miniature ball-bearings in Japan, provides a useful illustration. With a combination of entrepreneurial determination and the requisite technological competence, this medium-sized Japanese firm was able to establish a manufacturing operation in southern California.

NMB purchased a run-down plant in Chatsworth, California in 1971, from none other than SKF, a Swedish-based multinational firm and the world leader in ball-bearing products. Prior to this NMB had developed mass-production processes which enabled them to make commercial-grade miniature ball-bearings at internationally competitive costs. At the same time, NMB had been making inroads in the market for minature ball-bearings in the United States. Since this market in Japan was limited, because of Japan's lack of well-developed industries for precision instruments, aircraft, and other navigational equipment, NMB vigorously cultivated the U.S. market. With judicious use of "volume discounts" and "sales-through-consignment," by 1970 NMB captured about 40 percent of the American market for commercial-grade ball-bearings. Meanwhile, NMB's sales activities in the United States were enhanced by the invitational programs, which were implemented to attract important opinion leaders among potential American users of miniature ball-bearings to visit NMB's plant in Karuizawa, Japan. Once the confidence of customers in NMB products was won, NMB's position in the United States was firmly established.

Early in 1971, NMB was exploring ways to further penetrate the United States market for miniature ball-bearings. Like other markets for industrial goods, this one was divided into two parts: one consisting of standard products of commercial grade, and the other of specialized products of high skill content.* Price competition plagued the former market, while entry into the latter market required effective services for sales engineering, which in turn demanded closer interaction between sales engineers and the manufacturing plant.

NMB had neither the production skills necessary for higher grade production nor the experience in managing American sales engineers in the United States. As in the past, NMB could have hired foreign engineers to bring production know-how of specialized products to its plant in Karuizawa, Japan. Instead, NMB chose to close the learning gap in sales and engineering by opening the manufacturing plant in the United States. The close interaction between market and plant was essential for the effective penetration of a specialized product into the U.S. market. This consideration ruled out servicing the market from Japan.

In spring 1971 the U.S. Department of Defense made a move which forbade the use of imported ball bearings in defense-related products. This action by the United States government precipitated NMB's search for a plant site in the United States. Prior to this move, however, NMB was already evaluating potential plant sites. When NMB heard, through a close American customer, of SKF's intention of selling its miniature ball-bearing plant in Chatsworth, it barely hesitated before making a cash offer. In a matter of two hours, the deal was concluded. The earlier search for a plant site had provided NMB with sufficient information to evaluate SKF's asking price.

Once consummating the acquisition of the SKF plant, NMB chose, on its own accord, to invite all the employees of the SKF subsidiary to remain, with full credit given to anyone with accumulated seniority. This was a natural move for NMB, a firm bred in Japanese corporate culture which respects an employee's seniority and guards his well-being. At the time, NMB did not realize that this typically Japanese treatment of employees helped spread an in-plant atmosphere which was later conducive to plant improvements. This

---

*The quality of ball-bearings is classified into nine categories, ABEC 1 (American Ballbearing Engineering Classification) through ABEC 9. Generally, grades ABEC 1 through 5 are considered commercial grades of catalogued items. And products of higher grades 6 through 9 are often produced to the exact specifications provided by customers. At the time of its entry into the U.S., NMB conceded that it had experience only with commercial grade products.

practice on the part of NMB, and the prospect of expanded operations, even succeeded in attracting back a number of able workers and plant managers who had earlier left the SKF subsidiary.

With the goal of expanding plant operations, NMB initially planned to ship equipment from its plant in Japan to the one in the U.S. The Japanese seaman's strike, which paralyzed the shipment of machinery from Japan to the U.S., led the NMB team in Chatsworth to the fruitful discovery of the "synergistic effect" of mixing Japanese with American ways of production. NMB was thus saved from making costly mistakes, due to its own innocent assumption of the similarity between Japanese and American production processes.

While the strike continued, and while the shipment of production machinery and equipment from NMB's Karuizawa plant in Japan was held up, the NMB plant in California had to make do with the resources it had—leftover SKF machinery and, more important, machinists, engineers and workers who had to make do with little interference from the NMB plant in Japan. By the end of the strike, the NMB management had discovered that the engineering experience and manufacturing skills embodied in the machine/man interactions at the U.S. plant were far more relevant to the U.S. operations than those at its Japanese plant.* In essence, American production methods are designed to maximize the utilization of scarce man-hours. The breadth of skill of American machinists and technicians often permit them to operate multifunctional machines at much higher speeds and with greater precision than their Japanese counterparts.

On the other hand, the Japanese methods of smoothing the flow of manual handling and finishing of goods permits a longer production run for standard operations. American engineers of the NMB plant in California adapted the Japanese method of breaking up multifunctional operations into a chain of simple, specialized operations, and successfully designed a one-machine operation of bearing rings which drastically reduced the rejection-rate of this item from 30 percent to less than 5 percent per production batch. Later, automatic sorter-testers for finished products, which NMB had developed for mass-production methods in its Karuizawa plant, were installed in the Chatsworth plant; thus increasing in less than ten months the entire production capacity of the U.S. plant far beyond any peak reached by the old SKF plant. This achievement was remarkable in

---

*Accordingly, when production equipment finally arrived after the strike, NMB had long since realized its mistake in attempting wholesale transference of production processes from Japan to the U.S. The first production equipment to be delivered to the U.S. was shipped off to NMB's plant in Singapore in 1973.

view of the fact that at the time of NMB's takeover, the plant capacity was down to less than one-tenth of the previous peak during the SKF period.

The new learning methods also benefited the parent firm in Japan. In 1972, the Karuizawa plant adopted various U.S. production processes, and realized an immediate reduction of 80 man-years (40 men per shift per year) in the finishing processes for ball bearings. The Karuizawa plant had grown accustomed to its way of hand-finishing inner-rings of ball-bearings. It had never questioned this method until it was provoked into reassessing the process through its exposure to the American subsidiary's innovation. In 1972, the Karuizawa plant was re-evaluating all its operational methods so that the U.S. methods could be adapted more closely to Japanese methods. In the days of labor shortage and high manpower costs the Japanese plant manager at Karuizawa realized the advantage of gaining a closer tie with the U.S. manufacturing operations.

The advantages of the synergy between Japanese and American ways was not only limited to the production of miniature ball-bearings. NMB in 1972 was trying to diversify into spherical ball bearings, rod-ends, micrometers and precision instruments. The California plant provided a close contact with the engineering and marketing bases for these new products in the United States. It also enabled the firm to utilize some of the managerial talent in the U.S. in fields like cost and inventory control, financial expertise in mergers and acquisition, management information systems for better plant-market interactions, and management of sales engineers. By hiring able managers and specialists for its subsidiary in California, the NMB system as a whole was able to share directly in the surplus managerial capacities of its American plant. This management energy was devoted in 1973 to the expansion of operations in the U.S. through product diversification. New plant construction, as well as the acquisition of existing firms, was being planned and implemented.

NMB's success in riding its international cycle of product and technology upward into the United States gave new confidence to its management. In order to ride the cycle out to developing nations, NMB began its Singapore plant in the spring of 1973, to which the manufacturing operations for standard products of commercial grade would be increasingly transferred from Japan. In developing nations suffering from a much more acute shortage of manufacturing skills and experience than Japan, the manufacturing processes which NMB (Japan) had developed a decade earlier to fit the realities of its own plant in Karuizawa appeared to be far more relevant than current

U.S. methods. By pooling its Japanese and American experience, NMB hoped to work from three manufacturing bases, the United States, Japan and Singapore.

The new vistas for the NMB system as a whole have begun to open out to even corporate financing fields. By placing the shares of NMB (U.S.) over-the-counter on the American equity market, NMB had acquired yet another source of capital. NMB (Singapore) would enable the firm to tap the Asian dollar market of Singapore, as well as to pool the earnings of the NMB system as a whole at Singapore during the initial period of exemption from corporate income taxes which was granted under the Singapore Development Plan.

MARKET PENETRATION (II)—THE CASE OF CONSUMER PRODUCTS

The preceding account also applied, in principle, to firms which produced consumer products requiring extensive customer services. It was not coincidental, therefore, that the knock-down assembly operation of tables and chairs was the sole manufacturing representative of "consumer" products during Period I. In order to cope with frequent but minor design changes in standard furniture on the American market, one small furniture firm of Japan in 1965 established its assembly plant in the U.S. Purchase orders for such products needed to be filled immediately if the firm was to retain its customers. The communication and transportation networks between Japan and the U.S. required too much time for Japanese firms to compete in standard furniture markets in the U.S.

In Period II there appear different types of consumer products seeking deeper market penetration in the U.S. Knock-down assemblies are being carried out in the U.S. for expensive and sophisticated lines of 35mm single reflex cameras, color TV sets, air conditioners for passenger cars, and stereo equipment. Thus, large firms of Japan have come to dominate the investment scene. The Sony Corp. (U.S.), which became the first to open an assembly plant for color TV sets in the U.S. in 1972, expanded its operation in 1973 to the manufacture of picture tubes for its newest product, the Trinitron TV set.

After 1971, even ostensibly labor-intensive products in the apparel field such as men's and women's shirts, men's suits, baby wear and diaper covers, canvas shoes, and products in other fields such as throw-away cigarette lighters and artificial grass lawns have been manufactured by Japanese subsidiaries in the U.S. In 1973 many more Japanese firms were seriously contemplating production abroad of those products which hitherto had been exported to the U.S. from their plants in Japan.

Detailed analyses of these large Japanese firms revealed their investment motives to be related to six strategic considerations. First, when the revaluations of the Japanese yen in 1971 and 1973 vis-a-vis the U.S. dollar were taken into consideration along with the rising wage costs in Japan, production operations of even standard labor-intensive products in the U.S. became economically feasible because of sizable savings in transportation costs and import duties. Second, production operations in the U.S. were expected to soothe American hostility toward products imported from Japan. Production plants within the United States not only provided visible job opportunities for Americans, but also the importation of semi-finished parts and components—rather than finished products—from Japan to the U.S. made Japan far less vulnerable to "dumping" charges. In the case of apparel, on-site production in the U.S. was deemed the surest way to circumvent strict import quotas placed on textile products. Third, in order to keep up with supplying the growing U.S. market, Japanese manufacturers needed to expand their total production capabilities. Since additional plant sites were either not available in Japan or prohibitively more expensive than in the U.S. (20 to 50 times the costs for serviced industrial lots in the U.S.), additional production sites located in the U.S. had become not only economically attractive, but also necessary. Fourth, given the well-developed nature of labor, product and service markets in the U.S., investing firms of Japan found it easier to procure, based on their own needs, manpower, professional services and input materials from U.S. markets. Fifth, many firms already had a foot in the U.S. door through their past years of exporting from Japan. Thus, production bases in the U.S. could be immediately utilized to further penetrate the American market by placing familiar products in established distribution channels. Sixth, production bases in the U.S. were expected to aid Japanese manufacturers in monitoring the new technological and market activities of their American competitors, and in recognizing and seizing new business opportunities for product and market diversifications. Thus, it was not too outlandish to see a Japanese garment manufacturer in 1973, producing men's and women's garments right in New York City for the local market and for export to Japan. Not only did the claims of "high fashions from New York" carry considerable snob appeal to Japanese consumers, but the New York location provided the firm with readily available labor, cheaper than that available in Japan.

In sum, the preceding types of Japanese direct investment in the U.S. are likely to increase markedly in number and size during the balance of the 1970s. In this regard, the Sony Corp. (U.S.) is the harbinger for most Japanese direct investments.

Beginning with the birth of the portable transistor radio about twenty years ago, Sony has rapidly built up its electronics capabilities to the point where it is surpassing its American competitors in introducing innovative versions of consumer products such as video recorder units and color television sets to the U.S. market. Sony's growth strategy has been based on innovative R&D endeavors, with the specific aim of riding an international product cycle all the way from the United States to Japan, and then further on to other countries.

In order to establish itself in the major markets of the world, notably the United States, from the outset Sony has chosen to market its products under its own brand name and through its own distribution channels. It has also made extensive efforts to establish worldwide networks for customer service. Sony's conscious strategy of investing time, money and energy in building up its own marketing facilities abroad had enabled it to add new products to the existing marketing channels in the United States and Europe, even when the Japanese market was not ready for them. By the time Japan becomes ready, Sony will have accumulated sufficient experience in the manufacture of such products to outproduce any follower-imitators in Japan, or in any other country for that matter.

In order to realize its worldwide market strategy, Sony long ago established itself in the financial markets of the United States and Europe, thus freeing itself from the limitations of the financial markets of Japan, and also establishing the firm's image in the business and consumer circles of the U.S.

In order to set an example of a good mental attitude for "international" activities for Sony's Japanese employees, the present head of Sony, Morita, had himself chosen to experiment with living in New York City, the business center of America, and moved there for a period of time rather than continuing the direction of his U.S. operations from Japan. The message to Sony employees was loud and clear: the supreme commander of the firm paid his central attention to the U.S. operations.

Thus, Sony was the first to open a substantial scale of manufacturing operations in the United States. Increases in the sales of Sony's color TV sets in Japan and abroad, especially in the United States, had for some time been forcing the firm to operate at or beyond its production capacity. In 1971, the market for color television sets in Japan was showing signs of approaching the saturation point with over 60 percent of urban households owning at least one color television set. The United States, as opposed to Japan, had a population twice as large and a greater income per household. Yet it still showed strong potential for further growth, with only about 40 percent of urban households owning at least one color television set in 1972. When this opportunity for growth in important U.S. markets was evaluated, along with the potential for savings in transportation costs of large finished products, and the lower procurement costs in the United States for such assembly components as cabinets and semiconductors, Sony began in 1972 to assemble color television sets just outside San Diego, California.

Sony's color television sets were recognized by American consumers and traders as innovative products, commanding a $30 to $50 premium price per set more than comparable American products. Sony was thus able to mitigate the risks of higher production costs in the U.S. In addition, its "Trinitron" feature contained only one electronics gun as opposed to the usual three guns used in U.S. sets, resulting in savings in labor in the assembly of the whole set—all the more important in a high wage country like the U.S.

Once Sony was able to overcome the misgivings of American dealers and consumers concerning the workmanship of the "made-in-U.S.-Sony," it expanded its manufacturing capacity, so that in the near future over half of the Sony TV sets sold in the United States would come from its plant in California.

In 1973, Sony began to manufacture color picture tubes in its San Diego plant, so that a more integrated operation could provide them with an additional advantage. Also, as its sales in Europe expanded between 1972 and 1973, Sony began to manufacture color TV sets in the U.K., in essentially the same manner as for its U.S. venture— and for the same strategic reasons.*

EXPORT-LED INVESTMENTS

In case after case—from Sony, NMB, Yoshida (YKK), Mitsubishi Heavy Industry, to other early-comers to the United States—a common theme arose. Japanese firms' export successes eventually pulled firms into direct investments in the industrialized nations like the United States. Unlike the defensive measures they had employed in coping with import substitution attempts of developing countries, however, Japanese investors in the United States and to some extent, in Europe, aggressively entered the United States and other industrialized markets as the logical sequel to investors' export successes.

*Early in 1972, upon the basis of my own investigation of Sony's overseas investments, I predicted that Sony would commence its manufacturing operations of color TV sets and picture tubes in the U.S. and Europe. Subsequent events fulfilled this prophecy.

And these investors' entries were based on their strengths arising from specific product- and process-related technologies which they had earlier perfected in Japan.

As their sales in the host countries expanded well beyond the supply capabilities of their plants at home, Japanese investors became motivated to expand manufacturing operations in the host countries. For instance, in 1973, Yoshida (YKK) decided to build a component plant in Macon, Georgia. In its onstream stage in 1974 with an initial employment of about 350 American workers, Yoshida (YKK) was supplying its five zipper assembly plants in the United States and Canada with assembly components entirely from its Macon plant. A history of YKK's entry into the North American market, 1959-73, illustrates the step-by-step progressions which YKK used in expanding its involvement in the industrialized market: namely, export of finished products from Japan (Step 1); establishment of local sales offices in the North American area with assembly facilities (Step 2); and opening of a local component plant as the supply center for the North American site (Step 3).[9]

The progression from Step 1 to Step 2 took place when YKK's regional sales reached about the $1 million a year level. In 1972, YKK started an assembly operation in the Boston area. The characteristic mobility of YKK's assembly operation was made possible because YKK had designed its own automatic zipper assembly machine. Only one operator was required to handle four assembly machines at a time, which was adequate in reaching a one million dollar sales volume per year. Including packer, shipper and product inspector, the YKK "assembly shop" could be set up with four to five persons in a corner of the warehouse attached to the YKK sales office.

Export-led investments characterized the Japanese manufacturing firms which opened manufacturing plants in the United States and Europe. In the mid-1970s, there appeared at least one dozen other Japanese firms in industrial products which were on the verge of commencing manufacturing operations in North America and Europe.

R&D CONTRACTS—DIRECT ACCESS TO STIMULI OF AMERICAN MARKETS

In Chapter 1, we observed that Japanese firms had endeavored to absorb and to improve both product- and process-related technologies initially developed by U.S. and European firms. We also observed that by 1970, many manufacturing firms of Japan had caught up technologically with American and European leaders in their respective industrial fields. As Japanese firms came to compete in the world markets with American and European firms, the latter two began to refuse the licensing of new product- and process-related technologies to Japan. Consequently, an increasing number of Japanese firms which had previously accumulated their technological competency through licensing agreements, began to open their R&D-related manufacturing operations mainly in the U.S., but also in the U.S., West Germany and France. In view of the fact that the development of products and processes requires frequent and close interaction between development labs and markets, subsidiaries seeking R&D contracts are also engaged on a limited scale in production and sales of their products, including those products imported from Japan.

In the preceding section, we observed NMB of Japan commencing production operations in the U.S. through its acquisition of an existing plant supplied with its own experienced technicians and production workers. In this move, NMB was consciously exploiting the new opportunity to acquire managerial and technological capabilities for diversification into new products. Today, there are many Japanese firms attempting to emulate NMB.

In addition to R&D necessities, two reasons were most frequently cited by Japanese firms in 1974 as the most important conditions which triggered their entry into the U.S. markets.* First, by 1974 the annual salary rates of experienced technicians, scientists and engineers in Japan were approaching or even surpassing the annual costs of their American counterparts. Even before 1974, salary and fringe benefit costs of skilled Japanese technicians, engineers and scientists, who required about ten years of in-company training, were often greater than those of their American counterparts. Furthermore, Japan suffered from an acute shortage of R&D personnel, while the U.S. experienced dismaying surpluses of scientists and engineers in its depressed economy.

Second, in the U.S. industries which concentrated on expanding technological frontiers, there were many small or individual operations which were "spun-off" by the R&D personnel formerly associated with large leading firms. This type of enterprise often sought investment capital from firms which promised not to demand a full

---

*Sample checks of Japanese firms that carried out R&D types of investment contracts in the U.S. were made in Japan. Early in the spring of 1972, and again in summer 1973, the author published articles in Japan predicting as well as recommending direct investments of this type. See Yoshi Tsurumi, "Nihon Kigyo no Takokusekika no Jyoken," *Toyo Kenizai Quarterly* (July 1973).

control of the new venture or a complete change of the acquired firm's management. Japanese firms often seized on such opportunities in order to obtain immediate access to technologies held by such spun-off firms. Thus far, electronics parts and equipment, heat foundry processes, peripheral computer equipment and the like, have been the industries Japanese investors seeking R&D contracts in the U.S. have chosen. In 1972, Fujitsu, the leader of the Japanese computer industry bought a 20 percent equity interest of Amdahl Computer Corporation of the United States, a research oriented firm spun-off by a former IBM scientist. By guaranteeing the purchase of the new Amdahl Computer that supplemented Fujitsu's products, Fujitsu not only became overnight a full-line supplier to the world market but obtained advanced Amdahl technology. In other instances, Tateishi Denki, which lagged behind its competitors technologically in the Japanese market of desk-top calculators and electronics parts, established the OMURON Co. in the United States as its research base of American scientists.

Japanese firms specializing in industrial products have spearheaded R&D explorations in the U.S. This can be attributed to the fact that substantive technological progress occurs more frequently in production processes and intermediate products than in finished forms of consumer products. Besides, the successful marketing of industrial products often requires R&D efforts to tailor applications of both product—and process—technologies to the specific needs of the customers. And such R&D efforts can only be undertaken "on-site" in the United States.

Technological innovations in consumer, as opposed to industrial, products usually stress product appearance and simplified performance so as to appeal to even non-technical consumers—e.g., in the past Japanese exporters of consumer products to the U.S. often found it easier to improve on products which had already been introduced into the U.S. market by American innovators. This kind of follower strategy of Japanese consumer appliance firms required little R&D efforts to be undertaken "on-site" in the U.S. market.

However, now that Sony and other firms oriented to consumer products have been for some time directly exposed to market stimuli in the U.S., the Japanese direct investments involved in consumer products will conceivably seek, in the future, market penetration in the U.S., by competing with American firms in product innovation. Direct investments for the purpose of R&D contacts may also grow to seek deeper market penetration of the local markets. All told, Japanese direct investments in the U.S. for purposes of both market penetration and direct investment for R&D contact may well converge. And the apparent differences between the two may blur in future endeavors.

MATERIAL PROCUREMENT—CLOSER LINK-UP WITH COMMODITY MARKETS

The U.S. is a leading supplier of such agricultural goods as dairy products, wheat, soybeans, corn and cotton. It is also endowed with rich timber supplies and other natural resources. Such products as scrap iron, chemicals and other intermediate goods are produced from the extensive manufacturing operations in the U.S.

Many Japanese manufacturers processed these imported materials and then re-exported them to the rest of the world, including the United States. The transportation and raw material costs which Japanese firms ordinarily had to pay, however, put them at a disadvantage with manufacturers in the United States. In order to overcome these handicaps, many Japanese manufacturers endeavored to make their production processes more efficient than those of the U.S. and to conserve raw materials by reducing waste in production. When efforts like these were added to the benefits of the large-scale of production afforded by the big Japanese market and to the generally lower wage rates, Japanese manufacturing firms were able to compete, at least in the past, in the American market.

As noted earlier, wage differentials between Japan and the U.S. have narrowed substantially since the early 1970s. Many Japanese firms are now searching for additional plant sites outside Japan. The world commodity markets are registering shortages. In light of these developments, Japanese firms which possess proprietary technologies related to production processes superior to those of the U.S. have increasingly begun to locate their branch plants in the United States, where they are able to find immediate access to necessary materials.

In addition, the embargo on soybeans and timber that the United States government suddenly and unilaterally instituted in 1973 renewed the persistent fear of Japanese firms dependent on various commodities from the United States. As a defensive measure, many of these firms are now weighing the wisdom of locating their processing plants in the United States.

In the case of food processing firms, the above observations hold patently true. For instance, the Kikkoman Company of Japan has perfected an indigenous process of soy sauce making, and since 1972 has located its soy sauce brewery in the middle of the soybean belt of the United States.[10] The Tsuzuki Cotton Spinning Company, which in 1965 led the Japanese direct investments in the textile spinning field, brought to America its technique of blending various grades of raw cotton—this technique was again unique to the Japanese cotton industry—and located its spinning plant in the middle of the United States cotton industry. The Kyoei Steel Company developed in Japan a method of increasing the number of daily charges possible per electro furnace (to over 50 percent of the industrial average in the U.S.). As mentioned earlier the firm began in 1973 to build its mini-steel mill in an upstate New York town, where it could collect scrap iron and tap a ready labor force. Similar accounts can be made of ceramic tile, concrete pile, and stereo cabinet-making plants, although the process-related technologies involved in those fields were not the decisive factors in their investment decisions, compared to their dire needs for particular raw materials.

Since the oil crisis of fall 1973, Japanese firms that use petrochemical products as raw material have seriously been investigating opportunities to locate their processing plants in the United States and Canada, where they believe the current and future supply outlook is far better than in Japan. I predict that during the balance of the 1970s, an increasing number of small- and medium-sized firms of Japan, dependent on petrochemical products, will begin opening up processing plants in the oil belts of the United States and Canada. They will outmove the larger firms mainly because small- and medium-sized firms of Japan have historically had to succumb to their larger competitors every time a supply of scarce intermediate products was to be allocated under the direction of MITI. Rather than hope for oil rations at the mercy of larger firms, a number of enterprising small- and medium-sized firms may attempt to maintain a physical proximity to suppliers in the United States and Canada outside the jurisdiction of MITI. If these ventures prove to be successful, other Japanese competitors may follow suit lest they be outmaneuvered by smaller firms.

In 1975, the Mitsubishi Corporation was seeking to acquire grain elevators in the inland Midwest areas and the seaport areas as well. When the grain shortage appeared to remain, the trading firm found it difficult to assemble and purchase grain from American farmers.[11] Mitsubishi and other Japanese importers of American grains had for some time been complaining of fraudulent adulterations of American grain grades. Apparently, various shoddy practices had been condoned by U.S. grain inspectors, who had succumbed to pay-offs rampant in the industry. Grain elevators had become the place where "skillful mixers" blended such foreign particles as rice hulls and broken kernels into corn and other grains delivered by farmers. Thus, Mitsubishi found it necessary to open and operate its own grain elevators in the United States in order to have direct access to quality grains in adequate quantity. It remains to be seen whether Mitsubishi will enter into further contractual arrangements with American farmers.

Taiyo Fishery, the largest fishing company in Japan, has formed joint fishing ventures with American and Canadian fisheries and canneries along the Pacific Coast. A number of trading firms are operating canning and packing operations for salmon and herring in British Columbia and Alaska. Salted and packed herring roes are exported to Japan as coveted delicacies. By extending their territorial fishing waters to the United States and Canada, Japanese trading and fishing firms could be motivated to operate as the corporate residents of these countries. Joint ventures with local fishing fleets and packing firms might be preferred by Japanese investors who wish to reduce the political visibility of "Japanese firms" operating inside the "territorial waters."

EXCHANGE OF HOSTAGES AND ACQUISITION OF AMERICAN AND EUROPEAN FIRMS—THE "FUTUROLOGY" OF JAPANESE INVESTMENTS?

From 1973 to 1974 there appeared different maneuvers on the part of Japanese oligopolistic firms, which perceived themselves to be in direct competition in the worldwide markets with large firms of other nations. As of the mid-1970s, however, none has surfaced to attract public attention. Yet I sensed for example, from the fall of 1973 to the spring of 1974, that a leading tire manufacturer of Japan, Bridgestone Company, was actively seeking to purchase a tire plant in the United States. On a further analysis, I had to conclude that their maneuver was mainly motivated by the firm's desire to improve its bargaining position with the American licensor that might open a tire plant in Japan. Although Bridgestone's plan was shelved by its management late in the spring of 1974, for a long while Bridgestone was speculating that would-be American competitors in Japan and active American competitors elsewhere in Asia might well be restrained from overt predatory moves in Bridgestone's territory if Bridgestone posed a direct threat to them in the United States market.*

Now that leading firms of Japan in consumer electric and electronic appliances have opened plants in the United States, the future expansion of their American plant operations may well be motivated by strategic considerations in attempts to counteract American firm's pressures in Asian markets and particularly in Japan. At this juncture, however, this is mere speculation. But in view of the fact that these Japanese firms had followed on the heels of American firms in opening their offshore production bases in Taiwan and Korea, and in view of the fact that in the fields of color TV sets, portable electronic calculators and electric appliances Japanese firms are competing strongly with American firms in the United States and increasingly in Japanese markets, the stage appears to be already set for an oligopolistic struggle involving Japanese firms in their attempts to secure hostages in the key markets of the world.[12]

Since the end of the 1960s Matsushita has intensified its own efforts to sell color television sets and other electronic consumer goods under the Panasonic brand rather than private brands of American distributors. In July 1974, Matsushita acquired *in toto* the television division of its American competitor, Motorola, for a cash transaction of 10 million dollars. Ever since Sony opened its San Diego plant, Matsushita was seeking to equalize its own competitive stand. With this manufacturing base in the United States, Matsushita was also expected to take on RCA and Zenith in the color television market in the United States. Matsushita (U.S.) was counting on the technological, marketing and financial backing of its Japanese parent which had already organized its own worldwide market coverage of household electronic appliances. By latching onto the economies of scale that the worldwide system of Matsushita permitted, Matsushita (U.S.) was expected to succeed where the television division of Motorola failed. Meanwhile, Motorola acquired full control of its

---

*In the world automobile tire industry, fierce competition is being waged among five oligopolistic leaders: Michelin, Dunlop, Goodrich, Goodyear and Uniroyal. In order to counteract American tire firms' competitive pressures in Europe, Michelin opened its first plant in North America in Canada in 1971 and a second plant in the United States in 1973. Bridgestone of Japan is endeavoring to hang on to the sixth place in the world of the automobile tire market.

Japanese plant of integrated circuits and other electronics parts formerly established together with a Japanese electronics part manufacturer, Alps Electric. Since in 1974 semiconductors became the "liberalized area" in which a fully-owned foreign subsidiary would be permitted by the MITI, Motorola, Fairchild and Texas Instruments are posing serious threats to fledgling Japanese semiconductor producers, including Matsushita. Thrusts and counter-thrusts among Japanese and American electronics firms on both sides of the Pacific are now becoming intense.

Interesting though, the preceding account of Matsushita's acquisition of an American firm signalled that in North America, as in Europe as well, Japanese firms would be pursuing the acquisition opportunities of American and European firms as an expedient way of entering into a further expansion in the industrialized countries. This is mainly because such acquisitions are increasingly seen as providing Japanese firms with immediate access to distribution channels and managerial talents in North America and Europe. In particular, in these countries where the public stigma of working for "Japanese firms" still tends to pose difficult hurdles to Japanese investors, acquisitions of on-going concerns "as is" have been preferred by Japanese investors.

In the United States and to a lesser extent in Europe, firms of various types are often "traded in" on the market. Hopeful sellers who seek the highest bidders often contact Japanese firms. In 1975, at least in the United States, there was a distinct sign that Japanese purchasers' preference for keeping (or purchasing) the American managers and employees was favorably viewed by potential sellers of existing firms in the United States.

Chapter Five

Large Trading Companies: Industrial Cyclops or Maligned Phoenix?

The political and economic aftermath of the oil crisis of fall 1973 led to a strained relationship between government and business circles in Tokyo. In January 1974, The Fair Trade Commission (FTC)—the antitrust regulatory agency of Japan), charged the country's six leading general trading companies with exercising unduly strong influence over economic activities in Japan. The FTC concluded that the six leading companies—Mitsui, Mitsubishi, C. Itoh, Sumitomo, Marubeni and Nisho-Iwai, were wielding monopolistic power over the pricing and distribution of various commodities and manufactures.[1] The six companies were found to own voting equity interests in a total of 924 firms, comprising over one-half of the firms listed in stock exchange markets in Japan. The FTC recommended the enactment of a law by the Diet which would prevent large trading companies from restricting market competition.

Mass media and consumer groups in Japan had already been blaming the trading companies for the rampant inflation. The involvement of trading companies in land, commodities and stock markets was viewed as a source of evil. Consumer groups like the Japanese Housewives Federation remembered the quadrupling of the prices of soybean products—a standard protein source in the Japanese diet—early in 1973. These groups charged that the large trading companies were hoarding scarce soybean supplies, pocketing large differences between the lower prices in the forward-purchase contracts of soybeans and the inflated levels of the spot market prices.

Several questionable practices of one or two trading firms had come to light, and the public grew wary of them. On January 29,

1974 Yano, the leader of Komeito (one of the more vocal opposition parties in Japan), exposed before the Diet that Tomen (Japan's seventh largest trading company) and Marubeni had been found guilty by the National Tax Agency of using their respective subsidiaries abroad to evade over 3.5 billion yen in income taxes. About one month later, C. Itoh was investigated by the Ministry of International Trade and Industry for its alleged act of hoarding scarce products in its branches and warehouse, thus manipulating prices. C. Itoh admitted to MITI's charge. The Ministry, which for some time had been exploiting public demand for price controls to regain both *de facto* and *de jure* control over the various commerces and industries of Japan, responded by reaffirming its intention to direct and supervise Japanese manufacturing and trading firms in order to fulfill its "social responsibilities" at home and abroad.

Politicians quickly moved in and took advantage of the public's fear of the firms. In their efforts to appear to fight the evils of "big business," they turned the trading firms into easy scapegoats. The Diet summoned to public hearing the presidents of the seven largest trading firms, and the three private Japanese banks which had extensive dealings in foreign exchange. For three consecutive days, these ten business executives were harshly criticized for their failures to restrain their respective firms from evading taxes and speculating on scarce products. The trading companies' public images appeared tarnished beyond repair. A number of daily newspapers even reported incidents at primary schools where the children of trading company employees were maliciously teased by their peers for the alleged actions of their parent's employers.

The political visibility of large trading firms made attacks inevitable. As we saw in Chapter 1, the division of tasks among manufacturing, financial and trading firms has succeeded in delegating the role of "middle man" to the trading firms. And the middle men have always been singled out by voters and politicians as the culprits responsible for the souring of the national economy. Under mounting political attack, the six largest trading firms maintained a low and silent image. They knew that any attempt on their part to "explain" their positions would be construed as arrogant rejoinder. Very few Japanese knew what function was filled by the firms, let alone how or why they had grown so large.

Corporate culture among large trading firms naturally varied from one to another. The diverse economic and political backgrounds of each was woven into several different histories. What worked for C.

Itoh and Marubeni, for example, might not have been conceivable for Mitsui.

A common characteristic of trading firms, however, is the pursuit of overall economic gain. But one should not dismiss too lightly as a public relations ploy an action such as that taken by Mitsui, when she plunged herself into a large-scale agricultural venture in Indonesia, on the basis of the firm's dedication to technically and financially assisting a fledgling farmers' cooperative. She thus fulfilled a role ignored by the Japanese government. Mitsui has become accustomed to making large-scale investment decisions not only on the basis of private gain, but also on the basis of what it believes is best for Japan as a whole. This explains why Mitsui has not abandoned the Mitsugoro project (Mitsui-Kosgoro joint venture in Indonesia). Up until 1975 Mitsui had run up well over $3 million in cumulative losses for the Mitsugoro Project in Lampung, South Sumatra. In 1976, after eight years of struggle, the Project was finally halting its cash drain. However, there was no denying that the Project had benefited surrounding subsistence farmers.[2] Neither the Indonesian nor the Japanese government has provided much financial support for the pilot farm project, although both have been liberally heaping rhetorical support and praise upon the project.

When Kosgoro, a local farmers' cooperative, requested help in 1967 from a Mitsui executive to open and cultivate what had long been considered barren fields in Lampung, the executive knew that Mitsui's incumbent president, Mizukami, would accept the challenge as worthy of Mitsui's effort. Hiroshi Ohara, who was sent to Lampung as the head of the Mitsui team, later recalled:

> Just before my departure to Indonesia, .. I went to Mr. Mizukami. He told me two things to keep in mind. First, the Mitsugoro Project is the project of Japan, not the commercial project of Mitsui. What is good for Kosgoro and Indonesia should guide the project. Second, I was told to report directly to him [Mizukami] if I needed anything. . . .

Having long operated as a "flagship" of Japan, not only of Mitsui, and having an identification with the ups and downs of Japan, Mitsui executives were motivated to undertake the Mitsugoro Project in the context of what Japan could do for Indonesia.[3]

In sum, the public image of industrial cyclops coexists with that of the maligned phoenix in the minds of the Japanese public cautiously eyeing large trading firms such as Mitsui. Who, then, are the large general trading firms? What are they doing abroad?

GENERAL TRADING COMPANY OF JAPAN (SOGOSHOSHA)

There are over 5000 trading companies in Japan. Some are exclusively engaged in the physical distribution of a limited range of merchandise at home. Others specialize in either the importation or exportation of a limited variety of products. In general, a small-size trading firm attempts to find a market "niche" by narrowing down the kind of services and products it handles for either domestic or overseas markets. At the apex of these numerous trading companies lie the large general trading companies.[4] The "general trading" companies (*sogoshosha*) are characterized by a wide breadth of products and services with which they deal, and by the large size of their annual turnovers and number of employees. Their diversity is captured in the popular Japanese saying, "General trading companies handle everything from peanuts to guided missiles."

THE TEN LARGEST TRADING FIRMS

Of the thirty or so general trading companies now present in Japan, the ten largest dominate the scene. These account for approximately 80 percent of the sales volume handled by all the Japanese trading

Table 5-1. The Ten Largest General Trading Companies of Japan As of 1974

Company	Annual Turnover 1973 (A)	Number of Employees (B)	Annual Turnover Employee (A)/(B)	Annual Profit after Taxes
Class A				
(Largest)	¥18,035 Bil	20,539	¥878 Mil	¥28.0 Bil
Mitsubishi	9,408	10,064	935	14.0
Mitsui	8,627	10,475	824	14.0
Class B				
(Medium Large)	19,903	28,603	696	26.0
Marubeni	5,548	8,040	690	9
C. Itoh	5,232	7,717	698	4
Sumitomo	5,181	5,775	886	7
Nisho-Iwai	6,006	7,071	566	6
Class C				
(Least Large)	8,929	15,449	578	9.0
Tomen	2,444	4,094	697	2
Kanematsu	2,321	3,901	595	2
Ataka	2,095	3,498	599	3
Nichimen	2,069	3,956	503	2

Source: Annual Reports of respective firms, 1974.

Table 5-2. Percentage Breakdowns of Annual Turnover of Ten Largest General Trading Companies by Product and by Activity As of 1974

Trading Company	Annual Turnover by Product						International Trade to Total Turnover
	Textile	Metals	Machinery	Food	Chemicals	Others[1]	
Mitsubishi	9%	32%	14%	13%	14%	18%	46%
Mitsui	9	34	16	15	12	14	44
Marubeni	20	27	20	13	10	11	44
C. Itoh	30	15	16	12	11	16	46
Sumitomo	—	36	18	12	17	9	41
Nisho-Iwai	10	39	19	11	—	21	49
Tomen	22	23	21	14	—	6	35
Kanematsu	26	23	11	19	8	22	49
Ataka	17	36	12	—	15	20	40
Nichimen	19	25	13	20	11	12	56

1. "Others" include the importation of timber trade and of crude oil, coal and pulp products.

Source: Annual Reports of respective firms, 1974.

firms. Their combined sales turnovers in 1974 were roughly equal to 30 percent of Japan's GNP. From the data seen in Tables 5-1 and 5-2, one can make the following four observations about the large trading companies: (1) the export-import business (international trade) amounts to less than 50 percent of the total annual sales turnover; (2) the two largest trading companies, Mitsubishi and Mitsui, have reduced their dependence on textile products to less than 10 percent of the respective total sales turnovers; (3) the larger the number of the firm's employees, the greater the sales turnover per employee; and (4) the larger the number of the firm's employees, the greater the net profit earned per employee by the company. One can speculate from these observations that the emergence and subsequent growth of a general trading company is related to the economies of large-scale organization in the given firm. The large general trading companies derive their competitive strength at home and abroad from the fact that their stronghold over the distribution of products in Japan can be linked to their hold over the international trade of merchandises and services, or vice-versa. The advantage of dealing in a wide range of products obviously enhances their opportunities to barter various products for diverse client-firms with different needs. In fact, the internal workings of a large general trading company like Mitsui remind alert observers of a large "marketplace" where diverse merchandise, services and information are traded domestically as well as internationally. The trading of information among company employees even extends into off-business hours. Make a surprise visit after 6 P.M., to one of the numerous bars and restaurants which have sprung up around the trading firms. One might discover the employees swapping business deals and information well into midnight.

Today, with the use of large and small computers, employees of trading firms are able to stay in touch with the rest of the organization. Informal and formal organization has evolved around these companies' communication networks. For instance, the formal groupings of Mitsui employees by product and geographical areas facilitate intra-firm bidding on merchandise and service within the entire organization. The internal organization of Mitsui has evolved so as to allow for the retrieval or trading of vital information within the firm.

The advantage gained by relying on a trading company for export or import activities is obvious for the manufacturing firm whose overseas sales or purchases have not yet developed in any single country market to the level of warranting the opening of an overseas marketing office. For a commission of 1 to 2 percent of gross sales, any Japanese trading firm will connect a manufacturing firm, small or large, with overseas markets. The trading firm needs to gross only $100,000 to $200,000 per month if it is to cover the out-of-pocket expense of supporting one missionary sales representative in a designated country market. In order to generate a gross sales of this volume, the trading firm deals in various products involving ten to twenty manufacturing firms in Japan. As the large trading firm becomes fully grown, any addition of overseas sales offices and communications terminals adds only marginal costs once the initial networks linking Japan with such key country markets and key points of overseas procurement as the United States and Europe have been laid out.

Large general trading companies have built up, within their own organizations, the flexibility to exploit diverse business opportunities which crop up in various corners of the world. Consider the following example:

> An employee stationed in Peru by the Mitsui Trading Company of Japan learns that a Peruvian copper mine has a surplus stock of copper ore. He immediately feeds that information into the worldwide telex networks of his firm and asks for an international bidding offer to process the Peruvian ore somewhere else in the world. Another person, in the Japanese head office, happens to know that a Japanese copper smelting firm is willing to produce blister copper for a fee because it has surplus processing capacity. Another man stationed in Bombay, knows that one Indian firm is willing to buy blister copper if the price is right. Through the internal telex networks, the three men get in touch with one another and consummate the deal. None of them haggles over the internal transfer prices of the product involved from ore to blister copper. They intuitively arrange the entire transaction in such a way as to maximize both the visible and invisible contributions to their firm as a whole.

The preceding account approximates what actually happened in the summer of 1972 within one of the largest general trading companies. It illustrates the kind of transactions involving diverse goods and services that large general trading companies are emphasizing today in order to exploit their ability to seek and organize multi-party business deals. In theory, an alert copper smelting firm of Japan, or of anywhere in the world, should be able to duplicate the kind of three-point transaction consummated above by the Mitsui Trading Company. From any single manufacturer's viewpoint, however, it may not be wise or profitable to invest in building up look-out posts for uncertain business deals all over the world. Accordingly, the manufacturer may decide to rely on trading companies for uncertain and random business deals that may crop up from time to time.

In addition to physical movements of industrial raw materials and manufactured goods between Japan and overseas markets, trading companies have thrived in the role of searching and bringing back product and process technologies for Japanese firms. The strength of Japanese trading firms in transferring technologies from abroad has been reflected in the number of foreign manufacturing technologies that trading companies have directly obtained through licensing agreements. Indeed, over one-half of the technologies licensed to Japan have been channeled through large trading firms.

The foreign product and process technologies coveted by Japanese manufacturers have aided the trading firms in cultivating business relationships with manufacturing firms. Nowhere has this pattern been more apparent than between trading firms and various machinery industries, from electric equipment to machine tools, or from transportation to earth-moving equipment. In fact, from 1949 to 1970, the annual growth of sales turnover in the machinery divisions of the ten largest general trading firms was strongly and positively related to the number of technical licenses that had been obtained directly from foreign manufacturers of various machinery. The greater the number of new foreign technologies that a given trading company purchased on its own accord from foreign manufacturers and eventually passed on to its Japanese client manufacturers, the greater was the volume of the trading company's business transactions in machinery products.

LARGE GENERAL TRADING COMPANIES— INEVITABLE DEVELOPMENT?

Why and how has even a "specialized" trading company, dealing in a single line of products, metamorphosed into a large general trading company? The appearance of many of these general firms in Japan, which deal in diverse goods and services at home and abroad, is distinctly a post-World War II phenomenon. What were the economic and political situations in Japan after the war that forced trading companies to grow in size and diversity in order to insure their survival? Why, after having been broken up into over one hundred separate firms, did Mitsui & Co. and Mitsubishi Co. coalesce and rise again from the ashes?

Type I—Vertical Integration of Trading and Banking Houses into Manufacturing Activities. The model of Mitsui & Co. represents one pattern of trading company development in which a merchant banking and trading house, dating back to the feudal days of Japan, had the foresight during the 1860s to rally around the emerging oligarchy of the Meiji leaders.[5] While other merchant traders of the feudal days remained closely tied to the Tokugawa Shogunate up until the last years of the feudal regime, the House of Mitsui concluded from its own intelligence sources that the new regime headed by the Emperor and anti-Tokugawa activists from Satsuma and Chosu Domains would triumph over Tokugawa. Thus, when the expeditionary forces of this new anti-Tokugawa group exhausted their finances on the way to a final attack on Tokugawa's Edo (Tokyo) in 1867, it was the House of Mitsui that extended financial aid to them. When Japan began to industralize under the Meiji oligarchy after 1868, Mitsui continued to add, on a piecemeal basis, various manufacturing firms to the industrial group gradually forming around the original Mitsui Bank and Mitsui & Co., the trading arm of the Mitsui organization.

Mitsui & Co. often took the initiative in creating various manufacturing subsidiaries. These manufacturing firms were often created as product divisions of Mitsui & Co. such as the fertilizer-producing division, and they were later reorganized as manufacturing subsidiary firms belonging to the House of Mitsui. Mitsui & Co. provided the marketing and often the financing services for all these manufacturing subsidiaries. Exports and imports involving any members of the Mitsui group were handled by Mitsui & Co. Machinery, raw materials and consumer goods were imported. And the leading export products, like cotton and silk yarns, coal and blister copper, were developed by Mitsui & Co. The fact that the House of Mitsui had been given a vast interest in the leading coal mines in Japan by the Meiji Regime placed it in the center of both domestic and international trading activities involving heavy and chemical industries.

The model of Mitsubishi Trading Co. represents another pattern of growth involving vertical integration. Mitsubishi (the three diamond trademark of Iwasaki's business) was founded in the mid-Nineteenth Century by Yataro Iwasaki whose humble origins were somewhat obscured by his later success. Iwasaki first demonstrated his shrewdness by procuring weapons, ammunition and other necessary goods for the Tosa Domain, one of the four local domains whose combined challenge to the Tokugawa Shogunate finally replaced it with the Meiji Regime in 1868. Iwasaki inherited a fleet of steam-powered vessels from the Tosa Domain, and later one from the Meiji Regime as well. He continued to accumulate wealth by transporting goods and soldiers for the internal and external expeditions of the Meiji Government. Like the House of Mitsui, Mitsubishi expanded its presence into the heavy and chemical industries of the new Japan. Shipbuilding and related manufacturing activities (machinery and metal fabricating works) came to form the key activities of Mitsubishi. The Mitsubishi Trading Company evolved as the marketing arm of the Mitsubishi industrial group (*Zaibatsu*); and Mitsubishi Bank evolved as the financial service center of the organization.

The cases of Mitsui and Mitsubishi reveal that from the outset, these trading companies grew as general trading firms dealing in diverse goods and services both at home and away. The general trading company evolved as the marketing arm of the respective industrial group. Unlike its rival Mitsubishi, Mitsui & Co. had long acted as creator of diverse manufacturing subsidiaries of Japan. After Suzuki Shoten—Mitsui's only competitor of comparable size and the creator of manufacturing subsidiaries such as Kobe Steel Company—went bankrupt during the 1920s, Mitsui had grown to be the uncontested leader of the larger general trading firms of the prewar days, handling about 15 percent of Japan's exports and about 21 percent of her imports by 1940. The annual sales turnovers of Mitsui & Co., that did involve Japan and that were carried out between foreign countries (including Japan's colonies), constituted at that time about 50 percent of Mitsui's total sales turnover per year.

Of late, only the Toyota Tsusho Trading Company has shown some sign of success in duplicating the type of growth pattern of Mitsubishi. Begun as the marketing arm of the Toyota group, and engaged in manufacturing activities of automobile and textile machinery and related metal fabricating industries, it has been trying to grow. Its future, however, appears to be rather uncertain unless various manufacturing firms associated with the Toyota group continue to farm out their domestic and international trading activities to Toyota Tsusho.

Type II—Successful Diversification Moves of One-time "Specialized" Trading Companies with a Single Product Line. Eight firms other than Mitsui and Mitsubishi have evolved from trading companies whose main line of business was limited to a single line of products. Sumitomo, the oldest of these, is representative of one end of the spectrum as far as the historical origin of the "specialized" trading company is concerned.

Sumitomo is the only remaining house of yesteryear except for Mitsui. Unlike Mitsui, however, the Sumitomo House accumulated its wealth by operating copper and other non-ferrous mining and smelting operations. Despite its close relationship with the old regime of Tokugawa, Sumitomo was shielded from the direct upheaval of the political changes of the 1850s and 1860s because its mines were geographically located far away from Edo, Tokogawa's capital. In addition to Sumitomo's political resiliency in surviving the uncertain years of the New Meiji Regime, the fact that the technologies and experience of mining, smelting, and distributing non-ferrous products had for centuries been accumulated within the collective institution of the Sumitomo House made any attempt at either imitating or taking over Sumitomo's activities impossible. Its presence, however, in domestic and international trade of goods and services other than non-ferrous products remained small in comparison with Mitsui and Mitsubishi.

On the other end of the spectrum, seven newer firms appeared which until rather recently had grown as domestic and international traders of single product lines such as steel and iron products, cotton textiles, woolen textiles, food grains, and particular kinds of machinery. The birth of the single-line firm is closely related to the way in which Japan added new industries (products)—from cotton textiles (Tomen, Marubeni, Nichimen, C. Itoh), woolen yarns (Kanematsu), Metal-working machinery (Nisho-Iwai) to steel and iron products (Ataka)—to its existing industrial structure.

From the late 1950s to the early 1960s, many single-line trading firms either became absorbed into the orbits of the large general trading firms such as Mitsui, Mitsubishi and Marubeni, or chose to diversify the ranges of goods and services they handled both domestically and internationally. The latter pattern is represented today by such firms as C. Itoh, Nisho-Iwai, Kanematsu, Tomen, Nichimen and Ataka, which are ranked within the ten largest general trading companies.

The preceding accounts still leave one pondering two central questions concerning the growth of general trading companies. First, why were trading companies able to find a vital niche in the Japanese economy? Secondly, why has the survival of the large trading company depended upon diversification?

Up until August 1947, when the General Headquarters (GHQ) of the Allied Occupying Forces permitted private Japanese firms to participate directly in international trade, the imports and exports of Japan had been handled by GHQ itself. GHQ imported products and channeled them to the International Trade Agency of the Japanese government, which in turn rationed the imported goods among many trading companies. In order to obtain imported products for the purpose of resale in Japan, many trading firms competed to handle products outside their traditional lines of business. They only needed the clerical ability required to process the documents of importation and the subsequent warehousing of merchandise preselected for them by the government of Japan and GHQ.

From the beginning of 1947, the trading companies that were initiated into handling products outside their prewar line of business formed departments within their respective companies designated to handle machinery, grain, fertilizer and industrial raw materials. These companies were anticipating the reopening of "private international trade" in which they would be allowed to directly handle not only imports of diverse products, but more important, exports of machinery and chemical products as war reparation payments of defeated Japan to her Asian neighbors.

From 1948 onward, however, even when private trading firms were permitted to engage in international trade, and even when the Japanese government chose to deal with trading firms rather than with manufacturing firms for international trade, the acute dollar shortage that was experienced by Japan and the importers of her products forced trading companies to execute barter trades. In exchange for crude sugar, products such as ammonium sulphate fertilizer, iron slabs and whale oil were exported. Importation of crude oil was bartered for galvanized iron sheets, nails and rubber products. Raw cotton was exchanged for barbed wire. Accordingly, in order to survive, trading firms had to develop adequate internal abilities to effect barter trades. This pressure also motivated a number of atomistically scattered trading firms to merge.

With the success of barter trade, the Japanese government began in 1953 to formally implement the use of "Linking Trade." Imports of lucrative products and raw materials were specifically linked with exports of heavy and chemical manufactures specifically designated as vital to the growth of the Japanese economy. The importing licenses of such lucrative consumer goods as bananas, whiskey and crude sugar were given to the trading firms that had already captured the export targets of ships, rolling stock and machine tools. The amount of imported raw materials allotted to the manufacture of products (e.g., cotton clothing, staple fiber, steel and iron) was based on the extent of export of these products already attained by each trading firm. This practice of "Linking Trade" lasted well into the late 1950s. It inevitably precipitated the diversification of goods and services handled by any single trading firm.

In addition to the traditional behavior of staying one step removed from international trade activities, the practice of "Linking Trade" further prevented Japanese manufacturing firms from getting involved in international trade. Most of them were "single product" firms and lacked both the will and the ability to embark on barter trade in the uncertain world of international trade. The dependence of manufacturing firms on trading firms became thus complete during the immediate postwar era.

In retrospect, however, it was not the bartering requirement of "Linking Trade," but the recurring booms and bursts of the postwar business cycles that forced general trading business into the hands of the ten largest general trading firms. From 1949 to 1963, the Japanese economy experienced six severe business downturns. In particular, the "Pot Bottom Recession"—a humorous Japanese phrase referring to the extended trough of the business cycle—in 1951 triggered severe price crashes in three commodities—rubber, hide and animal fat. The business downturn lasted for four years and drove many trading firms to financial insolvency.

It was during this recession that remaining small- to medium-sized trading firms—born out of the dissolutions of Mitsui and Mitsubishi —were forced to merge with one another into a semblance of re-creating the old Mitsui or Mitsubishi. The Mitsui and Mitsubishi Banks each played a key role in regrouping their respective clients of small- and medium-sized firms. Likewise, other city banks that by then had extended large amounts of loans to their respective clients, began to execute mergers among bankrupt or near-insolvent trading firms.[6] When newly regrouped trading firms emerged around 1955 out of the "Pot Bottom Recession," they had become large general trading firms, and had also come to be associated more closely than ever with the few select banking groups.

Later, in 1957, again in 1959 and then in 1961, the Japanese economy experienced recurring balance-of-trade deficits. In order to cope with these short-term adjustment problems, the Japanese government repeatedly evoked a tight money policy. Trading companies had long overextended themselves in financing the sales and inventories of such key goods as iron and steel products, nonferrous metal products and textile yarns, and they were hardest hit by this tight money policy. Throughout this period, trading companies were earning at best from 2 to 3 percent as an average gross margin on sales. Their sales and administrative expenses were running at around 1.3 percent of gross sales. The average collection time for their accounts receivable was well over 110 days. Most firms had borrowed from banks more than ten times the amount of their paid-in capital. Accordingly, any tight money situation, where a staggering amount of accounts receivable remained uncollectable, easily squeezed them out of financial solvency. The less diversified trading firms that had earlier survived the "Pot Bottom Recession" and had refused to become absorbed into the emerging groups of large general trading firms, finally succumbed to forced tie-ups with the larger companies. It was not by accident in 1959 that Mitsui Bussan and Daiichi, the last two remaining and contending firms of the old Mitsui, agreed to a merger, thus recreating Mitsui & Co. By the mid-1960s, the trading business of Japan became concentrated in the hands of the ten largest general trading firms.

TRADING FIRMS AND THEIR DIRECT INVESTMENTS ABROAD

As seen in Chapter 3, approximately one-half of the Japanese manufacturing subsidiaries abroad that had been established by about 1972 included at least one Japanese trading firm as one of its initial participants. Both large-sized and small- to medium-sized Japanese manufacturing firms demonstrated a strong propensity toward including trading firms in their respective manufacturing subsidiaries abroad.

Table 5-4 illustrates the geographical and functional profiles of the overseas subsidiaries in which trading firms of Japan had participated during the years 1950-71. In such industrialized areas as North America and Europe, the sales subsidiaries dominated the overseas

Table 5-4. Overseas Subsidiaries of Japanese Trading Firms Established During 1950-1961 Classified by Their Function and by Their Operating Area

Operating Area	*Function of Subsidiaries*				*Total*	
	Sales	Manufacturing	Natural Resource Development	Others[1]	No. of subsidiaries	As % of Total
Asia	96	392	31	16	535	46.4%
Latin America	52	69	20	5	146	12.6%
Middle East and Africa	19	37	5	1	62	5.3%
Oceania	32	19	24	3	78	6.8%
Canada and the U.S.	195	17	20	2	234	20.3%
Europe	85	12	—	2	99	8.6%
Total No. of Sub.	479	546	100[2]	29	1,154	100.0%
As % of Total	41.5%	47.3%	8.5%	2.7%	100.0%	

1. Service industries, agricultural and fishing projects.
2. Seven subsidiaries engaged in development of natural resources had more than two trading firms as participants. These projects were assigned to the "lead firm."

Source: Tables 5-4, 5-5, and 5-6 were compiled by the author on the basis of the Japanese government documents reported in *Kigyobetsu Kaigai Toshi, 1972*, Keizal Chosakai, Tokyo and, upon validation of the information through fieldwork in Japan.

investments of Japanese firms. In such developing areas as Asia, Latin America, the Middle East and Africa, however, the participation of Japanese trading firms in manufacturing subsidiaries had come to outnumber their sales subsidiaries. In Oceania (Australia and New Zealand), the number of manufacturing subsidiaries where the parent firm included at least one trading firm, lagged behind those subsidiaries engaged in sales activities and developments of natural resources.

In order to illuminate the economic and political forces abroad which might have produced the overseas investment profiles of Japanese trading firms, all 1,154 overseas subsidiaries in existence by the end of 1971 were classified by their year of entry, by the function of their operation, and by the size of the parent trading firm. These results are summarized in Table 5-5. Trading firms are grouped into three categories: (1) the "largest ten" (general trading firms); (2) "others" (trading firms other than the ten largest); and (3) "captive firms" (fully-owned by large manufacturing firms). From this table, one can deduce the following observations concerning the investment behavior of Japanese trading firms.

Throughout the years 1950-1971, about three-quarters of the subsidiaries established abroad by Japanese trading firms belonged to the ten largest trading firms, whose operations were more diversified than other medium- to small-sized special trading firms. For example, even in the category of sales subsidiaries, the ten largest trading firms until the early 1960s led other trading firms in opening the networks of their sales subsidiaries abroad.

Only in the mid-1960s did medium- to small-sized trading firms, most of which were specializing in a limited number of product groups, begin to open their own sales subsidiaries in export markets, while the ten largest trading firms had long since established their own marketing bases. The fact that the sales subsidiaries established by the ten largest trading firms outnumbered those established by other trading firms during the period 1968-1971 simply reflected the renewed trend that the ten largest trading firms began to expand their geographical (market) coverage not only by increasing their number of sales subsidiaries in North America and Europe, but also by opening new sales subsidiaries in developing nations previously serviced by their sales branches. Given the historical record the medium- to small-sized trading firms followed the precedents set by the ten largest trading firms, one may reasonably expect that during the 1970s more specialized trading firms will expand their market coverage by opening their own sales subsidiaries in areas previously covered by their "traveling salesmen."

Table 5-5. Overseas Subsidiaries of Japanese Trading Firms Established During 1950-1971 Classified by Their Year of Entry, by their Functions and by the Characteristics of Their Parent Firms

Year of Entry and Parent's Characteristics	Function of Subsidiaries			Total Number of Subsidiaries
	Sales	Manufacturing	Development of Natural Resources and Other Projects	
1950-55 Total	*54*	*4*	*1*	*59*
By Largest ten	44	2	—	46
By Others	8	1	1	10
By Captive Firms	2	1	—	3
Average per year[1]	*(9)*	*(1)*	—	*(10)*
1956-61 Total	*124*	*61*	*17*	*202*
By Largest ten	73	43	12	128
By Others	43	17	3	63
By Captive Firms	8	1	2	11
Average per year[1]	*(21)*	*(10)*	*(3)*	*(34)*
1962-67 Total	*164*	*215*	*32*	*411*
By Largest ten	59	149	22	230
By Others	86	58	11	155
By Captive Firms	20	8	—	28
Average per year[1]	*(27)*	*(36)*	*(5)*	*(69)*
1968-71 Total	*137*	*266*	*79*	*482*
By Largest ten	65	196	66	327
By Others	49	59	12	120
By Captive Firms	23	11	1	35
Average per year[1]	*(35)*	*(67)*	*(20)*	*(121)*
Total No. of Sub.	479	546	129	1,154

1. Rounded to the nearest figure.

In terms of a general sequence of overseas investment, one can see from Table 5-5 that trading firms followed the familiar pattern of beginning with sales subsidiaries and then of entering into manufacturing activities. Only during the period 1962 to 1967 did manufacturing subsidiaries of Japanese trading firms abroad come to outnumber those of sales subsidiaries; this was not altogether unanticipated. As shown in Chapter 3, the manufacturing subsidiaries of Japanese manufacturing firms abroad were established, on the whole, as expedient responses to attempts by host countries to substitute imports for domestic production operations. Japanese trading firms, large and small, which had been functioning as the international marketing arms of Japanese manufacturing firms were merely responding to the threat of losing their export markets by joining manufacturing firms in establishing production bases. The spreading patterns of manufacturing subsidiaries in which Japanese trading firms had come to be involved approximated the patterns of manufacturing operations abroad by Japanese firms as a whole.

In Table 5-6, manufacturing subsidiaries of trading firms that were established in the period 1950-1971 are classified by their operating area as well as by the characteristics of their parent firms. One can see that manufacturing subsidiaries of trading firms other than the ten largest were relatively more concentrated in Asia. This does not mean, however, that manufacturing subsidiaries of more specialized trading firms will not increase in number in Latin America and other areas. Chances are that as their sales subsidiaries are established, manufacturing operations will be increasingly added to the sales subsidiaries.

Historically, it was the large trading firms that had procured industrial raw materials abroad for manufacturing firms in Japan. As shown in Chapter 2, the large trading firms, which toward the end of the 1960s became increasingly concerned over the problems of maintaining access to adequate supplies of necessary raw materials, began to purchase their way into mines already owned and operated by foreign firms or began to conclude mining and other concessions abroad on their own. In the main, however, development projects in the area of natural resources remained the exclusive domain of the ten largest trading firms. Table 5-5 shows that the subsidiaries of medium- to small-sized trading firms involved in natural resources or related projects were, in fact, involved solely in the service industries and small-scale operations in agricultural and fishing projects. Again, this was not altogether unanticipated because the development of natural resources required a greater amount of capital outlay, usually an outlay beyond the means of the smaller-sized firms.

MANUFACTURING FIRMS VS. TRADING FIRMS

The division of labor between manufacturing and trading firms worked well as long as Japanese exports were dominated by standard consumer and industrial manufactures. The overseas sales of standard and less technology-intensive products rarely required special after-sale customer service or pre-sale engineering services.

However, beginning in the mid-1960s, Japanese exports came to

Table 5-6. Manufacturing Subsidiaries of Japanese Trading Firms Established During 1950-1971 Classified by Their Year of Entry, by Their Operating Area and by Characteristics of Their Parent Firms

Operating Area	1950-1955			1956-1961			1962-1967			1968-1971			Total
	By Largest Ten	By Others	By Captive Firms[1]	By Largest Ten	By Others	By Captive Firms[1]	By Largest Ten	By Others	By Captive Firms[1]	By Largest Ten	By Others	By Captive Firms[1]	
Total	2	1	1	43	17	1	149	58	8	196	59	11	546
Asia	1	1	1	27	14	1	97	44	7	141	49	9	392
Latin America	1			12	3		26	7	1	16	2	1	69
Middle East and Africa				3			16	4		12	2		37
Oceania													
Canada and the U.S.				1			5			8	3		17
Europe							3	1		6	2		12
Total		4			61			215			266		

1. "Captive firms" are mainly the fully-owned sales subsidiaries of large-sized electronics and electric appliance firms of Japan. In substance, these "captive firms" are the equivalent of international divisions of the respective parent firms.

be increasingly dominated by such specialized consumer products as color television sets, desk top calculators, automobiles and diverse appliances.[7] Even in such fields of industrial production as chemicals, ball-bearings and machine tools, pre-sales engineering as well as after-sales customer service became increasingly vital if the Japanese manufacturers were to acquire lasting exporting volume. This customer service required a manufacturing expertise which trading firms were ill-prepared to provide.

Under these circumstances, many large manufacturing firms which had traditionally depended on trading firms to cultivate initial sales contacts abroad, began to station their own sales personnel and service engineers in the key export markets. Once the volume of their business in these markets had grown large enough to support their own sales subsidiaries, these firms began to take primary marketing responsibilities away from trading firms. Trading firms were often left with such residual tasks as the transportation of goods, warehousing, financing merchandise, and international transmission of business communications through their worldwide telex networks.

In the marketing of consumer products such as electronic appliances and automobiles, the roles played by Japanese trading firms became far more perfunctory than those they played for the manufacturers of industrial products. For one thing, as had been the case with pharmaceutical and cosmetic products, Japanese manufacturers of electric and electronic appliances and automobiles had chosen to market their products under their own brand names in Japan. These firms grew to appreciate the importance of defending their brand images and of monitoring their own distribution channels. They often chose to sell their "private branded" products directly to large volume retail chains and manufacturers in the United States which were looking for low-cost supplies abroad. A number of them even chose to invest time, money and energy in building up their own distribution networks in such key export markets as the United States, and later Europe. Only the marginal markets whose business volumes did not warrant, at least for the time being, the full-time attention of the manufacturers' marketing activities were conceded to trading firms.

Therefore, it was not by accident that Toyota Automobile Co. let Canadian Motors Inc. (CMI), a fully-owned sales subsidiary of Mitsui & Co., sell Toyota models in Canada while keeping the American market to itself from the outset. From the viewpoint of Mitsui & Co., it had been necessary to acquire CMI from a Canadian entrepreneur-promoter so that Mitsui's sales network in Canada could become attractive enough to be coveted by Toyota. However, as the sales of Toyota models increased in Canada, and as the demand for a guaranteed supply of cars and frequent feedback of Canadian market information to Toyota plants in Japan increased, CMI found it expedient and at the same time necessary to accept Toyota as a part-owner of CMI. Thus, in late 1971, Toyota bought a minority position in CMI.[8]

The case of Mitsui & Co. vs. Toyota is not atypical. As Japanese exports came to include more and more high-technology products, trading firms were confronted with the choice of either setting up customer service networks with or for Japanese manufacturers, or of being reduced to handling only low-technology products and bulky commodities. Under these circumstances, trading firms attempted to combine their financial and marketing strengths with the technical expertise of manufacturing firms by involving themselves in sales subsidiaries in the industrialized countries, dealing in the newer consumer and industrial products that Japanese manufacturing industries began exporting in increasing quantity after the mid-1960s.

In Asia and Latin America, where host governments made outright attempts to stop or reduce the importance of light manufactures from Japan, trading companies actively began opening manufacturing subsidiaries either through the outright purchase of necessary technical expertise from Japanese manufacturing firms, or through the formation of joint ventures abroad with Japanese manufacturers. Often it was the trading firm that took the initiative in drawing Japanese manufacturing firms into overseas manufacturing operations.

The first initiatives by Japanese trading firms, notwithstanding the relationships between Japanese trading firms and manufacturing firms which had jointly established manufacturing subsidiaries abroad, have frequently been known to change from an initial phase of mutual accommodation (complementary) to subsequent conflict (rivalry). For instance, of the approximately 1500 manufacturing subsidiaries abroad which were established by Japanese manufacturing firms by the end of 1971, the number of overseas manufacturing subsidiaries in which at least one trading firm invested directly displayed the following trend.

Prior to 1959 when overseas direct investments by Japanese firms were few and far between, over three-quarters of them were established by Japanese manufacturing firms alone. During the first half of the 1960s, Japanese trading firms came to be involved in more than half of the manufacturing subsidiaries established abroad. During the years 1966 to 1967, however, the involvement of Japanese trading firms in newly established overseas manufacturing subsidiaries was abruptly reduced to about one-third, and during the balance of the 1960s, this ratio of involvement never exceeded the one-third level. From 1971 to 1972, this ratio further declined to one-fourth.[9]

The scenario that underlies the preceding phenomenon is what one might expect. During the 1950s, trading firms were preoccupied with exporting activities. From the end of the 1950s to the early 1960s, they actively persuaded Japanese manufacturing firms to open operations abroad in order to defend their familiar export markets. The in-depth analyses of the initial stimuli that influenced Japanese manufacturing firms during this period of time concerning their overseas ventures, revealed that Japanese trading firms enticed and even cajoled reluctant manufacturers into overseas ventures. This was also true for instances where Japanese manufacturers eventually became the sole Japanese owner(s) of their overseas subsidiaries. Trading firms assisted these firms in negotiating with host governments and local partners.

While trading companies kept up their involvement in Japanese manufacturing operations abroad during the second half of the 1960s, those manufacturers who were already involved in overseas operations began to take the initiative for themselves in setting up ventures overseas. By this time, a number of manufacturing firms had come to possess expertise and experience in dealing with host governments. Besides, as manufacturers became aware of the strategic value of linking their subsidiaries more closely to their home plants in Japan, they found it cumbersome to have trading firms as their communication intermediary. Furthermore, even those firms which were establishing their first overseas manufacturing subsidiary, avoided joint ventures with trading firms, as they saw their competitors doing without trading firms in their second and third overseas subsidiaries.

THE RESPONSES OF JAPANESE TRADING COMPANIES

Meanwhile, large trading companies in particular attempted to maintain their presence in direct Japanese investments abroad. They expanded their overseas investment projects in the fields of agri-products and natural resources, which they had long procured for Japan. During the first half of the 1970s, they increased their direct involvement in agricultural, cattle-grazing, and fishing activities abroad. They also increased the number of long-term purchase contracts with overseas agricultural plantation and fishing operations whose ownership remained with foreign entrepreneurs. In order to facilitate volume purchases of foods abroad, trading firms opened warehouses, grain elevators and cold storage points in the key purchasing bases.

In the field of manufacturing the defensive responses of trading companies have been two-fold. On the one hand, they have been trying to get involved in as many diverse subsidiaries of Japanese manufacturing firms abroad as possible. Under these circumstances, trading companies have often settled for about 10 percent of equity ownership of a subsidiary. In order to gain a toe-hold in the overseas manufacturing subsidiary, the trading firm acts as organizer and coordinator of the overseas manufacturing activities. By offering worldwide procuring and marketing networks, as well as long-term financing, trading firms hope to make foreign and Japanese manufacturing firms dependent upon their organizational trading skills. The Mitsubishi Corporation was eager, toward the end of the 1960s, to present itself to the Korean public as a firm committed to the economic development of Korea, not merely as a trading and financing firm benefiting from the economic and political recovery of Korea. Thus, when a Korean brewery requested that Mitsubishi organize a three-way joint venture of glass bottle-making in Korea by a Japanese bottle manufacturer as well, Mitsubishi impatiently swallowed the suggestion. Even when the Korean government objected to the Japanese equity ownership of the joint venture, Mitsubishi demonstrated remarkable flexibility and resiliency. Instead of employing outright equity ownership in the venture, Mitsubishi offered convertible debentures which were to be converted into common voting shares as soon as the Korean government loan to the joint venture was cleared. Meanwhile, the Japanese bottle manufacturer was content to receive a royalty for the bottle-making technologies licensed to the Korean firm, in exchange for initial subscription to the convertible debentures of the licensee firm in Korea. In 1975 the Mitsubishi Corporation was growing ambivalent about its shaky involvement in this bottle-making venture. Was it possible that from the outset, the Korean brewery and the Korean government exploited Mitsubishi's eagerness to please Korea? Would the convertible debentures ever be converted into common voting shares?

On the other hand, trading companies have annually increased the number of their own manufacturing subsidiaries abroad. To accomplish this, they are simply acquiring requisite product- and process-related technologies from Japanese manufacturing and engineering firms. The technologies are transferred directly abroad so that the investing trading firm can commence—often with local partners—manufacturing operations oriented to the local economy. A case in point is the C. Itoh Trading Co. In 1972 the firm took a plastic bag-making technology, which they had bought from an engineering firm in Tokyo, to Brazil where they opened a bag-making plant jointly with the largest instant coffee company in Brazil. This joint venture was created to replace jute bags with plastic bags in the packaging of Brazilian agricultural products. C. Itoh scanned Japanese manufacturing sectors for the requisite technologies and found an engineering firm willing to sell the necessary technologies.

When requisite technologies and ready access to markets could be acquired locally through the acquisition of an on-going local firm, trading companies often purchased local firms. In particular, in North America, where acquisitions of on-going firms are rather readily made, large Japanese trading firms have become especially active since the early 1970s in seeking candidates for acquisition. The Mitsubishi Corporation (U.S.) presently leads its other Japanese competitors, Mitsui and Marubeni, in the total number of American manufacturing firms purchased, even though Mitsui's purchase of a 50 percent interest in AMAX's aluminum subsidiary puts it ahead of the other Japanese firms in terms of total assets in the United States controlled by Japanese firms.

Upon realizing that many small- to medium-sized manufacturing firms of Japan often suffer from limitations of financial and managerial resources required for successful operations abroad, and that they are far less willing than large firms to risk jeopardizing their reliance on trading firms for both domestic and international marketing activities, trading firms have become increasingly inclined to tie up with these small- to medium-sized firms in promoting their manufacturing activities abroad. A case in point is the mini-steel firm that commenced operation in the spring of 1975 in an upper New York State town (already referred to in Chapter 4). This firm, Ataka Trading Co., which had been dealing in steel and iron products and raw materials inside and outside Japan, brought its financial and scrap iron-procuring skills to bear upon the first "steel" mill operated in the United States by a Japanese firm. The requisite manufacturing technologies for this project are being provided by a medium-sized electro-furnace operator in Japan, which became a minority partner in the joint venture with Ataka.

The preceding counter-efforts of trading companies of Japan are summarized in Table 5-7. Of the total of 546 manufacturing subsidiaries which were established abroad during the years 1950 to 1971 with the equity participation of Japanese trading firms, eleven involved the "captive trading firms" of large manufacturing firms of Japan. The remaining 535 subsidiaries are classified by the year of their establishment, by the Japanese parents' characteristics and by the percentage ownership of the subsidiaries belonging to the Japanese parent firm(s). The table reveals that for both categories of

Table 5-7. Overseas Manufacturing Subsidiaries Established by Japanese Trading Companies, 1950-1971

	Prior to 1955	1956-59	1960-63	1964-67	1968-71	Total
Established by trading companies alone and Japanese ownership:	3	7	19	23	53	105
50% or more	1	2	7	10	24	44
25%-49%	1	3	10	9	26	49
Less than 24%	1	2	2	4	3	12
Established by trading and manufacturing firms and Japanese ownership:	0	15	83	119	213	430
50% or more	—	9	46	61	134	250
25%-40%	—	5	28	44	67	144
Less than 24%	—	1	9	14	12	36

Source: The Data Bank of the Multinational Enterprise Project, Harvard Business School.

Japanese investing parents—trading firms alone and the combination of trading and manufacturing firms—the propensity of investors to retain at least initially the majority ownership of the manufacturing subsidiaries markedly increased after the mid-1960s. It also reveals that the propensity of trading firms to establish manufacturing subsidiaries abroad without the equity participation of Japanese manufacturing firms increased visibly from the end of the 1960s to the early 1970s.

MITSUI VS. MITSUBISHI

The ten largest trading firms of Japan combined accounted for about three-quarters of all the overseas manufacturing subsidiaries of trading firms; and the top two alone—Mitsui and Mitsubishi—accounted for about 150 subsidiaries, or one-third of the total number. Mitsui in particular has been the leader, with Mitsubishi lagging behind by about four years in terms of getting involved in overseas manufacturing activities. By 1963 Mitsui & Co. was visibly demonstrating its new strategy of involving itself in manufacturing operations abroad, while the Mitsubishi Co. entered the manufacturing scene abroad at about 1967.

The differences in investing behavior between the two leading general trading compaines of Japan give rise to a number of hypothetical explanations concerning the impact of organizational differences upon the timing as well as the extent of trading firms' involvement in manufacturing activities. However, for the present the following two plausible scenarios provide tentative reasons why Mitsui & Co. was the first to be actively drawn into manufacturing activities abroad.

As was shown earlier in this chapter, Mitsui has traditionally acted as the key organizer and creator of the so-called Mitsui industrial group while its leading competitor, Mitsubishi, has been organized as the marketing arm of the Mitsubishi industrial group. As a result, the corporate culture of Mitsui has long focused its attention upon the individual initiatives of "Mitsui-persons" as shrewd traders and entrepreneurs. Unlike their Mitsubishi counterparts, Mitsui employees often cultivate business opportunities inside and outside Japan with relative freedom from the formal boundaries of business tasks and responsibilities assigned to other internal organizations. In their *de facto* matrix-organization of product-wide and area-wide profit responsibilities, Mitsui distinctly emphasizes the business area-wide profitability and business volume. The Mitsubishi Co., on the other hand, places its emphasis upon the vertical links of product-wide groups cutting across various geographical areas. Mitsubishi has centered its behavioral norms around de-emphasizing individual employee actions beyond what is assigned to the formal organizational unit within the firm. Accordingly, it may be logical that Mitsui persons stationed in overseas area offices react more urgently and quickly to the host countries' moves of import substitution by commencing manufacturing operations. Mitsubishi persons, on the contrary, might react to a similar situation by changing their merchandise within the same product group from those products threatened with local substitution to those that are complementary to local production.

Moreover, compared to the Mitsubishi industrial group, the Mitsui group has lacked a strong orientation toward shipbuilding, heavy industrial machinery and equipment. The strength of the Mitsui industrial group centered around the Toray group of synthetic fibers. Many of the remaining manufacturing firms with which Mitsui & Co. has dealt were, for the most part, small- to medium-sized firms engaged in the production of standard consumer and industrial products. While Mitsubishi Co. could count on a few large manufacturers of ships and industrial equipment for the bulk of its business and profit, Mitsui needed to scurry around among many smaller-scale manufacturers for business.

As a result, the exports of manufactures handled by Mitsui were more likely to be singled out as the targets of import substitution moves by the developing countries than those exports handled by Mitsubishi. When the difference in the composite of manufactures between Mitsui and Mitsubishi is coupled with their differences in corporate culture, it is not surprising that Mitsui has thus far led Mitsubishi and other large trading companies in manufacturing operations abroad.

JAPANESE TRADING COMPANIES AND DEVELOPING COUNTRIES: A CASE OF THE TEXTILE INDUSTRY IN INDONESIA

The preceding accounts of trading firms' overseas manufacturing ventures lead one to question whether their behaviors are conducive to the industrial goals of developing nations. A general evaluation of the developing countries' reactions to Japanese direct investments will be attempted later in this book. For now, we will look at the interactions in Indonesia among the two chief actors on the scene: Japanese trading firms and Indonesian textile firms.

THE DUAL CHARACTERISTICS OF THE INDONESIAN TEXTILE INDUSTRY

The textile industry involves the following production processes: yarn-spinning, weaving, dyeing and printing. Between the stages of spinning and weaving exist the material preparation stages of yarn warpping and sizing operations; between the stages of weaving and dyeing exist the subsidiary preparation processes of cloth scouring and bleaching. The modern integrated textile mill is a plant internally capable of handling all of these processes, from yarn-spinning to cloth dyeing and printing, without having to ship the cloth to subcontractors to handle the interim processes of material preparation and inspection. The finished quality of the cloth is determined not only by the quality of the yarn, but also by the thoroughness exercised in material preparation between the key production stages.

Each stage of the process from spinning to dyeing can also be separated and broken down into independent specialized operations. But the modern spinning operation that requires mechanized operation of spindles, as opposed to hand-operated spindles, can be carried out economically only by a plant operating over 20,000 spindles. As a result, cottage factories concentrate on stages of operation beyond the spinning stage. In the weaving sector, machine-spun yarns are woven by hand looms and power looms, thus giving rise to thousands of hand loom operators in addition to small-scale operators with 5 to 25 power looms in their control who are gathered around the limited number of mechanized spinning plants. The processes of such material preparation as yarn sizing and cloth bleaching are often handled in Indonesia by subcontractors operating cottage factories of this kind.

In 1969, at the outset of the first five-year plan for Indonesia, it was estimated that the spinning sector had over 400,000 spindles in use exclusively for cotton yarn production. It was also estimated that prolonged neglect of and lack of repair parts for the spindles had reduced the total utilization of the existing spindles by at least 75 percent. In addition, about one-quarter of the total usable power looms for cotton weaving were concluded to be over 30 years old. Most of the prewar looms were found in the larger factories, and about 95 percent of the more than 500 looms dated from the 1930s. The newer power looms were found in the larger factories, and about 95 percent of the more than 500 looms dated from the 1930s. The newer power looms were installed mostly in smaller-sized mills with 11 to 25 looms—an operation too small to be economical unless the price of the woven cloth was artificially maintained at a high level.[10]

By 1973 the structure of the Indonesian textile industry showed the composition depicted in Figure 5-1.[11] Joint ventures between Japanese synthetic textile firms and Indonesian former cotton firms dominated the top layer of the industrial structure. Over one dozen Indonesian former cotton firms also came to compete with Indonesian-Japanese joint ventures in products blending synthetic fiber with cotton. Since 1970, the new products of layers 1 and 2 have been grafted on top of the old layer of indigenous sectors engaged exclusively in coarse cotton textile products. Japanese textile and trading companies have been instrumental in transplanting the production of synthetic fibers to Indonesia.

In 1973 for example, the weaving sector of the synthetic fiber industry revealed financial and technological links between Japanese textile and trading firms on one hand and weaving operations in Indonesia on the other. For the two products involved—polyester-rayon and polyester-cotton—the largest operators were Indonesian (with Chinese ancestry) firms. Indonesian-Japanese joint ventures, however, were concentrated in the high quality product lines of polyester-rayon cloth and in the high quality lines of polyester-cotton cloth.

More important, Indonesian operations, large or small, have been supplied with necessary technologies, yarns (raw materials) and even

Figure 5-1. Product Composition of the Indonesian Textile Industry, 1973

Description	Products	Industry
Layer 1 High quality newest product (Local production began, 1971-73)	208 threads per square inch blending of synthetic fibers with cotton	Dominated by 7 Japanese-Indonesian joint ventures and 6-8 Indonesian operations with technical and financial assistances from Japanese textile and trading firms.
Layer 2 Low quality newest product (Local production began, 1970-73)	186 threads per square inch blending of fibers with cotton	Indigenous weaver and dyers who upgraded their operations with technical and financial assistances from Japanese textile and trading firms.
Layer 3 Low quality old products (Local production began, 1950-60)	Coarse cotton products (medium to lower counts)	Indigenous sectors. Co-existence of large plants and small cottage operations.

funds (trade credits) by a limited number of synthetic fiber firms and large trading firms in Japan. Even when these technological and financial links between Japanese and Indonesian firms were not apparent, my fieldwork in Indonesia uncovered instances where Indonesian operations of synthetic fiber textiles were invariably started by the active prodding of Japanese trading firms.

The history of Japanese involvement in the Indonesian synthetic fiber industry repeatedly reveals the following pattern: Entry into the local manufacturing operation often began with the dyeing operation in which bleached cloths were imported from Japanese plants and were printed or dyed to suit local demand in Indonesia. With the enforcement of the first five-year plan (1969-1973), Japanese exporters of bleached cloth hurriedly prepared themselves to integrate backward into the weaving operation stage. By 1973 Japanese weaving operations had completed their further backward integration into spinning operations. At the same time, a few leading

Indonesian weavers and spinners upgraded their products, enabling them to enter the premium product market hitherto held by Japanese operations. At this juncture, a leading Japanese synthetic fiber firm like Toray began to vertically integrate further into the local production of nylon and polyester materials.

Meanwhile, since 1969, the Indonesian demand for knit products (nylon and acrylic)—sport shirts, socks, knit wears—began to increase markedly as more and more Indonesians were brought into contact with industrial and urban life oriented toward consumer products. For the second five-year plan in Indonesia (1973-78), the production of both Indonesian and Japanese knit products was anticipated to increase. More interesting, however, Chinese operators who were based in Hong Kong and Taiwan were found in 1973 to be preparing themselves to enter production of knit wear in Indonesia. At the same time, Japanese investors were found to be positioning themselves locally as the suppliers of nylon filament and acrylic materials to Indonesian and Chinese manufacturers of knit products in Indonesia.

By the spring of 1973, Japanese involvement in the Indonesian textile industry showed the following four patterns of response in order to cope with increased competition from Indonesian and Chinese operations. First, the scale of the integrated operation from the spinning to dyeing process was often being doubled. The spinning and dyeing capacities were often greater than the internal weaving capacity so that surplus yarns could be subcontracted out to small-sized Indonesian weavers. Second, large Japanese firms like Toray and Asahikasei, which possess the manufacturing know-how for nylon, polyester and acrylic raw materials, positioned themselves as the "upstream" local monopolies for nylon, polyester and acrylic production. The rubber tire industry and the textile industry were to be supplied by plants in Indonesia. Their Japanese competitors quickly sought to expand their plant capacities for nylon and polyester materials already located in Thailand and scheduled in Malaysia. Third, the leading Japanese firm Toray began to tie up with a Hong Kong-based Chinese textile conglomerate, TAL, in order to expand the newly planned integrated operations from the spinning to dyeing processes. In this venture, Taiwanese and Hong Kong machinery and engineers rather than Japanese were to be used so that initial capital costs and annual operating expenses would be substantially lower. And fourth, a number of Japanese trading companies in 1973 began to explore the possibility of opening export-oriented plants for the manufacture of apparel and canvas shoes in Indonesia.

JAPANESE TRADING COMPANIES AS THE PROMOTERS OF INDONESIAN TEXTILE FIRMS

The fourth pattern of response that Japanese trading companies showed in Indonesian plays an obvious role in the Indonesian economy. The sharp competition among leading trading firms of Japan as well as among Japanese manufacturers of synthetic fibers and textile machinery has thus far facilitated the transfer of synthetic products and requisite manufacturing technologies to indigenous Indonesian operators.

When one trading firm and one synthetic fiber manufacturer of Japan obtained the Indonesian government's permit to commence its weaving operation locally, competing trading firms usually launched two simultaneous counteractions. First, they persuaded other Japanese synthetic manufacturers to commence manufacturing operations in Indonesia, so as not to be outdone by the first venture in the same industry. Second, trading companies persuaded indigenous Indonesian weavers and dyers to upgrade their product operations. Necessary machinery, technology, raw materials and finances were provided by the trading firms in the form of extended trade credits and technical assistance in operations.

At the initial stage of their entry into the Indonesian manufacturing industries, many Japanese manufacturing firms of such standard products as textile products, galvanized iron sheets and plastic products were helped by Japanese trading companies to overcome their unfamiliarity with local conditions, their lack of managerial talents seasoned in the different cultures and languages, their lack of worldwide communication networks, and even their lack of experience in international finance. A strong case can be made that without trading companies, directly exposed to the local stimuli of Indonesia and to fierce competition among themselves, the development of the Indonesian synthetic fiber industry would have been further delayed.

It might be speculated that Japanese manufacturing firms would not have been anxious to foster indigenous Indonesian competitors too soon were there no visible benefit. Japanese trading firms that are not locked into any single firm or single product often find it expedient to sell necessary raw materials, technologies and machinery to Indonesian entrepreneurs. During the first five-year plan, 1969–1973, Indonesia had succeeded in transplanting the integrated operations of spinning to dyeing processes of synthetic fibers. By 1973, a few Indonesian operators began to enter the higher product market of polyester blended textiles, often with the technical assistance of Japanese trading firms.

THE FUTURE OF JAPANESE TRADING FIRMS

Japanese trading firms have thus far demonstrated organizational flexibility in coping with changes in their business environments at home and abroad. Inside Japan, as the Japanese government eased its restrictions on foreign investments, leading trading firms have been quick to conclude joint ventures with foreign investors. Foreign investors have realized that real barriers to entry to the Japanese market often turned out to be the near impossibility of recruiting freely the managerial and other necessary personnel in Japan. The Japanese labor market has remained closed to many foreign firms. The distribution channels of Japan are frequently subdivided into intricate mazes from which uninitiated foreign firms are often barred.

Under these circumstances, joint ventures with diversified trading firms have proven necessary and successful for many foreign entrants. They have found that Japanese trading firms offer new opportunities for diversifying their lines of business. Thus, even consumer-oriented firms, from Coca-Cola and Pepsi Cola to Kentucky Fried Chicken, have so far built up successes in Japan with the assistance of the leading trading firms.

Outside Japan, Japanese trading firms' tie-ups with foreign developers of natural resources were repeatedly discussed in Chapter 2. The developing nations possess raw materials but lack international marketing contacts. When Mitsui and Mitsubishi make respective marks in Indonesia, their competitor, C. Itoh, beat them to Brazil. Marubeni and other leading trading firms established their presence in Africa easily. And Mitsui entered Iran on a large scale. Such competition among trading firms is at the same time helping Japan to diversify in its procurement of natural resources. The developing nations possess raw materials but lack international marketing contacts. They are increasingly finding Japanese trading firms to be useful vehicles for international sales of raw materials.

In the field of trade with the Eastern European nations and China, large Japanese trading firms are proving to be formidable competitors of American and European manufacturers. For one thing, trading firms can offer much greater flexibility in barter trades with eastern European nations and China than can American or European manufacturers.[12]

Most indications point to the conclusion that it is too early to draft an obituary for the large trading firm of Japan. It has not only survived the oil crisis, but has also strengthened its bargaining strength vis-a-vis Japanese manufactures. This happened partly because Japanese manufacturers, out of necessity, began to diversify their supply sources of raw materials and semi-finished components on a worldwide basis. Large trading firms were quick to offer business assistance to such manufacturers. Phoenix or cyclops, the large trading company may well continue to grow, becoming a force to be reckoned with on the international scene.

At the same time, a pessimistic scenario can also be predicted even for the largest ten general trading firms. In particular, those trading firms which are rated as "Class C" in Table 5-1 may now well be stretching their financial and managerial capabilities too thinly as they become involved in overseas investments. If a severe economic downturn in Japan hits them hard, these over-stretched firms can easily find themselves being forced to choose between insolvency and humiliating acquisition by Class A and Class B firms. Thus, a strong case can be made that the multinational expansion of Japanese trading firms is likely to lead to the survival of the fittest even among large general trading firms.

Besides, all Japanese trading firms which have thus far become involved in diverse projects abroad would inevitably discover a painful message: some projects are successful while others turn out to be ill-conceived and ill-advised. As of the end of 1975, none of the largest ten trading firms seemed working on contigency plans for divesting themselves of the ill-conceived projects. Chances are that they will be caught unprepared by a sudden turn of events.

Whether the rosy or the pessimistic scenario will be in store for large trading firms is, of course, up to the management courage and wisdom of each firm.

Chapter Six

Are Japanese Banks Coming?

Both trading and manufacturing firms have gone multinational. But the banking and other financial communities of Japan are still dragging their feet, as it were, in venturing outside of the country.

Meanwhile, the Japanese equity and bond markets are becoming fused with those of New York, London and other European nations as more and more Japanese firms float debentures and list their shares in foreign markets. If the Japanese yen maintains its current stability in the international markets, more and more foreign governments and firms will float yen-dominated bonds in the Tokyo market. If Japanese banks and security houses remain shy in their involvement in this aspect of international finance, even their current influence over trading and manufacturing firms might become jeopardized.

Sensing such impending dangers, leading banks and security houses of Japan are now trying to gain entry into the financial world outside Japan. Will their attempts pay off?

As of summer 1975, Japanese commercial and investment banks were still far behind their American counterparts. Since around 1972 the gap between the two groups had not narrowed. As of the end of 1972, Japanese commercial banks possessed about 80 overseas branches, 70 overseas offices and about 60 equity participations in investment and commercial banks abroad; and the leading city banks came to possess from 10 to 17 overseas subsidiaries engaged in wide ranges of business from commercial to merchant banking. In terms of the number of overseas posts, the Japanese commercial banking interests ranked a distant third behind American and British banking interests. In 1972, the number of overseas branches of American commercial banks exceeded 520. There were more than 2,000 posts of American banking businesses abroad, including minority equity interests in foreign banks in over 100 countries.[1] At the same time, the EEC-based banks had been expanding their worldwide networks by joining international banking consortia led by American banks, as well as expanding their business operations in the United States.

By 1975, the number of overseas branches of American commercial banks exceeded 700, with a concomitant increase in the number of their foreign subsidiaries engaged in banking and nonbanking activities since 1972. The gap between American and Japanese banks even widened from 1972 to 1975.

The Ministry of Finance of Japan, which regulates both the domestic and international activities of Japanese banks and security companies, was partly responsible for the slow pace of Japanese multinational activities in finances. The Ministry of Finance appeared particularly afraid of exposing the yen to the pressures of international currency markets. This fear was intensified in late August 1971 when the confidence of the Ministry in its ability to stem speculative inflows of foreign currencies was badly shaken. As of 1975, the Ministry has still not recovered from the shock of 1971.

In August 1971, as soon as President Nixon suspended the convertibility of the U.S. dollar into gold and unilaterally devalued the U.S. dollar, European nations closed their foreign exchange markets in order to discourage massive speculation on their currencies. Japan alone kept her foreign exchange market open for four days until the Ministry of Finance grudgingly admitted its inability to control speculative pressures on the yen and closed the Tokyo foreign exchange market. Subsequently, the value of the yen floated upward. The Ministry of Finance had earlier counted on its varous controls over foreign exchange transactions to stem speculative inflows of foreign currency. It vastly underestimated the abilities of trading firms, banks and Japanese and foreign firms based in Japan, which brought in foreign currencies under the guise of "advances of export earnings" or "advance collections" of outstanding dollar-denominator loans abroad.[2] Long gone are the days when the Japanese capital markets were effectively shielded from foreign markets. And yet the financial officialdom indulged itself in the past.

The Ministry of Finance maintained that the use of the Japanese yen as an international reserve currency would push Japan onto the same disastrous path which the British economy had experienced with the burden on the pound as an international reserve currency. However, this insular attitude of the Ministry barely masked a true fear on the part of financial officialdom.

As we noted in Chapter 1, the rapid industrial growth of Japan after World War II was made possible by the tight control of capital markets which the Bank of Japan and the Ministry of Finance kept by rationing scarce foreign exchange and domestic capital among growth-oriented projects in heavy and chemical industries. The success, however, of this "capital rationing," which was the cornerstone of the indicative economic planning of postwar Japan, had also fostered political control by the Ministry of Finance over Japanese financial communities. The multinational spread of Japanese financial institutions meant that Japanese banks and security companies would slip away from the tight grip of the Ministry of Finance. To make matters worse, the Ministry dreaded that the entry of Japanese banks and security firms into foreign countries would force Japan to allow, on the basis of "reciprocity," foreign commercial and investment banks to operate in Japan. The Ministry knew that the internationalization of Japanese financial markets would involve Japan in the international politics of money markets. And as of the mid-1970s the financial officialdom of Japan still appeared unprepared to plunge into such politics. The Ministry of Finance was still withstanding the mounting pressures from foreign and Japanese financial communities to interlock Japanese capital markets with those of the rest of the world. This is why the so-called "Asia-dollar market" was created in Singapore, not in Tokyo, despite Japan's potentially overwhelming volume of capital transactions. And the creation of "Asia-dollar market" vividly illustrated the intensifying oligopolistic competition among large American and European banks for hegemony in the international markets.

ASIA-DOLLAR MARKET

In 1975, the size of the "Asia-dollar market" was estimated to be around six billion dollars. It was functioning as a sub-market of the so-called "Euro-dollar market" whose size in 1975 was estimated to be around 75 billion dollars. The Asia-dollar market was established and cultivated by the Bank of America toward the end of the 1960s.[3]

As the supply of loanable funds tightened in the mid-1960s in the United States, and as the supply of Euro-dollars at the same time became tighter due to the sudden increase in borrowings by American banks, Bank of America (based in California) made its first attempt at tapping the Hong Kong market. Having been beaten to the "Euro-dollar" market by such large New York-based banks as First National City Bank and Chase Manhattan, Bank of America had been for some time endeavoring to close a gap with the leading competitors. The Administration in Hong Kong, however, did not exempt its non-resident depositors from a 15 percent withholding tax on interest earnings. True or not, it was widely whispered throughout Asia that the British Colonial Administration of Hong Kong did not find it attractive to help American banks increase their influences over Hong Kong financial markets. It was obvious then that American banks, not British banks, would be the largest beneficiaries of the "Asia-dollar" market.

At this juncture, Bank of America turned to Prime Minister Lee of Singapore, who was related to the family involved in the financial circle in Singapore. Prime Minister Lee agreed to exempt non-resident depositors from a 40 percent withholding tax on interest earnings. The government of Singapore also exempted the non-residents deposits from reserve requirement and exchange control. It also reduced income taxes and stamp duties on merchant banking transactions involving the Asia-dollars. All these moves were aimed at increasing the yield attractiveness of non-resident deposits as well as at facilitating Asia-dollar transactions. In 1969, the Asia-dollar market was born, with the opening of the Bank of America's branch accepting dollar-dominated deposits from non-residents in multiples of $25,000 (as opposed to $100,000 in Euro-dollar deposits). Immediately, five other American competitors of Bank of America—First National City Bank of New York, Chase Manhattan, First National of Chicago, Continental Bank (Chicago), and American Express International—rushed into the Singapore market. Seven banks from Europe followed suit. One Thai bank and one Russian bank also opened shop in Singapore in order to tap Asia-dollars.

Seeing that the Asia-dollar market was being pre-empted mainly by American and European banks, the Bank of Tokyo and Mitsui Bank—the two Japanese banks which had been expanding their branch networks in Southeast Asia in pursuit of expanding Japanese trade transactions—persuaded the Ministry of Finance of Japan in 1970 to permit branches in Singapore. Other Japanese banks later opened offices and lookout posts in the Asia-dollar market. When the first round of staking out in the Asia-dollar market ended, over 70 foreign banks had entered the market and had created among themselves 50 licensed Asia-dollar banks. American banks numbering 21 dominated the market by carving out about two-thirds of the transactions. Japanese banks hardly constituted a force to be reckoned with.

Only in 1972, as an expedient measure to reduce the embarrassingly large official exchange reserves of Japan, the Ministry of Finance of Japan timidly eased its restrictions on the establishment of branches and subsidiaries abroad by Japanese financial institutions. Even inside Japan, in 1972, the Ministry of Finance permitted the opening of the call loan market of U.S. dollars. This move was immediately interpreted by both Japanese and foreign banks as the budding emergence of the Tokyo-dollar market. Foreign commercial and investment banks continued to open branches in Japanese capital markets. And Japanese banks quickly discovered that without their own extensive presence in foreign financial markets, even the Tokyo-dollar market might be pre-empted by large American and European banks.

As of the end of 1970, there were only seven foreign banks operating in Japan. By the end of September 1972, the number of foreign commercial banks which had opened branches mushroomed to as many as 34. In addition 56 other foreign commercial banks opened new representative offices. Moreover, leading American investment banks and stock brokerage firms also opened branches in Tokyo. They all appeared ready to capitalize on the undeniable trend that the Tokyo capital market was increasingly becoming an integral part of international capital markets. The increases in foreign banks in Japan in turn made Japanese commercial and investment banks eager to enter capital markets abroad where foreign banks had already established their operations.

JAPANESE BANKS GO ABROAD

Partly for the purpose of entering the business territories abroad of American and European banks which were entering Japan, and partly for the purpose of servicing overseas subsidiaries of Japanese manufacturing and trading firms scattered throughout Asia, Latin America, Australia, Europe and North America, from 1972 onward Japanese banks stepped up their overseas business activities. Compared with American and European banks, however, Japan came late to Asia, Australia and Latin America. Japanese banks often found these host countries had closed entry to foreign banks. As a result, Japanese entrants often chose to purchase their way into minority equity ownerships through existing local commercial and investment banks or international consortia banks. This partial acquisition of existing institutions not only eased Japan's entry problem but also permitted her instantaneously to acquire business contacts and "know-how" of local operations.

In Europe, from 1968 to 1970, there were created a total of three investment consortia banks consisting exclusively of Japanese banks. As much as Japanese banks wished to join the international investment consortia consisting of various parent nationalities, no existing prestigious groups permitted participation by the Japanese banks which were inexperienced in international operations. Prior to their admission to existing consortia of foreign banks, Japanese entrant candidates often formed their own "consortia" in overseas financial markets. As it were, these "consortia" in which no participant held a majority interest, served as practicing fields for the Japanese entrants who often shared equal risks with partners in the initial stages of international finance. Only in 1971, as the Japanese yen became attractive and as the Tokyo dollar market emerged, a number of Japanese banks were invited into international consortia banks led by Rothschild, Manufacturers' Hanover, Oraion Group (Chase Manhattan) and First National City Bank of New York.

FOREIGN OWNERSHIP PATTERNS OF BANKS

In over 80 percent of these subsidiaries, the Japanese equity ownership portion remained less than 30 percent. And none of these subsidiaries were established through Japanese initiative. The leading city banks of Japan averaged in 1972 from 4 to 5 overseas branches per bank.

In the case of American banks, such latecomers as Chase Manhattan and Continental chose strategically to catch up with First National City Bank and Bank of America by supplementing their own networks of subsidiaries and branches with multiple-party joint ventures (consortia) with European and other American banks. Having caught up in 1972 with First National City Bank and Bank of America in terms of both market and service coverage, Chase Manhattan concentrated on expanding its own overseas branch networks. Since 1972, about one-half of all American bank branches opened outside the United States belonged to the two leading banks, Chase and First National City Bank, which were vigorously competing with each other for the leader's position in international banking.

After the oil crisis of 1973, the fortunes of international consortia banks waned, as Arab oil exporters preferred to deal with named banks in Europe and the United States.[4] The Arab depositors of so-called petro-dollars were fearful that international consortia banks in Euro-dollar markets had no single sovereign government responsible for their operations. The customers' faith in the international consortia was badly shaken when Bankhause I.D. Herstatt of Cologne collapsed in June 1974 amidst turbulent convulsions of the Eurodollar markets. If a nation-based bank like Bankhause folded, people thought that a dismal fate must be in store for international consortia banks. With a shrinkage of business volume of international consortia banks, a number of English and American members decided to withdraw from such arrangements. Then, Japanese banks were often found replacing English and American banks that wished to get out of playing musical chairs inside international consortia.

STRUCTURAL INSTABILITY OF EARLY CONSORTIA BANKS

In the practice-stage consortia, commercial banks and their arch-rivals, investment banks (security companies) of Japan, were often found holding minority interests in the same consortia. Accordingly, one could easily speculate that the "practicing consortia" formed by Japanese banks would tend to be structurally unstable. As participants of these practicing consortia completed the initiation phase, some participants appeared liable to either break away completely from the consortia or to re-emerge as the majority owners of the respective consortium. With the completion of the initiation phase, innate competitive rivalry among participants forced their diverse interests and expectations to surface. Such growing pains of the practicing consortium would often become intolerable and break up the original structure of the consortium.

SLOW INTERNALIZATION OF JAPANESE FINANCIAL INSTITUTIONS

As of mid-1975, there still remained a distinct asymmetry between the underdeveloped presence of Japanese financial institutions abroad and the active presence of foreign financial institutions in Japan. As a result, a number of Japanese commercial and investment banks have chosen to cooperate with foreign banks in their intent to expand in Japan, in exchange for their similar assistance to Japanese financial institutions abroad.

Since the oil crisis of 1973 destroyed the relaxation by the Ministry of Finance on out-flows of foreign exchange from Japan for the financing of manufacturing and resource development ventures abroad, Japanese commercial and investment banks have renewed their efforts to obtain necessary funds abroad for multinational firms through business connections with American and European financial institutions. As the strength of the yen weakened vis-a-vis the U.S. dollar after the oil crisis, Japanese financial institutions once again renewed their efforts to borrow abroad for their client firms in Japan.

In a rough estimate, the internationalization of the Japanese financial world can be measured by the amounts of international placements of dollar- and foreign-currency-denominated common shares and debentures (including convertible debentures), as well as by the amounts of yen-denominated foreign bonds in the Tokyo market. Starting in 1961 and especially after the mid-1960s and up until 1974, 36 Japanese firms and public corporations raised altogether about 520 million dollars in the U.S. capital markets either through convertible debentures, American Deposit Receipts (ADR) or straight bonds. During the same time period, 71 Japanese firms and public corporations raised about 1.3 billion dollars in European credit markets. In the Hong Kong market, Toray and Teiji together raised a total of 5.6 million dollars. After 1970 in particular, when the Tokyo markets were somewhat opened to foreign borrowers, up until 1975 the equivalent of about 550 million dollars in yen-denominated bonds were floated by thirteen issuing foreign governments and such international agencies as the Asia Development Bank and the World Bank.

PROMINENT EMERGENCE OF LEADING JAPANESE FIRMS

Meanwhile, fourteen foreign firms (thirteen American and one French) issued new common shares in the Tokyo Equity Market. And there was every expectation in 1975 that the Tokyo Market has already become closely linked with other capital markets of the world. And at the same time, more and more Japanese firms are directly tapping foreign capital markets. During summer 1975, Sony, which has been the leader of Japanese investments in New York and other foreign capital markets, publicly declared that it would not be restricted by the "in-house" rules and regulations of the Tokyo Capital Market.[5]

As one might expect, of all the bonds and shares abroad by Japanese public corporations and firms, Japanese securities houses were involved in less than one-half. Of the Japanese security houses (investment banks), Nomura Securities Co., the leading investment bank of Japan, was far ahead of the remaining three "large" security houses, namely, Nikko, Yamaichi, and Daiwa. Nomura has underwritten about two-thirds of the issues in which Japanese security firms were involved. In 1975, Nomura alone appeared capable of being accepted by the international financial communities as a "fully grown" partner in international finance.

Nomura's reputation in the international financial markets and in Asian capital markets in particular was such that in 1973 Merrill Lynch (U.S.) and Barclays International (U.K.) agreed to join Nomura in the three-way consortium Trident, a merchant and commercial banking venture in Hong Kong. The three parent firms were to pool their business contacts and expertise in an effort to turn Trident into a viable merchant banking institution in the Asian theatre. Nomura's competitors in Japan wished to follow suit, but there were no prestigious foreign partners offering assistance. Thus, international activities were further enhancing the leading Japanese firm's position.

This three-way tie-up among a British commercial bank and Japanese and American investment banks has raised one tantalizing question: will that unique British institution, merchant banking, be able to compete with commercial banks and investment brokerage houses invading the realms thus far conceded to merchant banks? Unlike either commercial banks or brokerage houses, traditional merchant banks often lack the retail networks to collect bank deposits or to sell investment portfolios.[6] The business experience and technical know-how that merchant banks have amassed appear imitable by commercial banks and investment brokerage houses. And yet, the retail business networks of commercial banks and investment houses are far more formidable for merchant banks to duplicate. This asymmetry in the barrier to entry is likely to give an advantage to commercial banks and investment brokerage firms competing with British merchant banks in the world capital markets that have increasingly become merged with one another.

COUNTER-THRUST OF THE MINISTRY OF FINANCE

Meanwhile, the Ministry of Finance of Japan has persistently discouraged such foreign financial practices as sales of certificates of deposit (CDs) or direct placement debentures, from spreading widely to Japan. Only when the Ministry of Finance was pressured by the combined lobbying of large Japanese firms and the leaders of the ruling party, LDP, did it grudgingly permit direct placement of shares and debentures as well as sales of unsecured convertible debentures. CDs were not yet permitted in Japan as of mid-1975.

Multinational expansions of Japanese banks and security companies were seen by Ministry officials as "slipping away from their regulatory powers." As previously mentioned, the overseas expansion of Japanese banks and security companies would force Japan to accept, on the principle of reciprocity, further expansion and new entries of foreign banks into Japan. Thus, the Ministry seemed uneasy about the growth in Japan of foreign banks whose operations were controlled by headquarters located outside Japan. In theory, all the foreign financial institutions operating in Japan came under the supervision of the Bank of Japan or the Ministry of Finance. Yet in practice, both the Bank and the Ministry have been unduly timid in exercising their legal authority, even in making routine audits of the operations of foreign financial institutions. Such political timidity on the part of the Japanese "financial officialdom" puzzled both Japanese and foreign observers. But this timidity was perhaps indicative of the fact that the Japanese financial markets, shielded too long from international capital markets, had bred the fear of becoming involved in both political and economic repercussions abroad.

To complicate matters, Japanese financial institutions both inside and outside Japan have interlocked their business interests with foreign financial firms. To Japanese "financial officialdom," such business tie-ups appeared to have created potential alliances between Japanese and foreign business interests. Thus, the absolute control which the Ministry of Finance and the Bank of Japan have held in the past over Japanese financial firms was seen as eroding as foreign financial institutions began joining forces with Japanese business partners.

At the same time, after the oil crisis of 1973, the increased demand for Japanese importation of oil and other raw materials motivated the Japanese government to encourage its manufacturing and trading firms to raise necessary funds abroad. Since the overseas financing abilities of Japanese commercial and investment banks still remained underdeveloped, an increasing number of Japanese multinational firms turned to foreign financial intermediaries for obtaining necessary funds. The upshot of such developments might well have been the closer business relationships which developed, both in and outside Japan, between Japanese manufacturing and trading firms on the one hand and foreign financial intermediaries on the other. Ironical as it sounds, therefore, the fact that the officials of the Ministry of Finance and the Bank of Japan kept the multinational activities of Japanese financial communities underdeveloped out of fear of losing their pervading influence might well have precipitated the erosion of power they so feared.

COMMERCIAL BANK VS. SECURITY HOUSE

Starting in the early 1960s, with foreigners' portfolio investments in Japanese shares and the circulation of European and American Depository Receipts of large Japanese firms in the New York Stock Exchange, competition between Japanese security houses and commercial banks have been intensifying over the floatation of yen-denominated bonds in the Tokyo market, and over inflows of Eurodollars and petro-dollars to Japan. So long as banks and security houses were kept inside Japan, their business territories were clearly divided by Article 65 of the Security Trading Law. As commercial banks and security houses began infiltrating business territories outside Japan, however, and as the foreign financial markets became fused with those of Japan, the anachronistic demarcation of business territories between commercial banks and security houses became blurred.

The increased presence of foreign banks and security houses in Japan is complicating competition and cooperation among banks, security houses and life insurance companies. For the balance of the 1970s, Japanese financial institutions may indeed be forced to review and alter not only their time-honored business horizons and practices, but more important their time-honored personnel recruitment and subsequent training and promotion practices. For as is not the case with manufacturing and trading firms, there exists great room for innovative business dealings that alert and energetic individuals can accomplish in internationalized financial markets inside and outside Japan. It remains to be seen whether Japanese banks and security houses will help their younger and more individualistic personnel acquire international recognition as financial traders. If attempted, such endeavors are bound to erode the strict seniority-based job assignment that the firms have long practiced. In both commercial and investment banking businesses, products (services) and ideas are not patentable and business information travels rather freely worldwide from one capital market to the next. Under these circumstances, the international credibility of individual bankers and traders, whose personal integrity and business expertise become widely known throughout the international banking world, tends to provide a main source of competitive strength.

Chapter Seven

The International Transfer of Japanese Technologies

Critics of multinational expansion of private firms appear convinced that multinational firms bring "wrong" technologies into developing countries.[1] In these host countries, government officials are questioning whether Japanese direct investments have anything special to offer for the successful transfer of manufacturing technologies and management skills.

The success of Japanese manufacturing subsidiaries abroad requires substantive transfer of products and manufacturing processes from parent plants in Japan. Therefore, Japanese investors believe they are doing their best in transferring products and requisite manufacturing processes to their subsidiaries abroad. Why then, are the host countries apprehensive about Japanese firms' efforts? Are the Japanese technologies different from American and European technologies?

In the current controversy over the roles of multinational firms in international transfer of technologies the governments of host countries and the investing foreign firms have their own definitions of "international transfer of technologies." While the latter is preoccupied with successful transfer of various proprietary technologies and products to subsidiaries abroad, the former is concerned over two basic questions; first, the selection of products and technologies appropriate for local settings, and second, the diffusion of such products and technologies to local industrialists emulating foreign investors.

Manufacturing technologies and management skills often deny conceptual clarification. This adds further confusion to the politically sensitive controversy over the roles which multinational firms play in transferring manufacturing technologies and management skills from the industrialized nations to the developing countries.

THE NATURE OF TECHNOLOGIES

For analytical treatment of international transfer of technologies, it would be useful to classify "technologies" into the following three categories:

1. *Product-related technologies* emanating from identifiable products, which are new to the host countries. These technologies are often proprietary possessions of the investing parent firms. Although specific production-related processes are an integral part of such proprietary products, the technological advantage of the investing parent (foreign) firm stems from the fact that investing firms alone, or with only a few other firms, possess the products in question.
2. *Production process-related technologies* emanating from identifiable manufacturing processes. These technologies are also often proprietary possessions unique to the investing parent firms. Although specific products are concrete results (outputs) of production process-related technologies, the technological advantage of the investing parent firms stems from the fact that they possess unique manufacturing processes not held by indigenous local firms or by other foreign investors.
3. *Institution-related technologies* resulting from the body of experience that has grown out of a specific technology related to products as well as production processes of the investing firm. This operational experience is difficult to separate from the firm and employees effecting it. The firm's ways of organizing and motivating employees to produce specific products or services is but one example of such technology. What we often call "management skill" falls into this category. Proper flow of management information within a given subsidiary, as well as proper communication between an investing parent firm and its subsidiary form a part of the institution-related technologies unique to a firm.

Naturally, the demarcations between the above three categories of technologies is often more theoretical than real. The successful utilization of production process-related technologies depends upon successful manipulation of institution-related technologies in the inevitable interactions between worker and machine.

As shown in Chapter 3, the Japanese products which migrated to the developing countries in Asia were increasingly mature products becoming uneconomical to produce in Japan. The manufacturing technologies of such products had long been adapted to the economic and cultural environments of Japan. The developing countries, however, have not absorbed these manufacturing technologies nor, more often than not, are there indigenous manufacturing processes in the host countries upon which "Japanese" products can be grafted. Thus, the product- and production process-related technologies often confront a vacuum in the economic and cultural settings of the developing nations.

JAPANESE TECHNOLOGIES

Especially since 1950, Japanese manufacturing firms have absorbed both product- and process-related technologies mainly through licensing agreements from the United States. These firms have also invested an increasing amount of R&D effort in remodeling the licensed technologies so that both product- and process-related technologies fit the economic and cultural setting of Japan.[2]

Of late, Japanese firms have been forced to emphasize more independent R&D efforts as the past licensors, notably American firms, have grown reluctant or unwilling to sell their proprietary technologies, except in the case of cross-licensing agreements. That such efforts by Japanese firms are now registering a fair degree of success is reflected in the increasing "export" of Japanese proprietary technologies. In Tables 7-1 and 7-2 Japan's "balance-of-trade" of technologies is summarized for the years 1950-1969.

During the years 1950-69, the average of Japan's sales of technologies abroad was only 8.4 percent of the number of technologies purchased from abroad. Japanese industries throughout these years,

Table 7-1. Japan's Receipts and Payments of Technological Fees, 1950-1969 (In millions of U.S. dollars)

	1950-55	1956-60	1961-65	1966-69	Total 1950-69
Receipts (A)	0.7	4.3	49.0	126.0	180.0
Payments (B)	68.9	280.5	686.0	1,113.0	2,148.4
(A)/(B) x 100 (%)	1.0%	1.5%	7.1%	11.1%	8.4%

Source: *Gaikoku Gijutsu Donyu Nenji Hokoku, 1971*, Science and Technology Agency, Tokyo, February 1973, pp. 20-21.

Table 7-2. Japan's Sales and Purchases of Technologies, 1950-1969

	No. of Technological License Agreements Concluded between Japan and the Rest of the World, 1950-1969
No. of technologies sold by Japan	711
No. of technologies purchased by Japan	6,994

Source: *Gaikoku Gijutsu Donyu Nenji Hokoku, 1971*, Science and Technology Agency, Tokyo, February 1973, pp. 20-21; *Japan's Overseas Investment and Technical Export*, Jukagaku Kogyo Tsushinsha, Tokyo, 1970, pp. 382-415.

however, were improving their technological capabilities. There was a marked increase in the proportion of sales to purchases of technologies from the first year, 1950, to the last, 1969, when Japan's receipts for technological fees from abroad were more than 10 percent of her payments of such fees to foreign firms. The bulk of such payments went to the U.S., which supplied approximately 60 percent of the technologies Japan bought from abroad. The remaining 40 percent went to Europe.

In order to examine this pattern of technology trade, the manufacturing technologies sold abroad by Japanese industries during the years 1950-69 were classified by the country of their purchasers. The technologies sold abroad are also classified according to whether they are product- or production process-related (Table 7-3).

Foreign firms purchase technologies from Japanese firms basically because those technologies are, in the main, commercially or technically superior to what is available elsewhere. This is especially true since the recorded "exports" of technologies from Japan exclude the licensing agreements between Japanese parent firms and their overseas subsidiaries. Accordingly, one can glean the following observations from Table 7-3:

1. About one-half of the Japanese technologies sold abroad went to Asian countries. European countries were the second largest customers, followed by the U.S. The ranking order of customers was exactly the opposite of the ranking of foreign suppliers of superior technologies to Japan (first U.S. firms, then Europe, and practically no Asian countries). In short, in terms of technological competence Japan was positioned somewhere between the U.S. and Europe on one hand, and Asian and other developing countries on the other. This means, perhaps, that Japan was often acting as an intermediary through which the technologies of the

Table 7-3. Classification of Japanese Technologies Sold Abroad, 1950-1969, by Purchasers' Location and by Nature of Technology

Purchasers' Location	Product-related Technologies[a]			Production Process-related Technologies[b]			Total No. of Tech.	% of Total Tech. Sold
	1950-59	1960-69	Sub Total	1950-59	1960-69	Sub Total		
Asia	15	54	69	44	187	231	300	44
U.S.	4	33	37	3	91	94	131	19
Europe	5	40	45	4	127	131	176	26
Latin America	5	8	13	6	26	32	45	6
British Dominion and Oceania	0	4	4	1	22	23	27	4
Middle East	0	5	5	0	4	4	9	1
Africa	0	0	0	0	1	1	1	—
Total	29	144	173[c]	58	458	516[c]	689	100%

[a]Product-related Technologies are generally as defined earlier in this chapter. As a working criterion, however, when Japanese industries are the inventors of the products involved, or when Japanese renovations of prototype foreign products are substantive such as the case of compact electronics and electric appliances, requisite technologies are classified in this category.

[b]Production Process-related Technologies are generally as defined earlier in this chapter. As a working criterion, requisite technology was classified in this category when, of various alternative sources of similar technology, Japanese products and their process-related technologies were chosen because of the uniqueness of the Japanese process. However, most of the technologies classified into this category were clearly identifiable process-related technologies for the production of known products.

[c]The Chi-square test of the respectively recorded numbers (516 vs. 173) reveals that the difference between the two recorded numbers is statistically significant, thus supporting the inference that Japanese industries have thus far produced an overwhelmingly large number of technological innovations related to production processes compared to those related to products.

Source: *Japan's Overseas Investment and Technological Export*, Jukagaku Kogyo Tsushinsha, Tokyo, 1970, pp. 382-415.

U.S. and Europe were being passed on to the developing countries in Asia.
2. Compared with Japanese technological achievements of the 1950s, the relative superiority of Japanese technologies vis-á-vis the rest of the world in general, and the U.S. and Europe in particular, had distinctly improved during the 1960s, indicating that increased R&D efforts by Japanese manufacturing industries have been successful. In fact, I found that in steel and iron products, electronics, drugs, synthetic fibers and plastic products, Japanese process technologies in particular, and sometimes even Japanese product innovations, have been increasingly licensed out to firms in the U.S. and Europe.
3. More important, the Japanese thrust of technological superiority was particularly vigorous in the production process-related technologies. As shown in Table 7-3, approximately three-quarters of the Japanese technologies which foreign firms had judged to be sufficiently superior to warrant payments of licensing fees, were indeed those of production process-related technologies. And the relative importance of such processes in contrast to product-related technologies in Japan's exports of technologies increased during the 1960s, indicating again that the R&D efforts of Japanese manufacturing firms had been aiming mainly at improvements of production processes.

The nature of the innovation of a given country will reflect particular economic and cultural characteristics of that country.[3] This is partly because the stimuli for innovation, emanating from diverse economic and cultural environments, will vary from one country to the next. The available information about technological innovations in the U.S. indicates that American innovations have been dominated by product-related technologies.[4] Similar data on the United Kingdom shows English innovations to be rather balanced between product and production process-related technologies. Germany, France and Italy record more production process-related technologies than product-related technologies but to nowhere near the same degree as Japan.*

---

*More definite conclusions on innovations in the U.S., the United Kingdom, Germany, France and Italy need to await the results of a comparative study of technological innovations in Japan, the U.S., the United Kingdom, and continental European countries, a study which is now being undertaken under the supervision of Professor Raymond Vernon of the Harvard Business School. However, preliminary data from this study already tend to support the observations made here.

In Japan, industrialists have been concerned with the maximum utilization of expensive production equipment (capital), as well as with the savings of expensive and imported raw materials. Two and three-shift arrangements of workers have become a standard practice in Japan in order to utilize expensive capital equipment around the clock. And operational engineering as well as R&D efforts of Japanese manufacturers have been directed toward further utilization of the equipment. Thus, Japanese technologies are characterized by such innovations as continuous, automatically-controlled operations of cold strip mills in the steel plants, and improved catalyses to facilitate chemical reactions within blast and electro furnaces.[5] Synthetic fiber producers have invented a method which enables them to draw more than one polymer thread at a time out of the same polymer-making chamber. In Chapter 1, we saw how the shipbuilding industries of Japan had devised a means to cut down the delivery time (production lead-time involved) of their ships. Shorter delivery time meant a greater turnover (better utilization of expensive capital investment).

In the area of raw material savings, the earliest "technological breakthrough" that the Japanese cotton yarn producers accomplished, was the development of blending various grades of raw cotton in such a way as to produce a higher quality of cotton yarns. The industrialists' desire to produce cotton yarns for a growing market in Japan motivated the great inventor, Toyota Sakichi, to develop an automatic loom.

A country like Japan emphasizes improvement and adaptation of process-related technologies, which had been developed earlier by foreign innovators, for the production of new products. As a latecomer to the competitive scene for new products, Japanese firms often needed to design cheaper ways of producing the same products in order to survive, if necessary, price cutting battles on the world market in direct competition with earlier arrivals to the industrial scene.

When Japanese manufacturers succeed in developing technologies which permit the reduction of unit production costs and/or the improvement of product quality, a number of manufacturers in the U.S. and Europe become potential purchasers of these innovations. Perhaps these foreign firms are already feeling, in their own domestic and foreign markets, the prick of price competition as their products become mature and standard items in other markets. Thus, they often attempt to prolong their competitive positions by purchasing the Japanese production processes which are economically superior to their own. Both the increased export of steel products from Japan and increased sales of steel-making technologies from Japan to American and European steel firms followed exactly the pattern mentioned above.[6]

OTHER CHARACTERISTICS OF THE MANUFACTURING TECHNOLOGIES OF JAPAN

The Japanese technologies which have found eager purchasers in the developing countries, most notably in Asia, are distinguishable from those purchased by the developed nations. The recent fruits of Japanese R&D efforts in the fields of electronics, chemical and petrochemical products and processes have been mainly exported to the U.S. and Europe. New semiconductors such as diodes and synthetic paper are being licensed to American and European firms. And newer production processes such as operational know-how of cold strip milling of steel plants are also sold by Japanese firms to those of the U.S. In contrast, older techniques such as drawing wires and producing power transformers are purchased by firms in India and Taiwan. Standard machine tools and their production know-how are also purchased by firms in Asia.

A classification, by their entry date into Japan, of the 689 technologies that Japan sold to other nations during the years 1950-69 reveals that the newer the licensed technology, the greater was its chance of being purchased by firms in the U.S. and Europe. In fact, as measured from the time of its first commercial application in Japan to its final export, the average age of the Japanese technologies that were licensed to U.S.- and Europe-based firms was around two to three years, while the average age of both product- and process-related technologies purchased by Taiwan, Singapore and India were from five to fifteen years.[7] A potential purchaser country of Japanese technologies might be depicted as in the U-shaped curve shown in Figure 7-1.

The developing nations in Asia were purchasing manufacturing technologies held by small- to medium-sized firms in Japan. In the Asian nations, such countries as Taiwan, Singapore and India were the most frequent purchasers of old technologies that had only recently begun to lose their dominant presence in Japan. On the other hand, other Asian countries such as Thailand, Malaysia and Indonesia appeared technologically yet too weak to absorb Japanese technologies merely through licensing agreements. As a result they purchased older and more simple technologies from Japan mainly through "direct investments" of Japanese firms.

Figure 7-1. The U-Shaped Pattern of Clients and Their Purchases of Japanese Technologies

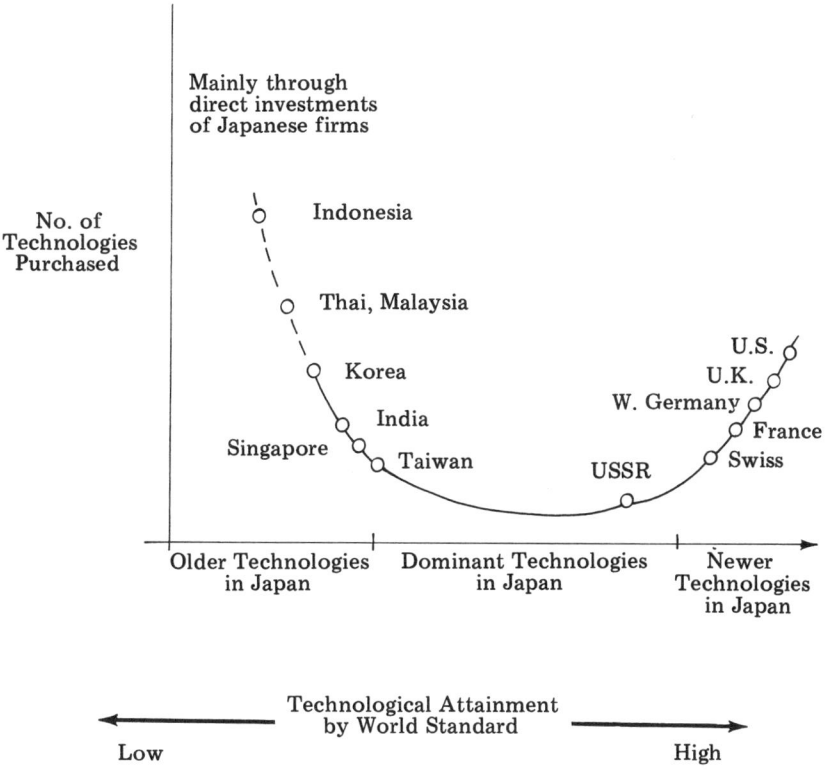

INTERNATIONAL TRANSFER OF JAPANESE TECHNOLOGIES

Since the 1870s, Japan has succeeded in overcoming her shortage of manufacturing skills and experience and has rapidly caught up with the "advanced" nations, mainly through the "division of tasks" among many individuals and firms. Firms in Japan have organized their employees, subsidiaries and subcontractors to allow one person or firm to perform essentially a single function, without having to wait for the single worker or firm to master the total breadth of skills needed for particular tasks. In order to compensate for the shortage of skilled workers in Japan, production processes imported from the West have often been broken down in Japan into a series of simple standard operations, to be linked up again by specialists. Because Japanese wage rates were much lower than those in the West, even this kind of division of labor involving many people permitted economically rapid assimilation of diverse manufacturing technologies in Japan.

Convincing historical documents point out that similar adaptive efforts were accomplished during the Nineteenth Century by U.S. manufacturing industries.[8] For, compared to the U.K., her major source of imported manufacturing technologies at that time, the U.S. was relatively skill-scarce. The case of Japan remains a curiosity at the present, however. Her adaptive efforts extended right into the 1950s, and she is the only developed country today where one can still find vintage 1950s process technologies and related products, particularly in her small- to medium-sized firms.

Efforts in individual specialization have also been accomplished in the fields of clerical and administrative works. This "group" or "human sea" (*Jinkai Senjutsu*) approach—in shortening the time required for a Japanese firm to attain a given level of technological and managerial competence—has remained very much intact in the older technologies still in use.

Accordingly, Japanese industries have produced individual engineers, skilled workers and technicians who possess a distinctly narrower breadth of expertise than their counterparts in, say, the U.S. For example, a typical journeyman machinist of Japan can often perform only a specialized job on one machine, a lathe for example, while an American machinist can perform jobs on several different pieces of equipment from lathe to milling machines. Such extreme forms of specialization have been perpetuated by the educational and vocational institutions which historically have been the products of Japan's concerted efforts to attain a high level of industrialization in a short period of time.

Within the typically Japanese environment, process-related technologies in particular have grown closely intertwined with the institutional idiosyncracies of Japanese corporate culture. Accordingly, the international transfer of Japanese technologies to foreign licensees and to Japanese subsidiaries abroad often required, at least at the outset, the simultaneous grafting of the "critical mass" element of institution-related technologies onto the economic and cultural roots of the host countries.[9]

CHOICE OF REQUISITE TECHNOLOGIES FOR JAPANESE SUBSIDIARIES IN ASIAN COUNTRIES

In a questionnaire, part of which was quoted in Chapter 3, several Japanese manufacturing firms surveyed during the fall of 1972 were asked to rank each of the six reasons shown below in determining requisite products and production processes of their manufacturing subsidiaries in developing nations. The numerical score given to each reason indicates the degree of relative importance collectively indicated by the two groups of firms in selecting the products and production processes of their manufacturing subsidiaries abroad. The greater the number, the more important is the reason. (See Table 7-4.)

The above results are consistent with the findings of Chapter 3. Regardless of the size of the parent firm, Japanese firms have chosen the oldest and most familiar products and production processes for their manufacturing subsidiaries in developing nations. Specific demands made by local business partners were far less influential in determining requisite products and processes than investing parent firms' motivations such as their desire to export the oldest and most familiar products and production processes.

Developing nations have persistently voiced the fear that foreign investors have been intolerably slow in adapting the product- and process-related technologies to local settings. Since the governments of the developing nations are concerned over the rise of urban unemployment, they believe that the use of "labor-intensive" processes by foreign subsidiaries could employ a greater number of locals. And many economists and politicians in the developing and developed nations still uphold the conventional axiom that labor-intensive technologies are best for low-wage countries burdened with unemployment. Rarely, however, do they investigate the economic and social factors which might predispose foreign manufacturers to choose mechanized operations over labor-intensive ones.[10]

In order to illuminate the decision-making problems involved in selecting requisite technologies, we need to examine the factors which the Japanese designers of new manufacturing operations consider in selecting specific production processes and products for their subsidiaries abroad. Interviews with the plant designers were supplemented with in-plant observations, and also compared with the operations of other foreign overseas subsidiaries in similar product Fields. The general pattern that emerged is summarized in Table 7-5.

Once an entry decision is made, the product and product quality for the subsidiary abroad is mainly determined by the constraints identified in Decision Step 2 of Table 7-5. Firms consciously maintain the brand images that they have established in their domestic

Table 7-4. Six Reasons Determing Products and Production Processes in Opening Subsidiaries in Developing Countries

Question: When you opened your manufacturing subsidiaries in developing countries, how important were the following six reasons in determining specific products and production processes of your subsidiaries?

Reasons	Japanese Parent Firm's Indicated Score*	
	Small- to Medium-sized	Large size
a. Local availability of necessary parts	-0.117	-0.137
b. Local availability of necessary raw materials	0.414	0.456
c. Oldest products and processes of parent plants in Japan. Familiarity and stability of product and process specifications	0.713	0.756
d. Local partners' specific requests	0.265	0.204
e. Local possibility to sell products to other Japanese firms	-1.690	-1.704
f. Export possibility of products to Japan, Europe and the U.S.	0.309	0.310
No. of Respondents	40	78

*For example, Respondent A rated on a seven-point scale the six reasons (a) through (f) as Xa, Xb, Xc, Xd, Xe, and Xf. The Respondent A's normalized score, Xn, for Reason (a) is computed as follows:

$$X_n = X_a - \frac{[X_a + X_b + X_c + X_d + X_e + X_f]}{6}$$

Then, calculate the arithmetical average of the normalized scores for each reason for the two groups of Japanese parent firms.
See Stopford and Wells, *Managing the Multinational Enterprise* (New York: Basic Books, 1973) pp. 104-105.

and export markets. Very few firms feel they can afford to jeopardize the quality images of their products. This preoccupation with brand image by investors is all the more important in the technologies chosen by the entering firm. Japanese parent firms have limited choices in selecting alternative technologies if they are to manufacture products of a predetermined and domestically accustomed quality.

Product specifications were determined in such a way as mainly to meet the requirements of the two constraints in Decision Step 2 of Table 7-5. The fact that Japanese investors were very conscious of present and future competition from other foreign firms and even from indigenous firms cannot be too strongly stressed. Japanese investors in manufacturing activities abroad often faced competition from other Japanese and non-Japanese firms. These competitors were generally capable of producing high quality products, and thus could

Table 7-5. A Typical Decision-Making Process of Japanese Firms in Selecting Manufacturing Technologies for Their Subsidiaries Abroad

Decision-Making Step	Key Decision-Maker and Relevant Information Used	Crucial Constraints on Decision Emanating from Foreign Environment
1. Entry decision	Parent's top management evaluates economic and political information on the target country	(1) Target country's trade policy (2) Japanese competitors' moves (3) Parent's worldwide strategy
2. Selection of product, its quality and production scale	Parent's middle management decides on the quality and the product lest they damage the firm's brand image	(1) Competitive strategy of the subsidiaries (domestic market-oriented vs. export possibility) against other foreign firms. (2) Difficulty of product imitation by indigenous firms
3. Decision on manufacturing technologies and processes: plant location, plant buildings and layouts, machinery and equipment.	Parent's engineers design plant and production scales in order to meet the "quality" of product that commands price premium in host country.	(1) Local laborer's work habits (2) Insufficient managerial skills of Japanese managers operating in foreign culture (3) Local availability of maintenance and repair services of equipment (4) Market uncertainty

exploit the degraded reputations of firms that unwisely introduced simpler and less dazzling products into the developing economies.

In the industries in which indigenous firms could quickly provide serious competition, as in the case of the weaving and dyeing branches of the textile industry, Japanese firms chose products and processes which were most difficult for indigenous firms to imitate. In this fashion, Japanese subsidiaries attempted either to pre-empt the market from other foreign subsidiaries in their host countries, or to avoid price competition from indigenous firms by producing products differentiated in quality from those made locally.

My field research, especially in Korea, Thailand, Singapore and Indonesia has led me to conclude that Japanese investors have been preoccupied with avoiding competition both from other foreign investors and from indigenous firms. Such preoccupation has produced two distinct biases in the selection of product quality and production scale. These were: (1) a preference for "high" quality products (and, for late-arriving firms, a notch "higher" than that of existing competitors); and (2) a propensity for building plants with larger production capacity than the initial market would warrant. Both biases were moves by the investors to insure against the risk of being out-produced by future competitors in terms of both product quality and supply capability.

In this regard, the following accounts of my fieldwork in two Asian countries, Indonesia and Korea, will further reveal the economic and social factors influencing the choice of technologies by Japanese investors abroad. These two countries were chosen mainly because they represent two opposite ends of the spectrum as far as the technological level of competence and cultural background of the host country is concerned. Culturally, Indonesia shares little with Japan, while Korea not only belongs, like Japan, to the East Asian cultural sphere but also has already a high literacy rate.

THE CASE OF JAPANESE SUBSIDIARIES IN INDONESIA: ORIENTATION TOWARD LOCAL MARKETS

In order to predict Japanese investors' moves in Indonesia, it is useful to remember that each investing firm is very conscious of what has happened in Taiwan, Thailand, Singapore and Malaysia, especially as the result of competition among Japanese subsidiaries. In Indonesia, the investing firm was endeavoring to either repeat its past successes or to avoid its mistakes elsewhere. There were enough past examples of unsuspecting Japanese investors abroad being prevented by latecomers from upgrading their product quality, or of being squeezed out of the price competition by late-comers who out-produced the earlier investors.

In the complicated operations required for high-quality products, plant engineers tended to rely heavily on semi-automatic and continuous processes rather than risk possible production breakdowns and deterioration of product-quality by using unskilled workers. In the dyeing processes of textile operations, for example, automatically-controlled, continuous processes are used rather than manually-controlled batch systems which require skilled artisan craftsmanship to produce quality products. Incidentally, this preference for automatic processes was not unique to foreign subsidiaries. Most notably, among indigenous textile mills in Indonesia, I found firms switching over to automatic processes once management had decided to upgrade product quality.[11]

Once product quality and production scales were determined, the parent company's engineers and cost accountants took over the final selection of manufacturing technologies and equipment. In this regard, my field investigations in Indonesia among foreign manufacturing subsidiaries (42 of Japanese origin, 5 of other), revealed the following constraints on the selection of manufacturing technologies and processes (Decision Step 3, Table 7-5):

1. *Local laborer's work habits:* Even when Indonesian workers are assigned to jobs which flow in sequence from one worker to the next, their ingrained attitude of "minding one's own business" tends to cause bottlenecks in the production flow. Rather than helping a fellow worker who lags behind, a fast-paced worker simply rests. And perhaps out of extreme reluctance to antagonize his peers, an Indonesian supervisor often fails to prod workers into maintaining a quick and continuous flow of work. As a result, many foreign plants have installed conveyor belts and semi-automatic machines to handle vital flows of materials. Even when labor-intensive production methods were feasible, with the extensive use of simple manual tools (knives, for example), initial attempts to employ them were often abandoned when such tools kept disappearing. Foreign managers have tended to solve these "control" problems by using "machine-paced" production processes. Foreigners substitute their lack of "training and supervising" skills with "capital" (machinery).

2. *Insufficient managerial skills of Japanese managers operating in a foreign culture:* Japanese managers are afraid that their ignorance of Indonesian customs and manners might inadvertently cause negative reactions from indigent employees. In order to avoid this risk, Japanese expatriate managers prefer machines to labor. Their hidden

rationale is that the fewer people there are to deal with, the less chance there will be for personal conflicts.

3. *Local availability of maintenance and repair service for equipment:* Like other developing countries, Indonesia is characterised by a severe paucity of skilled maintenance and repair technicians and of independent maintenance and service workshops. As a result, foreign engineers and technicians must train and develop teams of Indonesian maintenance crews inside their own plants and maintain and repair their equipment themselves. These obligations invariably lead foreign plant engineers and technicians to select processes and machines with which they are most familiar for their plants.

Of the 74 manufacturing subsidiaries which the author investigated, plant engineers in all but one echoed the following comment made by one engineer:

> No, we did not bring the newest model machines available in our country or elsewhere. We picked the second or third newest models, which we knew inside-out. We can fix these models blindfolded. More importantly, we can anticipate the breakdowns and prevent them on the basis of our experience back home.

More often than not, the equipment and processes thus chosen require more man-hours per machine than the newest models, and are also geared to a lower volume of production per machine. Consequently, the manufacturing processes that are moved to Indonesia tend at least at the outset to be more "labor-intensive," relative to the most advanced processes employed in parent countries, where comparable products are produced. It is worthwhile to note, however, that a foreign plant engineer's concern with maintenance of equipment often precludes the attempt to readjust the machines to fit other local conditions, such as the abundance of untrained workers eagerly seeking jobs.*

4. *Market uncertainty:* When market conditions are full of uncertainties, manufacturing firms are willing to pay a premium for

---

*One additional observation that can be made regarding the manufacturing processes of foreign subsidiaries in Indonesia is that the key machinery processes always have at least one identical back-up machine. When the plants are preoccupied with maximum utilization of machines (expensive capital), they can least afford a long down-time on key machinery or delayed production of key parts or intermediate materials. As a result, when measured by the ratio of labor to fixed assets, the overall capital/labor ratio in foreign subsidiaries in Indonesia is definitely greater than that in countries where maintenance and repair services are readily available.

flexibility in production volume. In this regard, labor-intensive processes which complicate firing or reassignment of workers are generally not as flexible as machine-intensive processes in adjusting production volume or production varieties. Foreign managers who prefer to avoid, at almost any cost, the possibility of confronting the unpleasant issue of antagonizing the labor force, government officials or politicians of the host country are likely to prefer machine- to labor-intensity.

The picture that has emerged from the preceding accounts of Indonesia is that of vulnerable foreign managers and engineers trying to minimize various political and business risks in their unfamiliar environment. According to one study of foreign manufacturing operations in Thailand, foreign subsidiaries became suddenly keen on "automating" and "mechanizing" their operations after the political upheaval in October 1973. Even the firms that had preferred workers to machines before the upheaval, reversed their predispositions after being subject to the militancy of Thai workers.[12]

THE CASE OF A JAPANESE OFFSHORE PLANT IN KOREA: TOTAL ORIENTATION TO EXPORT MARKET

As expected, the cultural (even linguistic) proximity of Korea to Japan reduces a Japanese manager's entry paranoia into a foreign culture. And partly because of the convenient geographical proximity of Korea, many Japanese firms are migrating to Korea to open offshore plants. The electric and electronics industry has been most actively involved in Korea in this offshore production activity.

One leading electronics parts manufacturer of Japan, which shall remain anonymous, opened a branch plant in Korea in early 1970. This venture was incorporated in Korea as a 50-50 joint venture with one of the emerging Korean industrial groups. This move was necessitated by the Japanese parent firm's desire to transfer technologically mature and standard products to a lower-wage country. In 1972, over 30 percent of the workers in the Japanese parent plant near Kyoto were engaged in product-testing and warehousing services for the products shipped in from the Korean plant. In terms of total production units, after two years, 83 percent of the products were produced in Korea. In terms of the varieties of the products involved, however, two-thirds of the combined production of the electronics parts of both the Korean and Japanese plants were still produced in the Japanese plant, indicating that the standardized products which permitted a larger lot-size of production than principal varieties in

Japan had been moved to the Korean plant. In Table 7-6, the shifts which had occurred by the middle of 1972 in the employment and production patterns of the plants in Korea and Japan are summarized. It took the Korean plant 18 months to record a gross productivity of labor comparable to the one maintained in the Japanese plant before 1970.

As shown in Table 7-6, combined production of the electronics parts between the Korean and Japanese plants declined from the peak of 1969 up through 1972. This provided more evidence that the product in question had long entered the maturity stage in its product life cycle before it was moved to Korea. Since the product was a standard mature product whose sales in the world market depended greatly upon price competition, neither the Japanese parent firm nor the Korean parent firm of the joint offshore venture could afford to risk loss of labor productivity while maintaining the strict product quality specifications.

Table 7-6. Changes in Employment, Output and Worker Productivity between Plant in Japan and Plant in Korea

	Production and Output Units in Thousands of Units						
	1969		1970		1971		1972
	I	II	I	II	I	II	I
Production units							
Japan	13,800	13,800	8,400	6,000	3,900	3,000	1,500
Korea	—	—	1,200	1,800	3,600	4,400	5,400
Workers							
Japan[a]							
Plant	1,640	1,640	1,500	725	510	435	240
Subcontractor	600	600	450	400	300	140	100
Korea	—	—	250	300	590	730	880
Output per worker							
Japan	62	62	43	53	48	56	44
Korea	—	—	48	60	61	61	62

Source: Corporate Data of one electronics parts manufacturer in Japan, for 7 semi-annual fiscal periods. One fiscal period is 6 months.

[a]It should be noted that the Japanese plant reduced the number of subcontractor employees as soon as the Korean plant commenced operations in 1970. The workers in the Japanese plant were reassigned to new tasks of producing more technology-intensive products, such as newly developed condensers and diodes.

With the use of a Bayesian estimation of micro-CES production functions—quantitative relations between plant output and such inputs as labor and capital—we can estimate econometrically the micro production functions of the two interrelated plants of the Japanese firm depicted in Table 7-6. This approach enables us to test, with econometric rigor, the question: which of the two plants, each producing a comparable commodity but located in a different country, possesses the more capital-intensive production process.*

The econometric comparisons of the micro production functions of the two plants revealed that both factories recorded increasing returns-to-scale. This means that both plants experienced greater economies of scale as production expanded. More important, however, the Korean plant turned out to be more capital-intensive than the Japanese plant. In addition the estimated value of the elasticity of substitution between labor and capital of the Korean plant was significantly larger than that of the Japanese plant. This means, perhaps, that for the Korean plant, mechanized processes were substituted for labor processes to a greater degree than for the Japanese plant.

The apparent "paradox" that a factory located in a less developed country is more capital-intensive than one in a more developed country can be logically resolved. Given the Japanese parent's purpose in building the offshore site in Korea—having the Korean plant produce standard and mature products that are no longer economical to manufacture in Japan but nevertheless will be sold to worldwide customers under the Japanese brand name—the Japanese parent firm could ill afford to risk allowing the product quality in its branch plant in Korea to slip. The lack of skilled laborers in Korea provided the firm with the incentive to introduce more standardized automatic processes. Thus, relatively unskilled workers could meet the production goals without jeopardizing the quality of the products.

The above events took place during the years when the Japanese yen was steadily appreciating vis-á-vis the Korean won. The equipment and materials exported to the Korean plant from Japan were becoming more and more expensive, relative to the wages needed to pay the Korean workers. And yet, the Japanese parent firm chose to compensate for the lack of experienced and skilled workers in Korea by continuing to ship out more mechanized processes of production.

---

*For the technical explanation of the Bayesian estimation method involved here, see Hiroki Tsurumi and Yoshi Tsurumi, "A Bayesian Estimation of Macro and Micro CES Production Functions," *Journal of Econometrics*, No. 4 (1976).

HOST GOVERNMENTS' PREOCCUPATION WITH NEW MACHINE

In addition to foreign investors' own preferences for "capital intensive" processes, the industrial policies of the host governments often reinforce such preferences. As a rule, the governments of the developing nations severely restrict foreign investors from bringing in second-hand equipment. The developing countries are gripped with nagging suspicion that foreign investors might burden them with obsolete equipment and production processes. As a result, even when foreign investors are able to install familiar and relatively labor-intensive processes with the use of their second-hand equipment, they are motivated through various government inducements to choose relatively newer and more capital-intensive production processes.

In order to arouse public interest in modern industries and manufacturing operations, the governments of the developing nations frequently sponsor trade fairs where foreign exporters exhibit varieties of "modern" equipment and gadgetry. Often, the selection of such equipment for public exhibition is left completely to the foreign participants in the fairs. These participants seldom bring in the equipment most appropriate for the economic and cultural settings of the host nations. The prospective investors are conscious of their competition with other foreign participants. They are aware of the public and government officials of the host nations who equate dazzle with technological competence. Accordingly, the demonstration pieces at the trade fairs tend to be too new and too modern to permit economical adaptation in the developing nations.

Moreover, from Taiwan to Korea to Singapore, the governments are eagerly professing that they no longer welcome "labor-intensive" industries. Their public stand is that only "capital-" and "technology-" intensive industries are welcome. Meanwhile, the general wage levels of these developing countries are rising at a rate of ten to fifteen percent a year, rendering the "human sea" approach to production less and less economical. Japanese and other foreign investors suspect that more developing nations in Asia, and elsewhere, will soon be following the lead set by Taiwan, Korea and Singapore.

There is, though, much room for improvement in the decision-making processes of Japanese investors selecting manufacturing technologies for their subsidiaries in developing countries. As shown in Table 7-5, once the entry decision was made by the top echelon of the Japanese management, the remaining tasks of selecting manufacturing technologies were often delegated to middle management and to the engineers. Often, major business risks are entailed in adapting domestically familiar technologies to the economic and political environments of the developing nations. Only the top management of an investing firm can make the strategic decisions, such as what technological and managerial resources of the firm would be appropriate for the manufacturing operations abroad.

Presently, none of the Japanese investing firms that I studied has revised its decision-making processes so as to involve the top management echelon in selecting technologies for their overseas subsidiaries. Nor did I find that the top management of Japanese investing firms has been adequately sensitized to the technological and employment needs of the developing countries.

JAPANESE EFFORTS TO TRANSFER PROCESS-RELATED TECHNOLOGIES ABROAD

We have observed that Japanese technologies are historically the products of the cultural and economic setting of Japan. In order for Japanese firms to transfer their process-related technologies abroad, therefore, they are confronted with the task of exporting their institutional "atmosphere" to the environment of the host countries. Instinctively, Japanese firms have thus far evolved a number of programs by which the transfer of technologies related to Japanese corporate culture has been attempted.

In realizing that such culture-bound technologies as Japanese production processes can only be successfully transferred into different cultures by persons thoroughly familiar with the specific corporate culture and production process, Japanese firms have frequently insisted on having their own Japanese managers assume the overall responsibility for production operations abroad. I found through my own field investigations that when Japanese firms do not obtain this arrangement, they have invariably placed one of their own men in an official position as second in command. Informally, this man will be the one running the plant. After all, an individual's selection of technology and machine is often more of "cultural" than a "scientific" or "engineering" matter. This explains why local nationals trained in Germany would prefer German machines, just as their competitors trained in Japan prefer Japanese machines.[13]

The preceding observations are supported by Table 7-7. Of 628 Japanese manufacturing subsidiaries abroad polled as of March 31, 1972 by MITI of Japan, about two-thirds still had the position of plant manager filled by a Japanese. Furthermore, the placing of a

Table 7-7. Percentage of Management Positions of Japanese Subsidiaries Abroad Filled by Japanese Expatriates

	Percentage Equity Ownership of Subsidiaries by Japanese Parent Firms					
Management Position held by Japanese	95% and above	94%–51%	50%	49%–25%	less than 25%	Average for all manufacturing subsidiaries, regardless of equity ownership
President	84.8%	71.7%	36.7%	21.6%	6.1%	46.8%
Treasurer-Controller	71.6	61.6	44.5	29.1	6.1	46.7
Sales Manager	58.7	45.9	32.2	23.1	15.2	36.6
Plant Manager	66.7	73.6	58.6	54.3	33.3	62.9
Industrial Relations Manager	39.4	18.2	6.3	5.5	3.0	14.2
Others	6.1	6.9	9.4	14.6	15.2	10.4
Total number of Subsidiaries surveyed	109	159	128	199	33	628

Source: *Wagakuni Kigyo no Kaigai Jigyo Katsudo,* Ministry of International Trade and Industry, Tokyo, October 1973, pp 81-82.

Japanese in the position of plant manager in overseas manufacturing subsidiaries is not too markedly reduced even when the percentage of equity ownership by the Japanese investor declines drastically, or when the percentage of Japanese in other management positions declines tremendously.

The MITI survey of March 1972 revealed that, on the average, a typical Japanese subsidiary abroad recorded 180 employees, and that most typically, of these, seven to eight would be Japanese expatriates permanently stationed in the subsidiary. During my own field investigations, I also ascertained that regardless of the employment level of the Japanese subsidiary, there were customarily six to eight Japanese managers and engineers stationed in each plant. Rarely did I observe the number of Japanese managers to be fewer than three.

Table 7-8 summarizes the observations I made during the first quarter of 1973 of 42 Japanese manufacturing subsidiaries in Indonesia. One should note that even when the employment size changes from less than 100 to over 400, the average number of Japanese expatriates found does not change. Even the smallest-scale operations with fewer than 100 employees were found to have six Japanese. And I might add that the Japanese subsidiaries located in

Table 7-8. Average Number of Japanese Expatriates per Manufacturing Subsidiary (As of the First Quarter of 1973)

Firm Scale	No. of Employees	Average Number of Japanese Expatriates to nearest whole number	
		All Categories	Engineers & Technicians[b]
1	100 or less	6	3
2	101-200	5	3
3	201-400	6	4
4	401-800	8	6
5	801-1000+	25[a]	8[a]
(Sample size = 42 firms)			

[a]This jump in the average number of Japanese managers and engineers is strongly influenced by the presence of integrated textile mills of larger scale than mere weaving and dyeing operations.

[b]Technicians and instructors of machine operators are included in this category.

other countries in Asia showed similar patterns to those observed in Indonesia.

In order to identify some factors other than the mere employment size of the subsidiary that might determine more significantly the number of Japanese managers in Japanese manufacturing subsidiaries, a further attempt was made in Indonesia to isolate the type of product- and process-technologies used by the manufacturing subsidiaries as a possible basis for estimating the number of Japanese expatriates likely to be found. In Table 7-9 the results of my field investigations in Indonesia are presented.

In Table 7-9, the products involved are classified into two categories on the basis of *prima facie* evidence of the level of complexity of manufacturing technologies required for successful production. Integrated textile mills are eliminated from the sample because these operations are undoubtedly far ahead of other groups of products produced in Indonesia in terms of technological complexity. Even when such obviously biased samples are eliminated, it is still apparent that a slight difference in the degree of complexity in technology affects the number of Japanese expatriates present in the manufacturing subsidiary. This reflects the nature of Japan's technological development at home, founded on the principles of high specialization and a high degree of division of labor. Thus, the narrower the breadth of technology possessed by a single person, in Japan or overseas, the greater the number of the persons required for a given production operations.

Accordingly, Japanese firms would send in a "task force" to operate their manufacturing subsidiaries abroad. This task force, often comprised of seven to eight Japanese, included the plant manager plus the other skilled technicians who act as "instructors" in setting the work pace for local production workers. During the start-up period of new plants the team is often supported by frequent "visiting assistants" from Japanese plants who help to operate and service the key equipment.

The task force approach, necessitated by the extreme form of work-specialization practiced by Japanese engineers, managers and workers, also fulfills two more "human" needs among the Japanese expatriates. Considering the fact that the seniority-conscious firms appoint Japanese usually in their 40s and 50s to management positions abroad, the Japanese in these age categories are the same persons who had been actively involved in Japan during the 1940s and the 1950s in improvising and adapting older production processes to the economic settings of that time (namely, lower wages, higher costs of industrial materials and limited availability of substitutable materials). During the 1960s and 1970s, the amassed experience of these

Table 7-9. Number of Japanese Expatriates per Manufacturing Subsidiary by Product Group (As of the First Quarter of 1973)

Product Group[a]	Modal number of the Japanese expatriates (all categories)[b]
I. *Simple Products* Instant noodles, charcoal makers, sawmills, plastic sandals, plastic films and bags, dry batteries, leather products, furniture, cigarette filters, bicycle assembly	2-3
II. *Less Simple Products* Galvanized iron sheets, steel and iron pipes and structures, drugs, cosmetics, diesel engine assembly, fishing nets, monosodium glutamate (MSG), stretch nylon yarns, electronics and electric appliances, modern printing operations	7-8

[a]A more rigorous test of the complexity of manufacturing processes involved can be used, such as the number of production processes involved and the required degree of machine operations, etc. But the field observations of these product groups and of the required degree of product quality control in the process, are adequate for the purposes outlined here.

[b]The difference in this modal value does not significantly change even if a few simpler products in Group II such as assembly of small stationary diesel engines are reclassified into Group I.

Japanese engineers and workers is found to be relevant to production problems encountered by Japanese manufacturing subsidiaries in the developing countries. Unlike the newer generation of post–World War II, these middle-aged Japanese usually find it emotionally intolerable to be left alone in a foreign culture. Thus, they prefer to form a task force whose members can empathize with one another both on and off the job.

More significant, that aspect of Japanese culture which highly praises "man-to-man" instruction is reinforced by the "lifetime employment" system of Japanese firms. This system has long supported Japanese employees as teachers, whereby managerial and technical knowledge is passed on from older to younger, from initiated to uninitiated, and from experienced to inexperienced. The pedagogical method is face-to-face communication emphasizing learning by doing. This cultural predisposition leads naturally to a task force approach in the problems of transferring culture-bound technologies abroad.

Besides, the process-related technologies of Japan can be transferred only through personal contact. Such invisible skills as the knack and feel of a Japanese worker for the handling of his machine or materials are often an indivisible part of the production process. Any attempt at transferring a body of such invisible skills from one cultural setting to another must require face-to-face instruction.

Japan's emphasis on the person-to-person instructional approach is not limited to her manufacturing subsidiaries in the developing nations. For instance, Kikkoman Shoyu Co. Ltd. of Japan, which has been producing organically brewed soy sauce in the U.S. since 1973, has placed 15 Kikkoman employees from Japan in its Wisconsin plant. They have been assigned to work with about 40 American employees recruited locally. Production know-how for the fermenting of organically brewed soy sauce was developed by Kikkoman on the basis of indigenous Japanese techniques held only by Kikkoman personnel from Japan. Therefore, only personal tutoring would permit the transfer of requisite technology from Japan to the U.S. Once a nucleus of American workers masters the techniques, Kikkoman hopes by 1976 to double the production capacity and employment in its Wisconsin plant, without having to increase the number of Japanese stationed there.

The NMB U.S., which we discussed in Chapter 4, has also brought a team of five to six male and female production workers from its parent plant in Karuizawa to its plant in Chatworth, California. They have been strategically mingled with American workers in key operational sections like assembly lines, product quality testing and polishing of parts where manual handling of products was vital for total production. NMB hopes that the American co-workers will learn NMB methods of key manual operations by imitating the pace as well as the procedures of the Japanese workers placed among them.

In addition to the typical presence of Japanese "task forces" in overseas subsidiaries, there are six practices I have observed as the most frequently utilized methods of Japanese transfer of technology abroad. Although the degree of emphasis on each of these six practices varies from one firm to the other, and from one product to another, it is rather striking, indeed, to see that all six are employed by each of the 75 Japanese parent firms operating manufacturing subsidiaries abroad during my fieldwork from 1972 to 1974 in Korea, Hongkong, Taiwan, Thailand, Singapore, Malaysia, Indonesia, Germany, Italy, Canada and the U.S.

Creation of Little Japan

Little change is made in the production procedures in the transfer from the Japanese source (parent plant) to the overseas plant(s). Often, even the color and design of worker uniforms in the overseas plants are the same as those in their parent plants in Japan. Employees' benefits, including a company subsidized cafeteria and employees' recreational programs, are transplanted almost as is. The Japanese plant managers invariably emphasize that these institutional arrangements are essential for creating the "right" atmosphere conducive to employees' dedication to their production work.

New Plant

Where possible, Japanese manufacturers purposely avoid using old plant facilities which might be available in the developing countries. They even prefer a local partner who has no prior experience in manufacturing the given product. The Japanese investors often deliberately choose a plant location away from the areas where clusters of indigenous craft shops and small plants have developed a native working habit alien to "Japanese" methods. Japanese firms argue that it is easier for them to transfer their own institution-related technologies into an "unspoiled" environment than into a "spoiled" one.

As shown in Table 7-10, of 511 manufacturing subsidiaries that large Japanese firms established during the years 1956-1970, 432 of them or about 85 percent, were "newly formed" by the investors. And this dominance of newly formed subsidiaries had not changed from pre-1956 to the years 1968-1970.

Table 7-10. Method of Entry of Japanese Manufacturing Subsidiaries Abroad

	Date of Entry						
Method of Entry	Pre-1956	1956-58	1959-61	1962-64	1965-67	1968-70	Total
Newly Formed	31	13	41	74	96	177	432
Merger	1	0	0	0	1	0	2
Acquired	3	1	3	16	16	29	68
Others	6	0	3	0	0	0	9
Total Number of Subsidiaries	41	14	47	90	113	206	511
Ratio of Newly Formed to Total Subsidiaries	75.6%	92.9%	87.2%	82.2%	85.0%	85.9%	84.5%

Source: Multinational Enterprise Project, Harvard Business School.

Foreign Trainees

Japanese firms invite a group of foreign nationals to their plants back home for in-plant training. The in-plant training period varies from three to twelve months. During that time, the foreign trainees are assigned to the same operations and equipment that they will be working on when they are sent back to their own subsidiaries. Most typically, the invitational "tour of duty" is not limited to foreign nationals designated to become plant supervisors and engineers. A nucleus of production workers is, as a rule, included in the group. These worker-trainees are expected to act as pace-setters in their own plants.* Japanese firms are more than willing to invest time and money in exposing their foreign workers to the in-plant operations and production culture of the Japanese parent firms.

Japanese and Foreign Workers

In order to help local nationals become familiar with the plant operations and equipment, Japanese managers and skilled workers sent to manufacturing subsidiaries abroad try to involve as many

---

*The NMB Co. of Japan brought about 200 male and female workers from Singapore to its plant in Karuizawa, Japan for twelve months of in-plant training. In this way, when NMB completed its plant construction in Singapore in 1973, approximately one-half of its production workers in the subsidiary had not only become familiar with the production methods being transferred from Japan but also had been exposed to the attitudes and environments of Japanese NMB workers.

local employees as possible in the installing and testing the equipment shipped in from Japan. In this way, a group of workers is taught the routine maintenance of machinery as well as its operation. These workers, both male and female, are often given the official status of "instructor-worker" among the other locally recruited workers. This new status is made recognizable, say, by a difference in the color of their uniform cap. These practices are again straightforward replicas of in-plant practice in the home country.

Foreign Workers' Efficiency

Prior to their initial entry into a developing nation, Japanese manufacturing firms have worked out their expectations for individual worker efficiency for various countries. Interestingly, these estimates are closely and positively related to the Japanese engineers' subjective feelings of cultural proximity to the host country. The closer they feel to the host country, the less will they discount performance records of Japanese workers in Japan in arriving at an estimate for local workers.

For example, a common rule-of-thumb which Japanese plant engineers often used to measure the Indonesian worker's "efficiency" prior to their entry into Indonesia, is that Indonesians will accomplish 50-60 percent of the work done by their Japanese, Taiwanese, Korean or Singapore counterparts in the same amount of time, for simple man-and-machine labor, or simple manual work. Compared with their Thai counterparts, Indonesian recruits will be gauged at 70-80 percent of the former efficiency. The East Asian cultural sphere encircling Japan, Taiwan, Korea and Singapore permits Japanese engineers to generalize in gauging worker performance: the Thai's efficiency is assumed higher than that of the Indonesian merely because Japanese investors have for some time been involved in manufacturing operations in Thailand.

An assumption like this will initially lead the Japanese plant engineers to assign more Indonesian workers per piece of equipment or operation than is usual in other countries. However, after twelve to eighteen months of work experience, and closely supervised training, an Indonesian worker's efficiency is said to reach an average of 80-90 percent of the capacity of Japanese, Korean or Singapore workers (still for simple and manual operations). This means that after twelve to eighteen months, the "learning effect" can be substantially exploited in Indonesia.

However, the production records of Japanese manufacturing subsidiaries in all areas of Asia show that it usually will take from twelve to eighteen months in any case before the work pace and output of the Japanese plants begin to produce the anticipated results. This production lead-time appears to be universally experienced by Japanese investors when the products in question possess the technical complexity at least of the Group II type shown in Table 7-9. This may be due to the time it takes to transfer abroad such abstract and institution-related technologies as cost control, product quality control, inventory management and production scheduling. All of these methods are necessary for successful production operations.*

Task Force Approach
It has been stressed that the Japanese firms' preference for a "task force approach" in the staffing of their overseas manufacturing subsidiaries has been necessitated by the idiosyncrasies of Japanese technologies. The complement to this form of international transfer of technology is always the pattern of communication between Japanese plants and their branch plants abroad. This is particularly so when the technologies to be transferred are available only in the many individuals of the parent firm, each of whom has absorbed through personal contact both the knowledge and the atmosphere of the particular corporate culture of his firm.

In other words, the styles and procedures of decision-making in Japanese parent firms often require that key posts in their overseas subsidiaries be held by persons who have grown thoroughly familiar with the informal and often implied communication patterns peculiar to each specific firm.[14] Hence, Japanese firms' preference for a "task force approach" in their overseas subsidiaries is reinforced or even necessitated by the communication patterns among Japanese parents and their overseas offspring.

Japanese firms have evolved the so-called "bottom-up" procedure of *Ringistyle* decision-making in which the middle management often initiates decision proposals and seeks the approval of other middle managers and upper echelons of management. This process requires not only vertical, but also lateral communication among multiple echelons of corporate organization. This means that for any key decision concerning, say, the production operations of an overseas subsidiary, not only the production manager, but also the managers

---

*During my field investigations of Japanese plants abroad, I came across many instances in which product quality and often production itself suffered drastically when a team of expatriate Japanese quality-control experts left for Japan after teaching in-plant workers for only three to five months. Often, they had to be called back in and had to be stationed for longer than one year before local trainees could be left on their own.

of finance, sales and all other functions need to keep in touch with their counterparts at the headquarters offices and plants in Japan.

In the milieu of Japanese corporate culture, any requests and messages from outposts such as overseas subsidiaries tend to be processed and compiled in accordance with the amounts of implicit credits and favors the overseas managers have in the past built up with the key persons in the Japanese parent firm who will receive and screen these messages. Unless these message screeners see to it that all bases have been properly touched and persuaded to accommodate requests from their overseas subsidiaries, the subsidiaries may remain helpless.

In an organic organization such as a Japanese corporate system, no key decision will be made without taking pains to let all the relevant subunits within the firm readjust themselves adequately to any waves made at home through requests from overseas subsidiaries. The more sympathetic the recipients of overseas requests are to problems peculiar to their overseas subsidiaries, the more receptive they will be to requests from abroad. This means that all the managers of the overseas subsidiaries, regardless of their functions, need to keep their counterparts in Japan informed of business developments. The communications networks are too fine to be handled by any single overseas representative, such as the president of the overseas subsidiary.

During the fieldwork which I conducted among the overseas manufacturing subsidiaries of Japan in 1972 and again in 1973, I kept running into middle management members who regularly wrote "personal" reports to "their men" back home. These reports were designed to substitute for the intimate face to face communication relied upon at home. The personal nature of these reports was such that drafting them could not possibly have been assigned even to other Japanese expatriates from the same corporation.

Without an intuitive feel for *what* to tell *whom*, and *when*—which can only be developed by an intense sharing of corporate values and experience—the delicate, intimate trading of information and favors through letters would have been impossible for the overseas subsidiaries. Therefore, for the time being, unless the present multilateral base-touching among individuals in Japan and abroad is changed radically, Japanese subsidiaries abroad will not be able to bring even the most able local nationals into meaningful communication roles with their headquarter offices and plants back in Japan.

Thus far, many Japanese firms have resisted a drastic change in the communication patterns between headquarters and overseas subsidiaries, mainly because effective native communicators, able to serve as "gatekeepers" between Japan and overseas, have not yet been developed.*

---

*The vital role of "gatekeeper" has been identified in non-Japanese corporate culture as well. In the U.S., engineers and scientists who are assigned to separate R&D tasks but who find it necessary to maintain active "trading" of information and favors among various groups are found to evolve their own "gatekeepers." See, for example, Thomas Allen, "Roles in Technical Communication Networks," in Nelson and Pollock, eds., Communication among Scientists and Engineers (Lexington, Mass.: D.C. Heath & Co., 1970), pp. 191-208.

 Chapter Eight

The Quest for Majority Ownership

A popular myth still prevails among several critics of multi-nationals concerning the apparent over-propensity of Japanese firms to settle for non-controlling ownership of their joint manufacturing ventures abroad. Since local participation in foreign investment is politically popular with host governments, the Japanese tend to gain favor by sharing otherwise unpopular foreign investments. Does such a myth contain an element of truth? Will Japanese joint ventures abroad escape future conflicts and stresses that might well arise between Japanese and local partners?

OWNERSHIP OF JAPANESE SUBSIDIARIES

Table 8-1 shows the subsidiary ownership patterns of 2749 Japanese overseas subsidiaries that I found operating as of the end of 1972. These subsidiaries had been established by both large and small parent firms. Of the 2749 subsidiaries, 1605—about 58 percent—recorded Japanese parents as the majority owners.

Regional differences in subsidiary ownership patterns were related to the major functions of the subsidiaries. Since over two-thirds of the subsidiaries in North America and Europe were sales subsidiaries, majority ownership by Japanese parent firms predominated in these areas. In contrast, in Asia, where about 80 percent of the Japanese subsidiaries were engaged in manufacturing, in Latin America, where 65 percent of the subsidiaries were engaged in manufacturing, and in the Middle East and Africa, and the British Dominions and Oceania, where 72 percent and fifty percent, respectively, of the subsidiaries

Table 8-1. Japanese Parent Firms' Ownership Profile of Overseas Subsidiaries by Invested Area As of the End of 1972

Invested Area	Parent's Ownership of Subsidiaries					No. of Subsidiaries
	Over 51%	50%	49-26%	25-11%	below 10%	
Asia	41%	17%	32%	7%	3%	1,339
Canada/U.S.	87	6	3	3	1	614
Europe	74	11	9	4	2	275
Latin America	68	11	14	4	3	267
Middle East and Africa	41	17	22	17	3	108
British Dominions and Oceania	58	17	14	9	3	146
No. of Subsidiaries	1,605	362	546	162	74	2,749

Source: Compiled on the basis of field research in and outside Japan, and on the basis of *Kigyōbetsu Kaigai Tōshi of 1972* Keizai Chosa Kyokai, Tokyo, 1973.

were engaged in manufacturing, the Japanese have tended to settle for non-controlling ownership.

This tendency is also supported by Table 8-2. The table indicates the percentage of ownership of manufacturing subsidiaries abroad by the investing parent according to the size of the investing parent (small, medium or large), and also according to whether the specific subsidiaries were set up by the investing parent alone or through joint efforts with other Japanese investing partners. In all cases, Japanese firms in the main settled for non-controlling ownership. This pattern did not change even when Japanese investors went abroad alone, and was little affected by the size of the parent firm.

This ownership pattern did not change, even over time, from those subsidiaries established prior to 1955 to those set up early in the 1970s. This ownership pattern has indeed come to be a distinguishing characteristic of Japanese manufacturing subsidiaries abroad as opposed to those established by U.S.- and Europe-based multinational firms. A comparison of Japanese ownership profiles with those of other nation-based overseas manufacturing firms is shown in Table 8-3.

The entering Japanese firms generally commenced a limited scale of simple manufacturing in a joint venture with a local partner who had formerly been the Japanese firm's import agent. For example, I found in Indonesia that about 83 percent of the Japanese manufacturing subsidiaries operating during the first quarter of 1973 had as

Table 8-2. Ownership Profile of Japanese Manufacturing Subsidiaries Abroad by Size of Parent Firm As of the End of 1972

		\multicolumn{5}{c}{Parent's Ownership of Manufacturing Subsidiaries}	
Investing Firm		Over 51%	50%	49-26%	25-11%	Below 10%	No. of Subsidiaries
Large	Alone	44%	17%	26%	9%	4%	270
	Group	41	14	31	11	3	307
Medium	Alone	29	26	34	11	—	38
	Group	50	15	6	5	—	20
Small	Alone	42	24	29	3	2	289
	Group	40	27	25	5	3	162
For all Firms		42	20	28	7	3	1,086

Source: Compiled on the basis of field research in and outside Japan, and on the basis of *Kigyōbetsu Kaigai Tōshi of 1972* Keizai Chosa Kyokai, Tokyo, 1973.

Table 8-3. Ownership of Overseas Manufacturing Subsidiaries by Nationality of Largest Parent Firms[1] As of January 1, 1971[2]

Parent's Nationality	\multicolumn{5}{c}{Parent's Ownership of Subsidiaires}				
	95-100%	94-51%	50%	49-26%	25-5%
France	38%	23%	9%	18%	12%
W. Germany	56	22	9	10	5
Italy	65	13	5	12	4
Belgium Luxembourg	52	21	6	10	13
Netherlands	65	18	7	7	2
Sweden	80	9	4	5	3
Switzerland	62	25	6	5	3
Canada	68	12	7	10	3
Japan	27	8	7	25	33
United Kingdom	51	15	14	11	9
Average of Non-U.S. Firms	53	18	7	12	10
U.S. Firms[2]	71	\multicolumn{2}{c}{20}		9	

1. "Largest" parent firms are defined as those investing firms recorded in *Fortune*'s list of 500 Largest Firms in the U.S. in 1967 and *Fortune*'s 200 Largest non-U.S. Firms in 1970.
2. The U.S. data are as of January 1, 1968.

Source: The Data Bank of the Multinational Enterprise Project, the Harvard Business School.

their local partners either former import agents or indigenous manufacturers who had formerly imported semi-processed products from Japan. Over one-half of the Japanese manufacturing subsidiaries which were not directly related to local government-owned business had their former import agent as their local partner. Similar patterns were observed through East and Southeast Asia and Latin America.

Rather than insisting on majority ownership of a subsidiary that might well fail, the Japanese parent investor often spread the risks by involving other Japanese partners and more than one local partner in the venture. The local market orientation of the Japanese manufacturing subsidiaries, which did not insist on bringing sophisticated technologies into the host countries, gave the local partner greater bargaining strength in demanding a sizeable, even majority, ownership. Even when the local partners did not provide their share of capital, either in kind (plant sites, etc.) or in cash, the Japanese parent firms would still extend loans to them. In the case of Japanese investments in Indonesia over one-third of the Japanese manufacturing subsidiaries had loaned money to their local partners with which the latter paid for their share of the joint venture.[1]

Elsewhere in Asia, similar practices by Japanese investing parents were rather widespread and well accepted by local partners. Little did Japanese investors realize then, however, that such expedient forms of entry into host countries would later come to haunt them, starting from the mid-1970s on.

JOINT VENTURES ABROAD OF JAPANESE MANUFACTURING FIRMS

The results of my own questionnaire survey among Japanese parent firms clarified the perceptions of Japanese investors regarding their joint ventures abroad. The relevant question and responding firms' answers regarding their joint venture partners are reproduced in Table 8-4.

The degree of importance that responding firms placed on each contribution expected from their local partner varied little with the size of the parent firm. The most common expectation Japanese firms had of their local partners—general management skills—can be summarized as the ability of local partners to supply sales personnel and knowledge of local customs, manners and political situations. It should be added that this ranking order also varies little from one industry group to another.

Compared with large-sized firms, small- to medium-sized firms expected a great deal more from their local partners in terms of the

Table 8-4.

Question:	In selecting a foreign (local) partner of your joint venture abroad, how important were the following seven contributions expected from such local partners?

	Japanese Parent Firms Normalized Score*	
Expected Contributions from Local Partner	Small- to Medium-sized Firms	Large-sized Firms
a. General managers and general management skills	1.129 (1)	0.930 (1)
b. Capital funds	0.054 (5)	-0.514 (5)
c. Ability to supply sales personnel	0.679 (2)	0.250 (3)
d. Ability to distribute local imports from Japan	-0.367 (6)	-0.098 (4)
e. Joint venture made condition for local sales of products of subsidiary (speed of entry)	-1.611 (7)	-0.735 (7)
f. Knowledge of local customs and political situations	0.373 (3)	0.584 (2)
g. Ability to procure necessary raw and input materials locally	0.222 (4)	-0.515 (5)
No. or Respondents	40	82

*The numbers in parentheses indicate the descending order of the relative importance of each contribution expected from local partners.

latter's ability to supply capital, sales personnel and necessary input materials that were available locally. Large-sized firms counted more significantly on their local partners' ability to distribute additional goods imported from Japan, and also placed relatively greater importance than the smaller firms on their partners' knowledge of local customs, manners and political situations.

In-depth interviews with the responding firms indicated that large-sized firms of Japan were more politically sensitive about their public visibility in the host countries than small- to medium-sized firms. This reflected the political and economic realities of fall 1972 in Japan and abroad (the date of the questionnaire survey), when Japanese mass media and government agencies like MITI were sounding increasingly alarmed over the "behaviors of Japanese investors abroad." In the midst of such an atmosphere in Japan, large-sized firms were not only already more politically vulnerable than smaller ones, but were also more concerned with any political damage that might tarnish their worldwide image, through the mishandling of politically sensitive matters anywhere abroad in the course of their more abundant overseas expansion.

The expectations of Japanese investors concerning their local partners' contributions do not differ greatly from those of American investors except on one point. Stopford and Wells found that American investors mentioned "speed of entry" as the second most important contribution expected from the local partners of their joint ventures.* Local partners' "general knowledge of local economy, politics and customs" was the most important contribution that American firms expected from their joint venture partners.

In contrast, neither small- to medium-sized firms nor large-sized firms of Japan rated Contribution (e), "speed of entry" (where a joint venture is the entry condition for local sales of products involved) significantly high. Further interviews with randomly selected respondents revealed that Japanese firms, large or small, perceived the joint venture with local partners as a vehicle for sharing political and economic risks. This meant that even when joint ventures were not mandatory for entry into a host country, Japanese investors actively chose them nonetheless as their initial entry format.

EMERGING STRESSES BETWEEN LOCAL PARTNERS AND JAPANESE INVESTORS

It is widely assumed by host governments of both developed and underdeveloped countries that local equity participation not only assures local influence in the management of the joint venture, but also facilitates local absorption of the manufacturing skills and managerial talents of the multinational partners.[2] This belief is so widespread among government planners and economists that one developing country after another has now come to demand local equity participation or even controlling ownership in both new and existing foreign investments.

The notion that the joint venture with local equity holders— Indonesian, Korean or Mexican as the case may be—makes the subsidiary more "local" than the fully-owned subsidiary of foreign parents presupposes the active involvement of local partners in the

---

*Stopford and Wells, *Managing the Multinational Enterprise* (New York: Basic Books, 1972) p. 103.

key decision-making processes and the management of the joint ventures.

In light of the fact that Japanese investors have preferred joint ventures in order to share start-up risks with local partners, one might expect that local partners of Japanese manufacturing subsidiaries would be substantially involved in and consulted on the management of the joint ventures, especially in the developing nations. However, today in Japanese and other foreign investments in Asia, some notable exceptions notwithstanding, few local partners of the foreign subsidiaries are generally involved in the key decision-making processes or strategic decisions of the joint ventures.

In the day-to-day operations of the joint ventures, local partners are expected to help foreign managers negotiate with various levels of the host governments and with the local distributors of their products. But local partners are rarely involved in the strategic process of selecting new products and new markets for the joint ventures.

The following comments made in March 1973 by the presidents of two European subsidiaries in Indonesia describe the situations prevalent during the years 1971-1974 elsewhere in Asia.[3] And similar comments are increasingly being repeated by Japanese investors describing the notable absence of their local partners' influence in strategy formulations:

President A (pharmaceutical firm)
... He (the Indonesian partner) is given the major job of distributing our products as our distributor-agent. He forwarded hardly any cash when he thought the manufacturing subsidiary was not going to pay dividends for at least three years. Meanwhile he is happy to make substantial wholesale commissions as our distributor...

President B (electrical appliance firm)
... The expansion of this joint venture is determined by our parent company. Changes in the line of products of this firm or developments of export markets are beyond my responsibility. I don't think that the increase in legal ownership by local partners, even to a controlling percentage, would make much difference so long as this firm depends on our parent firm for new products...

Especially after 1971-1972, Japanese manufacturing firms began regrouping their manufacturing subsidiaries which were atomistically scattered throughout Asia and Latin America. From 1972 to 1974 more and more Japanese firms were found to be linking up previously disjointed operations of overseas subsidiaries. The case of offshore production bases built by Japanese manufacturing firms was but one extreme form of the close links required between Japanese parents plants at home and their branch plants abroad.

With such substantive changes in the attitudes of Japanese investing firms toward the roles of their manufacturing subsidiaries abroad, their present or previous preferences for joint ventures are undergoing substantive changes as well. For example, in the case of four leading firms producing electric and electronics appliances, Hitachi, Toshiba, Matsushita and Sanyo, as of 1973, they owned a total of 66 manufacturing subsidiaries abroad. Twenty-one of these 66 firms were offshore production bases whose main function was to supply their respective parent firms with products destined for export markets including those of Japan. The average percentage of ownership of these offshore manufacturing subsidiaries by the parent firm was, as shown below, significantly greater than that of the non-offshire subsidiaries. This reflected a favorable attitude by developing nations toward offshore production bases of foreign firms. In fact, eleven of the twenty-one offshore manufacturing subsidiaries were fully owned by Japanese parent firms. And the more recent the date of their establishment, the greater was the Japanese parent firms' propensity to set up fully-owned manufacturing subsidiaries abroad.

The host countries of these offshore manufacturing bases oriented to export markets, permitted Japanese investing firms to own fully their respective subsidiaries. But from the Japanese investors' point of view, why was it necessary to insist on majority ownership of their offshore manufacturing bases? Their expressed reasons for desiring majority ownership illuminate the fundamental shift in attitude of Japanese investing firms toward joint ventures abroad, from their earlier attitude concerning such entry into risky and uncertain markets abroad.

Table 8-5. Equity Ownership of Off-shore and Non-offshore Subsidiaries

	Offshore Subsidiaries	Non-offshore Subsidiaries
Average Percentage Ownership of a Subsidiary Held by Japanese Parent Firm	80%[1]	44%
No. of Subsidiaries	21	45

N.B. [1] The Chai-square test of this value shows that it is significantly greater than the average of the percentage ownership of the non-offshore subsidiaries.

THE QUEST FOR MAJORITY OWNERSHIP

Japanese investments in Indonesia provide a clue to the preceding question. Indonesia began to attract Japanese manufacturing operations mainly after 1970. Indonesia represented Japan's latest entry efforts in terms of the chronology of overseas investments. By 1973, when Japanese direct investments in Indonesia showed a marked increase not only in number but also in breadth of products, Japanese investing firms were already awakening to the strategy of linking their manufacturing operations in Indonesia with manufacturing subsidiaries elsewhere.

Of eighty-seven Japanese manufacturing subsidiaries that I found operating effectively in Indonesia during the first quarter of 1973, eighty had a Japanese partner(s) owning over 51 percent of equity interest. The ownership of five subsidiaries was split 50–50 between Japanese and Indonesian partners. The remaining two subsidiaries had Japanese partners owning only 49 percent of equity trust. In fact, over two-thirds of the subsidiaries had Japanese partners owning over 80 percent of equity interest. This trend, where over 90 percent of the Japanese investors insisted on the majority ownership of their manufacturing subsidiaries in Indonesia, did not change either during the balance of 1973 or thereafter.

The products involved covered diverse manufactures. The ownership patterns of Japanese manufacturing subsidiaries in Indonesia (especially in the 1970s), were not specifically related to any one group of products or firms, but were significantly related to the change in Japanese investor's attitudes toward overseas manufacturing operations.

The questionnaire survey that I conducted during the fall of 1972 among various sized Japanese parent firms, uncovered such changes in attitude toward ownership of manufacturing subsidiaries abroad as has been alluded to. The results are shown in Table 8-6.

Generally speaking, Reasons (a) and (b), to desire the *de jure* controlling ownership of their subsidiaries abroad, loomed as strategically important considerations for both small- and large-sized Japanese firms. The firms that were surveyed during the fall of 1972 distinctly perceived their legal control over their subsidiaries as critically important if they were to act as the strategic organizers of their multinational marketing and manufacturing activities located (or to be located) outside Japan. When planning both the product and production schedules of their joint ventures abroad, they did not

Table 8-6.

Question:	When you desire to own over 51 percent of the equity of your overseas subsidiaries, how important are the following six reasons?

	Japanese Parent Firm's Normalized Score*	
Reasons	Small- to Medium-sized Firms	Large-sized Firms
a. Worldwide consistency of sales policies	1.124 (1)	1.284 (2)
b. Parent's choice of production schedules and products of overseas subsidiaries	0.830 (3)	1.447 (1)
c. Uncertainty of local customs and greater distance from Japan	0.908 (2)	-1.144 (6)
d. Avoidance of confusion of export markets	0.717 (4)	-0.781 (5)
e. Maintenance of secrecy of production processes and sales strategies	0.005 (5)	-0.331 (3)
f. Dividends from subsidiaries	-0.362 (6)	-0.494 (4)
No. of respondents	40	82

*The numbers in parentheses indicate the descending order of the relative importance of each reason for the two groups of Japanese parent firms.

wish to be constrained by demands of local partners. Such attitudes toward joint ventures were different in tone and substance from the earlier disposition toward joint ventures as an expedient means of sharing operational risks with local partners.

Both small-, medium-, and large-sized firms placed rather low expectations on the dividends received from their subsidiaries abroad. Additional interviews with the responding firms revealed that Japanese investing firms preferred and exercised other means of repatriating "profits" from their overseas subsidiaries. One method was the use of technical and management fees, or increased sales of goods and services from parent plants in Japan to their overseas plants. Furthermore, at the time of these interviews (fall 1972), Japanese firms were more preoccupied with expanding the networks of their overseas subsidiaries than with collecting immediate inflows of dividends from them. As a result, the importance of dividends was not a major consideration.

Large-sized firms, on the contrary, considered Reasons (e) and (f)—maintenance of secrecy of production processes and sales strategies, and dividends—as far more important factors in seeking the majority ownership of their overseas subsidiaries. Reason (c), the reduction of communication problems between themselves and subsidiaries arising from their unfamiliarity with local customs, as well as Reason (d), the avoidance of confusion occurring in their demarcations of export markets assigned to plants in Japan and abroad, were of lesser importance.

Further interviews with the respondents revealed the following scenario as the most plausible explanation for the expressed differences in attitudes toward joint ventures between large-sized and small- to medium-sized firms. By fall of 1972 large firms had already trained a number of individuals in the management and operation of subsidiaries abroad. Thus, they were less frightened by the prospects of expanding their operations into unfamiliar foreign environments. On the other hand, smaller firms whose overseas operations had been confined to a few limited-scale operations in one or two countries in Asia, were genuinely concerned about operating in unfamiliar territories. This anxiety and fear often led them to assume that with the majority ownership of their overseas subsidiaries, they would somehow withstand the initial shocks of initiation into a new local environment without losing their effective control.

Small- to medium-sized firms, however, knew that their products and processes were not secretive, but were imitable eventually by foreign partners. Consequently, they resigned themselves to the fact that they could not indefinitely contain the leakage of their products and processes. They did, however, believe that with increased leakage to foreign producers and partners, they would have to protect their own export market territories from unwelcomed competitors. These small-sized Japanese parents firms tended to count on the legal control of their subsidiaries as a means of preventing foreign subsidiaries from raiding their export territories. On the other hand, large firms, with their wider range of product lines, used product differentiation in their respective production bases inside and outside of Japan in order to protect their export markets.

In the future, Japanese multinational firms, like their U.S.-based counterparts, will also attempt to secure, where and when permitted, effective control of their overseas subsidiaries. Long gone are the days when Japanese firms preferred positions of minority owners, while going through trial and error practices of managing their overseas ventures.

Still in 1974, Japanese manufacturing firms, large and small, were practically all single-industry operators whose lines of products rarely involved more than one industry group, as defined by the two-digit classification of the SIC (Standard Industrial Classification). Accordingly, their new preference for majority (even 100% ownership) of their overseas subsidiaries resembles similar motives that U.S.-based multinational firms with single-industry lines of products have expressed in order to maintain uniform worldwide sales strategies, to avoid confusion in export market demarcations, and to regulate the production plans and products of overseas manufacturing subsidiaries.[4]

CONFLICTS INVOLVED IN THE JOINT VENTURE

A total of 132 firms ranging from large- to small-sized (as measured by the respondent's paid-in capital as of fall 1972), rated the following ten plausible sources of conflicts with the foreign partners of their joint ventures. Unlike the results of earlier questions that were analyzed in this chapter, the responses of the 132 firms to each of these ten sources of conflicts were remarkably the same from the largest to the smallest firms. They collectively produced the responses shown in Table 8-7. The sources of conflicts are arranged in a descending order from that of "most frequently experienced" to that of "least frequently experienced."

Table 8-7.

Question: Of the requests that you received from the foreign partners of your joint ventures abroad, and of the conflicts that you encountered from your foreign partners, how serious and frequent were the following ten sources of conflicts?

Conflicts of Interest	Means of Indicated Score*
1. Transfer prices of parts and semi-processed materials shipped from Japanese parent to joint ventures.	4.08
2. Timing and extent of expansion of equity of joint ventures.	3.18
3. Transfer prices of products produced by joint ventures and shipped to Japanese parent.	3.03
4. Dividend policy.	2.97
5. Quantity of products produced by joint ventures.	2.92
6. Selection of products to be produced by joint ventures.	2.90
7. Specifications of quality of products produced by joint ventures.	2.85
8. Demarcation of export markets of joint ventures and direct shipments of exports from joint ventures.	2.69
9. Uses of trademarks and brand names.	2.49
10. Budget of sales promotions of joint ventures.	1.73

*The scoring scale is from "6" (most frequent and serious) to "0" (least serious).

It should be noted that two of the three conflicts considered to be "above average," are related to transfer pricing decisions of products flowing between Japanese parent firms and their subsidiaries abroad. The second most serious conflict, which Japanese firms had already experienced by the fall of 1972, concerned the timing and extent of capital expansion of their joint ventures. In particular, Japanese parent firms often encountered stiff resistance from their foreign partners when they sought to finance the expansion of their joint ventures by increasing their equity bases.

The multinational strategies effected by Japanese firms from 1972 to 1974 required that they oversee and police the cross-hauling of goods and services between their parent plants at home and overseas subsidiary plants, and also between their overseas subsidiary plants. The transfer prices of such goods and services internationally cross-hauled comprise the key elements of Japanese multinational strategies. These strategies often require parent firms to expand the operational scopes of their overseas subsidiaries, or to change the products being produced far more frequently than in the case of overseas subsidiaries oriented exclusively to their own local markets.

As the majority of offshore manufacturing subsidiaries of the four leading electric and electronics appliance firms, Hitachi, Toshiba, Sanyo and Matsushita earlier exemplified, control of overseas subsidiaries would prove to be most pressing for the Japanese manufacturing subsidiaries as they became pressured by the host governments to export. And yet, local business partners would demand greater say in the management of the joint ventures as they began to absorb product- and process-related technologies. The seed of the first inevitable conflict of interests was budding, therefore, between local and Japanese partners of joint ventures abroad.

On the eve of the oil crisis that befell Japan in October 1973 the country was replete with domestic manufacturing firms hoping to increase and expand their manufacturing activities abroad, if permitted by host governments and local partners. The ensuing oil crisis, as well as the crisis in other natural resources, caused many more Japanese firms to relocate their additional manufacturing subsidiaires abroad. Will Japanese firms be able to carry out these multinational strategies without causing fatal conflicts of interest with foreign governments and business partners? Some sources of conflicts have already appeared.

During the two year period, 1970-1972, in sixteen out of eighty-four Japanese manufacturing subsidiaries surveyed, which corresponded roughly to 20 percent of the Japanese manufacturing subsidiaires in Thailand, the Japanese ownership decreased. Two Japanese subsidiaries were closed down because of conflicts of the ownership interests between Thai and Japanese business partners.[5] The operations of these eighteen "unstable" subsidiaries were patently characterized by such standard and least-technology intensive products as towels, blankets, weaving operations, steel pipes, and insecticides. Meanwhile, there were two manufacturing subsidiaries which had increased Japanese ownership during the two year period. They not only expanded their equity bases by over 30 times, but also upgraded their products to electronics parts and filament textile spinning. The Japanese parent firms of the remaining "stable" subsidiaries were well advised to heed the inevitable message: upgrade or expand production and export, or face divestment.[6]

In Indonesia, after January 1974, all the foreign subsidiaries were asked to step up their promises of phasing out (divesting) foreign ownership elements. At the same time, expatriate managers were also to be phased out. Japanese manufacturing subsidiaries appeared unprepared for this sudden rise in Indonesian economic nationalism. In Korea, in 1975, Toray of Japan conceded the majority ownership of its subsidiary, Hanguk Nylon, to the Korean partner. And the Korean partner expanded the spinning and weaving operations with the hope of exporting products to Japan.

Because of these changes taking place abroad, Japanese firms will need to draw up either a coherent contingency plan of "divestment" or one of "expansion." In particular, in the planned process of divestment, the parent firms should strive to separate their own legal ownership from the issues of defining the scope and nature of their subsidiaries' activities—what to produce and how much, where to sell—as well as the royalties to be paid by subsidiaries.

Not only Japanese firms but other multinational firms have also singularly ignored such contingency planning thus far. In a brutal atmosphere of office politics, the divestment of any on-going operation implies some kind of shameful failure to the persons involved in the operation. Thus, a planned divestment—not much more than a method of coping with a complex scenario—becomes taboo. The existence of the divestment plan—a contingency plan—does not necessarily force firms to divest operations, but could motivate firms to periodically review the changing environment of their overseas subsidiaries. As a result, a firm would be able to keep readjusting both the scope and nature of its overseas operations to the changing local environment. And yet, this obvious step by multinational firms has vanished from their ordinary corporate planning as well as from the curricula offered in international business courses in business schools. Everyone seems to be keen on the idea of entry. But the need to service local subsidiaries, let alone the usefulness of a contingency planning, still escapes the minds of many multinational managers. And Japanese firms are no exceptions.

An inordinate degree of interest is expressed in the excitement of entry, but not in the problematical exit. This lopsided situation has been fueled by the corporate emphasis on avoiding risk. Both explicit and implicit rules of conduct are heavily weighted toward penalizing small mistakes and failures, and toward ignoring rewards for successes. Since human attempts at success often entail mistakes and failures, the corporate atmosphere of risk avoidance motivates individuals to preserve their own hide even at the risk of overlooking serious problems in the making.

Japanese subsidiaries abroad are just now beginning to feel the gathering need for change in the scope and nature of their operations. Will these firms be able to withstand such external pressures for divestment or expansion? Will Japanese firms be able and ready to cope with both the internal and external changes that many Japanese firms are experiencing today as their multinational activities expand? In the next chapter, we will evaluate Japanese corporate culture as well as emerging internal structure of overseas divisions designed to cope with such changes in the business environment of Japanese multinational firms.

❊ Chapter Nine

Japanese Corporate Culture and Overseas Divisions

Several years ago, a fire broke out in a department store in Tokyo on its regular off-business day. When radio and television stations broadcast the incident, most of the company's rank-and-file employees rushed to their store. As they reached the scene of the blaze, they voluntarily assigned themselves immediate tasks. Some joined the police in helping direct traffic, and others helped fight the fire or remove whatever merchandise was left in the store. From the upper management to the youngest novice employees, they were totally occupied with one single objective: to save their own store.

In preparing reports of the incident for the media, no reporters even bothered to mention that most of the store's employees had abandoned their holiday and rushed to the scene of the disaster. The public simply took it for granted. Indeed, if the employees had not acted as they did, that would have made the news of the day.

What are the apparent characteristics of Japanese corporate culture? How have they been cultivated? Has Japanese corporate culture produced a "Japanese" way of overseeing and organizing firms' activities abroad?

Let us consider the following three manifestations of Japanese corporate culture that often bewilder foreign observers:*

---

*See also, "Convergence of Japanese and American Management Practices" in Tsurumi *Multinational Management: Texts, Readings and Cases*, Ch. 3. Cambridge, Mass.: Ballinger Publishing Co., 1976.

Case 1: Kinki Coca-Cola Bottling Co.

The product is distinctly "American," and yet the ways by which the familiar product is bottled and delivered to customers by the largest Coca-Cola bottler in the world are distinctly "Japanese."

> The film "New Days" that Kinki produced in 1969 for its recruitment and trainees, contained messages that young Japanese high school graduates like to hear from prospective employers. The film traces the life of Kazuo Takagi, a young southern Japanese, in his early 20s. In three years Takagi matures mentally and physically by leading a self-disciplined and devoted life with his fellow employees at Kinki. In scene after scene, the film hammers out the following messages: (1) Kinki is an effective training institution worth devoting one's life to; (2) togetherness of all members of the Kinki family, from President down to youngest helpers of route salesmen; (3) happy and harmonious way of life with Kinki; and (4) indivisibility of the fortune of Taskagi, one single Kinki member, from the entire fortune of the "Kinki Coca-Cola" body. Nowhere throughout the forty-minute film are such details and trivia as pay scales, working conditions or fringe benefits. The film repeatedly depicts the running theme that so long as you help Kinki grow and maintain harmony among its members, your economic and social needs will naturally and automatically be taken care of.

Case 2: Two Surveys

From 1969 to 1971 I conducted a study on attitudes and aspirations of employees of a leading soft drink industry in Japan. The average age of the employees was around 20. The plants are scattered throughout Japan. Attitudes and aspirations common to all the bottlers can therefore be safely regarded as representing a national trend among individuals within a similar age group. During the same period of time, similar observations were collected on employee attitudes and aspirations from a leading pharmaceutical firm of Japan. The following often-heard comment in essence summarizes the anxiety and hopes of rather young rank-and-file employees in these enterprises:

> I joined this company because it was said to be a growth firm. I am now in sales (or plant or accounting, as the case may be). I hope that the company will teach me as much as possible about this firm's business. I often wonder, though, what I will be doing in this firm, say, at forty years of age ... I don't want to be in this sales (or plant or accounting, as the case may be) job all my life. After all, I have a high school (or university) diploma.

The same people were asked to choose between two hypothetical bosses as preferable people to work under. One boss was characterized as a bright and sharp person, who, while severe in his evaluation of subordinates, is always fair. He assigns jobs according to the proven capabilities of subordinates and avoids socializing with them after work. The other boss is characterized as emotional. He often bawls out his subordinates but means no malice. His evaluation of subordinates is not always fair. He attempts to assign interesting jobs on a rotational basis to his subordinates, regardless of proven ability. He often takes his subordinates out for drinks and dinner after work and listens to their personal problems. In a young employee's popularity polling the "emotional" boss wins over the "bright" boss with an almost three to one margin.

Case 3: Japanese Employees' Dedication to Their Communal Goal

The job security of lifetime employment within Japanese firms guarantees that individual employees will not be discharged except in the case of such gross unethical conduct as embezzlement of corporate funds. So long as individuals exercise initiative for the good of the organization, they can even make mistakes without being punished. As a matter of fact, this system maintains a tremendous tolerance for individual errors so long as they arise from the employees' genuine desire to do what is believed to be for the good of the firm. This system therefore does not necessarily inhibit individual initiative.

This is why people often hear of young clerks of an automobile firm, for instance, rushing to a typhoon disaster area on their own accord, in order to help their distressed customers. They hurry to the scene, paying their own way, or walking day and night if communication and transportation are severely cut. It does not occur to them that they might be punished by their superiors for abandoning their office work or that the expenses they incur might not be reimbursed. Alert individuals initiate rescue moves with the conviction that their work in the office will either have to wait or be filled by someone else. After all, this is a clear-cut case of job priority for the good of the entire company. Even when such individual initiatives unauthorized by their higher-ups entail mistakes and losses for the firm, the purity of their motives (*doki no junsuisei*) is not to be questioned. And their mistakes are not only pardoned but praised as the proofs of individuals' dedication to their communal goals. Indeed, the Japanese emphasis on the purity of motives, not necessarily on the outcome of individuals' actions, characterizes the criteria by which individuals, leaders and rank-and-file members alike, are rewarded and punished in a closely-knit corporate atmosphere.

JAPANESE CORPORATE ATMOSPHERE

The preceding illustrations point out that Japanese corporations have cultivated, since around 1870s, the cultural predisposition of valuing highly the cohesive harmony of the group.[1] This value of group harmony has been refined by various management practices. Employee relations focus on individual group members' acceptance of, and common trust in, what they perceive to be good for the group. And their firm defines the ultimate boundary of the group.

When, in the early 1870s, Japan chose to industrialize rapidly, the oligarchy of the Meiji Era (1868-1911) inherited much of its cultural and technological legacy from the Tokugawa feudalism.[2] Three main cultural and practical legacies of the Tokagawa era turned out to be useful and rewarding endowments for the government and business leaders of the Meiji Era. First, Japan emerged out of the Tokugawa Era with the notion of Japan as a single sovereign state ingrained in the minds of both the *Samurai* (warrior) and merchant classes alike. The central and local administrations (e.g., the collection of taxes and enforcement of laws and regulations) that the Central Tokugawa Shogunate government and the local domain governments had developed were immediately made the basic administrative machinery of the Meiji government. Second, the Japanese emerged from the Tokugawa Era with an attitude predisposed to practical values of "learning" and "training." This culminated by the 1870s in a substantive rate of literacy among the general population. Third, the agrarian way of life in Japan required intensive cooperation among village members for the successful cultivation and harvesting of rice and other crops and produce. Amidst a repressive atmosphere of punishing nonconformists, the administrative governments of the feudal domains held a group of peasants, merchants and craftsmen (consisting of five family-units much like the system of "Gonin Gumi," five-member group) collectively responsible not only for the group members' tax payments, but also for the conduct of the individual members as a whole. Thus, the Japanese masses had long been conditioned to regard the individual as an integral and indivisible element of the group.[3]

Ideologically, the prevalent ethical codes of conduct that emanated from the Japanese interpretation of the Chu'si school of Confucianism governed the ruling class of *Samurai*. This school of thought regarded devotion to the master as the supreme form of virtue. And in turn the master (the leadership) was expected to be an exemplar of benevolence, sagacity and purity.[4] Masters (leaders) who failed to demonstrate such qualities were belittled as "small men" in the eyes of observer-critics cultivated in the Confucian tradition. This moralistic standard by which the leaders were evaluated still lingers within Japanese institutions. Under this master-follower relationship, subordinates were not only expected, but obligated to help their master attain exemplary conduct; even such extreme forms of self-sacrifice as disemboweling themselves and thereby performing the "protest of death" were not unheard of. The merchant class emulated such ideologies of the ruling class of *Samurai*.

POST-WORLD WAR II PHENOMENON

The current practices of management-employee relations in Japan were formed during the post–World War II period of industrial reconstruction. During the War both white and blue collar employees of a given firm organized into an enterprise-based unit of "Collaborating with the Great Reign of the Emperor." This practice effectively erased class and status differences between production and office employees. The practice of placing production employees on a monthly salary also spread during the war. As a result, when Japan emerged out of the defeat and ruins of World War II, its firms by then had perfected the internal structures upon which their rapid post–World War II industrial growth depended.

Incidentally, the Allied Occupying Forces at that time purged surviving corporate managers of war-time "collaborating" firms from their businesses. Thus, the young and ambitious echelon of the middle management were left free to pick and choose what they considered to be useful management-employee practices of the past, just as the young leaders of the Meiji Oligarchy were given a similar mandate during the 1870s to pick and choose the useful elements of the social and political legacies of the Tokugawa Era. The crisis atmosphere of post–World War II brought all employees of Japanese firms closer together. The job security of individuals, from the president down to novice employees, was to be collectively protected. The slogan "Each for all and all for each" carried a serious message: employees disciplined themselves to stay with their firm for a long time and to postpone personal reward or enjoyment long into the future.

Once employees are trained to share the objectives of the firm, their cooperative work is vital to the firm. The firm's job security and resultant no layoff principle guards the employee's interests. In turn, employees are motivated to guard the whole welfare of their firm. Thus, the job security is not a product of Japanese paternalism, but a necessary economy to all persons in the firm.

Not until the 1950s did this form of job security come to be established practice in all Japanese firms. Many Japanese firms discovered that it was a most effective means of making rank-and-file employees identify their own individual interests with those of the corporation.

In their approach to division of labor, the Japanese could not afford to jeopardize cooperative work among employees by arbitrarily ranking one man's specific task above another's. Regardless of task, individuals needed to be treated as equals in their worth to the organization as a whole. As a result, it was a social anathema to tie one's specific task too closely to an economic or similar kind of reward.

A cultural egalitarian norm of Japan presupposes that members of the same sex are born with equal potential, and that differences in one's diligence and self-discipline separate the successful from the unsuccessful in life.[5] This means that a Japanese firm can only afford to reward its individual employees differently on the basis of socially accepted manifestations of differences in cumulative diligence. Thus, such obvious factors as age (seniority), educational background and sex have been made the bases for wage determination and promotion within Japanese firms.

In the past, when contemporary conventions were formed, corporate life was far more simple. Various post-secondary educational institutions screened job candidates for preselected roles in firms and government offices. The students of these post-secondary institutes were by and large selected on the basis of strict, competitive entrance examinations. And the best schools, from municipal secondary schools to national universities, with very few exceptions, were, and still are, publicly supported institutions. Children of families with limited economic means were not condemned to second or third rate public schools.

The Japanese educational system has thus been the accepted device for separating the "more diligent" from the "less diligent" candidates. The scarcity of university graduates was a sign demonstrating their knowledge and training to be superior to that of "high-school" or "middle-school" graduates. Thus, those with university training have often commanded respect from non-university graduates. Women rarely joined firms or government offices as anything other than plant workers or subordinate office clerks.

A man's role and resultant modes of interaction with superiors, peers and subordinates is more or less indirectly defined and understood by him and the people around him when he enters a firm or government office. In order to survive within the organization, he must master various "traditions," "conventions," and implicit sets of rules. This exercise is certainly not unique to Japanese organizations. However, with the Japanese corporate system of limited promotional opportunities and lifetime employment with one firm, an individual's need for both patience with, and comprehension of, implicit rules of conduct within the firm is obviously greater than in the case where one is encouraged to exploit job mobility from one firm to the next.[6]

Within this system of corporate tradition, the elders, who were the guardians of custom and convention, commanded respect from the young. They could genuinely teach something to the young. And the young in turn craved the information and knowledge that only their elders could impart. Under these circumstances, few questioned the seniority supremacy system of promotion within the firm. Not only was the system compatible with the Japanese mores of respecting the elderly, but it also fostered a sense of job security—employees could predict what they would be doing, or how much they would be earning in ten or twenty years.

LONG WORK TIME-HORIZON OF EMPLOYEES

Under the job security of lifetime commitment, Japanese employees, management and rank-and-file alike, develop substantially longer work time-horizons than their American counterparts. The Japanese firm reviews an individual's performance every five or ten years. American employees' performances are reviewed hourly, quarterly or annually. In America, an individual's rewards and punishments are closely linked to these short-term evaluations.

Furthermore, the Japanese practices of job rotation and job security enable the firm to reassign production and office work rather freely. Organizational changes or introduction of new machinery creates little resistance within the corporation. Frequent job rotation, especially among upward middle management and management candidates, tends to nurture the goals and profits of the total firm, rather than the goals and profits of specific subunits within the firm.

As Case 2 pointed out earlier, the Japanese emphasis on job rotation has shaped employees' career aspirations inside their firm. They "join" an established firm with growth potential rather than sell their specific "expertise" to the highest bidding firm. Once an individual joins a firm, he expects the firm to know how to keep him occupied until the mandatory age of retirement (55 to 60 years of age), *with* steady promotion that is *due* him given his sex, educational background and years with the firm. While rising in rank, he expects to be rotated from one type of work to another for as great a variety of experience as possible.

VOLLEYBALL TEAM MODEL

Individual employees in a given Japanese firm may be likened to individual players in a volleyball team competing against another team. Each individual's position and expected role at any given point is determined and understood by his teammates. But during the game a surprise ball may come around to the back liner. His team has only one chance left to return the ball to the opponents. Although his usual play is to return the ball to his team's setter, he does not hesitate in smashing the ball directly back across the net. The team's overriding goal is to beat the opponent according to the volleyball rules. To attain this shared goal, individuals are encouraged to exercise discretion and to deal with emergencies. When the team wins, the victory belongs to everyone. Frequently, behind fine individual plays there lies the intricate teamwork that makes these unrestricted individual moves possible.

The anology of the volleyball game has been used to illustrate the interaction of Japanese employees at their best within their respective corporations. The size of the team is small enough to permit intimate face-to-face communication among the team members. Although individuals are expected to develop their own expertise and special plays, they rotate not only the server's role but also the defense positions. By practicing together and by sharing both personal and team lives, the members get to know one another so well that their mode of communication takes on implicit phrases and expressions rather than explicit verbal discussions.

The popularity of volleyball in Japan might indeed be attributed to the fact that the game is nothing but a condensed replay of Japanese organizational life. Accordingly, one might be tempted to venture that the popularity of football in the United States can be culturally traced to its condensation of American organizational rules. Football demonstrates the vital importance of preplanned strategies and total division of labor (special plays and expertise) among several players crowding the field. The exemplary American corporate model, often studied in business schools in the United States, sometimes comes close to this successful, dazzling, preplanned execution of American football plays.

JAPANESE AND AMERICAN CORPORATE CULTURE

In order to better understand Japanese and American corporate cultures, I have in the past attempted to identify the favorite platitudes that top executives of Japanese and American corporations tend to repeat concerning the goals and values of their organizations. The contrast between the two cultures is often marked, at least on a surface level, by the following three concepts of management-employee relations:[7]

Recruitment of Employees
U.S.: "We hire specific expertise" (labor man-hours and skills).
Japan: "We accept a total personality, a whole person to become a member of our firm."

As the expression "hired hands" epitomizes, American corporations "hire" only labor skills. Employees are often expected, figuratively that is, to leave other parts of their anatomy, especially their head, at home. Individual employees are working to sell their services for a fee. On the other hand, Japanese firms "accept" not only a prospective employee's total personality, but also that of his or her immediate family members. And Japanese employees in turn expect their firms to satisfy their social and personal needs as well.

Ownership of Corporation
U.S.: "The firm belongs to the stockholders. We need to make profits for them."
Japan: "Legally, the firm belongs to the stockholders. But more important, morally speaking, the firm is the collective property of all the members, from the president down to the rank-and-file."

In reality, both Japanese and American stockholders are so widely dispersed among many individual and institutional shareholders that the professional management class commands vast power over the firm. In Japan, however, the prevalent notion of "moral ownership" tends to render the top management leadership effective only so long as that leadership, in the eyes of all employees, acts to improve for the total worth of the corporation. The Japanese corporate leaders are expected to act as trustees of the collective interest of all members of the firm.[8]

Motivation and Responsibility of Employees

U.S.: "We motivate employees through specific reward and punishment. We mete them out through frequent reviews of their work performance. The boss hires his subordinates. The fear of job loss keeps them aware of who is in charge. Layoff of the workers is unavoidable. Labor unions acknowledge the management's right to lay workers off."

Japan: "When management miscalculates or when economic chips are down, the responsibility should be borne from the top down. Dividends should be cut. Then, top executives' salaries should be cut. The middle managements' salaries and expenses should be reduced before the management can ask the rank-and-file employees to shoulder economic burdens of business downturn. Job security maintains the basic order in the firm. The fear of an individual's job loss cannot be used to motivate employees.

The exemplary organizational models that Japanese and American corporations have thus far cultivated may be best illustrated by the diagram shown in Figure 9–1. The triangular figure in the middle denotes the ordinary hierarchy of any formal corporate organization, from the president down to rank-and-file employees, whether in Japan or the U.S.

American corporate culture and control systems are designed such that the individual's commitment to the firm's goal and his concept of a time horizon form the shape of an inverted triangle. For example, the very top echelon of management in both Japanese and American firms is expected to maintain the broadest commitment to,

Figure 9-1. Japanese and American Corporate Culture

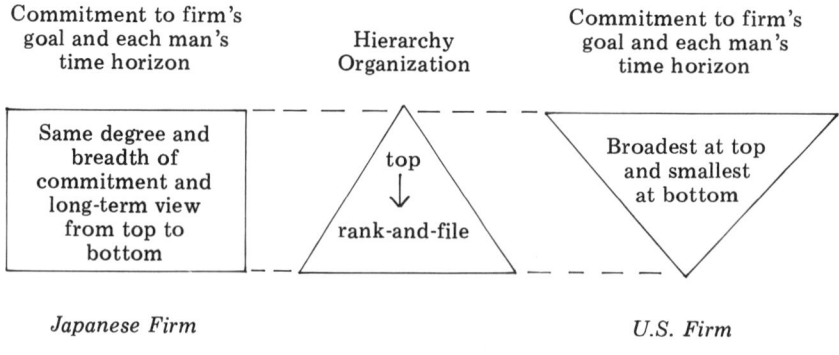

and most acute interest in, the long-range future of the company. In American corporations, as the individual's hierarchical position in the firm declines, his commitment to the firm's goals and future objectives tapers markedly. At the very bottom of the triangle are rank-and-file employees of American firms, who are merely expected to perform pre-designated jobs from one hour to the next. In contrast, Japanese firms have cultivated their corporate culture and concomitant management-employee relations so that even the lowest rank-and-file members of the firm maintain not only the broadest commitment to their firm's goal, but also a long-term interest and vision in their firm's future.[10]

DECISION-MAKING PROCESSES OF JAPANESE FIRMS: "RINGI SEIDO" REVISITED

This type of individual commitment to the widely accepted goal of the firm has produced the often cited decision-making system of Japanese firms called *ringi seido*.* Observers of this decision-making process will see that new proposals, marketing or investment decisions for example, are often initiated by the lower to middle echelons of the firm.[11] And these proposals are passed through the hierarchy collecting seals of approval or minor revisions on their way to the president. Informally, the initiators or collaborating-bosses of such proposals are busily engaged in pinpointing the key personalities needed for support. Some proposals fade or die on their journey to the top echelon. But those proposals that do survive cannot be attributed to the initiator(s) only. By the time the proposal is accepted by top management, it will have received corporate consensus.

This process of building consensus among the individuals who will be affected by a decision takes the decision out of the hands of a specific initiator or implementor. The decision-making process of Japan can barely be separated from the later process of implementation. On the other hand, in American corporate culture, the party and process that initiates decisions is separate from the party and process that carries out the decision. This explains why American managers often complain of the long time it seems to take Japanese managers to make decisions. And Japanese managers in turn complain of the delays American managers face in carrying out their

*The terminology *"ringi seido"* literally refers to the procedural aspect of the decision-making, in which people concerned with the implementation of a proposal are literally consulted from one individual to the next. The phrase "touching bases" in American jargon may capture some physical aspects of the procedure called *"ringi seido."*

decisions. It is inconceivable to Japanese managers that any decision can be made without consulting the internal workings of the organization. The specifics of such an arrangement might be time consuming. But when a decision is made and communicated to a third party such as the customer, this process is deemed tantamount to the commencement of implementation.

The "consensus building" practices in the decision-making process of Japanese firms have created two distinct Japanese characteristics: namely, (1) the substantive involvement of middle management (section chiefs to department heads) in making strategic decisions; and (2) the presidential leadership being expected to cope mainly with crisis situations or with abrupt and clear-cut changes in the direction of the firm. Once the general direction of the firm is communicated to the middle management echelon, both operational decisions and incremental changes tend to be entrusted to the initiative of the lower to middle management echelons.

In actual practice, the conceptual demarcation of roles between top and middle echelons in the Japanese corporation is often blurred. Generally, one can view the top and middle echelon as a group, concerned not only with the day-to-day fine tuning of the firm's accepted strategies, but also with the search for new strategic moves. In this context, the middle management of a Japanese corporation act as planning aides and advisers to the top echelon management, as well as day-to-day supervisors implementing agreed-on strategies. In turn, the top echelon is expected to take an active interest in the details of the middle management's activities while staying one step removed from any actual involvement.

This benign "surveillance" by the top echelon over the actions of the middle management is reciprocated by an equally benign and often polite "scrutinization" of the top echelon's decisions by the middle management. Consequently, in Japanese corporate culture, the middle management may often politely disagree with the top echelon on various key issues. Since the middle management is likely to be with the firm longer than the top management, because of the system of lifetime employment, it is accustomed to reviewing the long-range implications of top executive decisions.

More specifically, when new decisions originate from the top echelon, they must be sold to the middle management, rather than given to them as directives. When new suggestions originate from the middle management, as they often do, anticipated implementation problems are ironed out among themselves before being passed on for approval to the top echelon.

The deep-rooted feeling that the Japanese corporation belongs to all its members accounts for the behavior of middle management in Japanese corporate culture. This belief also breeds the attitude on the part of middle management that it should behave as a trustee for the collective interests of all members. At minimum, the middle management is expected to initiate questioning when it is not convinced of the wisdom of a specific top echelon decision.

In the case of American subsidiaries that I have studied in Japan, this notion of middle management roles in respect to the top echelon authority has caused a great deal of conflict between Japanese employees and American managers. Frequently, able Japanese personnel have resigned when they were confronted with hostile reactions from newly arrived American managers. These employees, working for the long-term goals of their firm, tended to challenge actions on the part of superiors that they might have deemed detrimental to the good of the firm. These Japanese employees expected explanations from their superiors as to how certain actions would benefit the firm for a longer period of time than American managers cared to consider. Most American managers took such requests as personal affronts to their management prerogatives. American managers, who had been bred in American corporate culture, expected Japanese middle management to follow their decisions. Least of all did they expect to be confronted with questions concerning their decisions.

In the case of Japanese subsidiaries that I have studied in the U.S., American plant and sales managers were often bewildered when they discovered that they were expected to solve problems among themselves without bothering Japanese top executives. American managers would report problems to the Japanese president, together with suggestions for solutions. The Japanese president would politely suggest that if American managers could identify the problem and knew the solution, they should have quietly gone ahead and solved it. Once American managers learned that the *de facto* delegation of managerial authority was materially prevalent in the Japanese corporate environment, and that this culture tolerated managerial mistakes far more readily than the American culture, American managers began enjoying a position of managerial authority that in their former U.S. corporations only belonged to a higher level of management.

PRESIDENTIAL LEADERSHIP

The style of presidential leadership in Japanese firms varies significantly according to the size of the firm. The smaller the firm, the greater is the involvement of the president in routine operations.

While this may be true of firms of various nationalities, the Japanese president is expected to behave more as a "constitutional monarch" than a "prime minister" as the organization becomes larger and the business becomes more diversified. Furthermore, the president, who is also the founder-entrepreneur of the firm, is often permitted to become involved in detailed and operational ends of the firm's organizational activities. However, from the second generation president on, the leader is expected to maintain the position of sagacity and his personal influence is expected only in times of clear-cut crisis or like situations. Until such situations arise, the president's task is to motivate his lieutenant-executives to maintain harmonious order within the organization.

Japanese corporate organizations often discourage the worship of specific personalities and attempt to substitute abstract ideals like "the firm's institutional goal" or "institutional tradition" for the cult of enshrining specific leaders. One can detect this trend in Japanese folklore; an individual member of the firm can never be greater than the collective expression, the "institution." Even the founder-entrepreneur does not escape this cultural process of ridding the institution of personality worshipping.

For example, let us compare the following two corporate anthems. One belongs to IBM (U.S.) and the other to Matsushita, the leading Japanese electric and electronics appliances firm.

IBM Anthem, Second Chorus

EVER ONWARD—EVER ONWARD!

We're bound for the top never to fall!
Right here and now we thankfully
Pledge sincerest loyalty
To the corporation that's the best for all!
Our leaders we revere, and while we're here
Let's show the world just what we think of them!
So let's sing, men! SING, MEN!
For the EVER ONWARD IBM!

Matsushita Anthem

For the building of a new Japan
Let's put our strength and mind together,
Doing our best to promote production,
Sending out goods to the people of the world
Endlessly and continuously,
Like water gushing from a fountain.

Grow, industry, grow, grow, grow!
Harmony and sincerity!
Matsushita Electric!

The IBM Anthem emphasizes the supreme importance and worship of its leaders. The Matsushita Anthem, which is still sung today all over the world in diverse languages by diverse nationalities, is a reminder of the employee's expected dedication to the export status, organizational growth and harmony and national goal. By simply changing the word "Japan" in the first line, to the more general word "country," the verse can transcend national boundaries. In passing, it should be noted that Matsushita is renowned throughout Japan for the personal influence of its founder-entrepreneur, Konosuke Matsushita. And yet, this firm is seriously attempting to eternalize its organizational goals away from specific leader type influence.

In practice, therefore, the president and top management echelon of Japanese firms need to communicate new presidential decisions to the rest of the organization in the form of institutional messages rather than personal mandates. This is particularly necessary if the entire organization is to readjust to the firm's new direction. The rest of the organization, engaged in other on-going activities, will be called upon to supply manpower and financial resources for this new corporate direction.

The multinational activities that Japanese firms began to undertake in the early 1970s often required such all-out organizational commitments within each firm. How was this message communicated internally to the rest of the organization, and more important, externally to outside groups.

THE RAISON D'ETRE OF "KAIGAI JIGYOBU" (OVERSEAS DIVISION) FOR THE JAPANESE MULTINATIONAL FIRM

Of the 52 large manufacturing firms of Japan that made *Fortune's* list of the 200 largest non-U.S. firms in 1970, by the end of 1970, all but five had at least one overseas subsidiary. By summer 1972 when these top multinational firms were approached for data collection concerning their overseas activities, of 47 firms, 24 already possessed the internal organizational subunit called "Kaigai Jigyobu," to be abbreviated KJ Division (Overseas Division) for the balance of this chapter.

Very few of these multinational firms had the KJ Division even as late as 1970. After 1971, one firm after another began to establish its own KJ Division. The sudden appearance of the KJ Division often coincided with the firm's new commitment to cross-hauling goods and services between overseas manufacturing subsidiaries and between them and plants in Japan.

In the *MITI Survey of 1973*, as well as in my own field surveys in 1972, the Japanese manufacturing operations abroad were graded according to scale; the overseas activities of investing parent firms fall between the arithmetical average of 1 and 2 per cent of the parent's total sales. During the fall of 1972 and again during the spring and summer of 1973, my field surveys of overseas manufacturing subsidiaries of Japanese firms revealed that a typical subsidiary employed between 200 and 300 nationals of the host country, usually for a two-shift operation per day; many plants had less than 100 production workers. In textile plants involving spinning, weaving and dyeing operations, where expensive equipment was used, a three-shift day was standard. Relevant data, as of the spring of 1973, indicated the scale of operations of overseas manufacturing subsidiaries relative to their Japanese parent firms. These results are summarized in Table 9-1.

Accordingly, one might ask why the KJ Division was suddenly created in the early 1970s within large Japanese multinational firms at a time when their overseas manufacturing operations were small. Is the KJ Division of the Japanese firm similar to the International Division of an American firm? Is the KJ Division likely to remain a viable internal subunit of Japanese multinational firms as their overseas operations take on additional complexities in the near future? Even partial answers to these questions require a review of the evolutionary process which created the typical KJ Division within the Japanese multinational firm.

During the latter half of 1972, I visited 47 of the large firms in order to obtain relevant operational information on their overseas subsidiaries. In Table 9-2, the specific internal organization of each firm from which I obtained information is classified according to the number of manufacturing subsidiaries abroad each parent firm possessed as of fall 1972. One can glean relevant observations from this table concerning some of the characteristics of a KJ Division within the large Japanese firm.

First, the KJ Division is found mainly within firms possessing more than three overseas manufacturing subsidiaries. In fact, the chronological birth records of 23 KJ Divisions possessing greater than three manufacturing subsidiaries abroad as of the fall 1972, revealed that these births were critically related to the total number of overseas manufacturing subsidiaries: three subsidiaries proved to be a magic number.

Table 9-1. Relative Size of Overseas Manufacturing Subsidiaries as Compared with Parent Firms' Operations in Japan as of March 31, 1973

Industry Ratio	Textiles	Chemicals	Ferrous & Non-ferrous Products	Electric Machinery	General Machinery	Transportation Machinery	Precision Equipment	Misc.	For all the Industries
Ratio of Subsidiary's Sales to Parent's Sales (%)	2.6	6.4	0.7	0.3	0.7	1.1	0.9	2.7	1.3
Ratio of Subsidiary's Assets to Parent's Assets (%)	5.1	0.3	1.1	1.2	0.6	1.1	0.9	3.6	1.7
Ratio of Subsidiary's Employment to Parent's Employment (%)	12.8	1.5	1.8	5.6	1.8	2.7	1.9	10.2	5.0

Source: The *MITI Survey of 1973* reports the above data, indicating the scale of overseas manufacturing subsidiaries relative to parent firms' operations in Japan for 606 investing firms.

Table 9-2. The Internal Organization of 47 Large Japanese Multinational Firms, Possessing Relevant Information on Their Overseas Subsidiaries As of Fall 1972

Internal Organization	No. of Product Lines of the Firm*	Number of Overseas Manufacturing Subsidiaries				Total Firms
		1-2	3-5	6-8	Over 9	
Kaigai Jigyobu (K.J. Division)	Multiple Product line firm	None	3 firms	3 firms	7 firms	13 firms
	Single Product line firm	1 firm	3 firms	4 firms	3 firms	11 firms
Export Department or Export Division	Multiple Product line firm	None	None	None	None	None
	Single Product line firm	1 firm	1 firm	1 firm	1 firm	4 firms
Miscellaneous Staff Organizations e.g. president's office, planning department, department of related business, foreign department	Multiple Product line firm	None	None	None	None	None
	Single Product line firm	11 firms	2 firms	1 firm	5 firms	19 firms
Total Firms		13	9	9	16	47

*Multiple product line firm manufactures more than two products which are classified into different product categories according to the two-digit industry classification of SIC (Standard Industrial Classification).

Second, the firm with a single product line (SIC two-digit classification) retained its own internal organization and did not adopt the KJ Division format. The firm with more than two product lines created the KJ Division as its overseas operations began to exceed three or four. The responses of the 24 firms did indeed strongly indicate that the firm with more than two product lines showed an earlier propensity for creating the KJ Division than the firm with a single product line. And it should be pointed out that ten of the thirteen firms utilizing the KJ Division and having more than two product lines were internally holding each product division responsible for its profit budget. Such a product division did indeed operate as a profit center.

Third, with the exception of 4 firms—all of them automobile firms—the remaining 43 internally separated the responsibility of exporting activities from the responsibility of overseeing manufacturing subsidiaries abroad. In fact, it was more an exception than a rule that the KJ Division of a large multinational firm of Japan was entrusted with the responsibility of exporting activities.

The miscellaneous departments to which the 19 multinational firms shown in Table 9-2 assigned the responsibility of coordinating and overseeing overseas manufacturing activities were: the president's office, the planning department, the department of related businesses and the foreign department. The common characteristic of these staff organizations was that they all reported directly to the president of the firm, or to the second-in-command, such as the executive vice president (in charge of internal coordination of various functions such as personnel, finance and management information systems).

The 24 KJ Divisions that I studied as of fall 1972 revealed relevant information as to the evolutionary and organizational processes within the large Japanese multinational firm. As pictured in Figure 9-2, of these 24 KJ Divisions, 18 were created primarily out of miscellaneous staff organizations like the president's office, the planning and coordinating departments, or the department of related businesses. The remaining six were created mainly by expanding the functions of foreign departments.

This observation leads one to speculate that sooner or later the miscellaneous staff organizations of the 19 multinational firms (Table 9-2) will adopt the *de facto* or *de jure* Kaigai Jigyobu (KJ Division). In particular, the 11 firms that by fall of 1972 had assigned the coordinating and reporting activities of their overseas subsidiaries to miscellaneous staff organizations, might already be contemplating the creation of a KJ Division as their overseas activities expand. What then does a typical KJ Division accomplish?

Figure 9-2. Evolutionary Process of KJ Division

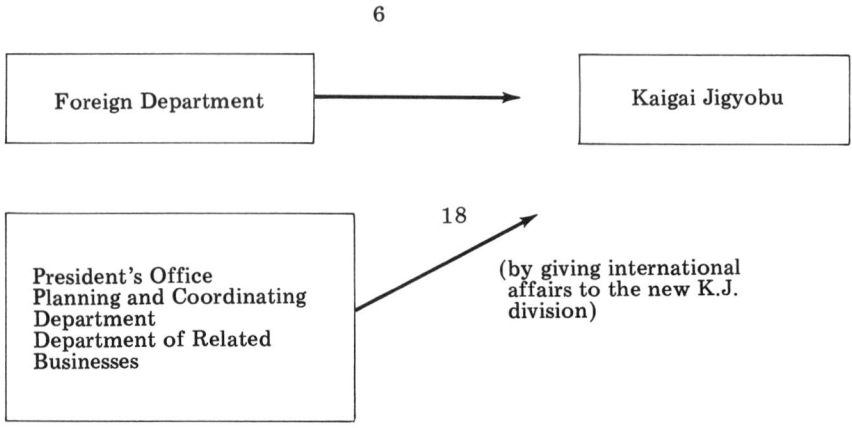

FUNCTIONS OF KJ DIVISION

The most striking characteristic of the KJ Division is that in all firms but one it was formed as a specifically "non-profit center." This similarity of assigned function, varying little from single to multiple product line firms, can only be explained in the context of the Japanese firm organization. The overwhelming majority of Japanese international divisions (KJ Divisions) today are functioning as advisory staff. They have no direct profit responsibility. Their responsibility is in the formal monitoring of overseas subsidiaries: keeping their records, evaluating their performance and looking after their personnel needs.

Another salient characteristic of the 24 KJ Divisions is the fact that all but a few had come by the fall of 1972 to be headed by a corporate officer, often with the rank of managing director, or at least that of corporate director. In fact, even in the case of the other 23 manufacturing parent firms that did not have the KJ Division in the fall of 1972, 19 of them had put a managing or corporate director in charge of overseeing their subsidiaries abroad.

The Japanese corporate culture, both internally and externally, deems the rank of corporate directorship and above as the peak echelon of the management hierarchy. Internally, for example, the appointment of a top manager to a new head position of any given function or department draws the attention of all members of the firm. Such an appointment is the explicit "body" language of the firm that communicates to its loyal members the increased importance of the specified activities headed by a ranking officer. Such "body" language calls for new dedication and cooperation from all corporate members.

The sudden appearance of KJ divisions within Japanese multinational firms in the early 1970s were indeed explicit attempts on the part of Japanese top management to point their firms in a new direction. By elevating the obsolete "foreign department" to the KJ Division, or by consolidating international responsibilities and businesses of various staff departments into a single KJ Division unit, Japanese firms were seeking to communicate to their members the newly expanded direction of their multinational activities. And these moves coincided with the time in the early 1970s when more and more Japanese multinational firms were awakening to the need to expand and coordinate their manufacturing activities abroad. One could observe a uniformity of KJ Division growth in the early 1970s, across various manufacturing industries, because of these common needs.

Apart from the function of communicating the firm's new activities, the actual influence and function that the KJ Division performed internally varied from one firm to the next. Generally speaking, however, like any other newly created subunit of a Japanese firm, the KJ Division increases its internal influence gradually by establishing its own organizational legitimacy. This is usually done first by accepting necessary but uninteresting chores that other subunits do not wish to perform. In the case of the KJ Division, such chores vary from travel services to regular shipment of "care packages" to employees stationed abroad.

As the KJ Division continues to perform such personal services for employees involved in overseas activities, it begins to accumulate personal credit and favors with the rest of the firm's organization. The formal appointment of the influential corporate executive to the head of the KJ Division no doubt enhances the legitimacy of the division. With such an appointment, the KJ Division is given the additional responsibility of drawing up operational budgets and recording the economic performance of overseas subsidiaries. When this happens, the KJ Division is finally well on its way to the full fledged staff position of overseeing and planning for overseas activities of the firm.

When the KJ Division is fully grown to coordinating the overseas activities of the firms, the common arrangement for sharing these responsibilities with other units of the firm would look like the diagram pictured in Figure 9-3. Here again, one needs to recall that Japanese corporate culture has prepared its employees and management as well to operate in the organically arranged networks of both lateral and vertical communication. The shared experiences of the corporate employees enhance their expected commitment to the overall goals of the firm. This is even true when the product or area division is being used as a profit center.

For administrative reasons, the technical and management personnel sent abroad are first formally "transferred" on paper to the KJ Division, then reassigned to appropriate posts overseas. This "on paper appointment" is vital in Japanese corporate culture so that the KJ Division might secure the formal responsibility of "overseeing" persons stationed abroad. In this way, managers and engineers sent abroad can legitimately maintain their multiple loyalty to the KJ Division and to the product division from which they came. For the actual daily management of plants abroad, Japanese managers can rely on the informal stock of personal credit that they have built up with various individuals in the corporation.

GROUP DECISION-MAKING

This arrangement, which might appear to be a charade to people bred

Figure 9-3. KJ Division and Its Relation to Product Division

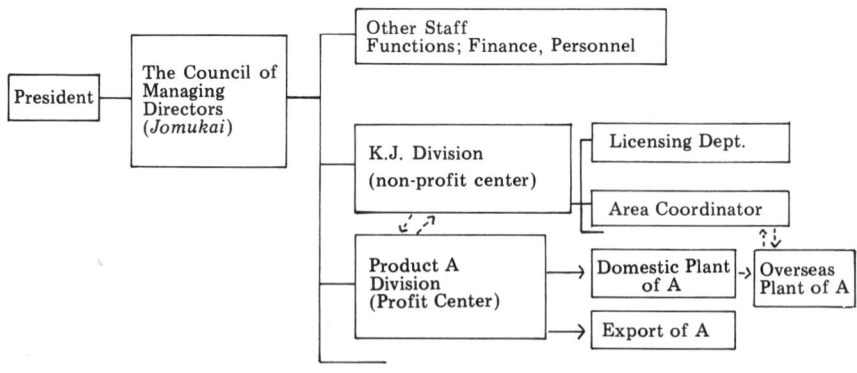

Key ← → Formal flows of manpower and financial information
⟵⟶ Formal flows of technology, products, production schedulings

in North American corporate culture, actually works in Japanese corporate culture. This is partly because such matters of personnel administration as rotation and promotion of various corporate employees belong solely to the president and are centrally controlled by the personnel department. The personnel department of a Japanese firm commands greater prestige and authority than it does in the American firm. Since the staffing of the KJ Division is done with the blessing of the personnel department, the KJ Division has legitimate control over its employees.

In addition, it is an accepted practice that Japanese multinational firms have an internally developed and supreme group decision-making body called *Jomukai* (the council of managing directors). Strategic decisions such as those concerning the timing, location, scale, products and major markets of the overseas manufacturing bases are the joint responsibility of the council of managing directors, (or equivalent decision-making body that is often chaired by the president). As a result, every corporate member is expected to cooperate with the KJ Division on the implementation of a decision reached by *Jomukai*. The KJ Division can in turn legitimately solicit cooperation from the rest of the organization.

The KJ Division is responsible for drawing up a concrete proposal to be scrutinized by *Jomukai*. Naturally, this process requires extensive and in-depth consultation and bargaining, although informal, among key persons in the divisions and departments to be affected by the proposed investment. The overriding concern is to create an argument that is convincing for the good of the company as a whole. The president can and does influence the direction of strategic decisions by deeply involving himself in the process of intense bargainings. The president's wishes do carry weight, especially in persuading skeptics of the good of a new corporate venture. The "new venture" and "crisis" situation are, after all, the president's traditional legitimate domain.

The strategic decision that formally results from *Jomukai* is the shared responsibility of all the *Jomukai* members. All key division and department heads are appointed *Jomukai* members. This is why it is important for the KJ Division to be headed by a corporate officer who is a voting member of *Jomukai*. Thus, it was explicit in the organizational structure of Japanese multinational firms that the KJ Division came to be headed by a corporate officer holding the rank of managing director or higher. The message of the rest of the corporate organization was that overseas activities were going to be given not only presidential but also organizational attention, making them worthy of the total commitment of all corporate employees.

The operational decisions or routine services of the overseas subsidiaries are settled amongst managers and their assistants, who report to the members of *Jomukai*. Only those portions of the operational decisions that cannot be settled by the practicing managers are sent upward to *Jomukai* for final arbitration. Discord at the level of practicing managers is often interpreted as a sign of incompetence or uncooperativeness by the supervisors. Thus, the practicing managers are strongly motivated to decide on present operational decisions according to previously approved *Jomukai* objectives. Here again, "presidential wishes" are often used as the overriding guideline for operational decisions. When the operational decisions are made by the practicing managers, the *Ringi Report* is sent to *Jomukai* merely to inform it of operational decisions. Informal consultations are often held between practicing managers and members of *Jomukai*. Thus, when practicing managers grope their way toward consensus, the personal reactions of *Jomukai* members will be taken into account.

As a buffer between *Jomukai* and *Ringi* procedure of operational decisions, a number of firms have a management committee that often consists of the same members as *Jomukai*. But this committee is clearly defined as a "discussion" group in which strategic decisions are freely evaluated. This seemingly redundant forum serves well in Japanese corporate culture to identify sensitive issues and diffuse oppositions, without committing anyone to a specific position. Since the managers' process of decision-making is one of consensus building, hot, volatile debate is almost a must. As a result, the forum-like "discussion group" in which disagreement amongst participants becomes the "norm" is frequently used within Japanese corporations.

KJ DIVISION IN TRANSITION?

As we have seen thus far, the *Kaigai Jigyobu* (Overseas Division) of Japanese multinational firms is different in substance from the International Division of American multinational firms.[12] The latter is, as a rule, a profit center within the firm and tends to practice "adversary" or "competing" relationships with the rest of the organization. The KJ Division of Japanese multinational firms, as of the mid-1970s, mainly performs the coordinating staff functions and thrives on "cooperative" relationships with the rest of the firm's organization.

In view of the fact that the overseas manufacturing activities of Japanese multinational firms still occupy a relatively small portion of the sales and production activities, the non-profit center role of the KJ Division may be appropriate. However, it remains to be seen whether the intricate networks of communication among the KJ Division, its overseas subsidiaries, and the rest of the organization will be able to handle the increasing complexity of parent-subsidiary relationships in the near future.

One way to make the KJ more responsive to the socioeconomic needs of its subsidiaries abroad might be to turn it into a profit center fully responsible for the political and economic health of its subsidiaries. In this way, the KJ Divisions could become more motivated to protect the interests of their overseas subsidiaries, more rigorously than the politically weak coordinating body presently handling the interests of these subsidiaries abroad.

As of the mid-1970s, the Japanese multinational firms which have made their KJ Division fully responsible for the profit and loss of their manufacturing subsidiaries abroad are still few and far between. However, as a profit center, the KJ Division is invariably accompanied by one of the two following such methods of giving formal or informal credit to the product or domestic division for its contribution of the success of the overseas subsidiary:

(1) *Internal Licensing Agreement and Royalty Payment:* Product divisions have a standard price list for their know-how and consulting services. These are open to negotiation. The schedule of payments is also open to negotiation. The KJ negotiates its royalty fees and schedule of payments as the need arises. The products that the KJ purchases from the domestic plants for its overseas subsidiaries are priced according to the export prices of comparable products.

(2) *Internal Identification of Contributions by Product Division:* All profits and losses of overseas subsidiaries are formally registered by the KJ. But the KJ does biannually declare and publicize each product division's contribution to the total performance of the firm's overseas manufacturing subsidiaries. The product division does not include its "declared" contributions in the performance report. It does, however, share in the glory of overseas success, if any.

Given the organizational commitment to overseas ventures, the above methods of dividing the "reward" and "profit" of overseas ventures between the KJ Division and domestic divisions tends to facilitate cooperation within the organization. The firms that initiated the above methods invariably admitted that they made the KJ a profit center in order to be more directly responsive to the political and economic needs of their subsidiaries. The staffing of the KJ Division as well as the rotation of key managers between the KJ and the domestic divisions were, however, invariably handled by personnel departments. Thus, the organizational rivalry between the KJ Division and the domestic division was either kept at a minimum or substantially diffused. The expectation that any manager might be forced to rotate between the KJ and the domestic division conditions him to cooperate with fellow employees as much as possible. And there is always the *Jomukai* group to remind each division of its joint responsibility to the success of the overseas ventures.

All in all, since the early 1970s Japanese manufacturing firms have entered a new and expanded phase in their multinational activities. In changing their strategic course, Japanese manufacturing firms tend to create internally a separate subunit like *Kaigai Jigyobu* as a focal point of their new activities. However, unlike the American international division, the Japanese *Kaigai Jigyobu* keeps intact its indivisible links with the rest of the firm organizations. The end result of such organizational adaptation of the Japanese *Kaigai Jigyobu* may well enhance the role of the KJ Division as the parent firm expands its multinational activities. In the case of many American firms, organizational subunits like the international division often broke up as the parent firm expanded its overseas activities.[13] In the case of the Japanese KJ Division, the opposite fate may well turn out to be true.

Chapter Ten

The "Ugly Japanese" and Their Dilemma Abroad

For ten days, from October 6 to October 16, 1973 Thailand was shaken. Students and city dwellers staged bloody revolts against the military regime that had been in power for over twenty years. When the two strong men of the miliatry regime, Thanom and Prapass, fled by night from Bangkok into exile on October 14, 1973, the students emerged as victors whose singular success in replacing the military regime with a civilian government set Thailand apart in Asia from the opposite and more general trends of increased repression in the old South Vietnam under Thieu, in Cambodia under Lon Nol, in Taiwan under Chiang Kai-shek, in the Philippines under Marcos and in Korea under Park.

The successful revolt was touched off on October 6 when a group of twelve students, instructors and minor political figures were arrested by the National Police for distributing leaflets near Thammasat University, Bangkok. The leaflets called for the early promulgation of a constitution—a direct criticism of the military regime that labelled this constitution drive "a sinister plot" to overthrow the government.

Even to date it is not quite clear why literally hundreds of thousands of students and city dwellers were able to topple the military regime after staging such fierce prolonged assaults on police and military stations in Bangkok. Their outbursts of anger surprised both foreign and Thai residents who were accustomed to Thais' long-suffering Buddhist acceptance of the hierarchical authority. Undoubtedly there were many pressing social issues that had for some time bred anger among the Thais—rising prices, scarcity of rice, chronic unemployment and widespread corruption in the government. Yet most of these issues had been conditions of Thai life for some time. What then prepared the students' increasing militancy against the Thai authority—the very militancy that had been swelling almost to the boiling point prior to October 6, 1973? The issues which Thai students and city dwellers seized to criticize their military regime prior to the October uprising might shed some light on this tantalizing question.

Prior to October 1973 Thai students staged prolonged demonstrations against the issue of Japanese investments in Thailand—thus demonstrating that their previous sporadic outbursts had finally culminated in a rallying force to be reckoned with by Thai authority. They not only called for the boycotting of Japanese goods, but also charged the Thai government with being corrupted by Japanese investors. In Bangkok, the first mass protest against the Japanese businesses was touched off in fall 1972. Ostensibly, the Thais' anger over a newly opened Japanese gymnasium devoted to "Thai kickboxing"—the sacred martial art of Thailand—triggered mass demonstrations calling for the boycott of Japanese products. The Japanese-run department store in Thailand, Daimaru, also became the target of waves of mass protests not merely because the store was located next to the Japanese gymnasium but also because the store was viewed as the symbol of the Japanese domination of the Thai economy. Once aroused, attention on Japanese investments was immediately extended to include all foreign investments.[1] American investments in Thailand came to draw as much attention as those of the Japanese.

With the build-up of U.S. military forces in Thailand as back-up bases for Vietnam operations, the students became increasingly apprehensive of American soldiers corrupting the delicate fabric of Thai society. When the Japanese domination of the Thai economy became apparent, students came to question the foreign domination of Thai society and the complicity of the government in permitting political and economic domination by alien groups. As they began to articulate these anti-foreign and anti-Japanese sentiments in particular, the students earned themselves the implicit support of a wide portion of Thai society, and thus came to command much influence among the population.

In June 1973 a sensational scandal concerning the military regime broke out in Bangkok. A group of high-ranking military officers were exposed by the newspapers as having taken several well-known movie actresses on a safari to a large government game reserve where hunting was strictly forbidden. It was reported that their helicopter, to be used for hunting and supplied by the United States, was actually for the ostensible mission of checking "communist rebellion." Angered students seized on this incident to expose corruption in the top echelon. Japanese and American investments were frequently cited as having corrupt influence on the Thai government. Yet the demonstrations were staged against Japanese firms. These demonstrations often appeared dominated by Thais of Chinese ancestry whose traditional family businesses and commerce were rumored to be threatened by Japanese direct investments.

Thus, in Thailand a vocal dissident group like the university students, who first became irritated at the visible presence of foreign (Japanese) investments, was able to politicize itself and other segments of the population by focusing on the entire issue of hateful foreign domination of Thai society. And their increased political awareness led them to criticize what they saw as the duplicity and complicity of their own government elites in personally benefiting from graft and other favors extended by foreign firms.

In 1975, the sudden disappearance of "border trade"—a euphemism for contraband trade to Laos, Cambodia, Burma and Vietnam—struck a severe blow to fledgling textile industry in Thailand. Until this incident about 30 percent of Thai textile manufactures found their way into the neighboring countries. The twenty-six firms that belonged to the Thai Textile Manufacturers' Association broached the Thai government with proposals for government assistance in exporting Thai textile products. What country but Japan could afford to buy these products? After all, Japanese textile firms and trading firms had been very instrumental in coaching Thai into a rapid build-up of its textile production capacity. And yet Japanese textile workers and firms were already pressuring the government to restrict such imports. The Japanese-Thai economic interests now appear to be heading for collision. And their collision will certainly not help Thailand ease her anti-Japanese feelings.

Elsewhere, in Indonesia, students and unemployed urban dwellers, in January 1974, burned an effigy of the prime minister of Japan, Tanaka, who was visiting Jakarta. The demonstrators stoned Japanese businesses and burned Japanese cars. The hateful image of "ugly Japanese" seemed a strong enough issue to help rally otherwise politically apathetic students and city dwellers in Indonesia. When the protesters began to turn their attention to the complicity of Indonesian government elites, however, the Suharto regime decided to crack down. The fate that befell the Thai military regime in

October 1973 appeared to be very much on the minds of Indonesian government officials. But in the fall of 1975, the Indonesian newspapers suddenly revived their scathing criticisms of the Japanese investments and Japanese tourists. This eruption signalled that the government again chose to permit the Indonesians to vent their general frustrations on foreign investments. And Japan became an easy scapegoat.

In Korea, in July 1972, one popular television series of the Korean Broadcasting System featured a drama in which a Japanese policeman, stationed in a Korean village around 1941, was instigated by a Korean thug in the village to torture a wealthy Korean farmer and his son. The Japanese policeman was depicted as having sinister designs on the farmer's daughter-in-law. Regardless of the historical authenticity of this particular episode, its setting and motif exposed the deep-seated anger that the Korean public generally harbored against the brutal colonial experiences of the Japanese regime, 1910–1945, and against contemptuous Korean collaborators. Around the same time in Korea in 1972, newspapers and magazines began to question aloud whether Japanese direct investments succeeded where military endeavors before 1945 had failed; namely, the silent conquest of Korea, or its silent surrender to the Japanese hegemony. The television drama rekindled Korea's memories of the brutal humiliation suffered under the Japanese colonial administration. Furthermore, it succeeded in helping Koreans see the current presence of Japanese investments as an extension of the "colonized Korea."

From the end of 1972 to mid-1973, Korean public criticism of Japanese businesses was openly stepped up. For instance, from spring to fall of 1973, it was widely publicized that of all foreign subsidiaries, the Japanese had the lowest wage level. During the months of July and August 1973 while in Korea, I was repeatedly reminded of this fact. Such leading national newspapers as *Dong-A-Ilbo* and *Chosun Ilbo* frequently carried stories about "low wage rates" of Japanese subsidiaries on the basis of the data released by the Korean government. This survey evidence was singularly interpreted as evidence that Japanese firms were exploiting Korean laborers. The survey failed to take into account the fact that all Japanese subsidiaries cited were joint ventures with Koreans and that many of them were established by so-called medium- to small-sized Japanese firms, often owned and operated by Koreans residing in Japan. Although these subsidiaries pay higher wages than comparable small- to medium-sized firms of Korea, they were matched against American subsidiaries of such large firms as Fairchild, Motorola and Gulf Oil. The survey did not mention that the wage levels and working conditions of subsidiaries of large Japanese firms such as Hitachi, Toshiba, Sanyo and NEC were often better than those of their American counterparts in Korea.

Similar campaigns to reinforce public prejudices against Japanese firms during 1973 were spreading throughout Asia. However, in checking the chronology of the sudden appearances of public criticism of Japanese investments by the leading local newspapers, I found one distinct pattern is apparent. Local newspapers, which were often under government censorship, began to criticize Japanese investment policies when Japan appeared to be overtaking the United States as a leading foreign investor.

As Japanese investments increased their public visibility in the United States, Brazil, Europe and Australia, the image of the "ugly Japanese" began to appear throughout the mass media and political sector. Why was this so? Over and above the expected reactions of host countries to any foreign investments, was there something special about Japanese investments that tended to single them out as the "hateful investments" by various interest groups?

THE VIEWPOINTS OF THE DEVELOPING COUNTRIES

As in the case of a manufacturing firm, the industrial growth of a country requires such factors as (1) investment capital, (2) foreign exchange, (3) manufacturing technologies, (4) export market contacts and (5) managerial skills. Historically, different countries have chosen a number of ways to obtain and augment these five necessary factors. For example, at least up until 1973 when the Canadian Parliament passed the Foreign Investment Review Act—designed to regulate further efforts of foreign investments—and created the Canadian Development Corporation—designed in part to buy back selective foreign assets in Canada—this country had encouraged the inflows of foreign direct investment as an expedient way of obtaining a conglomerate package of the five necessary factors for Canada's economic development.[2]

On the other hand, the Japanese approach provides an extreme opposite example. Since the mid-Nineteenth Century and especially since the 1870s when Japan consciously chose to industrialize her economy, she endeavored to augment for herself these five necessary factors.

The Maoist economic development of China today presents a distinctly different pattern. In terms of the role of the central government and the emphasis on "human resources," the Chinese model contains many elements of the early Japanese model.³ But the similarity ends there. Rather than developing professional and ideological elites, as in the case of Japan or the Soviet Union, China emphasizes not only the "balanced growth" between agricultural and industrial sectors, but more important, the equitable distribution of economic wealth and political power. Indeed, China's economic development appears to be centered on the goal of attaining an equal distribution of wealth and political power. In order to achieve this goal, Chinese leadership resorts to so-called "cultural revolutions" from time to time in order to rid the industrial and party leaders of elitist thinking. In addition, her vast domestic market helps China chart her own course of "self-sufficient" industrial development with limited dependence on foreign trade.

Today, with the possible exception of Cuba, Tanzania, Burma, Cambodia and Vietnam, the leaders of developing nations tend to adopt an approach to industrial development somewhere between the Canadian and Japanese models, but often closer to the Canadian than to the Japanese model. This is partly because the living standards of advanced nations are demonstrated internationally. This makes developing nations reluctant to hold down their own levels of national consumption in order to squeeze necessary savings for reinvestment. In addition, the central governments of most developing nations do not yet possess internally the administrative efficiency or political strength required for successful execution of the early Japanese approach. Accordingly, as a matter of expediency, a foreign direct investment is counted on by the governments of developing countries as the package that will readily provide the five factors necessary for industrial growth. The resultant dilemma of the developing nations of today is, therefore: how much and for how long should they be burdened with the political and psychological dependency on foreign private firms in exchange for the benefits of the five factors. For the most part, foreign direct investments are perceived as a necessary evil that must be tolerated for as long as the intended benefits exceed the actual costs to the host country.

This tolerance of multinational firms based in Japan, the United States and Europe was not limited to non-socialist countries. Today, East European countries and even the Soviet Union appear to be embracing "industrial cooperation" with multinational firms of "capitalist countries," through which they desire to obtain proprietary technologies on a continuing basis.⁴

The upshot of all these considerations is that the conduct of private foreign subsidiaries tends to be judged in host countries by unstated but strong expectations for benevolent change, and those factors which will best facilitate the industrial development of the particular country. Worse yet, intellectuals, students and political opponents of the regime in power in developing countries tend to assume that unless foreign subsidiaries aid them in their unrealized tasks of drastic political and economic reform, they should not be tolerated. To make matters worse, many high-ranking executives of Japanese, European and American multinational firms publicly boast of their subsidiaries in developing nations as being the basic moving force for social development. Consequently, these executives of private multinational firms end up with unwarranted but self-serving boasts of power. These boasts are in turn taken at face value and summarized in popular books such as *Global Reach*; they confirm the suspicions journalist critics have long felt toward multinational firms in regard to their obnoxious global reaching powers.

Interestingly enough, however, from Latin America to East Asia, and from Southeast Asia to Africa, the popular criticisms which host developing countries harbor against foreign investments contain very similar themes. They can be grouped into the following five categories:[5]

(1) *Dependencia Theorems*: By accepting private investments from the "metropolis" of the world (developed countries), developing countries (LDCs) increase their technological and cultural dependency upon the "metropolis" nations. Various converts of this school of thought point out that foreign multinational firms implant in the host LDCs manufacturing technologies suited to their own purposes of quick profit-making but unsuited to the economic and social fabrics of the LDCs. The LDCs thus become perpetually dependent upon multinational firms for manufacturing technologies. Advertising campaigns which foreign multinational firms bombard on the middle-class populace of LDCs reinforce a decadent consumer mentality. The end result is that LDCs are drained of their own cultural identity and technological growth potentials.

(2) *Alliance with the Reactionary Forces*: Foreign multinational firms tie up politically and economically in the host country with the reactionary forces who resist necessary social changes. By aiding reactionary elements in increasing their economic and political power, multinational firms retard the political and social change of LDCs.

(3) *Corrupting Influence*: In order to bend laws and regulations of host LDCs to suit their own commercial purposes, foreign multinationals widely resort to bribing government officials and politicians. By offering higher salaries and greater material benefits than indigenous businessmen or government offices can afford, foreign multinational firms attract human resource and skills away from

the local plants and offices. Thus, the materialist mentality creeps into local elite groups in the government sectors as well as in the industries.

(4) *Reliance on Home Countries' Diplomatic and Military Powers*: When in political binds with host government of LDCs, foreign multinational firms call in their home country governments to apply diplomatic pressure. Thinly veiled threats of cutting off economic and military aid are an often used tactic of the "metropolis" nations. Thus, the acceptance of foreign direct investments makes host LDCs politically dependent on foreign powers.

(5) *Extraterritoriality*: Even if private foreign investors are reluctant to call in their home governments, they do use their private subsidiaries in LDCs as tools for upholding their foreign policies. Most commonly, home governments of the "metropolis" nations intervene in the foreign trade and investments of their subsidiaries abroad. Thus, the acceptance of private foreign investments by host LDCs at the same time brings the meddling of home governments in their domestic affairs.

Obviously, one does not have to look too far to find a number of specific examples of foreign subsidiaries in LDCs which appear to fit one or more of the above five categories. And to impressionist observers of multinational firms, these examples serve as irrefutable proof of the sins being perpetrated by multinational firms against LDCs. In reality, however, the closer one analyzes the various dimensions of multinational behavior (e.g., the selection of manufacturing technologies for their subsidiaries in LDCs or the actual management of their subsidiaries abroad), the less certain one becomes of the "cost and benefits" relationship between foreign subsidiaries and host LDCs.

In addition to the preceding five categories of criticism against multinational firms in LDCs, Japanese subsidiaries are often charged with the following three misbehaviors:

(1) *Exclusiveness*: Japanese expatriate managers and engineers exclude local managers and engineers from important decision-making processes of their subsidiaries as well as from important tasks of communicating with Japanese parent plants and offices located in Japan and elsewhere.

(2) *Too many Japanese Expatriates*: Compared with other foreign multinational firms, Japanese parent firms send too many Japanese expatriate managers and engineers into their subsidiaries abroad. They occupy not only the top management echelon of the subsidiary organization but the middle and lower management echelon as well.

(3) *Cultural Insensitivity*: Socially, Japanese expatriates keep to

themselves outside their subsidiaries. They seldom socialize with local residents. They remain insensitive to social and cultural "taboos" of host countries. They do not learn local languages. And they send their children to "Japanese" schools.

Accordingly, the public image of "ugly Japanese" in LDCs appears tarnished beyond repair. Of all the hated multinational firms, Japanese firms are labelled by intellectuals, students and politicians of LDCs as the most undesirable. How did this come about? Are the realities of Japanese multinational firms the same as the images they invoke in the minds of the "man on the street" in host LDCs?

PUBLIC VISIBILITY OF JAPANESE INVESTMENTS

It has been widely assumed among local residents and Japanese expatriates throughout East and Southeast Asia that Japanese direct investments are the largest of all foreign investments in each country. This impression was already visible throughout Asia by about 1970. By 1973, it appeared ingrained in the minds of local residents and Japanese visitors. Japanese investments thus became familiar to the public eye.

Nonetheless, the available facts pointed to a wide discrepancy between the prevailing impression and the reality of Japanese investments in Asia. In Table 10-1 the direct investments of the United States and Japan for the years 1971 and 1973, are summarized. The United States' investments in Asia were about four times as large as those of Japan in 1971 and were still about twice as large in 1973. In 1971, in every single country throughout Asia, Japanese investments remained a distant second to those of the United States. By 1973, excluding South Korea and Thailand, the United States was still the world's largest investor. And yet, each host country developed the impression that Japan had long dominated foreign investments.

When compared with U.S. or foreign investments in general, there are four characteristics of Japanese investments that make them particularly visible to the public eye. Politically negative reactions of host countries to Japanese investments are strongly related to these four attributes.

First, although Japan remained second to the United States in terms of the total value of assets invested, Japan surpassed all other foreign investments throughout Asia in terms of the number of subsidiaries involved. A large number of small-scale operations characterized Japanese investments; compared to the average size of investment in the U.S.–based firm, the average Japanese investment

Table 10-1. Accumulated United States and Japanese Direct Investments in Asia (Millions of U.S. dollars)

	United States			Japan		
Host Country	1971	1973	1973/71(%)	1971	1973	1973/71(%)
Sri Lanka	N.A.	N.A.	— %	2	3	150%
Taiwan	133	142	106	85	110	129
Hong Kong	286	291	101	139	180	129
India	329	332	101	12	15	125
Indonesia	512	812	159	241	344	143
S. Korea	277	301	108	33	310	939
Malaysia	] 307	162	] 297	50	121	242
Singapore		750		33	150	454
Pakistan	96	N.A.	—	5	6	120
Philippines	719	820	114	74	110	149
Thailand	124	172	138	91	200	219
Others including S. Vietnam	266	N.A.	—	14	15	107
Total	3,049	3,821	125%	779	1,574	202%

Source: The U.S. data for 1971 were obtained from *Survey of Current Business*, U.S. Dept. of Commerce. The Japanese data for 1971 are estimated by the author from *Tokei Geppo*, June 1972, Toyo Keizai, Tokyo, pp. 4-5, p. 8. The 1971 data appeared previously in Donald R. Sherk, *Foreign Investments in Asia: Cooperation and Conflict Between the U.S. and Japan*, Federal Reserve Bank of San Francisco, October 1973, p. 24. The 1973 data were estimated on the basis of information gathered through the fieldwork of the author in 1973.

was only one-fifth to one-tenth the size. Residents of each host country had a greater chance of encountering a Japanese subsidiary than any other foreign subsidiary. Hence, a greater public exposure to Japanese investments led people to assume that Japanese investments dominated the scene.

Second, Japanese investments in Asia and elsewhere were concentrated in manufacturing industries. As a matter of fact, in manufacturing industries Japan dominated every country in Asia both in terms of the total asset and the number of subsidiaries involved. Furthermore, as seen in Chapter 3, Japanese manufacturing operations tended to concentrate on light consumer goods industries. For economic reasons, the consumer goods plants were often located in or around major population centers of host countries. In order to sell these goods, producers resorted to massive advertisements on radio, TV, billboards and neon signs. Thus, the public visibility of Japanese investments was being cultivated by Japanese investors.

In other areas, it was widely rumored throughout Thailand from

1974 to 1975, that Japanese subsidiaries had more labor unrest than other foreign subsidiaries. This rumor was perpetuated by Thai government officials, academics, journalists and students. However, field investigations into these allegations revealed that from 1973 to 1974 the Thai economy underwent its worst economic slump, severely affecting fledgling manufacturing industries. The hardest hit victim was the textile industry, Thailand's leading manufacturing industry. Labor unrest and disputes swept through textile plants. It so happened that the textile industry was dominated by Japanese subsidiaries. Although the American and Thai owned textile plants were struck by the Thai Textile Workers Union as often, if not more often than Japanese-owned plants, the public visibility of Japanese textile industries led impressionistic observers to conclude that Thai workers hated Japanese plants.

Third, Japanese manufacturing subsidiaries in host LDCs were often producing products for domestic markets of host countries that were not technologically sophisticated. These products often became the first candidates for direct competition by indigenous manufacturers. Indigenous manufacturers, who were eager to oust Japanese products from their own home markets, often kept up political campaigns against Japanese investments. The oft-heard charge was that Japanese multinational firms brought only obsolete and simple products to host countries.

The first generation of products that migrated to Asian LDCs from Japan during the 1960s were taken over by the mid-1970s almost exclusively by indigenous entrepreneurs from Korea, Hong Kong, Taiwan and Singapore. Of late, Taiwan, Hong Kong, Singapore and Korea have become the chief suppliers of manufacturing technologies in a wide range of standard industrial and consumer products to Indonesia, Thailand and Malaysia. Newcomers to the field of "multinational activity," they absorbed much of their manufacturing technology from Japan by way of Japanese direct investment in their countries, by way of technology learned through licensing agreements with Japanese firms, or often by direct imitation of standard Japanese products.

When entrepreneurs from Taiwan, Hong Kong, Singapore or Korea seek to further their product and process technologies, they send one or two technicians on a training tour-of-duty into small- or medium-sized Japanese firms where such technologies are conveniently found. More often than not, six to twelve months in these plants is deemed sufficient enough time to round out their experience and skill. By combining the Japanese technologies they have learned, with the imitation of standard Japanese machines made in their own countries (made in Taiwan and Hong Kong for one-half the cost of those made in Japan), these entrepreneurs from outside Japan are able to set up manufacturing subsidiaries in Indonesia, Thailand, the Philippines and Malaysia. Through long kept personal contacts cultivated in East and Southeast Asia, investors from Hong Kong, Taiwan and Singapore in particular are increasingly able to overtake Japanese manufacturing product markets in Indonesia, Thailand and Malaysia.

For instance, of the total foreign direct investments in Indonesia made annually from 1967 to 1972, Hong Kong's dollar value investments increased over 14 times while Japan's equivalent figure rose only about 8 times. In 1972, investors from Taiwan appeared in Indonesia and signalled the beginning of Taiwan's expansion into Indonesia. One might also note, in Table 10-2, that direct investments in Indonesia from Singapore and even from Thailand, Malaysia and the Philippines increased during 1967-1972. In addition to direct investments cleared by the Indonesian government, a bulk of additional investments from Taiwan, Hong Kong, Singapore and other Asian countries flowed into Indonesia "invisibly" through their contacts with Chinese-Indonesian businesses. The upshot of all these events was that Japanese investments received increasingly adverse publicity from would-be Asian competitors, as well as from indigenous entrepreneurs.

The relative declines recorded by Asian investors from 1971 to 1972 in their combined dollar value share of the newly entered foreign investments in Indonesia was caused by an increased influx of investments from the U.S., Australia, Germany and the Netherlands. Japanese investors found themselves being squeezed out of the standard product market by other Asian investors, and waging new product market fights with American and other non-Asian investors. The end result was that Japanese investors were hit with much negative and vocal publicity from competing investors in a wide range of product markets.

Fourth, as shown in Table 10-1, the growth rate of Japanese direct investments in each Asian host country was often explosively high after 1971. This was caused mainly by the Japanese parent firm's desire to follow its competitors into overseas ventures. This situation produced the appearance of a "massive avalanche" of Japanese investments in Asian host countries. In 1973 alone, Japanese investments in Malaysia increased 700 percent from the 1972 level. In 1974 in Indonesia, Japanese investments became the largest of all foreign investments in terms of cumulative assets involved. Other Asian host countries began to fear that Japanese investments would soon overtake American investments.

Table 10-2. Approved Investments in Indonesia for Asian Countries 1967-1972

	Annual Moving Average of Approved Investments for Two-Year Period									
	1967-68		1968-69		1969-70		1970-71		1971-72	
Country	No.	$Mil.	No.	$Mil.	No.	$Mil.	No.	$Mil.	No.	$Mil.
(1) Asian Investors' Total	15.5	46.9	38.0	251.3	65.5	268.6	73.0	169.3	63.0	201.2
(2) Japan	5.0	10.1	11.5	58.6	21.5	74.4	27.0	78.4	23.5	88.0
(3) Non-Japan	10.5	36.8	26.5	192.8	44.0	194.2	46.0	90.9	39.5	113.2
S. Korea	0.5	24.0	0.5	24.0	1.5	2.4	1.5	2.5	1.0	2.3
Hong Kong	5.0	4.3	9.0	11.8	15.5	17.6	19.5	45.9	18.0	61.6
Taiwan	—	—	—	—	—	—	—	—	1.0	8.7[b]
Singapore	3.0	3.3	7.5	17.4	11.0	28.9	8.5	19.3	6.0	16.9
Malaysia	0.5	0.5	3.0	8.0	9.0	14.6	11.5	13.4	8.0	11.3
Thailand	—	—	2.0	1.6	2.5	1.9	3.0	7.0	2.5	6.7
Philippines	1.5	4.7	4.5	130.0[a]	4.5	128.8[a]	2.0	2.7	3.0	5.7
Japan's share in $ value		51.5%		23.3%		27.6%		46.3%		43.7%
Hong Kong's share in $ value		9.1%		4.6%		6.5%		27.1%		30.6%
Asian's share in $ value		22.9%		52.6%		55.5%		74.5%		60.4%

[a] Investments in logging operations that amounted to $255 M. in 1969 contributed to this marked increase.
[b] Taiwanese investments actually appeared in 1972, amounting to $17.3 M. for two projects.

Source: Compiled from Mimeographed Data, Foreign Investments Board, Djakarta, March 1973, and also ascertained through fieldwork by the author.

A similar avalanche effect was also being increasingly felt from 1973 to 1975 throughout Latin America, in Brazil in particular. For example, in 1973 alone, new Japanese investments in Brazil and Mexico trebled from the previous year. Subsequently, Japanese investments showed no sign of levelling off.

In Australia, in 1973 alone, new Japanese investments registered over a 600 percent increase from the 1972 level. From 1974 to 1975 there appeared distinct signs of similar avalanche effects throughout Europe and North America. Accordingly, by 1975 Japanese investments began to attract politically adverse attention even in the industrially advanced nations.

In addition to the public visibility of firms in host countries, the avalanche effect of Japanese investments inevitably threatened the delicate political power balances of various interest groups, political factions and businesses in host LDCs. As pointed out earlier in this chapter, a chronological analysis of the rise of anti-Japanese sentiments in each Asian country revealed the following. The first traceable appearance of anti-Japanese sentiments in the local presses dates from the time when Japanese investments approached one-third to one-half of United States investments in terms of cumulative assets involved. This was at the same time that Japanese investments became the most numerous of all foreign investments in terms of the number of subsidiaries involved. My own field observations in Korea, Taiwan, Thailand and Indonesia, however, led me to the following proposition.

As discussed earlier in this chapter, host LDCs chose grudgingly to tolerate foreign investments that provided them with desired economic and technological resources. Once adopting foreign investments, local business partners, politicians and government officials developed new balances of political and economic power among various interest groups and individuals linked with foreign investments. Being the first and the largest, United States investments served as the core which formed these new political balances of power among business elites and political leaders.

The infusion of such new alien powers as Japanese investments inevitably disrupted not only the existing balances of power but also the familiar external relationships of host LDCs. LDC diplomatic stances were based upon the premise that United States investments were the dominant economic force. With the rise of Japanese investments, local business partners, students, government officials and political leaders who chose to link themselves up with Japanese investments, began to improve their political and economic fortune relative to the "old guard," whose fortune was tied closely to United States investments.

The old guard, whose accustomed position of power was threatened by newcomers like the Japanese and their local partners, began to take a lead in singling out Japanese investments as the increasing menace to their society. This explains why staff personnel of American embassies often joined (albeit privately) adverse verbal campaigns against Japanese investments. While I was doing field research on foreign investments throughout Asia, I frequently ran into American embassy or consulate people recounting with relish adverse rumors about Japanese corporate behavior.* These diplomatic corps people were concerned with the declining influence of American businesses in Asian countries. In short, the four idiosyncracies of Japanese investments in host LDCs described earlier, provide inadvertent bases for the intentional negative publicity often contrived by the old guards in host LDCs.

From 1974 to 1975 Japanese investments in Brazil were overtaking German investments, which had long held the position of distant second to American investments. From 1973 to 1974 Japan surpassed France and the United Kingdom in the ranking ladder of foreign investors in Brazil. This was at about the same time when Brazilian newspapers began carrying statements and featured articles warning Brazil of Japan's "sinister" plot to monopolize the Brazilian market.

In 1973, of 223 foreign-owned firms that made the list of the largest 1000 firms in Brazil, only nine were Japanese-owned. With 82 firms on the list, the United States led all other foreign investors. France, the United Kingdom, Germany, Italy, Sweden, and the Netherlands together held 109 of the largest 1000 firms. Like their counterparts in Asia, Japanese investments in Brazil were characterized by small- to medium-sized firms. Only one Japanese related subsidiary, in which a Japanese partner had 10 percent ownership, made the list of Brazil's 60 largest firms, while United States and European nations dominated the list in competition with Brazilian federal government- or state government-owned firms. Again in Brazil, with over 330 subsidiaries having entered the country since

---

*In order to obtain the true feelings of American and European individuals concerning increasing Japanese influences, I often pretended to be any nationality but Japanese. The story that was popular among Americans and Europeans in Djakarta in 1973 was one about the more than 2000 massage parlors in Indonesia which catered mainly to Japanese businessmen and tourists. At that time, I estimated that on any given day, the total number of Japanese businessmen and tourists in Indonesia could not possibly be more than 2000. No massage parlor could survive commercially with only one customer per day. When this detail was pointed out, the usual reply was, "there must be tens of thousands of Japanese all over the country. They are bribing and corrupting Indonesians right to left."

1970, Japanese investments attracted the adverse attention of Brazilians of European ancestry and their friends in the government, business and academic worlds.

In order to allay fear amongst Brazilians, the Japanese Chamber of Commerce in Brazil issued the "nine codes of exemplary conduct" for Japanese subsidiaries, but these efforts were of no avail. Notwithstanding the Chamber of Commerce's good intentions, such an act of public declaration only confirmed the suspicions of the "man on the street" in Brazil. People wondered, "If the Japanese Chamber of Commerce must issue such codes of conduct, Japanese firms must be behaving really badly." Hence, the public campaign of the Japanese Chamber of Commerce provided yet another inadvertent proof of Japanese insensitivity to Brazilian culture. They were mistaken in their assumption that Brazilians would react favorably to such a campaign as the public in Japan would.

JAPANESE EXPORT DRIVE AND HOST COUNTRIES' REACTION

The public visibility of Japanese investments is naturally influenced by the domination of Japanese products in host country product markets. The man on the street does not distinguish between Japanese goods made locally and Japanese goods imported from Japan. Long before Japanese investors commenced their local manufacturing operations, Japanese products were being exported to Asia, Latin America and other developing countries. As we saw in Chapter 3, Japanese manufacturing subsidiaries abroad were initially set up in host LDCs in order to counteract import substitution moves by the host LDCs. As a result, inasmuch as Japanese direct investments were often mere extensions of Japanese export drives to host LDCs, the public visibility of these direct investments was naturally influenced by the preceding domination of Japanese imports in the host countries.

In addition, Japanese exports to host LDCs were often increased by Japanese manufacturing subsidiaries in host LDCs who continued to import intermediary manufactured goods from Japan. For example, in Table 10-3, imports of manufactures from Japan as a percent of total imports of manufactures are listed for nine selected host LDCs. By 1972 these host countries accepted over three-quarters of their goods from Japanese manufacturing subsidiaries abroad.

Table 10-3. Import of Manufactures from Japan as a Percent of Total Imports of Manufactures of Nine Selected Countries, 1972

Country	Import from Japan as Percent of Total Import	Balance of Trade with Japan
Korea	56.3%	Deficit
Taiwan	59.2	Deficit
Philippines	35.3	Deficit
Hong Kong	32.7	Deficit
Thailand	47.4	Deficit
Singapore	30.9	Deficit
Indonesia	31.2	Deficit
Brazil	8.0	Deficit
Mexico	3.8	Deficit

Source: *The United Nations Commodity Trade Statistics,* The United Nations, 1973.

N.B.: Manufactured goods are defined as the three-digit SITC product categories of 100's to 800's, plus foods.

Imports of such industrial raw materials as oil and ores, or nonprocessed foods such as grains, are not so publicly visible. But manufactured goods attract the attention of both consumers and businessmen. Lacking natural resources, Japanese exports consist exclusively of manufactured goods. Imports from Japan are thus more publicly visible than those of other countries. Throughout Asia, dependence of host LDCs on Japan for both consumer and industrial goods was deemed undesirable. To make matters worse, these LDCs often registered chronic trade deficits with the rest of the world and all nine of them registered chronic trade deficits with Japan.

Politicians and businessmen alike have regarded "trade deficit" as inherently bad for a country. They often believed that trade deficits with foreign investors were a sign that the investors were reaping exploitive profits twice—once through trade and the second time through direct investments. According to this folksy measure used to evaluate the "costs and benefits" of foreign investment, Japanese direct investments naturally again attracted adverse publicity. It was no wonder, therefore, that in most LDCs, Japanese direct investments became synonymous with the least desirable foreign investments. No one bothered to question why Japanese goods in direct competition with products of other industrialized countries, were in such demand in these LDCs. Was it because Japanese merchants brainwashed local residents through massive advertisement?

Or was it because Japanese products appealed to local consumers and industries both in terms of price and quality? A realistic answer would perhaps be closer to the latter than the former. But to those local politicians and intellectuals of LDCs eager to test the "social and political costs" of foreign investments, Japanese export drives were seen only as an exploitation of helpless consumers and businessmen.

The above perceptions of the social and political costs that the leaders, politicians, and intellectuals of host LDCs held against the highly visible presence of Japanese goods and direct investments, were aggravated by the apparently asymmetric relations that existed between Japan and Asian host LDCs. As shown in Table 10-3, Japan loomed as the dominant force in international trade to each Asian host country. And yet in terms of Japan's export market, all the Asian host countries combined were becoming, relatively speaking, less and less important. For example, from 1950 to 1970, Japan's exports to Asian LDCs declined from about three-quarters to one-third of her total exports. Each country in Asia had never constituted at best more than 5 percent of Japan's exports or imports. This asymmetric relationship between Japan and Asian host LDCs—of each host country's demand on Japan and Japan's sensitivity to such demand—inevitably produced a cleavage. To be sure, each host country expected Japan to pay special and individual attention to the fact that over one-third of the country's imports of manufactures came from Japan. Japan however, paid merely a fraction of her international attention to each host country, depending roughly on the part each country played in her total external trade. This unfulfilled expectation on the part of individual host countries bred frustration and resentment toward Japan.[6]

JAPANESE EXPATRIATE MANAGERS

The fact that Japanese direct investments appear ubiquitous in host LDCs automatically designates them as a prime target for host countries' wrath against foreign investments in general. Thus, the three "obnoxious" characteristics of Japanese operations pointed out earlier in this chapter appeared to be confirmed by casual observers of Japanese subsidiaries abroad. In particular, the charge that Japanese subsidiaries have too many Japanese managers is heard throughout Asia and Latin America. Host countries believe that Japanese have sinister plots to exclude local nationals from key decisions made by subsidiaries. Local nationals are capable, they say, of assuming greater managerial responsibilities. And yet, the Japanese are said to exclude them.

For instance, as shown in Chapter 7, my own field investigations in Indonesia during the first quarter of 1973 led me to observe that on the average a Japanese manufacturing subsidiary had five to six Japanese expatriates while a comparable manufacturing subsidiary of American and European investors had one to three expatriates. Furthermore, the maximum number of Japanese managers and engineers did not vary significantly with the total number of employees per subsidiary. Similarly, Japanese banks in Jakarta had about twice as many Japanese managers per office as comparable banks operated by American firms.

In Thailand as well, I observed that Japanese subsidiaries had a greater number of Japanese managers and engineers than American and European counterparts. This observation was corroborated independently by a separate piece of fieldwork.[7] During the summer of 1974, a researcher from Japan uncovered that for a comparable size as measured by the number of local employees, Japanese subsidiaries in Thailand had about two to four times as many expatriate personnel as American and European counterparts.

These data led casual observers to conclude that Japanese firms were excluding local personnel from managerial positions. As pointed out in Chapter 7, however, the seemingly ubiquitous presence of Japanese expatriates in a given subsidiary was caused by the idiosyncrasies of the production process-related technologies of Japan, as well as by the necessary and equally idiosyncratic patterns of communications between overseas subsidiaries and headquarters in Japan. As mentioned earlier, the institution-related technologies of Japanese firms that were often only implicitly ingrained in production process-related technologies, required person-to-person coaching on the job if Japanese technologies were to be transferred successfully to host countries.

These organizational idiosyncrasies of Japanese corporate systems are best highlighted by the ways in which Japanese expatriates are placed within the organization of a Japanese subsidiary. Compared with American and European counterparts, it is still common in a Japanese subsidiary that expatriates are placed very low on the hierarchical ladder of the firm's organization, even to include such first level supervisory positions as section chief or general foreman.

Besides, expatriate managers and engineers of American and European subsidiaries are often recruited locally from Americans and Europeans who have long been on the scene (since the end of World War II at any rate). These subsidiaries often employ expatriates whose nationality does not coincide with that of the firm. On the other hand, the expatriates of Japanese subsidiaries who hold key positions are not only Japanese but also the very Japanese who have been bred by the specific corporate culture of the investing parent firm. Thus, subsidiaries of Hitachi employ Japanese managers and engineers who have been bred in "Hitachi culture."

From the viewpoint of Japanese parent firms, the implicit and face-to-face mode of intra- and inter-organizational communication that evolved required that only "their own people" be placed in key posts within the overseas subsidiaries. Otherwise, communication that is vital to the constant flow of business and technologies between parent operations and their overseas subsidiaries breaks down. However, from the viewpoint of host countries, Japanese subsidiaries appear closed-minded not only to their own local aspirants seeking managerial positions but also to other non-Japanese expatriates wishing to land jobs with foreign firms. Both dissident viewpoints echo the mistaken but popular criticism that Japanese firms hire only Japanese. The truth of the matter is that it is not the Japanese nationality or even the Japanese language capability that is required for the effective transfer of technologies and managerial practices from Japan to subsidiaries abroad. Indeed, a trained dog or entertaining monkey could be hired for managerial positions by Japanese subsidiaries abroad. The only qualification would be that the prospective candidate understand the implicit modes of communication within Japanese corporate systems.

Notwithstanding the Japanese necessity for person-to-person training of local employees on the job, the available records of Japanese manufacturing firms indicated that after three to four years of such training, many of the Japanese "instruction managers" and "instruction technicians" successfully withdrew from their overseas manufacturing operations. Surely, a strong case can be made for the conclusion that the larger the initial number of Japanese expatriates assigned to a new venture, the quicker is their fade out.

The adverse public opinion of "ubiquitous" Japanese expatriates tends to be formed during the initial training years. The public opinion lingers long after a number of newly trained local managers and engineers are promoted to at least the first line of supervisory positions. Since new Japanese investments still tend to outnumber older, more established ventures in each host country, the public only see those Japanese subsidiaries with Japanese expatriate "trainers" who are working side by side the local trainees. Hence, casual observers adhere to the half-truth of the "exclusiveness" and "dominant presence" of Japanese expatriate managers.

CULTURAL INSENSITIVITY
OF JAPANESE FIRMS

Japanese firms are often ignorant of the lingering scars that their militarist government left in the minds of Asian neighbors from the events of World War II. In Korea, the Philippines, Singapore and Hong Kong, where the atrocities and brutality of Imperial Japan are still vividly remembered, Japanese firms are expected to be more sensitive to each country's social needs, even more so than their Western counterparts. As a retribution for the wartime destruction committed by Japan, these host countries expect that Japanese firms will make extra efforts in cooperating with the needs of the public.

In places like Indonesia, where the wartime Japan was initially remembered as a liberator that freed the country from Dutch colonialism, local politicians and intellectuals nevertheless expected Japanese firms to devote themselves to the goals of national construction. They expected Japanese investors to be more "Asian" and hence, more sensitive to local needs.

When Japanese subsidiaries appeared just as profit-minded and just as insensitive to public needs as any other foreign subsidiaries, the local expectations of "benign or repenting Japanese" were betrayed. And these delusions bred resentment toward Japanese firms.*

Japanese insensitivity to Asian host countries' stated and strong demand for Japanese repentance is one rather logical consequence of the self-serving efforts that the Japanese bureaucracy and the ruling party, LDP, expended shortly after 1952. At that time a campaign was begun to erase the wartime acts of Imperial Japan from all textbooks in Japanese primary through high schools.[8] With the regaining of her political independence in 1952, LDP and the Ministry of Education launched concerted efforts to place primary through high schools under the direct influence of the central bureaucracy and the conservative ruling party. In addition to abolishing elective local school committees and installing appointive school

---

*While I was interviewing high-ranking government officials of Indonesia in 1973 concerning their reactions to Japanese firms, one of them rhetorically asked me, "Why are Japanese firms concerned with their own sales and profits?" When I responded with an equally rhetorical reply, "Why do you expect Japanese firms to be different from other foreign firms? Why don't you call Japanese firms or Japanese businessmen 'banana—outside yellow but inside white?" This Indonesian official sadly agreed, "Perhaps we expected the Japanese to be different from Americans and Europeans."

committees, the Ministry of Education censured and screened textbooks. Any direct reference to the Japanese invasion of China, Korea and other Asian countries was quickly banished from social studies and history textbooks.

Concerted efforts to erase such a distinct chapter of Japanese history not only produced new generations of Japanese who were ignorant of Japan's actions during World War II, but more important helped the adult populace wipe the unpleasant memories and guilt feelings of these wartime experiences from its mind. Thus, the majority of Japanese, both young and old, have naively come to assume that since they themselves have been able to forget wartime memories, other Asians will have forgotten them as well. Only now is Japan beginning to see "her own chickens come home to roost"; the selective amnesia of haunted memories was not as potent outside Japan.

Nowhere else is other Asians' resentment stronger toward the forgetful Japanese than today in Korea. The following anecdote that I encountered might serve to illustrate the intensity of such deep-seated resentments:

> While I was engaged in fieldwork in Korea in 1972, I was one day invited to my Korean friend's home. He told me that his mother-in-law had gone to senior high school under the Japanese colonial administration. This meant that she was fluent in Japanese. I knew this much because the Japanese colonial administration banned the use of the Korean language in Koreans' daily life, let alone in their schools.
>
> As the evening meal and conversation continued (in English and my broken Korean), my friend's mother-in-law listened in intensely. A few hours passed without her joining our conversation beyond the most perfunctory greetings she had made earlier to me, the house guest. Then suddenly, she asked her son-in-law to translate what she was about to say to me. After ascertaining that I was too young during the war to be responsible for what happened, but old enough to remember it, she recounted the daily horror stories of her experience with Japanese teachers and schools, where Koreans were despised and punished savagely at the slightest sign of disobedience. I heard her out. I could not and did not say anything. To utter a word, I thought, would be flippant and disrespectful. It was clear that she gracefully tolerated my coming to visit her son-in-law's home. All this time, she refused to speak Japanese.[9]

The popular epithet, "economic animal," is said to have been coined by Thais, during the 1960s in order to describe Japanese firms' behavior in Thai. This slur reflects Thais' contempt of Japanese' inability to modify their behavior in Thailand—the so-called Japanese inability to adapt to a new environment. Sometimes, however, the self-serving ethnocentricity of Japanese, who insensitively superimpose their own familiar modes of behavior and values upon different cultures, produces inadvertent success among ordinary workers of host countries. In Indonesia for example, I observed time and again that the so-called paternalistic relationship of Japanese management to employees, happened to meet the expectations of rank-and-file workers.

Japanese firms intuitively attempted to transfer their own corporate system (culture) onto local settings that had not yet developed their own industrial practices. To the Japanese, it was imperative that employee cafeterias and recreational facilities be built as an integral part of the plant and that meals be provided to employees at the employer's expense. Quite unintentionally, this Japanese preoccupation with employee "fringe benefits" served to reduce daily absenteeism. Even the Japanese practice of person-to-person training of rank-and-file employees was well accepted by Indonesian workers. Under this system, high-ranking managers such as plant managers and even chief engineers mingle with workers and get to know them personally. The Japanese did not know however, that this mingling custom was not expected by the Indonesian supervisors (foremen). In Indonesian culture, supervisors are extremely reluctant to exercise their formal line of authority over fellow Indonesians and expect higher ranking managers to aid them in enforcing discipline and strict work rules.

Problems arose because the Japanese insensitivity to the delicate fabrics of local cultures made them draw wrong conclusions from their initial but inadvertent success with local employees. Rather than analyzing which components of Japanese management-employee practices produced success, Japanese managers embraced the sweeping myth that all aspects of Japanese corporate culture were transferrable intact into local settings and that Japanese firms always outperformed other foreign firms in the realms of fringe benefits and rank-and-file relations.

The first myth often served to alienate higher ranking local managers with university training, who preferred not to mingle too closely with rank-and-file employees and lower echelon managers. They often took it as a personal affront when asked by Japanese managers to emulate their example and go inside plants. Japanese managers in turn, bewildered by such incomprehensible resistances from local elites, came to write them off as "lazy" or "incompetent."

This resentment was strengthened by the Japanese practice that every corporate manager must rise through the ranks and go through long years of apprenticeship. The Japanese force local elites, often with missionary zeal, to do the same as an integral part of training for future management positions. Outside Japan, however, it is a general rule that local elites such as manager-candidates, do not start from the bottom of the organization. Local elites expect to be treated as such and to be visibly distinguished from rank-and-file employees. In developing countries, differences in educational level are often expected to carry different currency value. Therefore, high school graduates or people with university education expect to be paid accordingly and given jobs commensurate with their educational level.

The enforcement of so-called "Japanese classless societal behavior" among class-conscious local elites often ends up causing more resentment. They do not hesitate to articulate to outside politicians and newspapers that they perceive these imposed tasks to be both demeaning and humiliating. Hence, here arises one more source of inadvertent and unfortunate misunderstanding between Japanese expatriates and their local recruits.

The second myth, on the other hand, caught Japanese firms by surprise when other foreign firms, in the course of time, embraced the usefulness of fringe benefits like company subsidized lunches and recreation. This erased the competitive edge Japanese firms held in the local labor market. In Thailand in 1974, it was observed that American and European firms were providing as good if not better fringe benefits to Thai employees than were Japanese firms. Yet Japanese firms were naively asserting that their wage and fringe benefit packages were better than those of American and European counterparts. Little did they notice that other firms had long caught up with their customs.

INTERNATIONAL IMPACT OF GOVERNMENT AND BUSINESS RELATIONS IN JAPAN

It is a widespread cliché that Japanese business and government work hand in hand—thus the nickname "Japan, Inc." While sophisticated foreign students of government-business relations in Japan are now beginning to discard this mischievous generalization, there are many less rigorous observers who cling to the paradigm of "Japan, Inc." And again, rather unfortunately, there are ample and dazzling examples of close and almost collusive relationships between Japanese business and government. Consider the following two incidents:

... Two Palestinian guerrillas and one Japanese "volunteer" hijacked a Boeing 747 of Japan Air Line and diverted it to a remote airport in Dubai, an Arab shiekdom in the Persian Gulf. The Japanese government had no offices in Dubai, nor even a contingency plan to establish telex communication between Dubai and Tokyo. The only Japanese prescence in Dubai was limited to a small outpost of one of the ten largest Japanese trading companies. The manager of the office immediately and voluntarily suspended all business operations and directed his staff to handle the communication between the governments of Dubai and Japan. His intuitive decision of subordinating business interests to what he perceived to be the larger interests of Japan was subsequently reinforced when his Tokyo office instructed him to devote all efforts to aiding Dubai and Tokyo in coping with the hijack. Not only the Ministry of Foreign Affairs of Japan but also the private newspapers and television networks relied on the single telex contact between Dubai and Tokyo that was handled by the one private trading company. Hence, there unfolded a dazzling display of "Japan, Inc."—government, business and mass media all working in unison. Long after the "Dubai incident" was resolved, the rest of the world remained more and more convinced of the inseparability of business and governmental interests in Japan.

... In Jakarta during the 1960s, Japanese firms were experiencing difficulty in locating suitable office space. They decided jointly to build one high-rise office building. The Japanese Embassy, which was also hard pressed for suitable office space, invited itself to participate in the project. The Japanese firms obliged and let the Japanese Embassy occupy the largest and most choice space of the building compound. It did not occur to either Japanese firms or to the Embassy that the "co-habitat" of Japanese business and government would loom in the minds of Indonesians and foreigners as the massive evidence of a "Japan, Inc." Japanese businessmen pushed the co-op building only because it made economic sense. They reluctantly accommodated the request of the Japanese Embassy on the naive premise that business circles might do the same in Tokyo, under similar pressing shortage of office space.

Similarly, many Japanese firms have inadvertently aggravated the fears of host governments and local businessmen. Host governments and local businessmen have suspected Japanese businesses of calling on political clout by the Japanese government when deadlocks in negotiations occur between Japanese firms and host countries. For a quarter of a century, since about 1950, Japanese firms large and small have developed a habit of using the unstated and unspecified attitudes or rulings of the Japanese government as convenient and overriding excuses for their not being able to accommodate the wishes, bargains and licensing agreements of foreign businesses. Many

Japanese firms would say, "We would like very much to accommodate this request of your firm. But the Ministry of International Trade and Industry (MITI) would not go along with such an agreement . . ." These negotiating tactics were perceived to be effective by Japanese businessmen because foreign negotiators knew that such familiar MITI intervention was not a mere "bluff."

When Japanese firms negotiate in investments and licensing agreements with host governments and local businessmen abroad, they seem unable to resist liberal and mostly unfounded references to the "wishes" of the Japanese government. From Korea to Indonesia, and from Mexico to Brazil, many Japanese businesses used what they casually thought was effective negotiating rhetoric. The other side, however, took this rhetoric seriously.

What makes matters worse, is that Japanese firms have historically developed attitudes toward both their central and regional governments upon the basis of three idiosyncracies peculiar to the internal politics of Japan: namely, (1) omnipotently strong power of the central (national) government vis-à-vis regional (municipal) government; (2) continuous stability and everlasting longevity of the ruling political party; and (3) close and almost collusive cooperation between business and government.

When such attitudes, ingrained in the Japanese firm's perception of government roles and powers, are uncritically transferred to host countries for Japanese investments, they produce politically disastrous effects. In Thailand in 1973, Japanese firms, who had by then cultivated close ties with the military regime, were caught in the sudden shift of political power from the military regime to the new civilian regime. Or in Indonesia in 1973, Japanese firms, though unintentionally, seriously angered the regional governors in remote districts when they demanded that these governors implement the agreements reached between Japanese investors and the central government of Indonesia in Jakarta. Little did Japanese investors realize that the administrative and political power of Jakarta did not reach the remote corners of Indonesia.

Elsewhere, in Korea from 1973 to 1975, Japanese businesses came to draw criticism essentially from two groups of Koreans: one, a group of local businessmen who sought unsuccessfully to become business partners with Japanese investors and labelled Japanese ventures in Korea "neo-colonial expansions"; and two, a group of Korean businesses who concluded business tie-ups with Japanese firms and were mocked and accused of collaborating with such Japanese neocolonialism. University students, intellectuals, the Christian churches and politicians of opposition parties believed that Japanese business interests in Korea were aiding the dictatorial regime of President Park Chung-hee. After all, they said, President Park had been a lieutenant in the hated Kanto Army of Imperial Japan and had relentlessly persecuted the Korean underground resisters opposing the Japanese colonial regime.

In October 1972, President Park abolished the elective national assembly and created the appointive forum of five thousand "deputies," the collaborative arm of his regime—too close a replica of the Imperial Japanese "Great Collaborating Association" that replaced the elected Diet in 1940. President Park called for a referendum in which voters were asked to reject or support his concentration of power. Park and his supporters maintained that strong leadership was absolutely necessary in negotiating successfully with Prime Minister Kim of North Korea. Despite the overwhelming "yes" vote of the referendum, however, President Park was patently unable to quell the rising opposition among a wide spectrum of the Korean population.

In August 1973, one articulate opposition leader, Kim Dae-Chu, was abducted from a hotel in Tokyo by the Korean Secret Police and shipped back to Korea for an alleged secret execution. The uproar of protest involving Koreans, Japanese citizens and the mass media led President Park to detain Kim Dae-Chu in "house arrest" rather than "waste" him. From 1974 to 1975, President Park's confrontation with university communities and the news media worsened. In the spring of 1975, leading universities in Korea were ordered closed, as was done in the past every time President Park feared student protest spreading to the populace. Concurrently, anti-Japanese sentiment was rapidly rising in Korea. In that spring, in private one could overhear the forbidden but growing nostalgia for the deposed Rhee Shig-man (banished from Korea in the spring of 1960 as the result of student uprising); Rhee Shig-man at least kept those hateful Japanese out of the country. How did this sentiment come about?

JAPANESE INVESTMENTS IN KOREA

After the devastation of the Korean War, 1950–1951, the government of South Korea faced the problem of feeding and clothing a population of about 21 million which was growing at an annual rate of 2.5 to 3.0 percent. During the 1950s and 1960s, the surplus population continued to flow into the already congested cities and away from the agrarian sector, which until around 1952, had absorbed about 80 percent of the total population. Lacking natural resources, Korea embarked during the 1950s upon an "instantaneous" industrialization, mainly with the economic help of the United States.

Riding the waves of successful student uprising against the Rhee regime, Park Chung-hee staged a military coup and installed himself as the head of state. His promise of "turning" the power over to civilian rule was later carried out when Park himself discarded military uniform and donned civilian clothes as the "newly elected" president of the Republic of Korea.[10]

As part of a scheme to shift the economic burden of aiding Korea to Japan, the United States encouraged Tokyo and Seoul to normalize their diplomatic relations. The Park regime at that time was concerned with the dwindling amount of economic aid from the United States. Thus the Korea-Japan Treaty, that not only permitted economic dialogues between the two nations but also brought Korea reparation payments and government aid grants, became necessary for Park to bolster the sagging economy of Korea. In Tokyo, the sudden push that the ruling party and the Japanese bureaucracy staged in order to hasten the Korea-Japan Treaty was bitterly received in the Diet by the opposition parties. The treaty was viewed by the opposition parties as a device by which big business would re-enter Korea. Park's opposition parties and intellectuals in Korea also opposed the treaty out of fear that Japan would again exploit Korea. But in 1965, the treaty was railroaded through both in Seoul and Tokyo by the Park regime and Sato cabinet respectively.

The immediate economic pay-offs that President Park reaped for Korea through this treaty can be gleaned from Table 10-4. For the post-treaty years 1966-1969, foreign (mainly Japanese) private loans to the Korean government as well as to Korean business, together

Table 10-4. Inflows of External Funds into Korea, 1948-1969 (In Millions of U.S. Dollars)

Years	Foreign grants-in-aid (forgivable)	External Borrowings and Foreign Direct Investments			
		Government Borrowings	Private Borrowings	Direct Investments	Total
1948-50	354.8	—	—	—	—
1951-55	852.7	—	—	—	—
1956-58	1,030.9	—	—	—	—
1959-62	899.1	7.3	—	—	7.3
1963-65	497.1	59.9	72.3*	12.4	144.5
1966-69	413.5	414.5	887.0*	52.0	1,333.5

*In 1965 and 1969, the annual private borrowing by Korean businesses was $36.1 million and $386.9 million respectively.

Source: The Bank of Korea, *Economic Statistics Yearbook*, 1970, p. 322; the Bank of Korea, *Review of Korean Economy, 1969*, Seoul, 1970, p. 146.

with foreign (mainly Japanese) direct investments were offset by a more than steady decline in outright foreign economic aid. In particular, external borrowing by Korean businesses increased tenfold from 1965 to 1969.

The rapid economic growth of Korea was closely related to the above inflows of external funds as well as to the inflows of manufacturing technologies that accompanied the external borrowings and foreign direct investments. For instance, the gross national product of Korea began to grow after about 1963. During the second five year plan, 1967–1971, the GNP registered on the average an annual growth rate of over 12 percent. Accordingly, the per capita income of Korea increased from about $94 in 1960 to about $224 in 1970. Even a cursory macroeconomic analysis would reveal that the rapid growth of the Korean GNP was achieved through rapid increases in private and government investments. And, during the period 1963–1970, over one-half of these investments were financed by external borrowing and foreign direct investments. In particular, the growth of the manufacturing industries, which was the central theme of the second five-year plan, was attained through the inflows of foreign fuels and technology.

The thrust of the second five-year plan was: first to allocate these foreign technologies and funds to the manufacturing projects of import substitutions, and second to the exporting industries. As a result, the exports of Korea increased from about $33 million in 1960 to $1,880 million in 1970. During the years 1962–1972, about one-quarter of Korea's exports were directly related to inflows of foreign technologies and funds. As shown in Table 10–5, according to the Korean government the cumulative inflows of foreign funds and technologies during 1962–1970 produced net gains of about $1,173 million for Korea's balance of payments. In terms of macroeconomic benefits, therefore, the inflows of foreign funds and technologies were "beneficial" to the Korean economy up until 1970.

Beginning in the 1970s, however, the Korean government realized that the annual out-flows of foreign exchanges were increasing. At this juncture, the Korean government began to discourage outright external borrowings by businesses. It came to favor foreign direct investment. In 1970, in order to attract foreign manufacturing subsidiaries the Korean government instituted such measures as tax exemptions, legal protection, restrictions on strikes, and the designation of a single agency to oversee the actions of would-be foreign investors. In 1969, the first "free trade" zone was set up in Masan near the southern port of Pusan in order to attract offshore manufacturing operations of foreign investors. In 1971, the second "free trade" zone and industrial park was opened in Gumi near the central

Table 10-5. Balance of Payments of Korea Related to Inflows of External Funds, Foreign Direct Investments and Foreign Technologies, 1962-1970 (In Millions of U.S. Dollars)

Current Account Items	Charges in Current Accounts Related to the Following Sources of External Funds and Technologies			
	External Borrowings	Foreign Direct Investments	Licensing Agreements	Total
(A) Exports	+ 508.2	+70.3	+ 28.0	+ 606.5
(B) Import Substitutions	+1,252.8	+11.6	+210.3	+1,474.7
(C) Imports of Raw Materials	− 705.7	(−)	− 88.2	− 793.9
(D) Payments of Royalties, fees and dividends	− 95.1	−15.0	− 4.2	− 114.3
(E) Net Gains (A + B − C − D)	+ 960.2	+66.9	+145.9	+1,173.0

Source: The study by The Economic Planning Agency, Seoul, 1971, quoted in Kim Jyum-Hyung, "Kan-Nichi Keizai Kyoryoku no Hyoka," *Asia Koron* (August 1973) p. 72.

part of the city of Tague. This second "free trade" zone was coincidentally located near the village from which President Park came.

The Korean government's efforts to attract manufacturing subsidiaries of foreign investors were made at the same time that Japanese firms, both small and large, were increasingly looking for overseas locations for their manufacturing subsidiaries. As a result, an "avalanche" of Japanese investments descended on Korea. For example, during the first seven months of 1970, 53 out of the 66 new foreign manufacturing subsidiaries that were authorized by the Korean government came from Japan. In addition, the bulk of manufacturing technologies from abroad which Korean firms purchased through licensing agreements came from Japan.

As a result, by mid-1970, in terms of assets per industry, Japanese investors came to own: 63 percent of the hotel business, 55 percent in industrial machinery, 41 percent of construction, 40 percent of textiles, 32 percent of pulp and paper, 32 percent of metal fabrication, 31 percent of fertilizer, 30 percent of clay, glass and cement, 24 percent of electric and electronics products, 23 percent of fishery, 23 percent of water and sewage supplies, 20 percent of the automobile industry, 16 percent of transportation and warehouses, 16 percent of chemicals and 14 percent of electric power utilities. The leading firms in each industry mentioned above were either Korean-Japanese joint ventures or Japanese wholly-owned subsidiaries. When this presence of Japanese firms was combined with the various imports from Japan, the public visibility of Japanese "economic power" in Korea became magnified.

However, the preceding "static" snapshot of Japanese presence in Korea does not illuminate the reasons why Japanese investments have become so politically entangled in the fierce fights amongst old and new Korean "industrial tycoons." From 1951 to the early 1960s, under the regime of Rhee Shig-man, there appeared about ten "industrial families" that dominated the Korean economy. These families built up their economic power on the bases of their success in the cement, textile, sugar, flour mill, coastal and ocean freighter industries. Ten years later, in the early 1970s, none of these former "industrial tycoons" made the list of the ten largest industrial firms in Korea.

Instead, completely new personalities came to dominate the industrial scene. Many of these new "industrialists" were catapulted into the "big business world" from literally unknown "basement" or "cottage" operations dating back ten years. They owed their rapid industrial success to the fortune of having found appropriately large Japanese (and sometimes American) business partners. The Korean versions of "Horatio Alger" stories were in the main a symbol of Japanese firms' whimsicality in choosing business partners in Korea. As a result, new "industrial tycoons" like Kanjin emerged out of the late 1960s "Vietnam" boom as the leading force in the hotel, airlines, tourist, warehouse and transportation industries.

When the Korean government attempted to develop an electronic appliances industry for domestic and export markets, two leading industrial groups, Sum Sung (Three Star) and Kim Sung (Gold Star), competed with each other for contracting Japanese electronic firms. While Sum Sung linked itself up with Sanyo and NEC, Kim Sung covered itself by concluding joint ventures with Hitachi and Alps. The intensified rivalries among existing and emerging "industrial tycoons" thus inevitably involved Japanese and other foreign firms: Korean industrialism became a fight for survival of the fittest. The political and economic fortunes of Korean businessmen during this time were of course closely tied to the ruling party controlled by President Park.

This economic upsurge was soon to change. The oil crisis hit Korea hard in the fall of 1973. Not only were the import bills for petroleum products quadrupled, but the imports of many semi-finished industrial materials from Japan were either reduced or cut off. The price of Japanese goods and services, which Korea could not do without, were materially increased due to Japan's galloping inflation rate. Unfortunately, Korea received this economic blow at the same time that inflows of foreign investments were rapidly tapering off. Prior to the fall of 1973, Korea, who had become over-confident about attracting foreign (Japanese) investors, began demanding greater concessions in equity ownership for Korean partners as well as less stringent payment schemes for manufacturing technologies licensed by parents to foreign subsidiaries. These moves quickly dampened the interest of would-be investors in Korea. A decline in new foreign direct investments not only aggravated Korea's balance of payments but also threw a kink in the "investment-led" growth of her economy.

In short, from 1973 to 1975 Korea suffered from worsening economic recessions. President Park lost his once convincing excuse for dictatorial power. In the past, political apologies for President Park and business leaders never failed to convince Koreans that they owed their rapid rise in living standards to President Park's economic policies. As long as immediate economic gains were by and large visible, Koreans tolerated even the hateful Japanese investments. When these gains disappeared, dissident Koreans began to question the legitimacy of President Park's high-handed posture as well as the wisdom of increasing both political and economic dependence on Japan. Once Japanese investments became exposed to this political assessment by Koreans, the lingering memories of "Imperial Japan" made them the most politically vulnerable of all foreign investments.

All in all, the image of the "Ugly Japanese" has been firmly cemented in Asia and Latin America. Inasmuch as this image is produced by the investment patterns as well as the behavioral idiosyncracies of Japanese firms attempting to transfer Japanese technologies abroad, Japanese firms will have to live with it.

This does not mean, however, that Japanese business and government circles can afford to continue with the diplomatic negligences they have so far heaped upon developing nations in Asia and Latin America. In the next chapter, we will see what kind of problems may lie ahead for Japan. Today, multinational firms may hope, at best, to influence the grounds upon which they would be "hated" rather than "loved." But even this goal may prove elusive for Japanese multinational firms.

Chapter Eleven

Japan in a Conflicting World

THE OIL CRISIS AND ALL THAT

The oil crisis of fall 1973 aggravated Japan's galloping inflation that had earlier been touched off by Prime Minister Tanaka's ill-conceived expansion scheme of "remodeling the Japanese archipelago." Many Japanese watchers concluded that she had priced herself out of the world export market.[1] Japan appeared down and out. More perceptive observers pointed out that the rapid growth of the Japanese economy during the 1950s and 1960s was aided by the abundant availability of low-cost oil as well as by technological innovations turning out newer and newer exportable manufactures. The oil shortage destroyed the former. And the fact that Japan now needed to spend more on such non-productive R&D and manufacturing efforts as cleaning up polluted rivers, seemed to arrest the past innovation-led growth of Japanese exports. Simply put, their arguments went: new television sets and improved steel alloys were exportable; but the new technologies used in cleaning up the polluted Tokyo Bay might not be so exportable, not in league at any rate with the export of automobiles and other such manufactures.

As of 1975, however, the Japanese economy appeared to have survived the initial shock of the oil crisis. In September 1974, Japan's balance of trade registered a surplus. Since then, together with petro-dollars recycled to Japan, a continued trend of surplus in Japan's trade accounts has restored the confidence of both business and government circles. The feared drive of labor unions for substantial wage increases in the spring of 1975 was averted as one union after another closed its ranks with management in order to protect their common property, namely, the firm.² The "income policy" à la Japonaise—the general wage rise being contained by business firms that were told to hold tight by government and business leaders—was again functioning.

As a semblance of normalcy returned to the Japanese business and political circles in 1975, they lost any zeal for economic and social reforms that they themselves advocated amidst the crisis atmosphere of the oil shock of 1973-1974. The deceptive atmosphere of "business-as-usual" produced a latent but strong realliance between the deposed former prime minister, Tanaka, and leading financial supporters of the ruling party. Tanaka was shamed into resignation in December 1974, as his scandalous ways of amassing personal wealth through years of influence-peddling were exposed. At that time, the business circles found it expedient to abandon him.

By spring 1975, however, the leading personalities of Japanese "big business" grew disenchanted with the "moderate expansion policy" of Prime Minister Miki. Miki's commitment to moderate growth forced business firms to forsake the growth syndrome that Tanaka's expansionist policy once encouraged. As businesses one after another found it painful to trim their bloated physiques, as it were, business leaders yearned after good old Tanaka's days when government spendings and subsidies were plentiful. Meanwhile, Tanaka, who turned 57 in 1975, began to plot his political comeback for the near future when the current leaders (in their late 60s and early 70s) of various factions within the ruling party would be gone.

The anti-Miki alliance was gathering force throughout 1975. Then, the "Lockheed" landed on Tanaka. Lockheed and its Japanese import agent, Marubeni, were exposed of having bribed Tanaka and other leading politicians. The Lockheed Incident invoked, just as did the "Siemens Incident" of the mid-1910s, the wrath of the nationalistic public. Just as in the case of the Siemens Incident, the Lockheed exposé was made first by foreign investigations. In order to restore the public credibility, the Japanese investigative authority had to pursue the matter relentlessly. In August, 1976 Tanaka was indicted. Miki diffused the intra-party oppositions. However, there still remained unresolved serious political problems at home and abroad.

SEPARATION OF ECONOMICS FROM POLITICS

Perhaps partly because of the unpleasant results of Japan's defeat in

World War II, there had evolved within the Japanese bureaucracy and political circles the notion of keeping economic matters separate at least internationally from political matters (a policy known as *seikei bunri*). Japan was to concentrate on the former while the latter was to be left to the initiative of the United States. This policy was applied during the 1950s and the 1960s in Japan's approach to China, with a disastrous effect that culminated in the first "Nixon shock," caused by the U.S. restoring diplomatic dialogue with China while keeping Japan in the dark.

In the main, however, the policy of *seikei bunri* served to produce Japan's single pursuit of economic success both at home and abroad. The epithet "economic animal," described Japan's industrial success. The past dread of the "Yellow Peril"—and American and European fear of Japan's political and military might—came to be replaced by the nagging apprehension held by the rest of the world of Japan's economic might.

The rest of the world grew fearful that Japan might begin to flex her military might in order to protect her economic interests abroad. On the other hand, the Japanese naively assumed that the rest of the world also accepted her benign separation of economics from politics in international trade and investment. The Japanese thought that they would erase the memories of Imperial Japan, 1864–1945, from the minds of the rest of the world simply by unilaterally declaring this new and benign stance.

Unfortunately for Japan, during the 1950s and the early 1960s, the glutting of various national resources throughout the world permitted Japan to indulge in concentrating on economics (exercising economic bargaining strength only) in procuring these necessary raw materials. In exporting activities, Japan was aided by the United States in joining such international agreements as the General Agreement of Tariffs and Trade (GATT) and the International Monetary Fund (IMF). The ideology of freer trade that was strongly espoused by the world leader, the United States, helped Japan expand her access to markets of both developed and developing nations. Within government and business circles of Japan, her apparent success in extracting only international business increasingly came to be interpreted as an irrefutable proof of the "rightness" of Japan's *seikei bunri*. So long as this myth remained enshrined, subsequent Japanese approaches to the world market were predicated on the assumption that Japan's perception of the world was shared globally. Nowhere did this self-inflicted illusion surface more patently than in the following examples of Japan's expedient attempts at "resource diplomacy."

In 1967, the Ministry of International Trade and Industry and the petroleum firms of Japan produced their recommendation for the future procurement of crude oil for Japan. The timing of their deliberations coincided with the intense lobbying in the United Nations of the Organization of Petroleum Exporting Countries (OPEC), who were seeking the passage of a resolution on the sovereignty of host countries over natural resources. From 1966 to 1967, inside the United Nations, OPEC members successfully solicited the support of many less developed countries. Earlier, from 1962 to 1964, OPEC members had already made a historic breakthrough by having international oil majors recognize the price of crude oil as a negotiable item between foreign oil firms and the oil exporting countries. OPEC members had repeatedly been on record for their hostility toward oil importing nations that attempted to depress the price of crude oil. And yet, in Japan, the government and business "experts" of the world oil market publicly produced the recommendation that the price of crude oil should be further reduced by a minimum of 15 cents per barrel (about 7 to 9 percent of the then prevailing price). If Japan had calculated to anger OPEC members, she could not have chosen a better way. This diplomatic fiasco was made all the more tragically comical by the fact that the recommendation was nothing but an empty slogan lacking any credible program or policy commitment.

From spring to summer 1973, as the price of crude oil continued to rise, the MITI became concerned over Japan's past negligence in cultivating diplomatic ties with the Middle East nations. Japan hurriedly swept Nakasone, then Minister of MITI, through a one week tour of the Middle East countries. His visit would not have been so blatantly ironical had Nakasone and the Japanese government not been genuinely convinced that Japan would be more acceptable to the Arab countries and Iran than France, the United States and the United Kingdom. Japanese officialdom, including the Ministry of Foreign Affairs, unabashedly presumed that Japan's lack of past colonial presence in the Middle East would present her as an untainted and innocent suitor to the Arabs and Iranians who were rightfully suspicious of any foreign country's interest in their oil.

From 1973 to 1974 the steel firms of Japan took an initiative in promoting grandiose schemes of developing vast resources of oil, timber, coal and natural gas in Siberia. The Yakutsk project for coal and natural gas was officially begun by the Japanese business interests of steel and public utility companies. But their primary project, the Tyumen oil field in Siberia, was torpedoed by the United States Senate, which forbade American firms from using Ex-Im bank loans for proposed three-way business ventures between the governments of the Soviet Union, Japan and the U.S. Japanese business firms calculated that the participation of American business interests in the Soviet Union would diffuse hostile reactions by China. This scheme created by Japanese business circles was to hang Japan in the center of balanced powers between the Soviet Union, China and the United States. Although it appeared far more sophisticated than her earlier approach to the Middle East, Japanese business circles again naively assumed that the United States government and Congress would go along with the Siberian venture.

The preceding accounts of Nakasone's trip to the Middle East as well as the Siberian venture, reveal that Japan's past separation of economics from politics in international trade and investment had made both the Japanese government and business circles politically "tone deaf." In March, 1974 President Nixon sent his wife Patricia Nixon to represent the United States at the inauguration of the new President of Brazil. Japan sent an obscure Member of Parliament of the ruling party as her special envoy. Japanese residents in Brazil were extremely embarrassed by the Japanese government's lack of diplomatic sensitivity. Before this embarrassment was forgotten, Prime Minister Tanaka of Japan added injury to earlier insult by declaring that Japan would turn Brazil into the supply center for natural resources and foods.

When Japan hurriedly began making moves to mix economics with politics, the end result was a painfully crude orchestration of new "resource diplomacy." As of 1976 it still remains to be seen whether Japan's trial-and-error approach to mastering the fine tuning of politics and economics in international business will adequately prepare Japanese government and business circles for the complex world situations expected for the last quarter of the Twentieth Century. As discussed in Chapters 2, 3 and 10 of this book, Japan's future involvement in the economic and political processes of other nations will be far more complex than her past involvement.

For instance, in April 1975 we saw that the first attempt in Paris at a "group dialogue" between oil exporting and importing nations broke down. As was feared from the outset by the United States in particular, OPEC members insisted on acting as the negotiators for all Third World countries engaged in the exportation of various commodities to industrialized nations. The OPEC members thus appeared to be practicing the so-called "Eight-Point Action Program for a New International Economic Order" which was debated earlier at the Karachi Conference of the Third World Forum from January 5 to 11, 1975. The deliberations at this Karachi meeting among the OPEC and other "Third World" countries centered around specific negotiating tactics over the price of "primary commodities" between the "haves"—the industrialized world—and the "have-nots"—less developed countries that had collectively come to prefer the name "Third World" to "less developed countries" (LDCs). In their negotiations with the industrialized world, it was expected that OPEC members would exploit their bargaining strength to raise the prices of other commodities supplied by the Third World.

The success of the OPEC countries in regaining control of the pricing as well as production decisions of crude oil from foreign private firms, has become a political inspiration for Third World producers in such commodity markets as bauxite, copper ore, iron ore, coffee and even bananas. The successful tactics of OPEC in playing independent foreign purchases of oil off against those of international oil majors are bound to be emulated by other commodity exporters as well.

As shown in Chapter 2, those Japanese firms which attempted to break the oligopolistic controls of other foreign firms in various commodity markets in the Third World may well be helping the Third World countries increase their bargaining strength vis-à-vis U.S.- and Europe-based firms. This move of Japan, whose manufacturing and trading firms seem to be playing on "both sides" of the fence, as it were, may well find the Japanese government caught in the political conflict between the industrialized and Third World nations. Japan will find it necessary to balance the opportunities to join the international consortia of resource developments led by the U.S.- and Europe-based firms against the opportunities to conclude bilateral deals directly with Third World producers of various commodities.

In addition, there is a sign that various nations might become involved in scrambling for food. In 1975, the overall Japanese self-sufficiency in foodstuffs including fruits and vegetables was estimated to be around 70 percent. In cereal alone, Japan produced for herself only about 40 percent of her annual consumption. And it was estimated that she would grow more and more dependent on imports for her food.[3] In terms of arable land, this meant that roughly 8 million hectares—about 20 percent more than all the arable land in Japan—would have to be found outside Japan and be devoted to food growing for Japan. Where will Japan find such suppliers?

Forests in Japan have been over-cut. Japan needs import lumber from Canada, the United States, the Philippines, Sarawak and Indonesia. Tropical lumber resources in the Philippines and Sarawak, which Japanese trading firms helped develop, are on the verge of exhaustion. The last remaining source, East Kalimantan of Indonesia, appears to be running bare at a fast pace, as its tropical trees are being cut by Japanese, American, Philippino and Korean concessions. The day will come soon when the Japanese importers of tropical logs will have to aid the government of Indonesia in developing a way to conserve tropical tree resources.

The annual catch of the Japanese fishing industry has increased from about 4 million tons a year for the pre-World War II average to 10 million tons in 1973. Still today, over one-half of the Japanese intake of protein comes from sea produce. And yet, only a little over 40 percent of the annual catch is now made within the "200 sea mile" zone which is about to be declared as "economic territorial water" by the coastal nations. How vulnerable Japan has grown to political temperature of foreign countries!

The Ministry of Forestry and Agriculture has thus far been overshadowed by MITI. Now, it appears bewildered at the colossal task of reviving Japanese agriculture and coastal fishing. As of 1975, the "best" idea that the Ministry hurriedly proposed remains limited to the "stock-pile reserve" of feed grain items and soybeans. There is yet to be developed within Japanese officialdom an overall approach to the general questions of "economic security" for Japan. The fragmented rivalries within the Japanese bureaucracies are still denying an overall approach to international activities of Japan.

Finally, as discussed in Chapter 3, Japan's need for finding additional sites, fishing bases and labor outside Japan has not been limited to agriculture and fishing. A number of manufacturing firms have already begun searching for plant sites for offshore production arrangements. Will Japan then, be able to expand in her procurement of various commodities abroad as well as in her manufacturing operations abroad without changing her diplomatic stance in the post-Vietnam War era?

THE POST-VIETNAM WAR ERA IN ASIA AND JAPAN

It is almost passé to reiterate that the eventual unification of the two parts of Vietnam under the Vietnamese Communist regime was bound to restructure the political climate of Asia.

The victories of communists in Vietnam and Cambodia shocked Thais into a pensive review of the unwanted "urbanization" of the Thai population. Lured by the gaiety of cities which foreign businesses promoted, and aided by the military road networks which the United States opened to the Laotian and Cambodian borders, hordes of rural Thais are trickling into cities, only to join the swelling ranks of the urban unemployed. Similar urbanization trends which the United States forced on Vietnam and Cambodia not only created a horrendous stream of refugees into urban enclaves, but also made the poverty-stricken city dwellers totally dependent upon the economic hand-outs of an alien power, the United States. With the physical disappearance of the United States forces from urban centers, however, the National Liberation Forces tightened their grips around cities and choked them off. A string of cities, thus, collapsed from within as panicked city dwellers and demoralized soldiers fled. Although the Thai situation is somewhat different, ominous lessons from the unwanted urbanization trend in Vietnam and Cambodia seemed too close to be ignored.

The forced "de-urbanization" which the Cambodian communists adopted in earnest forced Thai intellectuals and students to question drifting along uncritically with the uncontrolled influx of population from countryside into cities. A steady inflow of jobless farmers to the cities reflected years of neglect of agrarian reforms and developments by the Thai government which had opted out for a quickened pace of industrialization in cities under the initiative of foreign businesses. Thais are now worried that the unwanted urbanization of its populace will make Thailand all the more dependent on the alien economic forces, namely, the Japanese and American businesses. Meanwhile, open insurgencies of the indigenous communists are rising in poor countrysides. Thailand is now confronted with a choice between the outbreak of a civil war a la Vietnam, or a drastic internal reform that would accommodate a more popular, pro-China and Vietnam stance than in the past. Whichever direction Thailand may go in the future, Japanese firms which have already been deeply involved in the Thai economy will certainly be affected.

In Korea, where Japanese firms' involvement in the domestic economy has also been substantial, President Park Chung-hee appeared to be driving South Koreans to internal strifes. In April 1975 Kim Il-sung, the leader of North Korea, suddenly flew to Peking after an interval of many years. It was feared that Kim had attempted to solicit China's support in his plan to invade South Korea. The fact that Peking publicly broke Kim's visit to the world and gave him a grandiose state reception, made seasoned China watchers conclude that China discouraged him from marching down to South Korea. Without overt intervention from North Korea however, President Park, who, as a lieutenant of the Japanese Imperial Army during World War II used to chase the Korean resistance guerrillas led by Kim Il-sung, was pushing South Koreans to bitter civil strife. As discussed in Chapter 10, South Koreans, who detested

President Park's dictatorial rulings, were increasingly becoming suspicious of the Japanese business interests in Korea. Accordingly, even against their own will, Japanese investors were becoming embroiled in South Korea's internal strife.

Meanwhile, in Malaysia, Indonesia and Singapore—the three countries bound together by the strait of Malacca—politicians were wondering whether Japan would send her naval force to defend her "life line," the Malacca strait, which links the oil of the Middle East and Japan. In 1974 the Japanese Navy's state visits to Singapore and Australia aggravated the suspicions of the Southeast Asian countries. People there never failed to point out that the Japanese fleet traced the same courses frequented during World War II by the Japanese Imperial Navy. Was the new naval force of Japan simply making a "practice run" for what was to come in the event that Japanese economic interests were jeopardized by political conflicts in Southeast Asia?

When the United Forces were driven out of Indochina, the fear of "old Imperial Japan" appeared to be returning to Asia. Interestingly, there were two different scenarios converging upon the expected behavior of Japan—that of the "cold war" mythology and the die-hard scenario of the "New Left" paradigm. According to the former school of thought, Japan would move in to fill the political vacuum left by the departure of the United States. After all, the implied argument went, these Southeast Asian countries would need the protective umbrella of a large and powerful country like Japan. The scenario of the "New Left" had it that regardless of the cosmetic touch-up of the so-called "new" Japan, the neo-colonialist Japan would be forced to protect her economic interests abroad with military might. Even if Japan would not want to do this, one argued, the United States would need now to maintain her political presence in Asia through her proxy nation, Japan.[4]

In business and government circles in Tokyo, however, these suspicions by the rest of the world were greeted with utter disbelief. The Japanese had long made themselves believe in the new self-image of "pacifist Japan," which renounced military violence as a means of settling international disputes. It had not occurred to Japan that the rest of the world would interpret her rearmament as a preparation for military expansion in Asia.

Business and government circles did not realize that the persistent attempts by the ruling party (LDP) at repealing Article 9 of the Japanese Constitution would also be construed by the rest of the world as Japan's preparation for military intervention in other countries. Article 9 specifically declares that "Japan renounces military interventions as her means of dissolving international disputes." The business and government circles had condoned the LDP's declared intention of repealing Article 9.

The rest of the world superimposed the rapid spread of Japanese multinational firms upon the familiar (and stereotyped) image of the collusive relationships between Japanese government and business circles. In this context, memories of the "old" Imperial Japan—the nation muscling its way into China, Korea, Taiwan and Southeast Asia under the banner of the "Great Asia Co-Prosperity Sphere"— were dredged up by the rest of the world. How then, can Japan erase the lingering fears of the "old Japan," especially among Third World nations?

For one thing, the business and government circles of Japan would need to communicate in words and deeds to the rest of the world that Japan would take Article 9 of her Constitution seriously. Ironic as it seemed, the future economic interests of Japan would now force the business and government circles to embrace the ideological stance of the opposition groups that had successfully defended the LDP's (and its industrial sponsors') attempts at changing the Japanese Constitution.

Similar changes in attitude would be required by business and government circles toward the rearmament of Japan. In 1975 Japan possessed conventional forces whose combined fire and striking powers were greater than those of the old Imperial Japan.[5] And the world knew that Japan possessed the technological capability to produce nuclear weapons including guided missiles. It was no wonder, therefore, that the rest of the world was already suspicious of Japan's intent in rearming herself.

Paradoxical as it seems, Japan was in the past much freer, psychologically and practically, to increase her armament beneath the protective umbrella of the United States' nuclear weapons. At that time, Japan and the rest of the world understood that Japanese armaments would be contained within the framework of the United States' defense posture in the Pacific. But Japan was jolted into her own diplomatic stance by the oil crisis as well as by the decline of American military and political influence in Asia after the Vietnam war. Under these circumstances, the expansion of Japan's military strength would be bound to be interpreted by Asian neighbors in the context of the spread of Japanese multinational firms.

Indeed, then, it was no accident that Premier Chou En-lai of China suggested early in 1975, that Japan maintain the U.S.-Japan Security Treaty. In the same vein, China would not oppose the continued stationing of U.S. forces in South Korea. According to this plan, the presence of U.S. forces would contain the civil strife of South Korea within South Korea, should it occur. The maintenance of the U.S.-Japan Security Treaty would contain Japan's armaments within the limits spelled out by the obligations of the Treaty.

This calculation by China proved to be beyond the comprehension of Japanese politicians whose political sensitivities at best, were limited to trading on political patronage and pet projects inside Japan.* According to the formula which business, government and political circles of Japan predicted for Chinese diplomacy, China was to encourage Japan to dissolve her security arrangements with the United States. Japan failed to note that, above all, China might prefer to avoid becoming engrossed anew in political instabilities throughout Asia, and instead further her own internal development because of external threats from the Soviet Union. Once again Japan witnessed her political and business leadership circles exposing their incapability of seeing how Japan might be perceived from other countries' vantage points.

Accordingly, Japan's political sensitivity to the goals and aspirations of other countries would need to be developed. In particular, Japan would need to eradicate the "official contempt," which Japanese bureaucracy and business had heaped upon Third World nations in the past. Japan has long divided the world population into three groups: namely, *gaijin* (foreigners), Japanese and *daisan kokujin* (third country people). Given the inferiority complex that is still strongly felt by Japanese in their forties and older toward the West, the first group, *gaijin*, has singularly consisted of white European races. Asians and the rest of the world are grouped in the third category. People say that Japan has much to learn from the technologies, ideologies and culture of the first group. But Japanese view themselves superior to the "third country" people. This racial prejudice has permeated various walks of life. Even in 1975 it was common knowledge that students from Asia and Africa had difficulty in locating housing in Japan.

It is beyond the scope of this book to go into a detailed psychoanalysis of Japan's economic history since the 1850s, as to what contributed to her worship of Western technologies and cultures as well as to her contempt for cultures of less developed countries. For the purpose of this chapter, however, it is sufficient to point out that the "third countries" have long been ignored within Japanese bureaucracy and industry.

*The late Chou En-Lai made the preceding remarks in the spring of 1975 to the visiting team of the Diet members of the Japanese Socialist Party and the Liberal Democrat Party.

For example, in terms of promotional opportunities within the Ministry of Foreign Affairs, the overseas positions in Asia, Africa, Latin America and the Middle East have been regarded as terminal jobs set aside for those officials who have fallen out of grace with the Ministry. The business firms have performed no better. From 1973 to 1975, more and more firms instituted programs of so-called "study abroad" for promising young employees. And yet, these firms have mainly sent their trainees to graduate schools located in the United States and Europe. Except for a few "language students" whom Japanese trading firms sent to Asia, Africa and Latin America, future managers of Japanese multinational firms are trained exclusively in North America and Europe. Thus, the "official" negligence of Third World cultures has been perpetuated in the hierarchy of Japanese multinational firms. It is no wonder, therefore, that the "official" contempt of Japanese educational institutions toward Asian neighbors continues to breed both the political and cultural insensitivity which Japanese business and government circles manifest toward Third World countries. In short, the future of Japanese multinational activities—for that matter, the future of Japan—will now also depend upon how soon Japanese government and business alike stop perpetuating their "official" contempt and neglect of the Third World.

In other words, nothing short of a drastic reversal in educational and diplomatic policies in Japan will help Japanese firms overcome the increasing resistance of host countries to Japanese investments abroad. As of 1975, however, both Japanese bureaucracy and business still seem to have failed in grasping this problem.*

All told, then, the future multinational expansion of Japanese financial firms was constrained in part by the insular attitudes of the government officials and business executives. No doubt, it is not unique to Japan that the governmental bureaucracy, like its counterpart in the entrenched private corporate bureaucracy, attempts to defend its vested interests. In the case of Japan, however, the governmental bureaucracy has not always shown aversion to change per se,

---

*Professor Saburo Ienaga of Tokyo Kyoiku University whose accounts of Imperial Japan and its expansions into Asia were censored out of school text books sued the Ministry of Education for unconstitutional interference in freedom of speech and learning. Ienaga won the first round in Tokyo District Court. The "Ienaga Case" reflects near-complete control of thought that the Ministry of Education has achieved through a series of administrative measures rather than through a due process of law. The Japanese government now appears intent on having the supreme court reverse the decision of the Tokyo District Court. But Japan might realize that the rest of the world is also watching the "Ienaga Case" to see the outcome of the Japanese governmental effort to rid Japan of its past wartime memories.

as shown by the initiative it began to take around the 1870s in the rapid industrialization of Japan. In fact, the Japanese bureaucracy has initiated and at the same time managed rapid changes in many dimensions of Japanese institutions—legal, educational, political and economic alike. However, these changes were often triggered by such drastic historical events as the Meiji Restoration in 1868 or the defeat of Imperial Japan in World War II in 1945.

Under these circumstances of historical crisis, as we noted earlier in Chapters 1 and 8, a new group of elite officials of the Japanese government acquired new mandates for change and set about to manage these changes for Japanese society. Once their newly designed courses of societal change took root, they often became enshrined as the "unalterable *modus operendi*" of Japan, only to be discontinued by the advent of a new historical crisis. This explains why it took the defeat of Imperial Japan in 1945 to make discernible changes in the institutional fabric of her society, which had previously been molded by the Meiji oligarchy during the last quarter of the Nineteenth Century.

It now remains to be seen whether the oil crisis and the political changes in Asia triggered by the final victories of the liberation forces in Cambodia and Vietnam in 1975 will provide sufficient impetus for changes in government-business relationships inside Japan as well as impetus for changes in Japan's external posture vis-à-vis the rest of the world. In view of the fact that there has not yet been any drastic change in the personalities within the Japanese bureaucracy and the political parties, however, one might wonder whether the governmental officialdom of Japan will continue to defend the *status quo*, effecting only marginal changes in its attitudes toward lessening (but not eliminating) the direction of governmental interference within Japanese multinational activities.

THE GOVERNMENT AND POLITICS OF JAPAN

For about one hundred years, the Japanese government has played a pivotal role in shaping not only the industrial but also the educational and political communities in Japan. As we discussed in the preceding chapter of this book, the continued legacy of pre–World War II Japan, with such acts as the censorship of primary and secondary school textbooks, produced among the Japanese a mass amnesia of what Japan did to her Asian neighbors during the years 1870–1945. The aftermath of this mass amnesia was increasingly felt toward the end of the 1960s, contributing to the tensions between

Japanese investors and nationals of Asian host countries. Indeed, there would be a tinge of irony if the Ministry of Education ever moved to tolerate, under pressures from "business establishments" interested in multinational expansion, "counter-official views" of Japanese history for primary and secondary school children.

In addition, as we saw in Chapter 1, the fact that the industrial growth of post–World War II Japan was steered by the Japanese government increased the government's influence over private businesses. Moreover, one distinct phenomenon of post–World War II Japan was that many elite government officials entered the world of politics and occupied key positions in the ruling party, LDP, upon their retirement from government service. Ambitious government officials have made it a rule to exploit their influence over Japanese businesses and various interest groups for their own political goals. This tendency on the part of the Japanese bureaucracy has come to breed collusive relationships between businesses and government in Japan. How did this happen?

Prime Minister Shigeru Yoshida—a former career bureaucrat of the Minstry of Foreign Affairs, who assumed the premiership intermittently between 1946 and 1955—disliked and distrusted career politicians so intensely that he filled not only cabinet positions but also executive positions in the ruling party (a forerunner of LDP) with former bureaucrats. Such favoritism shown by Yoshida and his followers, like Kishi, Ikeda and Sato—all former bureaucrats—has motivated ambitious career bureaucrats to enter politics upon their retirement from government bureaus.

Since the early days of the Imperial Japan, government positions have carried not only a position of power but also extremely high social prestige in Japan. The leading national universities in Japan, led by Tokyo Imperial University (currently Tokyo University), were designed to supply able administrators to the central government ministries.[6] Not only able but ambitious young Japanese gravitated to the leading national universities and then, to government positions. A series of competitive entrance examinations from secondary schools through universities, and then civil service exams, screened individuals for various career positions. Thus once Yoshida opened the way, there was no lack of ambitious officials who aspired toward careers in politics.

In addition, the "unwritten" policy of retirement that prevails within the Japanese bureaucracy necessitated many ambitious career officials to seek their post-retirement employment either in industry or politics. This "unwritten" policy expects retirement in a ministry from all members of a 'peer group" when one of its members reaches the position of Vice Minister, the highest rank attainable by career officials. This leaves many ambitious and vital men in their forties and fifties without jobs. Historically, this convention has evolved through the system of seniority-based promotion in Japanese ministries, so that senior elite officials can vacate their places to younger elite officials.

Since the Japanese politician's influences are mainly determined by the ability to manipulate and accommodate various ministries of Japan, former career officials who have risen through the ranks in influential ministries of Japan have easily out-maneuvered career politicians within LDP. As a result, LDP is now dominated by former elite government officials.

More important, however, three idiosyncratic aspects of Japanese politics have helped ambitious bureaucrats attain political power within LDP. *First*, except for the brief period from mid-1947 to early 1948, when the coalition cabinet of Socialists, Democrats and Kyodo (the liberal branch of the conservatives) was in existence under Premier Tetsu Katayama, the political strings in postwar Japan have been held exclusively by LDP. Thus, the elite officials have come to work closely with LDP rather than maintaining only an arm's length relationship with a political party uncertain of its political longevity.

This prolonged longevity of the ruling party has been partly made possible by the persistent erosion of the principle of "one voter-one vote," especially apparent in the national election of the Diet. The votes have been fixed for some time in favor of the farming and rural areas of Japan, where not only farmers' conservatism but also closely-knit structures enable LDP candidates to police their votes. This apportionment of the Diet seats is still based on the population distribution of 1946 when war-torn Japanese cities were deprived of resident voters. The subsequent trend of urbanization has increased the population of cities throughout Japan, but has long been ignored by the ruling party whose political strength still lies with the conservative farming population.[7]

Second, with no grass-roots organizations in Japanese political parties, elections for both the Diet (lower house) and the House of Councillors (upper house) have come to be determined by various interest groups such as labor unions, farmers' associations, craftmen's associations and various commercial and industrial associations. The government-led development of the post-war economy of Japan has enabled elite officials to wield economic and political power over the fate of these various interest groups. This has placed elite officials in strategic positions to accumulate political and economic favors from leading interest groups of the nation, which in turn sought government subsidies and special protection from foreign competition. When they run for public office, therefore, government officials often collect votes and campaign donations from the interest groups which they have aided.

Third, the three-year president of LDP today is virtually assured the premiership because of LDP's domination of both the lower and upper houses of the parliament. This president is chosen every three years by about five hundred LDP "delegates" at the party's national convention. This is not an impossible number of voting delegates for contending factions within LDP to manipulate. LDP has for some time been split among eight to twelve factions, depending on how finely one wants to group the various factions. Each faction fraternizes or feuds with the others, depending on the political gusts within LDP. Each faction which puts up a candidate for the presidency of LDP has long been cultivating its own political and financial ties with particular industrialists. And the bureaucrats with political ambitions have long discovered that the quickest way to the apex of the political pyramid is to identify with a winning faction and nurture it through political influence. Hence, collusive relationships are often formed between specific LDP factions and select elite officials of various ministries. The individual elite officials who have cultivated connections with various corporations and industry associations often act as the intermediaries peddling political influence between Japanese corporations and faction leaders of LDP.

Factional politics within the LDP require each faction to exact campaign funds from large corporations. Otherwise the faction leader would not be able to retain its LDP rank-and-file members in the Diet and the House of Councillors, who comprise the overwhelming bulk of voting delegates at the LDP convention. The campaign fund, not the ideological commitment, is the only binding currency which cements fund-starved rank-and-file LDP'ers to respective leaders vying for the premiership. The Japanese Election Law does not forbid corporations and labor unions from making direct political donations. Moreover, the Autonomy Agency (*Jichi Cho*), which oversees the campaign spending of candidates for public office, is too weak politically within the Japanese bureaucracy to enforce the legal limit ostensibly placed on the campaign budget of each political candidate.[8] Furthermore, the LDP presidential election convention is not covered by the Election Law and this is riddled with the outright purchases of delegate votes.

The channel of communication between government ministries and industries was to be supplemented on another level through dealings between government ministries and the Economic Confederation of Japan (*Keidanren*). The latter body, reformed in 1946, was the continuation of the war-time business association consisting of leading firms of various Japanese industries. This business association collaborated with the Imperial Japanese government. During the 1950s and 1960s, *Keidanren*, which had come to be dominated by the interest groups representing steel firms, public utilities and banking communities, built up its political influence and was performing three important functions for the government and the ruling LDP party: (1) it was building a consensus within business groups concerning the general directions to be pursued in Japanese industrial policy; (2) it was acting as intermediary in the distribution of political favors among various business interests and as negotiator of three-way dealings among the Japanese government, business circles and LDP; and (3) it was collecting and subsequently distributing political donations among various political parties (excluding the Communist Party), and more important, among diverse factions within the ruling LDP.

Since the bulk of Japanese industries were under the jurisdiction of MITI, *Keidanren* had long cultivated close ties with MITI in particular. This is why at every turn in Japan's industrial policies, when ushering in a new "bellweather" industry for the further growth of the economy, MITI relied on *Keidanren* to rally Japanese business interests in launching newly selected, target industries. Thus, the emphasis placed on steel and coal in the late 1940s was shifted subsequently to shipbuilding, and then to petrochemicals, synthetic fibers and automobiles. From the mid-1860s, the computer- and electronics-related industries came to be singled out as the industries worthy of the government's support.

However, close relations between business and government in Japan came to be afflicted with graft and corruption as various business and interest groups competed for the government's favors. This graft and corruption took the form of firms' political donations and rebate payoffs to various political parties, notably LDP, as well as to various factions within LDP. In the process, a number of LDP politicians filled their own pockets. In fact, LDP politicians who assumed important cabinet and party positions often died rich, leaving large personal estates that were amassed during their political careers.

If we may call such behavior "large corruption"—where bribers seek to have government rules and policies bent in their favor—post–World War II Japan has seen such "large corruption" institutionalized into the workings of its large corporations. Japanese society has remained relatively free from "small corruptions," where ordinary citizens and businesses are subject to persistent demands for petty graft, bribes, gifts and payoffs from government clerks, firm purchase agents, policemen and soldiers. However, where the public and the mass media would be aghast at isolated incidents of "small corruption," they have shown a greater tolerance through tacit acquiescence to "large corruptions."* As a result, many private firms have actively attempted to negotiate their business transactions with the government and LDP.

Those Japanese firms which grew prone to practice "large corruption" at home often fell easy prey to politicians and government officials of host countries who sought payoffs from foreign corporations. International exposés from 1972 and 1975 such as ITT's clandestine political operations in Chile, the United Brands' $1.5 million payoff to a Honduras president, and Gulf Oil's "protection" money to President Park of Korea indicated that "large corruption" was practiced by American multinational firms as well. Furthermore, those Japanese and American multinational firms which practiced "large corruption" abroad were, without exception, ardent practitioners of "large corruption" at home. Thus, such observations run counter to the widespread pronouncement that multinational firms only succumb to local customs of graft and corruption.

Interestingly enough, however, the preceding cases of corruption by American multinational firms were exposed by none other than the Securities and Exchange Commission of the United States and the United States Senate Sub-Committee on Multinational Firms. The kind of investigative reporting of American journalism—that gave rise to the famed performance by the *Washington Post* on the Watergate story—was also instrumental in publicizing the corruption of American multinational firms.

In contrast, neither Japan's regulatory agency, the Fair Trade Commission, nor the Diet of Japan has been concerned with possible "large corruptions" practiced abroad by Japanese firms. For example, in 1974, it was reported that Japanese firms headed the list of foreign investors in violation of antipollution rules in Singapore. In 1973 it was reported that two to three leading trading firms of Japan were found to have bribed Thai Customs officials into reclassifying the firm's imports into lower tariff categories.

From about 1970 onward, it was increasingly rumored in Japan and whispered throughout Korea that both Japanese and Korean

---

*The leading daily newspapers of Japan have thus far failed to demonstrate the kind of investigative journalism as shown by the *Washington Post* over the Watergate incident in the United States. It was a monthly magazine *Bungei Shunju*, not a leading newspaper, that relentlessly exposed Prime Minister Tanaka's scandal in the fall of 1974.

high-ranking politicians of respective ruling parties including Nobel Peace Award laureate, Sato of Japan, enriched themselves through financial manipulation of Japanese private and government loans to government agencies and private businesses in Korea. But, again, no official investigation either by the Diet or by the Fair Trade Commission was instituted in Japan. The mass media of Japan launched no investigative reporting to ascertain the authenticity of such rumors. The Japanese public was generally indifferent to the rumored cases of "large corruption" abroad by Japanese businesses and politicians. The reputation of Japanese multinational firms abroad, however, was tarnished as suspicions mounted concerning their "large corruption" and concomitant "bad" behavior. The lack of the Japanese government's concern over the rise of such suspicions abroad was again interpreted by host countries as the *prima facie* evidence that Japanese government and industry were tacitly colluding in order to corrupt governments and businesses in developing countries.

Accordingly, if the Japanese government, and notably, the Ministry of International Trade and Industry were genuinely concerned with the conduct of Japanese firms abroad, they should be enforcing at home tough antipollution regulations and regulating corporate donations to politicians. To begin, the Fair Trade Commission might place Japanese firms on notice that their covert cartels and unfair trade practices at home and abroad will be watched closely. Also, the Minister of Finance should amend the current disclosure practices of Japanese firms in their economic performance so that intracorporation transactions between Japanese parents and their subsidiaries abroad will be revealed to the public. These measures, which do not require new legislation, would be far more effective in motivating Japanese multinational firms to maintain "exemplary" conduct, than MITI's current attempts at drawing up a "nine-point recommendation for good corporate citizens" to deal with the conduct of Japanese subsidiaries abroad.

In other words, the multinational expansion of Japanese firms has come to require that various branches of the Japanese government position themselves anew, somewhere between the public interest and corporate interest in Japan. The oil crisis of 1973 helped MITI reemerge, much stronger than in the past, with legal authorities to regulate diverse dimensions of Japanese firms' behavior. As a result, the rest of the world would begin watching how MITI might use its newly acquired regulatory power.

Moreover, a growing segment of the Japanese public has come to articulate anti-big business sentiments. Internally as well, with the rapid industrial growth of post–World War II Japan, the government and ruling party have been confronted with the need to protect ordinary citizens from the abuses of large corporations in their economic and political power.

Consumer concern was also spreading to the pricing and distribution practices of manufacturers of such consumer products as household appliances. In fact, in 1970 consumer groups like the CO-OP Association of Japan and the Federation of Japanese Housewives successfully organized, on a national scale, the boycott of color television sets made by Matsushita (Panasonic) Co. because of the firm's practice of maintaining artificially high prices. Increasing public distress over continued price increases and environmental pollution began to materialize into the confrontation with MITI and LDP, with the demand that the Japanese government cease to protect only the interests of big business. *Keidanren* became, for the first time in history, the target of repeated demonstrations and picketing staged by labor unions, consumer groups and even small merchants and fishermen who were angered over industrial pollution destroying their fishing areas.

Meanwhile, the Diet and LDP majority members who were elected from non-industrial farming areas, remained unresponsive to the frustration and anger of city dwellers and coastal fishermen. As a result, the increased public criticism of three-way collusion between LDP, MITI and big business began to manifest itself by the driving out of LDP-related politicians from local and municipal offices in the urban and industrial areas. In such local elections, a semblance of the "one voter one vote" principle was maintained because public office holders were elected on the basis of local municipality-wide popular votes. By 1973 the defeat of LDP candidates in elections for mayor, governor and city councilman spread from such metropolitan areas as Tokyo, Yokohama and Kyoto even to small cities which had been thought of, until then, as safe "LDP" pockets. By 1973 out of about 650 municipalities throughout Japan, about one-quarter came to elect members of opposition parties—Socialist, Komeito (Clean Government Party) and Communist—to the mayorality. This was unprecedented in the history of Japanese politics. After over a quarter of a century of relative inertia, Japanese political processes were undergoing fundamental change.

From January to spring 1974 the Tanaka Cabinet came under mounting pressure from both consumers and labor unions who are demanding that the government arrest the inflation raging throughout Japan at the rate of over a 30 percent increase in the consumer price index from the previous year. As the public became aware by spring 1974 that the 1973 oil crisis had been exploited by various large corporations to increase the prices of their products, their anti-big business sentiments also came to be directed at the ruling party, LDP, and the Japanese bureaucracy, both of whom appeared to have failed in restraining price-fixing by large corporations. Various public poll results were casting ominous predictions for the House of Councillors (upper house as opposed to the lower house, the Diet) in the national election scheduled for July, 1974.

Unlike the Diet, 100 of the 252 members of the House of Councillors are elected on the basis of a nationwide popular vote. Accordingly, a limited semblance of the "one voter one vote" principle enabled urban dwellers to articulate their feelings by way of defeating LDP candidates in the nationwide riding. Inasmuch as the city populations throughout Japan had grown increasingly disenchanted with LDP, LDP's power in the House of Councillors had been eroded for some time. As a result, it even became highly probable in the election in July 1974 that for the first time in Japan's history, the opposition party members combined might well outnumber LDP members in the upper house.

In order to save LDP from a probable defeat in the election of the upper house, the ruling party machinery and *Keidanren* (representing large corporations) devised the so-called "Corporationwide Election Campaign." According to this formula, each large industrial group like Mitsubishi, Kajima and Hitachi was assigned one LDP candidate by the ruling party. The designated firm group was expected to promote its LDP candidate throughout the country by pressuring numerous employees, subcontractors and their family members to vote for the candidate. Employees' loyalty to their companies was often tested by the devotion they paid on their own time to the election campaign of the company-designated candidates.

Perhaps because the "Corporationwide Election Campaign" registered a limited success, and perhaps because the ruling party did well in the local constituencies, the July election of the House of Councillors did not produce the expected reversal of power within the House. Nevertheless, LDP's majority in the upper house was reduced to one seat. Only later, when conservative unaffiliated members joined LDP, was the party's majority increased to seven. A spectacular defeat, however, of the very candidate in the national riding whom the famed "Mitsubishi Empire" promoted vigorously, signalled that many voters rejected the blatant display of collusion that existed between big business and the ruling party. If it were not for this visible loss of the "Mitsubishi" candidate, the Asian host countries watching the outcome of the July election in Japan would have concluded that Japanese large corporations and the Japanese government did in fact look after their collective interests.

The lingering aftermath of having almost lost the upper house election to the combined opposition continued to haunt the LDP. It became not only "thinkable" but also "plausible" that the ruling party might not be able to arrest the voters' trend of abandoning LDP. This crisis atmosphere permeated the ranks of the LDP. It became so serious that when Tanaka resigned in November 1974 from the Premiership, Miki, not Fukuda, was selected by the party and business "king makers." The ruling party feared that Fukuda's past identification with the right-of-center factions within LDP would surely invite fierce resistance inside the Diet from the combined opposition parties. It was more than plausible in the crisis atmosphere of selecting Tanaka's successor in November 1974 that the ruling party might have split irreparably. Thus, Miki was presented to the public as LDP's reformist "Mr. Clean LDP." And he set out to mend political fences with the middle-of-the-road voters in urban and industrial areas.

The immediate test of Miki's political strength was the election of Tokyo's governor scheduled for April 1975. Ever since the populist candidate Minobe captured the governorship in 1967, which until then had been held by LDP-leaning conservatives, the Tokyo gubernatorial election came to symbolize the acid test of LDP's popularity with city voters. In April 1975, despite the all-out support of LDP and business interests to their favorite son candidate Ishihara, who boasts his ultra-nationalism, Minobe won again. It was thus confirmed, even to skeptics, that without drastic reforms within the ruling party, LDP and its allies within the Japanese bureaucracy, the governing of the increasingly dissident public would become more difficult. And anti-big business sentiments in particular continued to rise in Japan.

The way in which Minobe was genuinely drafted by grass-roots voters into running against Ishihara signalled that at least the political processes in urban and industrial areas were materially changing. When Minobe decided not to seek a third term governorship, Ishihara's victory appeared almost certain. Determined to deny Ishihara his ambition, a group of housewives, office workers and students voluntarily started sit-ins in front of the Tokyo City Hall in order to collect signatures from passers-by on the plea that Minobe be drafted to rescind his earlier retirement. The mass media, big business and even the Socialist Party belittled the sit-in appeals, only to be totally surprised by tens of thousands of signatures the genuine grass-roots campaign collected in a matter of a few days.

INTERNATIONAL REPERCUSSIONS OF ANTI-BIG BUSINESS SENTIMENT IN JAPAN

It even appeared that the anti-big business sentiment movement in Japan was finding political allies in the neighboring Asian countries growing critical of Japanese investments. It was, indeed, ominous for Japanese multinational firms that a public accusation like "exporting pollution," being increasingly vocalized throughout Japan, was immediately picked up in 1975 by the government officials of Asian host countries and Australia as *prima facie* evidence of Japanese multinational firms' "bad behavior." In the era of McLuhanistic "instant communication," the exposé of bad behavior by Japanese firms in Japan supplied instant ammunition to intellectuals, students and government officials of developing countries who were intent on shaming Japanese investors into desired concessions.

Accordingly, as is the case with the future success of multinational financial firms of Japan, the similar success of Japanese manufacturing firms has come to depend partly upon how soon and in what way the leading Japanese bureaucracies (like MITI) position themselves at arm's length, away from the inner camp, as it were, of Japanese multinational firms. No doubt, it would be in the interest of Japanese multinational firms if the Japanese bureaucracy would enforce strict policies at home of anti-pollution, policed tax evasion, anti-monopoly and reformed political campaign contributions. Thus, when approached by local extortionists, Japanese multinational firms abroad could fall back upon the new and strict regulations forbidding Japanese firms at home and abroad to accommodate extortionists' demands.

In the years ahead, both home and host governments will be increasingly called into disputes involving private multinational firms at home and with host governments. For instance, the Third World now appears intent on internationally emulating the tactics of "pattern-setting" and "pattern-following" which labor unions in industrialized nations have for years successfully applied in obtaining greater wages and working conditions for weaker unions. In the Third World Forum that was held in January 1975 in Karachi, Pakistan, OPEC was ideologically and tactically likened to the "strongest union," so to speak, negotiating with its adversary, the "industrialized countries" for oil price concessions. OPEC was expected by other developing countries to insist on including other non-oil commodities produced by the Third World in the negotiation of oil prices with the industrialized nations. The attendants at the Third World Forum repeated the hope that with the maximum uses of oil for bargaining clout, the developing countries could aim at the annual transfer of real economic resources from the few industrialized "have" countries to the many developing "have-not" nations. The target rate for such economic transfer was from 3 to 4 percent of the gross national products of the industrialized nations. This rate was to be considered analogous to the special income "taxes" levied on the "incomes" of industrialized nations.

Because of an incredible solidarity, the Third World, that put OPEC in the forefront, successfully weathered the test of international diplomacy in April 1975 in Paris where the oil consuming and oil producing countries met to discuss the future prices of crude oil. The Paris meeting was adjourned when OPEC's demand for simultaneously discussing the prices of other commodities was deadlocked with the equally persistent demand of the oil consuming nations who wanted to separate oil from other commodities. Less than two months after the collapse of the Paris meeting, the Secretary of State of the United States declared late in May, 1975, that he was prepared to discuss oil prices together with the prices of other commodities. It remains to be seen whether the United States' abandonment of her past posture of separating oil from other commodities might eventually pave the way to an "international commodity fund" or an "international commodity agreement," after the fashion of the International Monetary Fund.

In view of the fact that various multinational firms are actively involved in the international trade in various commodities, an attempted global solution to the allocating of natural resources and food items may well lead to a "General Agreement of International Investments and Multinationals" after the pattern of the General Agreement of Tariffs and Trade (GATT).[9] Even short of such international agreement among multinational firms, Japanese and other multinational firms will find themselves increasingly involved in transnational political dealings among sovereign states. Whether the familiar three-way tie-ups of the Japanese bureaucracy, the ruling party and big business can adjust themselves to new international pressures still remained uncertain in 1975.

Not the least of these uncertainties comes from future courses of action which Japanese labor unions might take. From the mid-1960s to the mid-1970s, Japanese labor unions still remained bystanders to the multinational expansion of Japanese firms. Occasional rhetoric notwithstanding, Japanese labor unions of various ideological shades that represented diverse manufacturing sectors of Japan, remained tacit supporters of Japanese multinational expansion.

JAPANESE LABOR UNIONS AND JAPANESE MULTINATIONAL FIRMS

The docility of Japanese labor unions in general can be explained by two idiosyncracies of the Japanese labor union compared to say, their European and American counterparts. First, the *Sohyo*, which is ideologically classified as the left-of-center group rejecting the notion of business unionism, happens to be dominated by government and public utility workers whose jobs are least likely to be jeopardized by the multinational emigration of various manufacturing activities out of Japan. The largest private industrial union within the *Sohyo* is the Japanese Steelworkers Union consisting of employees from leading large steel firms. Their jobs have not been affected by the partial emigration of galvanized iron sheet plants and other small scale operations out of Japan. Second, the Japanese union is organized on the basis of specific private "enterprises." Such private enterprises have practiced "lifetime commitment" to regular workers who are members of such "enterprise unions." Therefore, enterprise unions easily accepted or even took pride in the fact that "their firms" were expanding multinationally. Some rank-and-file union members and foremen were, on a rotational basis, sent abroad as "technical advisors"—the dream of going abroad on the company's expenses came true.

The international transfer of production-process technologies, unique to specific corporate (or plant) cultures of Japanese parent firms, could only be transferred abroad through workers' cooperation. As a result, Japanese rank-and-file labor union members were encouraged to regard the overseas ventures of their firms as if they were "their own" ventures. Under these circumstances, the union leaders' main concern was to make sure that the working conditions for their union members in overseas manufacturing subsidiaries were roughly the same as those at home.

Indeed, many union leaders demanded and successfully obtained the "right" to inspect, at their firm's expenses, their overseas manufacturing plants. Thus, union leaders also had access to overseas "inspecting tours." While I was engaged in fieldwork from 1972 to 1974, in Asia from Korea to Indonesia, I kept running into Japanese labor union leaders and shop stewards ostensibly inspecting the working conditions of Japanese expatriate plant workers. Not once did I observe these union leaders concerning themselves with the working conditions and workers' organizational rights of the local nationals. One could see in these acts the unsuppressed display of Japanese enterprise unions looking after the interests of their firms.

from the nationwide mobilization during World War II. Within each enterprise (firm), both management and employees were formed into the "Great Collaboration Unit." Thus, when the occupying forces encouraged the unionization of Japanese industries as one of the "democratization schemes" for the new Japan, literally thousands of enterprise-based unions were created overnight out of the wartime prototypes exemplified by enterprise-based employee associations.

When paternalistic management and employee relationships were superimposed on the emerging espirit de corps among corporate employees, rank-and-file workers were conditioned to identify with fellow "family members" of the same firm, rather than with similar rank-and-file plant and office workers of different firms across the street. Such Japanese behavioral trait that corporate employees tend to socialize with others of the same firm, remains strong even today. One foreign researcher, for example, observed that for years workers at one plant in Tokyo during their noon recess, shared the same public street with workers from the plant next door to play catch, without ever getting to know the workers from the other plant beyond the most perfunctory nodding and smiling.[10]

The strong identification of Japanese workers with their "own company" presented unsurmountable blocks to a few national labor leaders who had sought to strengthen Japanese unions' solidarity with international labor movements. Formally at least, Japanese national confederations of labor unions are divided between the left-of-center groups aligned internationally with the World Federation of Trade Unions (WFTU), and the right-of-center groups associated with the International Confederation of Trade Unions (ICFTU). In the past, two industrial groups affiliated with the ICFTU unions have been the most actively involved in international labor exchange programs; namely, the Alliance of Textile Workers (*Zensen Domei*) and an assortment of metal workers' unions ranging from automobile and electric workers to shipbuilding workers. The latter groups have been affiliated with the International Metal Workers' Federation (IMF) within the ICFTU, and since around 1960 have formed the IMF-Japan Council (IMF-JC) as the organizational umbrella encompassing metal industries-related workers across all different national union center affiliations.

During the early 1960s, the Alliance of Textile Workers actively aided textile workers in their emerging aspiration for unionization in neighboring Asian countries. However, as the Japanese textile industry lost its growth momentum during the latter half of the 1960s, internal strife appeared between enterprise unions related to synthetic fibers and enterprise unions related to such conventional yarns as cotton and silk. From about 1970, both synthetic fibers and conventional fibers came under increasing competition in Japan from imported yarns and textile products made elsewhere in Asia. At this juncture, enterprise-based union members of the Alliance of Textile Workers became preoccupied with their own firms' survival, even at the expense of competitors. They are preoccupied with unifying the front of textile workers against the onslaught of imported goods from Korea, Thailand, Hong Kong and Taiwan. Gone are the days when the Alliance of Textile Workers pledged solidarity with the textile workers of neighboring countries in Asia.

As in the case of the coal miners late in the 1950s, textile workers knew intuitively that both the Japanese public and other industrial workers would consider it a necessary "growing pain" to shed an internationally uncompetitive industry in favor of new and future growth industries. After all, the past history of Japan's industrialization has demonstrated ruthless shedding of declining products and technologies past their prime.

As a result, in mid-1975, metal workers' groups affiliated with the IMF-JC remained the only labor union groups in Japan which still possessed both the financial and political strength to confront the multinational expansion of their own firms. Originally, the IMF-JC dated from the fall of 1962, when the late Walther Reuther of the United Auto Workers (UAW) of the United States suggested to his union hosts in Japan the creation of a "Wage Research Center." Earlier, Reuther was instrumental in the formation of IMF and was the driving force behind the automotive division within IMF. He proposed the cooperation between UAW and Japanese labor unions in studying the growing impacts of "multinationalization of capital" upon worldwide labor movements. The proposed "Wage Research Center" was to provide "union-oriented" information on wages and other working conditions of various manufacturing industries in various parts of the world. Around 1966, after about four years of intensive exchanges between Japanese metal workers' unions on one hand and UAW and IG Metal Union (Germany) on the other, the IMF-JC emerged in Japan.

However, in mid-1975, the IMF-JC had not yet embraced the notion of international metal workers' solidarity. Judging from the publications, background papers and reports of the IMF-JC's positions on multinational firms in general and on multinational expansions of Japanese manufacturing firms in particular, the IMF-JC did not appear free from the kind of internal dissention, inactions and timidity that Japanese textile workers vividly demonstrated earlier over perceived costs and benefits of member union firms tackling diverse forms of multinational activities. Still remaining secure in the Japanese firm tradition of lifetime employment, respective enterprise-based unions' of IMF-JC are shielded from the expansion abroad of Japanese automobile and electrical firms, in direct competition with foreign workers whose economic fate has ebbed and waned with the economic vicissitudes of American and European automotive and electric firms.

Even when the lingering aftermath of the oil crisis of 1973 pushed the Japanese economy, during 1974 and 1975, into its worst "stagflation" since the mid-1950s, and even when many previously "secure and growth" firms, including Sony and other electronics appliance firms, resorted to the Japanese version of "layoffs" (with a callback guarantee), Japanese enterprise-based unions were still preoccupied with the defense of their "own company." Under the prevailing crisis atmosphere, Japanese workers' identification with their own "quasi-family members" within the same firm—perhaps a sentiment akin to the Japanese version of "tribalism" surviving intact well into the Twentieth Century—helped corporate employees close ranks with management, and *vice-versa.*

Accordingly, in the mid-1970s, it appeared extremely unlikely that Japanese labor unions would ever emerge, not only as tactical, but also as ideological forces behind the revitalization of international labor movements. A few leading personalities in the international labor movement, including Levinson of the International Chemical Workers Union, were still being cheered by anti-business onlookers both in and outside Japan to promote international labor solidarity against multinational firms.[11] Yet very few Japanese allies of such international labor union endeavors were found inside Japanese labor groups. Ironic as it may seem, the multinational expansion of Japanese corporations, large or small, would continue to be accepted by enterprise-based unions as a logical solution to the economic problems of their respective firms. To the extent that the political and financial leadership of Japanese national union centers continues to pass from a "once strong but declining" enterprise-based union to a "future bellwether" firm-based one, Japanese labor unions as a whole do not appear able to muster the solidarity necessary for pressuring the Japanese political process into considering a Japanese version of the AFL-CIO backed bill—like the Hartke-Burke Bill in the United States—that was designed to prevent American firms from expanding manufacturing activities overseas.[12]

CONCLUSION

The Japanese are, indeed, coming abroad in droves. As Japanese manufacturing subsidiaries followed Japanese exports into various corners of the world, Japanese hotels, restaurants, night clubs, resort facilities, housing developments, pinball (pachinko) game centers, and attractive sales girls of Japanese cosmetics are also coming abroad to benefit from the proliferation of Japanese investments, as well as from the exploding number of Japanese tourists and honeymooners abroad. And the public visibility of the Japanese presence abroad is soaring.

A rumor about Japanese wine merchants purchasing wine in Bordeau, France, is immediately picked up by foreign news agencies. By the time the story hits the streets, the Japanese are being blamed for "buying up all the wine in France," thus jacking up wine prices. When art dealers from Japan successfully bid in international auctions and secure coveted Western art pieces away from American or European buyers, the story is blown up to a spectre of all the Western arts being drained to secret collections in Japan. When Japanese race horse breeders purchased a few studs in England, the story had to be spiced up to say that the Japanese had bought up all the English race horse ranches.

There is no way to fight off this kind of public visibility. It would be a folly to even try. For the first time in history, a country and people neither European nor American has become affluent and somewhat arrogant in mass, and has gone multinational in direct competition with these other countries. Therefore, the curious reactions to the proliferation of Japanese activities abroad are likely to rise, rather than subside, in the decades to come. And the Japanese firms, government, individuals and labor unions possess, as we have seen throughout this book, many idiosyncracies that baffle and irritate foreigners. Foreigners' paranoid fear of the Japanese coming in droves, as it were, cannot be easily diminished by such cosmetic touch-ups as government-and-business-sponsored good-will missions. Nor will MITI's proclamations of "good conduct" for Japanese multinationals allay foreigners' suspicions. As we saw in this chapter, without fundamental realignment of political and economic actions and ideologies within Japan, the future of Japan might be unsteady.

Today some watchers of multinational firms speculate that the ownership of foreign subsidiaries by any multinational firm could prove to be an increasing liability in the decades to come. According to such a school of thought, that derives its deductive reasoning from the case of Chrysler in England, the ownership of local subsidiaries would lock multinational firms into mires of political entanglement with recalcitrant local work forces and politicians. When multinational firms become aware of such a problem of ownership, this school of thought predicts, they will revert to old ways of international trade. And Japan, which has not yet gone too far in owning assets abroad, it is speculated, will benefit most. Large trading firms of Japan could emerge as victors in the new world, as international flows of goods, loan funds and information are revitalized among independent bidders and traders.

This scenario describes predictable events in the case of a firm like Chrysler that has been caught for too long manufacturing uneconomical products in a country like England. And this should be a sobering message that all multinational firms should consider. A foreign investor initially brings such "uniqueness" as technology, economies of scale, export contacts and capital funds to a host country that provides, in exchange, such "unique attractions" as local market, lower wage and export platforms. But foreigners' initial uniqueness fades out in a rather short span of time. And the attractiveness of the host country also fades as newer and more attractive hosts emerge. Volatile, perhaps, and persistent change ought to be a "regular and familiar" way of life for multinational firms. Failure to cope with change renders the ownership of assets a distinct liability, as the case of Chrysler vividly demonstrates.

We have already seen that the first generation of Japanese products (and portions of industries) which emigrated to developing nations are being taken over by indigenous producers as well as by foreign investors from intermediate countries like Korea, Hong Kong, Singapore, Taiwan and India. What was earlier perceived as a wise solution, if not a panacea, to Japan's economic dilemma at home and abroad has produced a new set of dilemmas for Japanese firms.

Indeed, the moment literally hundreds of Japanese firms each made the incremental decision to go multinational, they unknowingly destined Japan to its present situation. That is to say, industrial structures, government-business relations, diplomatic stances and even corporate culture, that Japan has cultivated at home for over a century, have now become exposed to external forces to change. In short, a societal change of no less colossal magnitude than that which Japan faced 1868 and again in 1945 is now a crisis Japan is experiencing. And by 1975, Japan has already passed the point of no return, although few government and business leaders in Japan are aware of it.

This time, the external forces of change are not so visible as at the end of Tokugawa feudalism in 1868, or the defeat in World War II in 1945. But the required change is no less urgent. Anything less than complete appreciation of this reality may court further dissension inside and outside Japan. Some say that the Twenty-First Century is the century of Japan. If Japan does not wish to belie such a speculation, she has much to do in very little time. Are the Japanese aware of this? Perhaps not yet.

The multinational expansion of Japanese firms, which was necessitated by Japan's past successes in industrial development, is now forcing various segments of Japanese society to re-examine not only the "ideology" of industrial growth but also Japan's practice of separating politics from economics in international trade and investment. If Japanese business and government circles fail to heed this ironic turn of events, the multinational expansion of Japanese firms may well be doomed again like that discredited "Great Asia Co-Prosperity." The result of such a turn of events could prove just as disastrous as that which befell its predecessor.

In a rising atmosphere of economic and political confrontation today, between industrialized countries as well as between rich and poor nations, the bargaining chips, as it were, of Japan are essentially two-fold. First, both product- and process-related technologies that Japan has accumulated carry merchandisable values for other countries to covet. Second, that Japan has become such a large consuming nation of various commodities and manufactures attracts solicitous suppliers of diverse products. In short, Japan's latent bargaining power is derived from the possibility that both technologies and markets of Japan may be purposely withheld from soliciting foreign firms and nations. If and when excluded from any schemes of alliance with the firms or the countries in the Third World, it is feared that Japanese firms and government will proceed with bilateral deals with developing countries producing natural resources and food.

At the same time, since Japan can never hope to become self-sufficient in natural resources, food and manufactured goods, she is forced to pursue a delicate policy of interdependence in the conflicting world. Hopefully, this need for interdependency, when recognized, will make Japan somewhat judicious and even humble in exercising her bargaining power.

An exercise of bargaining strength—potentially a brute power—is treacherous. Japan's reappearance in the arena of world politics could be linked up immediately in the minds of other nations with their vivid memories and hearsay evidence of Imperial Japan victimizing her Asian neighbors. Unlike the Japanese who inflicted selective amnesia upon themselves about their past, the memories of the victimized are long and deep. They remember that Japanese soldiers, merchants, bureaucrats and the right-wing ruffians of Imperial Japan—the products of the excruciatingly oppressive system, totally devoid of compassion for human suffering and tolerance of dissent even at home—rampaged through Asia, venting on the helpless civilians their own frustration and anger with the dehumanized system. The victimized recall that Japanese bureaucracy and businesses were also willing participants.

Is the Japan of today more humane than the Imperial Japan of the past? Is Japan's lingering mass abhorrence of the war and mass violence—a by-product of the unpleasant and shocking experience of defeat in World War II—strong enough to restrain Japan from thinking of a military solution to the question of economic security? Without convincing proof of the peaceful "new Japan," Japanese attempts at bargaining exercises in the world economic markets and political arenas would prove counterproductive.

One such proof of the "new Japan" would be for Japan to articulate her ideological commitment to a universal goal which is ardently hoped for by developing nations. One such goal is expanding and promoting freer trade throughout the world. And Japan must make an exemplary move by opening the Japanese market to the developing countries.

Historically, free trade was advocated by the leader-nations that saw it to be beneficial to her own political and economic causes. After the United Kingdom slipped from such a pinnacle position of world leadership, the United States waved the banner of free trade. The U.S. found free trade to be inseparable from establishing American hegemony throughout the world, in direct competition with the socialist countries. Now that the United States has abandoned the advocate's role, the world sorely needs a new promoter of free trade. Who but Japan, in dire need of freer trade, is in a position to fulfill the advocate's role vacated by the United States?

In the world today, Japan is in the position to promote freer trade without linking it with the problem of political hegemony. Unlike the United States, the world knows that Japan is more dependent upon other countries than other countries upon Japan. When Japan can articulate her own ideological commitment to the goal of freer trade through the recognition of her dependence on the rest of the world, freer trade may be given a chance of survival, relatively free from the brutal contest for political hegemony exercised by the past advocates of such a goal. Now the Japanese firms have positioned themselves in every corner of the world, it would be folly for Japan to reject the role of preserving and promoting freer trade in direct competition with the rising practices of protectionism.

Will Japan realize this? It remains to be seen whether leaders of business and political circles in Japan—all of whom have grown older and have created a kind of mass senility of the leadership echelon—will be persuaded to entrust the task of promoting the "new Japan" to the younger generation. Despite their achievements since the last World War, few of the current leaders of Japan have themselves shed the attitudes and the perceptions of the rest of the world, fostered in the oppressive atmosphere of the "old Japan."

Notes

Except when appropriate references are available only in Japanese, the notes in this book are limited to documents and publications available in English. When the Japanese sources are cited, my own translations of their titles follow the romanized original title. Most of the Japanese sources cited here are available at the Yenching Chinese, Japanese and Korean Library of Harvard University.

CHAPTER 1

1. The Economic and Social Council of the United Nations adopted unanimously on July 2, 1972, the resolution to appoint a group of eminent persons to study the role of multinational corporations and their impact on the process of economic development in the developing countries. *The Report* of this group was published by the United Nations in May, 1974: E/5500/Add. 1 (Part I), and (Part II). This *Report* reflects the anxiety of the developing countries facing multinational firms. In the United States, from 1974 to 1975, Congress, the Departments of State, Commerce and Justice, as well as the Securities and Exchange Commission and Federal Trade Commission respectively formed or commissioned a task force to study foreign investments in the United States.

2. Barbara Tuchman describes this anecdote in her book, *Zimmerman Telegram* (New York: The Macmillan Co., 1966). While negotiating with Japan at the Portsmouth Conference to end the Russo-Japan War in New Hampshire in 1905, the Russian delegates exploited the "Yellow Peril" characterization of the victor, Japan, and turned the American and European public opinion against Japan.

3. This working definition of the multinational firms was adopted by the Multinational Enterprise Project of the Harvard Business School mainly to define the scope of the study of the U.S.- and Europe-based multinational firms. See Raymond Vernon, *Sovereignty at Bay*, Ch. 1, New York: Basic Books, 1971.

4. Yoshi Tsurumi, "Japanese Multinational Firm," *Journal of World Trade Law* (February 1973).

309

5. The evolutionary process of modern Japanese education is given in *Gakusei Hyakunenshi* (One Hundred Years of the Educational System) Vols. I and II by the Ministry of Education, Tokyo, 1972. For accounts of the Tokugawa Era and the early Meiji Era, one should consult the excellent work by R.P. Dore, *Education in Tokugawa*, Berkeley and Los Angeles: University of California Press, 1965.

6. Of numerous references available in English, I still recommend the following three works: B.K. Marshall, *Captialism and Nationalism in Prewar Japan; The Ideology of the Business Elite, 1868–1941*, Palo Alto, Calif.: Stanford University Press, 1967; T.C. Smith, *The Agrarian Origin of Modern Japan*, Palo Alto, Calif.: Stanford University Press, 1959; and the epoch-making work by the late E.H. Norman, "Japan's Emergence as Modern State" in John Dower, ed., *Origins of the Modern Japanese State: Selected Writings of E.H. Norman*, New York: Pantheon, 1974. Also, see Thomas C. Smith, *Political Change and Industrial Development in Japan: Government Enterprise, 1868–1880*, Palo Alto, Calif.: Stanford University Press, 1955.

7. The three works cited above in Footnote 6 are replete with the examples of the cooperative works between government agencies and private businesses in Japan in her industrially formative stage.

8. Toshihiko Yoshino, *Watashino Sengo Keizaishi* (My Memoire of the Postwar Economic History), Shiseido Shinsho, Tokyo, 1965, pp. 22–23.

9. This important historical occurrence was often ignored by many Japanese and foreign researchers writing about the economic recovery of the post–World War II Japan but was recorded in an obscure government document: *Nihon Keizai Saiken no Kihon Mondai* (Problems of Economic Reconstruction of Japan), Special Report of the Ministry of Foreign Affairs, Tokyo, September 1946.

10. Saburo Ohkita, *Gijutsu-Shigen-Keizai* (Technology-Natural Resources-Economy), Hakuyosha, 1949, p. 4.

11. I retranslated the statement into English on the basis of the Japanese version of the Report of the Science Advisory Mission of the GHQ quoted in Saburo Ohkita, *op. cit.*, pp. 4–5.

12. This industrial policy was popularly referred to as the "*Keisha Seisan Hōshiki*" (slanted production policy). The governmental efforts were to be "slanted" to tackle the critical bottlenecks in the economy. The mechanism of resource allocation of the coal-steel link system is described in Naohiro Amaya, "The Ministry of International Trade and Industry," Bulletin No. 24 (mimeograph), Socio-Economic Institute, Sophia University, Tokoyo, 1970.

13. This estimation is based on a series of *Honpō Keizai Tōkei* (Economic Statistics of Japan), Bank of Japan.

14. This plan was popularly called the "Dodge Plan" after a Detroit banker who imposed the so-called "9 Principles of Economic Stability." Dodge applied to Japan the very same drastic monetary freezes which he earlier applied to occupied Germany.

15. More details of the "planned shipbuilding" as well as the growth of the Japanese shipbuilding industry are shown in Shin Katayama, *Nikon no Zōsen Kōgyō* (Shipbuilding Industry of Japan), Nikon Kōgyō Shuppan, Tokyo, 1970;

Kazunori Echigo, *Nikon Zōsen Kōgyō Ron* (On Japanese Shipbuilding), Nihon Hyoronsha, Tokyo, 1956; H. Arisawa, ed., *Gendai Nihon Sangyō Koza* (Modern Japanese Industries), Vol. IV, Iwanami, Tokyo, 1959.

16. *Brazil Report*, Kokusai Keizai Sha, Tokyo, June 30, 1974, pp. 31–41; Yaseizo Nakagawa, *Ujiminasu Monogatari* (USIMINAS Story), Sangyō Nōritsu, Tokyo, 1974.

17. Yoshi Tsurumi, *Technology Transfer and Foreign Trade: The Case of Japan, 1950–1966*, Chs. 4 and 5, unpublished doctoral thesis, Harvard Business School, Boston, 1968.

18. Takeo Imamura, ed., *Kōdan Sengo Keizai Nijunen Shi* (A Popular Account of 20 Years of the Postwar Economy), Arachi, Tokyo, 1964, pp. 53–55.

19. For a convenient reference, one should check the chapter entitled "Computer Industry" in Japan: *The Government-Business Relationship* by U.S. Department of Commerce, February 1972. This publication also contains chapters on other manufacturing industries in Japan.

20. *Janome Mishin* (Janome Sewing Machine Co.), Diamond Group, Tokyo, 1965; and N.B. Macintosh and Y. Tsurumi, "Multinational Strategies for Survival" in the *Proceedings* of the Winnipeg Meeting of the Canadian Association of Schools of Business, June 1970.

21. The following literature would provide useful introductions to labor situations in Japan: Alice Cook, *Japanese Trade Unionism*, Ithaca, N.Y.: Cornell University Press, 1966; Japan Institute of Labor, *The Changing Patterns of Industrial Relations*, Tokyo, 1965; Solomon Levine, *Industrial Relations in Postwar Japan*, Champaign: University of Illinois Press, 1958; Yoshi Tsurumi, *The Industrial Relations System in Japan*, ICH 9-311-001, Harvard Business School, 1966; Ronald P. Dore, *British Factory—Japanese Factory*, Berkeley: University of California Press, 1973.

22. Yoshi Tsurumi, "R&D Factors and Exports of Manufacturers of Japan", in L.T. Wells, *ed.*, *The Product Life Cycle and International Trade*, Cambridge, Mass.: Harvard University Press, 1972.

23. Economic Planning Agency, *Keizai Hakusho* (White Paper on the Economic Situation), Tokyo, 1961.

24. Raymond Vernon, "International Investment and International Trade in the Product Cycle," *Quarterly Journal of Economics*, Vol. LXXX (May 1966); and L.T. Wells' survey article in Wells *ed.*, *op. cit.*

25. For a rigorous econometric test of the Product Life Cycle Theory as applied to the growth and export performance of the Japanese steel industry, one should consult Hiroki Tsurumi, "A Bayesian Test of the Product Cycle Hypothesis Applied to Japanese Crude Steel Production," *Journal of Econometrics* (forthcoming 1976).

CHAPTER 2

1. See Irvine H. Anderson; *The Standard-Vacuum Oil Company and United States East Asian Policy, 1933–1944*, Princeton, N.J.: Princeton University Press, 1975.

2. Yoshi Tsurumi, "Japan" in *Daedalus: The Oil Crisis in Perspective* (Fall, 1975); also in Raymond Vernon, ed. *The Oil Crisis* New York: W.W. Norton Co., 1976.

3. This estimation is computed from *Shigen Mondai no Tenbo* (Survey of Problems of Natural Resources), the Ministry of International Trade and Industry, Tokyo, 1973, p. 359.

4. These estimates are derived from field investigation data that I collected from Japanese mining firms during 1972–73. I also confirmed that my estimates were in line with the internal data gathered by the Ministry of International Trade and Industry.

5. These estimates are based on the data gathered by the Petroleum Development Public Corporation.

6. During the months of July and August 1975, I ascertained these facts in Tokyo from the individuals in government and business circles who were in an undisputed position to know the intricate background of the Asahan Project.

7. I confirmed this view with the firms involved while I was collecting data on Japanese multinational firms for the Multinational Enterprise Project of the Harvard Business School.

8. The detailed accounts of AMAX-MITSUI tie-up in the context of the world aluminum industry are analytically provided in the series of notes and cases that Professor Graham of MIT and I developed jointly. They are available from the Intercollegiate Case Clearing House of the Harvard Business School: *The World Aluminum Industry* (Order No. 9-375-351); *AMAX-MITSUI (A)* Order No. 9-375-350); *AMAX-MITSUI (B)* (Order No. 9-375-388); *AMAX-MITSUI (C)* (Order No. 9-375-389); also see Yoshi Tsurumi, *Multinational Management*, Ch. 6, Cambridge, Mass.: Ballinger, 1976.

9. For aluminum industry, see the *World Aluminum Industry* cited in the preceding footnote; For oil one should consult the articles by Edith Penrose and Mira Wilkins in *Daedalus* (Fall 1975) and the classic work by Edith Penrose, *The Large International Firm in Developing Countries*, London: Allen & Unwin, 1969. Also see U.S. Federal Trade Commission, *The International Petroleum Cartel*, Government Printing Office, 1952. In business history, one should consult I.M. Tarbell, *The History of the Standard Oil Company*, 2 Vols., New York: Macmillan, 1925 and Mira Wilkins, *The Emergence of Multinational Enterprise*, Cambridge, Mass.: Harvard University Press, 1970; also see M.S. Broan and John Butler, *The Production, Marketing and Consumption of Copper and Aluminum*, New York: Praeger, 1968.

10. See Yoshi Tsurumi, "Japan," in *Daedalus* (Fall 1975).

11. Quoted in Takeo Imamura, *op. cit.*, pp. 67–69; and Sazo Idemitsu confirmed this view in his *Idemitsu Memoire*, Idemitsu, Tokyo, 1968.

12. For the detailed accounts of the copper concessions of the Bougainville Copper Co. Ltd. see *Bougainville Copper Co. Ltd. (B)* (Order No. 9-174-109) of Harvard Business School.

13. Yoshi Tsurumi, "Japan" in *Daedalus* (Fall 1975).

14. This figure is estimated from the data held by the Petroleum Industry Association of Japan. The annual report, 1972, of this association contains the basic information concerning the oil concessions held abroad by Japan.

CHAPTER 3

1. Ministry of International Trade and Industry, "Wagakuni Kigyō no Kaigai Katsudō Chōsa" (Survey of Multinational Activities of Japanese Firms), mimeograph, 1971.
2. Ministry of International Trade and Industry, *Wagakuni Kigyō no Kaigai Katsudō* (MITI Survey), 1973, p. 73.
3. See Lawrence G. Franko, "The Origins of Multinational Manufacturing by Continental European Firms," *Business History Review*, Vol. XLVIII, No. 3, (Autumn 1974); and John M. Stopford, "The Origins of British-based Multinational Manufacturing Enterprises," *Business History Review* (Autumn 1974).
4. This means that the structural pressures of the "cost-push" inflation became apparent around the mid-1960s. And yet, both government and business circles in Japan accelerated their investments throughout the balance of the 1960s; thus, triggering the two-digit inflation long before the oil crisis of fall 1973.
5. The Ministry of Labor, *Rōdō Hakusho* (White Paper on Labor Situations), annual issues, 1966-1975. After the mid-1960s, these *White Papers* annually noted that for the under eighteen years bracket of the labor force, the ratio of jobs offered to the number of new job seekers increased exponentially to well beyond five to one ratios.
6. For accounts of the structure of the Japanese synthetic fibre industry, see Uegusa and Nanbu, "Synthetic Fibre," in H. Kumagai, ed., *Nihon no Sangyō Soshiki* (The Industrial Organizations in Japan), Vol. II, Chuōkōron, Tokyo, 1973.
7. I reached this deduction of the "locational theory" of the oligopolists' plants while I was investigating manufacturing operations of foreign firms in Indonesia. Both in pharmaceutical and in synthetic fibre industries, both non-Japanese and Japanese investors tend to locate their plants literally next to one another.
8. The literature on the "offshore production" is growing by day. The worldwide proliferation of electrics and electronics industries has motivated a number of empirical studies. See, for instance, John E. Tilton, *International Diffusion of Technology: The Case of Semiconductors*, Washington, D.C.; Brookings Institution, 1971; and Richard W. Moxon, "Offshore Production in the Less Developed Countries—A Case Study of Multinationality in the Electronics Industry," *The Bulletin*, Nos. 98-99 (July 1974), Graduate School of Business Administration, New York University. Also see Jose de la Torre, *Exports of Manufactured Goods from Developing Countries: Marketing Factors and the Role of Foreign Enterprise*, unpublished DBA thesis, Harvard Business School, 1971. The theory of offshore production is rather straightforward. Indigenous manufacturers face formidable barrier-to-entry into export markets (abroad) even after they become proficient in physical productions of products. The time and money that indigenous manufacturers would need to invest in order to develop overseas marketing contacts are not only enormous but require "lumpy" investments. On the other hand, foreign investors can easily utilize their organizational economy of scale by marketing the offshore products through their own existing channels under familiar brand names.

9. See also John J. Teeling, *The Evolution of Offshore Investment*, unpublished DBA thesis, Harvard Business School, 1976. Teeling also points out that offshore production bases of foreign firms located in Ireland introduced more mechanized and technology-intensive methods of production as the wage rates in Ireland increased. Thus, the viability of offshore production bases depends on the investors' flexibility to upgrade the technological level of their export platforms abroad.

CHAPTER 4

1. This steel mill has attracted national attention. Leading newspapers including the *New York Times* (September 9, 1974, p. 33) have run a feature story on the "Japanese steel plant."

2. I confirmed this incident through my own field investigation. I was struck again by the fact that the Japanese investors like other Japanese investments in the U.S. and Europe, totally ignored investigating and coping with political repercussions of the host residents.

3. R.T. Johnson and W.G. Ouchi, "Made in America (under Japanese Management," *Harvard Business Review* (September-October 1974).

4. American managers will be increasingly confronted with examples of proven counter-evidences to their conventional management-employee relations. Workers' participation in management decisions, especially in the fields of labor and personnel administration is practiced in West Germany, Denmark and Sweden. A Volvo plant experience in dismantling its auto assembly line is the best known example, today. There are already similar experiments in the U.S. See R.E. Walton, "How to counter alienation in the plant," *Harvard Business Review* (November-December 1972). However, I maintain that a successful overhaul of the American management-employee relations requires a fundamental rejection of the so-called principles of "Tayloresque" scientific managements. Long before Marx's famous thesis of alienation, Adam Smith warned that an extreme division of labor (specialization in a narrow breadth of work) would make human beings extremely dull and stupid (Adam Smith's Lecture on Justice, Police, Revenue and Arms at the University of Glasgow in 1763— recorded by Edwin Cannon, in his note of this lecture: Oxford: Clarendon Press, 1896, pp. 255-256).

5. Department of Commerce, *Current Survey of Business*, 1973 and 1974 series.

6. I estimated this investment figure from the data collected by the Bank of Japan about the authorization of Japanese investments abroad as well as from the questionnaire survey I conducted among the Japanese firms operating in the U.S.

7. G.R. Hall and R.E. Johnson, *Aircraft Co-production and Procurement Strategy*, Rand Report R-450-PR, May 1967.

8. "A Mitsubishi made in the U.S." *Business Week*, (June 6, 1970). Also see "Aircraft: Culture 'Shokku' in Texas," *Time* (November 22, 1971), pp 103-104; and "Mitsubishi Expands Market Share," *Aviation Week and Space Technology*, (January 25, 1971), pp. 54-55; and *Wall Street Journal*

(November 2, 1972). Naturally, there are many American and European managers who are baffled and frustrated by their cultural shocks with Japanese management style. See, for instance, "Japanese foreign investment machine," *Business Week* (March 24, 1973), pp. 52–57.

9. T. Nakagawa and M. Yokoyama, "Japanese Manufacturing Investment in U.S.A.," MBA Research Report, spring 1973, Harvard Business School.

10. See Harvard Business School case, *Kikkoman Shoyu Co.* (Order No. ICH 4-375-073).

11. See Harvard Business School case, *Mitsubishi Corporation* (Order No. ICH 4-576-085).

12. "Multinationals: Foreign search for U.S. acquisitions," *Business Week* (May 19, 1973), pp. 50–54. The oligopolistic investment behaviors of the "follow-the-leader" are presented in F.T. Knickerbocker, *Oligopolistic Reaction and Multinational Enterprise*, Boston: Division of Research, Harvard Business School, 1973; and the "exchange-of-hostage" hypothesis of oligopolistic foreign investments is analyzed by E.M. Graham, "Oligopolistic Imitation, Theories of Foreign Direct Investment, and European Direct Investment in the United States," Working Paper, WP817–75 of Sloan School of Management, M.I.T., October 1975. A classic work on the defensive motivations of foreign investments was first presented by Stephen H. Hymer, *The International Operations of National Firms; A Study of Direct Foreign Investment*, Cambridge, M.I.T. Press, 1976. In the case of Japanese firms, see Yoshi Tsurumi, "Nihon Kigyō no Takokuseki ka no jōken" (On Multinationalization of Japanese Firms), *Tōyo Keizai Quarterly*, July 1973. Also see Raymond Vernon, "Competition Policy Toward Multinational Corporations," *American Economic Review*, Papers and Proceedings, Vol. LXIV, No. 2 (May 1974).

CHAPTER 5

1. For a historical as well as political account of the Fair Trade Commission of Japan (Kōsei Torihiki Iinkai), see Eleanor M. Hadley, *Antitrust in Japan*, Princeton, N.J.: Princeton University Press, 1970. For the sudden rise of the political militancy of the FTC during the oil crisis of fall 1973, see Yoshi Tsurumi, "Japan," in Raymond Vernon, *ed. The Oil Crisis*, New York: W.W. Norton, 1976. A group of the "New Dealer Technocrats" who had grown disenchanted with the slow pace of social and economic reforms in the United States during the 1930s and 1940s, came to the defeated Japan as the special policy advisors to the General Headquarters (GHQ) of General MacArthur. During a short period of the immediate post–World War II era, 1945–1948, up until the conservative and military elements of the GHQ began to realign themselves with the conservative elements of the Japanese politicians and bureaucrats, including former convicted war criminals, the "New Dealers" within the GHQ implemented a series of social and economic reforms in Japan in collaboration with like-minded Japanese politicians and government officials. The FTC was one of the newly created agencies whose function it was to prevent the rise of industrial combines and monopolistic practices in Japan.

2. For operational details of the Mitsugoro Project, see Harvard Business

School case, *Mitsui & Co. Ltd.*, (Order No. ICH 2–576–080). Other accounts of the Mitsugoro Project are ascertained through my field investigation in Indonesia.

3. The newsletters that stated the objectives of the Mitsugoro Project were circulated during 1969–1970 among the employees and managers of Mitsui & Co. These documents as well as the personalities involved in the commencement of the Mitsugoro Project attest genuinely to the "public interest" of the Project (for the sake of Indonesia and Japan) that outweighed the "private interests" (commercial profitability of the Project) of Mitsui & Co.

4. *Sōgōshōsha Nenkan* (Year Book of General Trading Firms) published annually by Seikei Tsūshinsha, Tokyo, provide census types of information on trading firms and their activities. Journalistic accounts of some of the activities of the leading trading firms also became available in 1973 and 1974 from Mainichi Shimbun Sha and Sankei Shimbun Sha, Tokyo. In English, a Harvard Business School note, *Note on Japanese Trading Companies* (Order No. 9–374–136), provides a descriptive digest of Japanese trading firms.

5. For detailed historical account of Mitsui, see John G. Roberts, *MITSUI: Three Centuries of Japanese Business*, New York: John C. Weatherhill, 1973.

6. The banks have chosen to channel trade financing to various manufacturing firms through trading firms. The trading firms cushion loan risks for banks. The ratio of outstanding debts, short-term and long-term borrowing, to equity of a large general trading firm runs currently 15 to 1. However, in view of the fact that banks have equity ownership in trading firms, a large portion of seemingly outstanding "debt" extended by minority-owner banks would have to be reclassified as "quasi" equity.

7. Yoshi Tsurumi, *Technology Transfer and Foreign Trade: The Case of Japan, 1950–1966*, unpublished doctoral thesis, Harvard Business School, 1968, Ch. 3.

8. The background of CMI is found in Nobuyuki Uebara, "Toyota's Export Strategy in Canada," MBA Thesis of Queen's University, Canada, April 1970. I ascertained the later account of Toyota's purchase of a part interest in CMI away from Mitsui in 1972.

9. See Yoshi Tsurumi, "On Multinationalization of Japanese Firms," *Tōyō Keizai Quarterly* (July 1973), 1973.

10. W. Boucherie, "The Textile Industry," *Bulletin of Indonesian Economic Studies*, Vol. V, No. 3 (November 1969), Australian National University, Canberra.

11. Based on my field investigation in Indonesia in 1973.

12. These fears of Japanese trading firms were increasingly repeated from 1974 to 1975 by American and European firms interested in East-West and in China-West trade. Indeed, throughout 1975, large Japanese trading firms were stepping up their trade with China and the East European nations.

CHAPTER 6

1. For multinational expansion of American banks, see Andrew F. Brimmer and Frederick R. Dahl, "Growth of American International Banking: Implications for Public Policy," *The Journal of Finance*, Vol. XXX, No. 2 (May 1975);

and Andrew F. Brimmer's testimony, "Perspectives on Foreign Activities of American Banks," before the Subcommittee on Financial Institutions Supervision, Regulation and Insurance of Committee on Banking, Currency and Housing, U.S. House of Representatives, December 5, 1975, Washington, D.C.; and Steven I. Davis, "U.S. banks abroad: one-stop shopping?" *Harvard Business Review* (July—August 1971).

2. The irate Ministry of Finance of Japan published in summer 1972, the list of the "worst speculators" which listed specific trading firms and banks alleged to have made profits on currency transactions during the crisis of August 1971 and later during February 1972. The government's threat to tax these speculation profits did not materialize.

3. The information on the "Asia Dollar" market is derived from my own fieldwork in Tokyo, Hong Kong and Singapore during the years 1969-1975.

4. See, for example, Harvard Business School case, *Southwest National Bank* (Order No. 9-375-207); also for a general topic of international consortium banking, see Michael von Clemm, "The rise of consortium banking," *Harvard Business Review* (May-June 1971).

5. The Security Exchange Commission of the Tokyo Stock Market and the Ministry of Finance specify rigid "eligibility" terms for Japanese firms to float debentures and raise equity capital publicly. Sony's independence declaration would force the Japanese financial authorities to re-align their practices with those prevailing in New York capital markets.

6. See Samuel L. Hayes, "Investment banking: power structure in flux," *Harvard Business Review* (March-April 1971); and also Pierr Van Groethen, *The Americanization of World Business*, New York: Herder and Herder, 1972; also Yoshi Tsurumi; *Multinational Management*, Ch. 7, Cambridge, Mass.: Ballinger, 1977.

CHAPTER 7

1. See, for example, one of the basic criticisms of multinational firms in R. Barnet and R. Muller, *Global Reach*, New York: Simon & Schuster, 1974. In particular, according to the conventional wisdom of many economists trained in North American universities, the developing countries are advised to adopt so-called "labor-intensive" or "intermediate" technologies. This kind of simple minded broadside advice has produced confusion and bad advice.

2. A succinct history of modern Japanese technologies is contained in Yoshiro Hoshino, *Gendai Nihon Gijutsushi Gaisetsu* (A Short History of Modern Japanese Technologies), Dai Nippon Tosho, Tokyo, 1956; also, Yoshi Tsurumi, *Japanese Efforts to Master Manufacturing Technologies*, Harvard Business School, ICH 9-314-045.

3. See H.J. Habakkuk, *American and British Technology in the Nineteenth Century: The Search for Labor-Saving Inventions*, Cambridge: Cambridge University Press, 1972; also J. Schmookler, *Invention and Economic Growth*, Cambridge, Mass.: Harvard University Press, 1966; and Nathan Rosenberg, "The Direction of Technological Change; Inducement Mechanisms and Focussing Devices," *Economic Development and Cultural Change* (October 1969).

4. The Study of Technological Innovations of the Harvard Business School

(Professor Raymond Vernon) has already uncovered much evidence pointing to this deduction. See William H. Davidson, "Factor-Saving Innovation and International Trade Theory," MBA Research Report, April 1975.

5. The impact of this kind of technological innovation upon Japanese steel production is econometrically captured by Hiroki Tsurumi, "A Bayesian Test of the Product Cycle Hypothesis Applied to Japanese Crude Steel Production," *Journal of Econometrics* (forthcoming, 1976); see also the Japan Steel Foundation *(Tekko Renusai) Tekko Junen Shi* (Decennial History of the Steel and Iron Industry), 1969, and Kenichi Imai, "Tekko" (Steel) in N. Kumagai, ed., *Nippon no Sangyō Shoshiki* (Industrial Organization in Japan), Vol. II, Chuōkōron, 1973; and Nippon Kōkkan Co. Ltd., *Nippon Kōkkan Kabushiki Kaisha Rokujunenshi* (60 Years History of Nippon Kōkkan Co.), 1971.

6. Yoshi Tsurumi, Unpublished Doctoral Thesis, *op. cit.*, Chs. 4 and 5, Harvard Business School, 1968.

7. This conclusion was deduced from a systematic and firm-by-firm check of a randomly selected sample of the exported technologies against the date of first commercial and industrial application in Japan. The field research was conducted in Japan, in summers of 1973 and 1974.

8. Habakkuk, *op. cit.*

9. Yoshi Tsurumi, "Japanese Direct Investments in Indonesia: Toward New Indonesia Policies of Foreign Direct Investments," a Consultant Report submitted to Harvard Advisory Group, Bappenas, Jakarta, Indonesia, 1973. For relevant literature on international transfer of technology, see Yoshi Tsurumi, "The Myths that Mislead U.S. Managers in Japan," *Harvard Business Review* (July-August 1971); Jack Barranson, "Transfer of Technical Knowledge by International Corporations to Developing Economies," *American Economic Review*, Vol. LVI, No. 2 (May, 1966); V.N. Balasubramanyam, *International Transfer of Technology to India*, New York: Praeger, 1973; G.C. Hufbauer, *Synthetic Materials and the Theory of International Trade*, Cambridge, Mass.: Harvard University Press, 1966; E. Mansfield, "Technical Change and the Rate of Imitation," *Econometrica*, Vo. 29, No. 4 (October 1961); *Guidelines for the Study of the Transfer of Technology to Developing Countries*, UNCTAD Report, TD/B/Ac. 11/9, United Nations, New York, 1972; *The Channels and Mechanisms for the Transfer of Technology from Developed to Developing Countries*, UNCTAD Report, TD/B/Ac. 11/5, Geneva, 1971.

10. Louis T. Wells, "Economic Man and Engineering Man: Choice of Technology in a Low-Wage Country," *Public Policy*, Vol. 21, No. 3 (Summer 1973).

11. Japanese and other foreign firms' preoccupation with the quality image of their products stem from the fact that the multinational firms are also concerned with their market positions throughout the world. They feel that they can ill afford to risk the "product quality," the source of their imagined or real product differentiation.

12. Donald Lecraw, *Determinants of Capital Intensity in Low Wage Countries: the Case of Thailand*, A Ph.D. thesis in Business-Economics, Harvard University, 1977.

13. Donald Lecraw, *op. cit.*; A selection of "appropriate technology" is indeed more a cultural and psychological than an engineering or economic decision.

14. This observation calls for new theories of formal and informal organizational structures of such human institutions as corporations. The new theories need to be based on social and interpersonal communication within the same firm and between the firm and its external environment. And these new theories of organizational development need to be closely linked to intrafirm diffusion of product-, process- and institution-related technologies.

CHAPTER 8

1. Yoshi Tsurumi, "Consultant's Report to Harvard Advisory Group," Bappenas, Jakarta, Indonesia, *op. cit.*, 1973.
2. For example, this assumption permeates *The Report* of A Group of Eminent Persons of the United Nations, May and June, 1974 as well as such concerted efforts of developing nations as the Andean Group coping with the foreign investments.
3. Based on my field researches in Asia.
4. See, Stopford and Wells, *Managing the Multinational Enterprise*, New York: Basic Books, 1973.
5. Data Bank of the Multinational Enterprise Project of the Harvard Business School.
6. This conclusion calls for new research efforts concerning the problems of "disinvestment" of multinational firms. For a survey of current state of descriptive works, see, for example, a Harvard Business School note, *Note on Foreign Disinvestment* (Order No. 9–376–080).

CHAPTER 9

1. Chie Nakane, *Japanese Society*, Berkeley University of California Press, 1969; Kunio Odaka, "Industrial Workers' Identification with Union and Management in Postwar Japan," *American Journal of Sociology* (Spring 1954).
2. For analytical account of pre-Meiji social and political thought and attitude of the Japanese, see Robert Bellah, *Tokugawa Religion: The Values of Pre-Industrial Japan*, Glencoe, Illinois: The Free Press, 1957, and "Reflections on the Protestant Ethic Analogy in Asia," *Journal of Social Issues*, Vol. 14 (January 1963); also, Masao Maruyama, *Studies in the Intellectual History of Tokugawa Japan*, Princeton, N.J.: Princeton University Press, 1974.
3. In this atmosphere, the word "individualism" carried a negative connotation and was equated with "selfishness" as well as "childishness."
4. See Maruyama's book, *op. cit.*; for a succinct introduction into Confucianism, see, Arthur Waley, *Three Ways of Thought in Ancient China*, New York: Doubleday, 1939; also, Tsunoda, de Barry and Keene, eds., *Sources of Japanese Tradition*, Vol. I, Chs. 6 through 8, New York: Columbia University Press, 1958.
5. Once the feudal class system was officially abandoned, this "classless" notion produced the "technocratic" society where, regardless of one's birth, one's educational achievement and diligence almost guaranteed a leadership position in government or firm.

6. In the United States, a number of behavioral scientists has espoused the "matrix organization," as opposed to "mechanistic organization," in which both vertical and lateral communication and concensus building become crucial to implementation of strategic and operational decisions of the firm. If this is the case, the mobility of individual managers from one firm to another may well be reduced drastically because they would be ineffective in new organizational environment without transferring with them a "critical mass" of the peers and subordinates essential to their effectiveness in former organization.

7. Yoshi Tsurumi, "Multinationalism and Management: Incorporating Employees' Interest in Corporate Objectives," a paper presented at the Toronto Meeting of Canadian Association of Administration Sciences," June 2–4, 1974, (the *Proceedings* of Meeting); also "Convergence of Japanese and American Management Practices" in Tsurumi, *Multinational Management*, Ch. 3, Cambridge, Mass.: Ballinger, 1976.

8. The ideological origin of this expected role and style of leadership can be traced to the Japanese primogeniture system of the inheritance of the agrarian society. The eldest son legally inherited the lands but was expected to manage and improve on them for the collective interests of his family and kinship before he passed them on to his posterity.

9. These management-employee relations of Japanese corporations were often transferred even to a North American environment. But this transfer, I observed, required American managers in Japanese subsidiaries to "un-learn" many so-called American management practices such as threats of dismissal as crude motivating forces to intimidate employees.

10. This is why even the rank-and-file employees of Japanese corporations are interested in and familiar with the growth rates, sales, products, and other detailed operations of their entire firm. They seek such information. If the management withhold such information or appears reluctant to disseminate it to rank-and-file employees, they would regard it a sign of the management "distrust" of the employees.

11. This procedural aspect of the *ringiseido* is elaborated in M.Y. Yoshino, *Japan's Managerial System*, Cambridge, Mass.: MIT Press, 1968.

12. John M. Stopford, *Growth and Organizational Change in the Multinational Firm*, Unpublished Doctoral Thesis, Harvard Business School, 1968.

13. See Lawrence E. Fouraker and John M. Stopford, "Organization Structure and the Multinational Strategy," *Administrative Science Quarterly* (June 1968). This study points out that the International Division of American multinational firms were often broken up by political "coalition" of other competing division managers when the profit or sales of the International Division reached the smallest size of the domestic divisions within the same firm. This internal rivalry among the divisional managers held responsible for their divisional profit performance was no doubt intensified by the American corporate culture and its concomitant reward and punishment systems. For inner workings of International Divisions of Japanese firms, see M.Y. Yoshino, "Organization and Decision Making in Emerging Japanese Multinational Enterprises", in Ezra Vogel *ed.*, *Decision Making in Large Japanese Organization*, Berkeley and Los Angeles: University of California Press, 1973.

CHAPTER 10

1. See, for instance, Stewart Meacham, "The Ten Days that Shook Thailand," *International Affairs Report*, Vol. XX, no. 6 (November 1973), American Friends Service Committee, Philadelphia. For excellent background history and culture of the Southeast Asian countries, see George Coedes, *The Indianized States of Southeast Asia*, East-West Center, University of Hawaii, 1968; and Edward Conze, *Buddhism: Its Essence and Development*, New York: Harper and Row, 1968.

2. Canadian literature related to a rise of economic and cultural nationalism is increasing in number by day. For standard references, see, A.E. Safarian, *Foreign Ownership of Canadian Industry*, New York: McGraw-Hill, 1966; Report of the Task Force on the Structure of Canadian Industry (*Watkin's Report*), Queen's Printer, Ottawa, 1968, Kari Levitt, *Silent Surrender*, Toronto: Macmillan, 1970; *The Herb Gray Report*, a special edition of the Canadian Forum (December 1971).

3. For the list of standard references as well as for a survey of China, today, see Tsurumi and Toplansky, *China in the World Economy*, Harvard Business School, ICH 9–375–392, 1975.

4. For example, Control Data Corporation, an American computer firm, established a joint venture manufacturing operation in Romania in 1973 with the government of Romania. This plant was to produce parts and equipment for their sales in Comecon countries as well as in the western European nations. Soviet Union and East European nations were increasingly concluding technical licensing agreements with Japanese and European and American firms, from 1973 to 1975. See, Tsurumi, *Multinational Management*, Ch. 5, Cambridge, Mass.: Ballinger, 1976.

5. For analytical studies of the interactions between multinational firms and host countries in natural resources, see two excellent works, Charles T. Goodsell, *American Corporation and Peruvian Politics*, Cambridge, Mass.: Harvard University Press, 1974, and Theodore H. Moran, *Multinational Corporations and the Politics of Dependence: Copper in Chile*, Princeton, N.J.: Princeton University Press, 1974.

6. The developing countries in Asia were encouraged by the United States government and its academic allies, "modernization schools" of the Japanologists, to emulate the Japanese model, not Maoist China, for efforts toward industrialization. See, for instance, John W. Dower's superb introduction to *Origins of the Modern Japanese State*, New York: Pantheon, 1974. Accordingly, Japan was expected to provide not only economic but cultural and political leadership for its Asian neighbors. However, the Japanese treated their Asian neighbors as scarcely more than markets for Japanese goods.

7. Hideki Yoshihara, "Personnel Practices of Japanese Companies in Thailand," Discussion Paper No. 6 (mimeograph), Research Institute for Economic and Business Administration, Kobe University, Japan, 1975. For a problem of managing a modern plant in a traditional society, see Ann Ruth Willner, "Problems of Management and Authority in a Transitional Society: A Case Study of a Javanese Factory," in W.A. Faunce, ed., *Readings in Industrial Sociology*, New York: Appleton Century Crofts, 1967.

8. This process of "thought control" by the Ministry of Education and the ruling party, LDP, is documented by Ienaga Saburo, a scholar-crusader, in his prolific and rigorous accounts of the censorship of text books by the Ministry of Education. See, for instance, *Ienaga Saburo Kyōiku Saiban Shōgen Shū* (Testimonies at Ienaga Saburo *Trial of Education*), Hitotsubashi Shobo, Tokyo, 1972; *Kentei Fugōkaku Nihonshi* (Censored Text Book Accounts of Japanese History), Sanichi Shobo, 1974; *Kyōkasho Kentei* (Government Selection and Evaluation of Text Books), Nihon Hyoronsha, 1965.

9. For the impacts of Japanese colonial rule on Korea, see Chong-sik Lee, *The Politics of Korean Nationalism*, Berkeley: University of California Press, 1963. For President Park's attempts to rule Korea with manipulation of academic and intellectual communities in Korea and in the United States, see Sugwon Kang, "President Park and His Learned Friends: Some Observations on Contemporary Korean Statecraft," *Bulletin of Concerned Asian Scholars*, Vol. 7, No. 4 (October-December 1975); and for windfall earnings of U.S. dollars during the Vietnam War, see Frank Baldwin, "America's Rented Troops: South Koreans in Vietnam," *Bulletin of Concerned Asian Scholars*, Vol. 7, No. 4 (October-December 1975) pp. 33–40. For Japanese colonial administration in Taiwan, see a perceptive work by E.P. Tsurumi, *Japanese Colonial Education in Taiwan, 1895–1945*, Cambridge, Mass.: Harvard University Press, 1977.

10. This "model" of transfer of power from a military to civilian rule was later imposed on South Vietnam by the United States. Thus, President Thieu was installed in South Vietnam. With the fall of South Vietnam, President Park of South Korea became rightfully concerned over the possibility that a similar fate might befall him.

CHAPTER 11

1. In 1972 Tanaka won the presidency of the Liberal Democartic Party and the premiership by rallying the support of business leaders around the industrial expansion theme of "remodelling the Japanese archipelago." This theme, and the fervor that the theme generated coincided with the mounting trade surplus that pumped liquid funds into large manufacturing and trading firms. And massive speculative investments in commodities and land developments followed suit; thus, triggering the "two-digit" inflation from 1972 to 1973.

2. For the "pattern-setting and pattern-following" of Japanese wage determinations, see Yoshi Tsurumi, *The Industrial Relations System in Japan*, Harvard Business School, 1966, ICH 9-311-001.

3. See, *Nōgyō Zensō Report*, the Ministry of Agriculture and Forestry (mimeograph), November 1975, Tokyo.

4. For "New Left" views of Japanese investments abroad, see, for instance, Jon Halliday and G. McCormack, *Japanese Imperialism Today*, New York: Monthly Review Press, 1973.

5. See Herbert Bix's article in Mark Selden, ed., *Remaking Asia: Essays on the American Use of Power*, New York: Pantheon, 1974; and also Jon Halliday, *Political History of Japanese Capitalism*, New York: Pantheon, 1975. This book contains extensive bibliography and references for the rearmament and overseas expansion of Japan.

6. N. Fukutake, ed., *Nihonjin no Shakai Ishiki* (Social Consciousness of the Japanese), Ch. 1, Sanichi Shobo, Tokyo, 1960.

7. Foreign observers of Japanese politics have somehow ignored or missed this malfunction of the democratic process.

8. The Autonomy Agency publishes annually in *Kampō* (Government Notification) the revenues and expenditures of political parties and those of major factions within the LDP. But these publications are nothing but reproductions of whatever is reported by the filing parties to the Agency.

9. In reality, however, there is little chance that such an international agreement will be realized. This kind of agreement requires close cooperation and shared interest among diverse nations, and above all a strong leadership taken by leading powers. In the post-oil crisis world, there appears no cooperative atmosphere among many contending nations.

10. Robert E. Cole, *Japanese Blue Collar: The Changing Tradition*, Berkeley and Los Angeles: University of California Press, 1971.

11. Charles Levinson, *Capital, Inflation and the Multinationals*, New York: Macmillan, 1972. This book summarizes the attitudes of the international labor movements toward the spread of multinational firms. Under Levinson's leadership, automotive tire firms may well become the first targets of the "multinational labor fronts" vis-à-vis Japan-, U.S.- and Europe based multinational firms. The United Auto Workers of the United States at least coordinated under the leadership of the late Walter Reuther union activities among the subsidiaries of the "big three" U.S. auto firms. The coordinating body, the Auto Council was launched in May 1966, in Detroit, under the initiative of the United Auto Workers. But as of 1975, the worldwide coordination of collective bargaining with multinational auto firms, which Reuther dreamed of, had not taken place.

12. In the United States, the political leadership of the organized labor group has been held by the unions related to the manufacturing industries, the international competitive strength of which has weakened over time. And yet, the organized unions have failed to unionize the emerging "service-oriented" industries, food processing industries (agribusiness) and farm workers, and technology-intensive industries.

Index

Agriculture, and overseas expansion, 42-43
ALCAN, 52, 65, 66
ALCOA, 56, 65, 66
Alliance of Textile Workers (Zensen Domei), 300
Alumax, 65, 66
Aluminum:
  historical background of, 59
  and Japanese firms, 147
Aluminum firms:
  and Asahan project, 51
  and joint ventures, 50
  and oligopolies, 52
Aluminum industry:
  and future international oligopolies, 55-56
  and group approach, 49-50
  and international consortia, 65-66
Aluminum smelting, and overseas expansion, 44-45. *See also* Overseas expansion
AMAX, 52, 55-56, 147
American Deposit Receipts (ADR), 164
Anglo-Iranian Oil Company, 60
Arabia Oil Company, 61, 67
Asahan project, 56. *See also* Indonesia
  and aluminum firms, 51
Asia:
  and Japanese manufacturing firms, 71-72, 75
  and Japanese technologies, 176
  and synthetic fiber firms, 91

Asia dollar market, 159-61
Assets, of Japanese investments, 2
Ataka Trading Company, 101, 147
Auburn, N.Y., and first Japanese steel mill, 101
Australia, and the "beef incident," 69
Automobile manufacturing, growth of, 21-23
Autonomy Agency, 290

Balance of trade:
  and overseas subsidiaries, 77
  and size of trading companies, 137
Ball bearings, and U.S. investment, 108-112
Bank of Japan, 16
  and foreign banks, 166
  and manufacturing, 13
Banking and trading firms, alliance of, 132-33
Banks, and finance, 28-29. *See also* Capital rationing
Bougainville Copper Mine, 63, 65
Brazil:
  and diplomatic sensitivity, 279
  and direct investments, 3
  and Japanese investments, 257-58
  and synthetic fiber firms, 91
Business, and government:
  alliance of, 27, 283, 288
  early history of, 5-9
  and industrialization, 7
Business Week, 108

325

326   Index

Cambodia, urbanization in, 281-82
Capacity utilization, 40
Capital intensive production process, 187
  and undeveloped country, 188
Capital rationing, and banking, 14, 159
Captive trading firms, 147
Carl Urbricht Woolen Mill, 6
Chiang Kai-shek, 243
Ch'ing China, and trade deficits. 5
Cia Minera Condestable, 61-62
C. Itoh Trading Company, 146-47
Coal-steel linkage policy, 14
Coal production, 12. *See also* MITI
Collective bargaining agreement, and Thai corn, 53-55
COMALCO, 52
Commercial banks, 167. *See also* Foreign banks
Comparative advantage theorem, 33
Competition. *See also* Japanese, and American competition
  and foreign firms, 181, 182
  and government intervention, 21
  and Japanese firms, 24
  and overseas expansion, 92-93
Compulsory education, 7. *See also* Educational policies
Computer industry, 23-24
Computer lease finance company, 24
Consumer products, in U.S., 112
Copper industry:
  and group approach, 49-51
  and Japan, 62-64
  and large firm leadership, 50
  and new precedents, 61
Corn, 53-55. *See also* Collective bargaining agreement
Corporate system, and host countries, 265
Corporationwide Election Campaign, 295

Daisan kokujin, 285
Decision-making process, 227-29
DEMINEX (Germany), 68
Depression (1949-50), 16
Developing countries (LDCs):
  and foreign investments, 179, 249-51
  and freer trade, 306
  and import substitution, 88
  and industrial growth, 248-51
  and Japanese products, 258-60
  and local repair service, 184
  and oil crisis, 278-80

Diet, 289, 290, 294
  and trading companies, 126
Direct investments. *See also* Brazil; Overseas investments
  in Asia, 91
  and banking knowledge, 276
  fear of, 2-3, 249-51
  and geographical proximity, 71
  growth rate of Japanese, 254, 256
  and Korean government, 271-72
  and manufacturing technologies, 169
  and overseas expansion, 3-5
  and political insensitivity, 276
  and small firms, 107
  and Sony Corporation, 113-15
  and trading firms, 145-48
  in U.S., 102-103, 105, 120-21
Direct placement debentures, 165
Division of tasks, 27-30, 59, 78
  and Japanese manufacturing, 177-78
  and size of firms, 84-85
Dowa Kogyo, 64-65
Dual wage structure, 28

"Economic animal," 277
  and Thai resentment, 264
Economic Confederation of Japan (*Keidanren*), 290-91, 294, 295
  See also MITI
Economic Planning Agency, 15
Economics, and politics, 276-81
  separation of, 305
The Economist, 2, 3, 14
Economy, post-WW II, 10-11. *See also* Japanese economy Post-WW II; Second World War
Educational policies:
  early, 7
  effects of, 19, 222
  government influence on, 287-89
  and oil exploration problems, 48-49
EEC countries, 96-97, 103
Electronics industry:
  and Korea, 273
  and offshore production, 98-99
  and overseas expansion, 93-95
  in U.S., 122
Employees. *See also* Ethical codes
  attitudes of, 217, 219
  Japanese vs. American, 102, 223-224, 225-227
  and Japanese corporate attitudes, 109
  of trading firms, 130
Employers, Mitsui vs. Mitsubishi, 149

Enterprise unions, and multinational firms, 299-302
ERAP, of France, 67, 68
Ethical codes, 220-21, 222
Euro-dollar markets, 159-62
Europe, and Japanese investments, 1
Excise taxes, 39
Export/import, and large trading firms, 130-31. *See also* Large trading firms
Export-Import Bank of Japan, 17
Export market vs. domestic, 31-33
  and Japanese businesses, 7-9
  and overseas expansion, 75-78
  and size of firms, 79-81
  and small firms, 83-84
Export supremacy, 25
Exports, and industrialized nations, 115
Extraterritoriality, 250

FACOM, 73
Fair Trade Commission (FTC), 55, 125, 293
Federal Trade Commission, 56
Federation of Japanese Housewives, 294
First five-year plan, 15-16, 151, 152
First Japanese steel mill, 101
The First Opium War (1839-42), 5
First overseas investment, 16
First woolen mill, 6
Fish imports, and Japanese needs, 281
Food imports, and Japanese needs, 280
  in 1970s, 42
Foreign banks, 167. *See also* Bank of Japan
Foreign direct investments, 102-103. *See also* Direct investments
Foreign subsidiaries, 251-52. *See also* Japanese subsidiaries
Foreign technologies, 20-21. *See also* Process-related technologies; Product-related technologies
Fortune, 73, 78, 231
Friendship Highway, 54
Fujitsu, 118. *See also* Computer industry
Fukuda, Vice Prime Minister, 69
Funds, for industry, 13-16

Gaijin, 285
General Agreement of Trade and Tariff (GATT), 277, 298
Geographical proximity, 71

GHQ (General Headquarters), 11, 12, 14, 135
Glut conditions, 58, 277
GNP, 20, 44, 130
Government:
  and new technologies, 18
  post-WW II, 12
  and private industry, 6-7, 8-9
Government, and business, 15. *See also* Business, and government
  alliance of, 266-67, 283-86
  early history of, 5-9
  future role of, 287-96
  and overseas investment, 16-17
Government intervention, 21
  and competition, 23
  and internal Japanese market, 58-60
Great Collaboration Unit: enterprise-based union, the origin of, 300
Group approach, 46-47, 49-50, 52-53. *See also* Copper industry

Harvard Business School, 78
Heavy industry, 38-39. *See also* Japanese heavy industry
  effects of, 40
  growth of, 133-34
  and provincial government, 44-45
Hitachi, 93-95
House of Councillors, 289
  and interest groups, 290, 295

Idemitsu, Sazo, 60-61
IG Metal Union (Germany), 301
IMF-Japan Council (IMF-JC), 300
Import agents, 202, 204
Import substitution. *See also* Developing countries
  and developing countries, 32, 88, 115
  and overseas investment, 88-89, 95-96
  and small manufacturing firms, 83-84
Import tariffs, 39
Imports, of crude oil, 39, 40
Indicative economic planning, 14, 16, 159
Indigenous manufacturers, 253-54
  and Japanese products, 304
Individual specialization, 178
Individuals, and technocratic society, 7
Indonesia:
  and Asahan project, 51
  and direct investments, 254
  and Japanese imports, 43

328 Index

and Japanese managers, 261
and Japanese subsidiaries, 208-209, 263
and joint ownership, 203, 204
and manufacturing technologies, 182-85
and on-site processing, 45-46
Indonesian laborers, 183
Industrial pollution, 44
Industrial products, 105-107
Industrial reconstruction, 12-16. See also Post-WW II
Industrial policies:
  early, 7
  and growth, 247
Industries, classification of, 14
Inflation, 13. See also Post-WW II
Innovations, and Japanese technologies, 175
Inoue, Shōzō, 6
Institution-related technologies:
  defined, 170-71
  and Japan, 173-74
International Confederation of Trade Unions (ICFTU), 300
International consortia banks, 162, 163. See also Japanese banks
International Metal Workers' Federation (IMF), 300
International Monetary Fund (IMF), 277
International Nickel Company (INCO), 64-65
International product cycle, 31-32
International trade, 276-81
International transfer of technologies, 169-71
Iran, and Japan, 45, 68
Iron ore, and overseas expansion, 52-53
Ishikawajima-Harima Industry (IHI), 16
Itoh, C., 126, 135
Iwasaki, Yatarō, 133-34

Janome Company, Ltd., 25
Japan. See also Foreign banks; the West and foreign banks, 161
  and foreign competition, 57-58, 60-62
  and industrial growth, 247
  and information gathering techniques, 33
  and methods of expansion, 121-23
  need for "new Japan," 304-307
  need for political sensitivity, 285
  and the West, 5-6

Japanese, and American competition:
  basis for, 63, 119
  in banks, 157-59
  in management techniques, 102
  in manufacturing, 18
  in U.S. 101-105
Japanese, and Thai revolt, 243-47
Japanese banks. See also International consortia banks
  and Asia dollar markets, 160-61
  and overseas expansion, 157-59, 161-62
Japanese consulate officers, 8
Japanese direct investments. See also Direct investments
  and Korean government, 272-73
  and overseas expansion, 1-3, 37
  and public visibility, 251-54
Japanese economy:
  dual structure of, 28
  growth of, 2, 3, 30
  and oil crisis, 69
  post-WW II, 9-11
Japanese Election Law, 290
Japanese exports:
  changes in, 30-31
  to LDCs, 58
Japanese firms. See also Manufacturing firms; Trading firms
  and attitudes toward government, 268
  competition among, 20
  and cooperation overseas, 46-47
  and cultural insensitivity, 263-66
  and loans, 41
  and raw materials, 41
  and search for information, 21
  and "Ugly Japanese," 274
  in U.S., 119-20
Japanese government:
  and oil crisis, 67-69
  and overseas investments, 5, 68-69
  role of, 287-96
Japanese heavy industry, 40. See also Heavy industry
Japanese Housewives Federation, 125
Japanese imperialism, 38-39
Japanese managers. See also Employees; Employers; Management-employee relations
  and employee relationship, 265-66
  in Indonesia, 183-84
  and LDCs, 260-62
  role of, 225-27
Japanese manufacturing, 41-42
Japanese multinational firm:
  defined, 3

and Third World people, 286
vs. American, 292-93
Japanese products, 304. *See also*
   Indigenous manufacturers
Japanese shipbuilding, 18
Japanese Steel Workers Union, 299
Japanese subsidiaries, 250-51
Japanese trading firms. *See also*
   Trading firms
   vs. Indonesian textile firms, 150-53
   and overseas expansion, 41-42, 46-47
"Japan, Inc., " 9
Japan-Thailand Agreement of Maize, 53-55
Job rotation, effects of, 223-24
Job security, in Japan, 219, 221-22, 223-24
Joint ownership, 48-49
Joint ventures:
   of Dowa-INCO, 64
   and international major countries, 64-67
   of Japan and Indonesia, 151-53
   of Korea and Japan, 185
   and local partners, 204-206, 207-208
   new attitudes toward, 210-11
Jomukai, 239-40, 242

Kaigai Jigyobu (KJ Division), 231-32, 235-42
   as "non-profit center," 236
Kaihatsu Yunyu, 55
Kanematsu Trading Company, 6
Karachi Conference of the Third World Forum, 279
Kaya, Minister of Finance, 10
Keidanren. See Economic Confederation of Japan
Kikkoman, 102
Kim Dae-chu, 269
Kim Sung, 273
Kinzoku Kōbutsu Tankō Sokushin Jigyōdan, 68
Korea:
   and industrialization, 269-74
   and Japanese firms, 246-47, 282
   and resentment for Japanese, 264, 268-69
Korea-Japan Treaty, 270
Korean War, 16, 269
Kosgoro, and Mitsui, 127
Kyoei Steel, 101

Labor intensive processes, 184, 188
Labor market, 58, 155

Labor saving method, and shipyards, 17
Labor unions, 299-302
Large manufacturing firms. *See also*
   manufacturing firms
   change in, 143
   and U.S. investments, 104-105, 113-15
Large trading firms, 128, 130-32. *See also* Trading firms
   growth of, 132-37
   and joint ownership, 204, 205, 206, 210-11
   and overseas investments, 84-85, 86-88, 145-48
Latin America:
   and direct investments, 3
   and Japanese investments, 1, 71-72
   and manufacturing firms. 75
LDCs. *See* Developing countries
LDP, and factional politics, 290-91, 294-96
   and government officials, 288-89
   and military intervention, 283-84
Licensing agreements, 19-20
   and U.S., 171-72, 174
Light Metal Resource Development Company, Ltd., 50
"Linking Trade," 136-37
Loan-related procurement contracts, 41-42
Loans, and Japanese firms, 41
Local equity holders, 206-208. *See also* Joint ventures
Lon Nol, 243
Long-term purchase contracts, 40-42
   and Thai corn, 54
Lumber, 43
   and Japanese needs, 280-81

Machine-intensive processes, 188
Majority ownership, 210-11
Management-employee relations, 265-66
Manufacturing firms:
   and developing countries, 75
   and direct investments, 252-53
   early, 6-7
   and economy, 11-13
   and export market, 31-32
   functions of, 28
   funding for, 13-16
   increase in, 1
   in Indonesia, 154
   and joint ventures, 202, 204-206
   and pollution demands, 44-45
   small size, 78

vs. trading firms, 132, 136-37, 138-41, 154-56
and vertical growth, 133
Manufacturing technologies, 7, 18. *See also* Technologies
Marcos, 243
Market information, 8
Market investments, 25-26, 37
Material saving method, 17. *See also* Shipyards
Matsushita, 93-95, 102, 122, 123
Medium-sized firms, 85-88
Meiji Regime, 133
"Mēkā" role, of manufacturing firms, 28-29
"Meritocracy," 7
"Metropolis" nation, 249-50
Middle management, 228-29
Mid-1960s, changes in, 82. *See also* 1960s; Overseas expansion
Miki, Prime Minister, 276, 296
Ministry of International Trade and Industry (MITI), 12, 13-16, 19, 23-24, 64, 66, 69, 75, 126, 189, 190, 205, 268
 and aluminum companies, 56, 59
 and corruption overseas, 293
 and *Keidanren*, 291, 294
 and leadership, 51
 and multinational firms, 297
 in 1950s, 89
 and oil exploration, 49, 278, 281
 and small firms, 47, 120
 and structural approach, 59
Ministry of Finance, 161, 163, 165, 166
 and funds for industry, 13, 14, 15
 and overseas banking, 158-59
Ministry of Forestry and Agriculture, 281
Ministry of Trade and Commerce, 12
Mitsubishi Corporation, 120, 146-47
Mitsubishi Heavy Industry, in Texas, 102, 107, 108, 115
Mitsubishi Kinzoku Company, 50
Mitsubishi Trading Company, 53-55, 130, 133-34, 135, 148-50
Mitsui and Company, 65, 66, 130, 143, 144
 and AMAX, 55-56
 and corn imports, 53-55
 history of, 132-33, 134, 135-37
 vs. Mitsubishi, 148-50, 155
 and Mitsugoro project, 127
Mizukami, 127
Morita, 114
Multinational Enterprise Project, 78

Multinational firms, 99, 157
 attitudes towards, 248-49
 and contingency planning, 214, 215
 and host governments, 297-98
 Japanese vs. American, 240-41
 and KJ Division, 231-32, 235-42
 and need for change, 304-305
 and politics and economics, 305
 United States vs. Japanese, 4-5
 roles of, 169

Nakasone, 278-79
National income, 44
"National wealth," vs. "trade surplus," 8
Nationalistic attitude, 7-9
Natural gas (Iran), 68
Natural resources:
 and developing countries, 50-51, 52, 60-62
 Japan's need for, 305
 and large trading firms, 141
 in 1950s-1960s, 277
 and oil crisis, 278-81
New York Stock Exchange, 167
1950s:
 and automobile industry, 21
 exports in, 18
 imports in, 39, 40
 and shipbuilding, 18
1970s and 1980s:
 and on-site processing, 45-46
 and overseas raw materials, 41
1960s:
 and computer industry, 23-24
 imports in, 39, 40-42
 and offshore production, 96-99
 and wage increases, 81
1963 MITI Report on Current State of Technologies, 21
Nippon Light Metals, 52
Nippon Mining Company, 45, 50, 61-62
Nippon Steel, 66-67
Nixon, President, 158
NMB, 108, 109-12, 193, 194
 influence on firms, 117
Nomura Securities Company, 164-65
Non-mineral resources, 42

Offshore production, 95-96
 and Japanese needs, 281
 and Korea, 185-87
 and manufacturing firms, 207-208
Oil crisis of 1973, 67. *See also* Developing countries
 effects on banking, 162, 163, 166

effects on government and business, 125-26
and Japanese economy, 275-76
and Korea, 273-74
and labor unions, 302
and overseas subsidiaries, 213
Oil industry:
fragmentation of, 48-49
and group approach, 47-49
and Japanese entry, 61
and structuralist approach, 59
Okubo, Toshimichi, 6
Oligopolistic firms:
and market positions, 92
and overseas expansion, 55-56, 88
and shared monopoly, 50
and U.S. expansion, 121-23
OMURON Co., 118
Organization, of large trading firms, 130. *See also* Large trading firms
Organization of Petroleum Exporting Countries (OPEC), 278-79, 280
and natural resources, 297-98
Overseas Development for Import, 55
Overseas expansion. *See also* Direct investments; Electronics industry
and aluminum firms, 52
and competition, 181, 182
and copper, 50
and developing countries, 60-62, 95
and direct investments, 43
and electronics industry, 93-94
and import substitution, 88-89
increase in, 1-3
and information gathering, 33
and labor unions, 299-302
and natural resources, 37
and non-mineral resources, 42
and oil exploration, 48-49
and on-site processing, 45-46
reasons for, 43, 75-78
and resource diplomacy, 67-69
and sea produce, 46
and synthetic fiber industry, 92-93
Overseas subsidiaries, 1-2
and cooperation of Japanese firms, 46-47
and developing countries, 60-62, 95
and economic changes, 82
and government interactions, 68-69
and Japanese government, 5, 16-17, 283-84, 287-91
and Japanese owners, 201
and Japanese technologies, 172, 179, 181
and KJ Division, 232, 235, 236-38
and manufacturing firms, 41-42, 78-82, 83-84, 86, 88, 89, 138-39
need for change, 212-215
and social changes, 82
and task force approach, 192-93, 194
and trading firms, 41-42, 53-55, 139-41, 144-45, 148
and transfer of products and processes, 169

Park, President Chung-hee, 243, 267, 270, 273, 274, 282
Pechiney, 65
Petrochemical industry, 45
Petroleum Development Public Corporation (SKK), 48-49, 67, 68, 69
Political incidents, 68-69
Political power balances, 256-58
Politics, and economics, 305. *See also* Economics, and politics
Pollution control, 44-45
Post-Vietnam War, 281-87
Post-WW II. *See also* Employees
and Japanese industry, 9-16
and management-employee relations, 221-22
Pot Bottom Recession, 137
Prapass, 243
President (corporate), 229-31
Private banks, 17
Private trading firms. *See also* Trading firms
and international trade, 136
and overseas cooperation, 49, 52
vs. public, 15, 16, 25-27, 48-49
Processing firms:
effects of small size, 47
of natural resources, 64-67
Process-related technologies, 96. *See also* Product-related technologies
defined, 170-71
effects of, 305
and Japan, 172, 174, 261
and overseas expansion, 84, 178, 189, 193
and world markets, 116-17
Product Life Cycle Theory, 33
Product-related technologies, 96, 116-17, 170
effects of, 305
and labor unions, 299
and overseas expansion, 84
and trading firms, 132
Production processes:
American vs. Japanese, 110-11
partial emigration of, 98

Products:
  and overseas expansion, 85, 253-54
  and size of firms, 78-80
Public Corporation to Promote Non-ferrous Metal Ores Exploration, 68
"Public domain" vs. "private domain," 9
Public visibility, 258-60, 303
Purchase reservation credit, 25-26

R&D activities, 18, 19
  expenditures for, 20-21
  of Japan, 171, 174
  and pollution control, 275
  for shipbuilding, 17
  and U.S. development, 116-19
  and utilization of equipment, 175
Raw materials:
  and change in access to, 59-60
  and Japanese imperialism, 38-39
  in 1950s, 58
  and on-site processing, 45-46
  and overseas expansion, 68-69
  and vertical integration, 57-60
Reactionary forces, 249
Reconstruction Financing Agency (RFA), 14, 16
Regional integration, 97-98
"Resource diplomacy," 277, 278
Reuther, Walter, 301
Ringi Report, 240
Ringi seido, 227
Rio Tinto Zinc, 62-63, 65
"Risk minimizing," 91
Rockefeller Research Institute in Thailand, 54

Sakichi, Toyota, 175
Samurai, 220, 221
Sanyo, 93-95
Science, and Japanese economy, 11
Sea produce, 46
Second five-year plan (Korea), 271
Second World War, effects of, 9-13. *See also* World War II
Security Trading Law, 167
Seikei bunri, 277
Self-sufficiency, and direct investment, 43
Sewing machine manufacturers, 31-32
  and Japan, 25-26
Shared monopoly, 50
Ship Technology Institute, 17
Shipyards, 16, 17
Shoten, Suzuki, 134
Showa Denko, 52, 56, 57
Singapore Development Plan, 112

Single-line trading companies, 135
Size of firm. *See also* Balance of trade
  and division of tasks, 84-85
  and overseas manufacturing, 78-82, 139-41
Small manufacturing firms, 104-105
Small- to medium-sized firms, 107
  and direct investments, 108
  and joint ventures, 204-206
  vs. large firms, 78-82, 210-11
  and 1950s technology, 178
  and overseas manufacturing, 82-84
  and presidential leadership, 229-31
Small trading firms, 128
  and "Pot Bottom Recession," 137
Sodium processing plants, 44-45
Sogoshosha, 128
Sony Corporation, 112, 113-15
Steel industry, 38-39, 40
Sum Sung, 273
Sumitomo Chemicals, 52, 56, 65
  and MITI, 57
Sumitomo House, 134-35
Sumitomo Trading Company, 107
"Survival of the fittest," 13, 24
Synergistic effect, 110, 111
Synthetic fiber industry, 97
  and Brazil, 91
  history of, 151, 152-53
  and Mitsui, 149-50
  and overseas expansion, 88-93

Taiyo Fishery, 121
Takashima, 101
Tanaka Cabinet, 294-95
Tanaka, Prime Minister, 275, 276, 279, 296
Task force approach, 192-93
  and overseas subsidiaries, 194, 197-98
Technologies. *See* Institution-related technologies; Process-related technologies; Product-related technologies
Teijin Co., Ltd., 21, 89, 91-93
Territorial waters, 121
Texas, and Japanese firms, 102, 107, 108
Textile industry, 150, 151, 153
Thai Board of Trade, 53-55
Thai revolt, 243-47
Thailand:
  and Japan, 261, 268
  and synthetic fiber firms, 92
  and U.S. aid, 54
Thanom, 243
Thieu, Ngyuyen Van, 243

Third World Forum, 297
Third World people, 286
 and LDCs, 280
Tokugawa era, 220
 and the West, 5
Tokugawa Shogunate, 133
Tokyo Equity Market, 164
Toray Co., Ltd., 21, 89, 91, 92-93, 97, 153
Tosa Domain, 133
Toshiba, 93-95
Total emigration, 96-97
Toyota Tsusho Trading Company, 134
"Trade surplus," 8
Trading firms:
 classification of, 128, 139
 competitive strength of, 130
 and developing countries, 75
 and economic gain, 127
 and FTC, 125
 future of, 155-56
 in Indonesia, 150-53, 154
 and natural resources, 52-53
 and oil firms, 49
 and overseas expansion, 53-55, 138-41
 and politics, 126
 role of, 28-29, 31, 55, 83, 126, 131-32, 143
 specialized vs. diversified, 134-37
 and steel producers, 53
Tsuzuki Cotton Spinning Company, 120

United Auto Workers (UAW), 301
United States:
 and Japanese investments, 1, 43, 108-112
 and Japanese loans, 15-16
 and Japanese steel mills, 101
 and large Japanese firms, 113-15
 and medium-sized Japanese firms, 108-112
 and multinational firms, 4-5
 and new Japanese technologies, 176
 and product-related technologies, 174
United States, and Japan, 31-32
Urbanization, of Cambodia, 281-82

Wages, 119
"*Wakon Yosai*," 6
The West. *See also* Japan, and the West
 and acceptance of Japan, 3
 and competition with Japan, 8-9
 vs. Japan, 5-9, 13
Women vs. men, 222. *See also* Employees
Workers (Japanese), 175
World Federation of Trade Unions (WFTU), 300
World War II. *See also* Second World War
 effects of, 277
 and industrial growth, 288

Yakutsk project, 278
Yamashita, "Manchuria Taro," 61
Yano, 126
"The Yellow Peril," 3
Yoshida (YKK), 115-16
Yoshida, Prime Minister Shigeru, 288

Zaibatsu, 12, 16, 134

About the Author

Yoshi Tsurumi is Professor and Director, Pacific Basin Economic Study Center, University of California, Los Angeles. Professor Tsurumi previously taught at Columbia University, Harvard Business School, Queen's University, Canada, and Keio University, Tokyo. He has published extensively in the fields of international transfer of technology and managerial skill, multinational firms, politics of oil and other natural resources, and economic development. In mid-1976, he began supervising an international team of researchers in the agricultural development of southern Sumatra, Indonesia. He is also the author of *Multinational Management: Texts, Readings and Cases* (Ballinger Publishing Company, Cambridge, Massachusetts, 1976), and *Japanese Business: A Research Guide with Annotated Bibliography* (Praeger Publishers, Inc., New York, New York, 1978).